AIR LAW

A comprehensive sourcebook for
Southern African pilots

AIR LAW

A comprehensive sourcebook for
Southern African pilots

Philippe-Joseph Salazar

First published 2019

© Juta and Company (Pty) Ltd
First Floor, Sunclare Building, 21 Dreyer Street, Claremont, 7708
www.jutalaw.co.za

This work is protected by copyright under the Berne Convention. In terms of the Copyright Act 98 of 1978, no part of this work may be reproduced or transmitted in any form or by any means, electronic or mechanical, including photocopying, recording or by any information storage and retrieval system, without permission in writing from the publisher.

Whilst every effort has been made to ensure that the information published in this work is accurate, the editors, publishers and printers take no responsibility for any loss or damage suffered by any person as a result of the reliance upon the information contained therein.

ISBN: 978-1-4851-3314-8

Production Coordinator: Deidre Du Preez
Editor: Martin Rollo
Proofreader: Linda van de Vijver
Indexer: Lexinfo
Cover design: Drag and Drop
Typeset by CBT Typesetting & Design

*In fond memory of Anita Saunders,
and of her silver biplane*

Acknowledgments

This book would not have come to fruition without the encouragement of colleagues, aviators and friends, and the occurrence of the right circumstances.

First, I owe a debt of gratitude to my long-time colleague and friend Professor Hugh Corder, former Dean of the Faculty of Law at the University of Cape Town, who put me in touch with Ms Linda van de Vijver at Juta, who championed the project and steered it to completion, with good humour and great caring. Due recognition goes to my colleagues in the Faculty of Law, Advocate Richard Bradstreet (Department of Commercial Law), son of renowned SAAF Major (ret.) Arthur Bradstreet, Associate Professor Tobias Schonvetter, Director of the Intellectual Property Unit; Dr Sifiso Eric Ngesi (Portfolio Committee on Transport, SA Parliament), and aviation medical examiner, Dr Lourens de Kock. For their conversation and advice, I am grateful to SAA Captain (ret.) Koos de Jager, Guy Leitch, Editor of *SA Flyer*, Ross Leighton, chairman of the Morningstar Flying Club, Alan Evan-Hanes, former General Manager of the Aero Club of South Africa, as well as to the 'grande dame' of aviation radio and navigation procedures in South Africa, Dietlind Lempp. Pilots who, one way or another, played a role in my writing this book are recognised: Alitalia Captain (ret.) Maurizio De Pol, Training Captain Robert Hall (Susi Air), Giovanni Titus (SAA), Pablo Fraga (Cathay Pacific), Sebastian Chennells (Flight Training London, UK), Yannik Le Roux (Aerosport at Wintervogel, and Susi Air), and last but not least, Colin Gray (Flight Training Adelaide, Australia).

Something would be amiss if I were not to mention fellow members of Aéro-Club de France for congenial dinners at the historical café-brasserie *L'Oiseau Blanc* in Paris, where pilots have met since the early 1920s, the Royal Air Force Club in London and the Army & Navy Club in Washington, DC, in whose rich libraries I delved whenever I stayed there.

Sadly, as I was putting the final touches to this book, I received news of the death of a friend, Mike Lomberg. He had embarked on a round-the-world trip with other 'handipilots'. He was a former distinguished SAAF test pilot, and an accident had deprived him of the use of his legs, but he had taken up flying again. He crashed his plane on 30 December 2018, having flown singlehandedly from Switzerland to Thailand, over the Alps, the Mediterranean Sea, the deserts of Arabia, the hallowed Ganges and the jungles of Burma. Mike was reserved in demeanour, straightforward in opinion, and determined in endeavour: a pilot and a gentleman.

Philippe-Joseph Salazar

July 2019
Cape Town

Contents

ACKNOWLEDGEMENTS vi

ABBREVIATIONS AND ACRONYMS xvi

PART ONE: BEFORE FLYING

CHAPTER 1: INTRODUCTION 1
1.1 This book has six types of reader in mind 2
1.2 A scenario-based book. 3
1.3 The components 5

CHAPTER 2: WHAT IS AIR LAW? 7
2.1 The Convention on International Civil Aviation. 8
2.2 Aviation law or air law?. 10
2.3 The South African Civil Aviation Authority. 11
    2.3.1 What does SACAA do?. 12
    2.3.2 Differences between ICAO and SACAA regulations and standards 13
    2.3.3 Civil Aviation Regulations 13
    2.3.4 Civil Aviation Technical Standards 14
2.4 CARS and CATS 15
    2.4.1 How regulations are written 15
    2.4.2 CARS and CATS are read in tandem 17
2.5 Integrated Aeronautical Information Package 19
    2.5.1 What is the AIP and its related components? 19
    2.5.2 Definitions of types of aeronautical information 20
    2.5.3 Understanding the AIP 25

CHAPTER 3: MEDICALLY 'FIT TO FLY'? 28
3.1 The medical certificate of fitness 28
3.2 The DAME in your life 29
3.3 Medical certificates: Five classes 31
3.4 Medical certificate validity 33
3.5 The application procedure 35
3.6 Duty to report being unfit. 36

PART TWO: BECOMING AND BEING A PILOT

CHAPTER 4: BECOMING A PILOT 43
4.1 Your first paperwork: your student licence and logbook 44
    4.1.1 Applying for a Student Pilot Licence 44
    4.1.2 How to maintain a valid SPL. 46
    4.1.3 Your logbook matters! 46
4.2 Privileges and limitations. 48
4.3 The legal framework of your training 50
4.4 The theoretical syllabus and examinations. 50
    4.4.1 The 7 +1 examination papers. 51
    4.4.2 Syllabus vs exams 52
    4.4.3 When should I study? 52
    4.4.4 Radiotelephony 53
    4.4.5 Do you speak English? The Language Proficiency Certificate . . 53
    4.4.6 Examination time-line issues 55
4.5 Practical flight instruction 58
    4.5.1 Flying exercises 58
    4.5.2 Airmanship 59
    4.5.3 Making a call: student prefixes 59
    4.5.4 Debriefs. 60
    4.5.5 Endorsements. 60
4.6 Towards your first solo 60
    4.6.1 The path to solo 61
    4.6.2 Satisfactory progress: dual progress checks 62
    4.6.3 Failing to meet the standards for going solo 63
    4.6.4 Dual competency check flight before first solo 64
    4.6.5 Dual check after solo 65
    4.6.6 Unsatisfactory progress after solo 65
    4.6.7 Flying solo is being on a long leash: rules 66
4.7 Logging flight time 66
    4.7.1 Logging flight time: what, how, who 66
    4.7.2 But, are you sure you are logging as the correct sort of pilot or as the legal PIC?. 68
4.8 The Private Pilot Licence Skills Test 70
    4.8.1 When am I allowed to test?. 70

| | | Contents | ix |

	4.8.2	Pre-test ground evaluation	72
	4.8.3	The Skills Test can be split into two or more flights	73
	4.8.4	What does the Skills Test consist of?	73
	4.8.5	Should you fail	75
4.9	At last! The 'brown book'		75

CHAPTER 5: BEING A PILOT 78

5.1	Keeping your PPL valid		78
	5.1.1	What does 'valid' mean?	79
	5.1.2	How do you observe the 'period of validity'?	79
	5.1.3	The three validity rules: competency, currency fee and medical	80
	5.1.4	The Competency Check Report and rules for revalidation	81
5.2	Privileges and limitations of a PPL		84
	5.2.1	Privileges	84
	5.2.2	Limitations: general and human performance	84
	5.2.3	Limitations linked to 'recency'	86
5.3	A PPL is a licence to learn: add ratings		88
	5.3.1	Category ratings	89
	5.3.2	Class and Type ratings: definitions	89
	5.3.3	Class and Type ratings training prerequisites	91
	5.3.4	Conversion training	92
	5.3.5	Turbojet or turbofan mentor programme	93
	5.3.6	Ratings for special purposes	93
	5.3.7	Endorsement and validation of rating and conversion	95
5.4	Categories of aircraft and aeroplanes		96

PART THREE: LET'S FLY!

CHAPTER 6: BEFORE YOU CALL 'CLEAR PROP' 103

6.1	Action 1: I'M SAFE?		104
6.2	Action 2: Airspace		106
	6.2.1	Check your airspace	106
	6.2.2	Airspace structure and classes	108
6.3	Action 3: Check your weather		111

	6.3.1	Determination of meteorological minima under VFR	111
	6.3.2	Weather at departure, en route, and at destination	112
	6.3.3	Check VFR minima	114
	6.3.4	Check special VFR (SVFR) weather minima	116
	6.3.5	VFR weather and airspace operations	117
	6.3.6	Weather and aerodrome operating minima IFR	120
6.4	Action 4: Check your aerodromes		122
	6.4.1	Alternate, adequate and suitable aerodromes	122
	6.4.2	Where can you take off or land?	124
6.5	Action 5: Flight plan—to file or not to file?		126
	6.5.1	To file or not to file for a VFR flight?	127
	6.5.2	How do I file?	128
	6.5.3	When do I file?	128
	6.5.4	When do I activate my flight plan?	129
	6.5.5	What is a flight plan valid for?	129
	6.5.6	What right does the flight plan give me?	130
	6.5.7	When do I close my flight plan?	130
6.6	Action 6: Aircraft inspection: nine checks		130
	6.6.1	Fuel supply	132
	6.6.2	Operating lights	135
	6.6.3	Oxygen	135
	6.6.4	Communication and navigation equipment	136
		6.6.4.1 Communication equipment capability	137
		6.6.4.2 Flight plan communication and navigation capability	138
	6.6.5	Compulsory instruments	139
	6.6.6	Fire extinguisher	141
	6.6.7	Safety belts and harnesses	141
	6.6.8	Stowage, baggage and cargo	142
	6.6.9	First aid kit, universal precaution kit and strips	142
6.7	Action 7: Paper plane!		144

CHAPTER 7: READY TO TAXI! 148

7.1	Where are you taxiing and what are these areas called?	149
7.2	Light signals	150
7.3	Taxi rules and right of way on the ground	152
7.4	Runway markings and displaced thresholds	154

	7.4.1	Various runway markings	154
	7.4.2	Displaced thresholds	155
	7.4.3	Pre-threshold area unfit for normal movement of aircraft (yellow chevron)	156
7.5		Runway and taxiway mandatory and information signs	156
7.6		Aerodrome signalling panel and signalling area	156

CHAPTER 8: FLYING AWAY, EN ROUTE! 158

8.1	Collision avoidance: 'Rules of the air'		159
	8.1.1	The general rules	159
	8.1.2	The specific rules	159
8.2	Collision avoidance: Right of way		161
8.3	Collision avoidance: Flying under pressure and Flight Levels		165
	8.3.1	Altimeter setting, transition altitude and level	166
	8.3.2	Altimeter setting scenarios	166
8.4	Collision avoidance: Semi-circular rule, Flight Levels		169
	8.4.1	Semi-circular rule and magnetic track	170
	8.4.2	About operations with RVSM, FL290 – FL410	171
	8.4.3	Flight level and magnetic track	172
8.5	Collision avoidance: and the ground below?		173
	8.5.1	General regulation	174
	8.5.2	En-route safe altitude, minimum safe altitude	175
	8.5.3	Minimum Sector Altitude, Minimum En-route Altitude, Minimum Off-route Altitude	176
	8.5.4	Minimum heights	178
	8.5.5	Line features	178
	8.5.6	Minimum height over people	179
	8.5.7	National Parks (NP) and World Heritage Sites	180
8.6	Collision avoidance: what about speed?		180
8.7	Collision avoidance: Fun stuff you can or cannot do		181
8.8	Rules for collision avoidance: Communicate!		182
	8.8.1	In uncontrolled and information airspace	183
	8.8.2	In controlled and advisory airspace	185

CHAPTER 9: UNPLANNED EVENTS EN ROUTE AND WHAT YOU SHOULD DO ABOUT THEM 190

9.1	From VFR to IFR	190

xii Air Law

9.2 Can I change my flight plan en route? 192
    9.2.1 Deviations from a flight plan 192
    9.2.2 Changes to a flight plan 193
9.3 Being warned off an area that is off limits 193
9.4 Declaring an urgency 194
    9.4.1 What is an urgency? 194
    9.4.2 How to declare an urgency 195
    9.4.3 Priority over other aircraft 197
9.5 Declaring an emergency 197
9.6 Interception! 199
9.7 Search and Rescue (SAR) 202
    9.7.1 The five golden rules 202
    9.7.2 SAR procedures 203
9.8 What to do after a crash 204
9.9 Radio failure in controlled airspace, and arriving safely under VFR ... 206

CHAPTER 10: AT YOUR FINAL DESTINATION 208
10.1 How does the law define 'approach'? 208
10.2 Apply transition level and reset altimeter 209
10.3 Radio calls on approach to an uncontrolled airfield 210
10.4 Cancel Search and Rescue and close your Flight Plan 210
10.5 Observe right of way and rules of operation 211
10.6 Observe lights, signals and markings 214
    10.6.1 Precision approach path indicator (PAPI) 214
    10.6.2 Aeronautical light beacons 215
    10.6.3 Runway markings and runway and taxiway mandatory and information signs 215
    10.6.4 Visual ground signals and markings 216
    10.6.5 Pyrotechnical signals (flares) sent from tower 218
    10.6.6 Light signals from tower 218

CHAPTER 11: RUNWAY VACATED! 220
11.1 Taxi rules of interest to a landing aircraft 220
11.2 Signals from or on the tower 221
11.3 Marshalling signals (A) 222
11.4 Back to paper plane 224
    11.4.1 Arrival report in case of a flight plan 224

11.4.2	Filling in the aircraft flight folio	225
11.4.3	Logging of flight time in your pilot logbook	227

CHAPTER 12: HOW TO REPORT AN INCIDENT OR AN ACCIDENT ... 229

12.1	The PIC must report incidents and accidents	229
12.2	Definitions: incident, accident, hazard	230
12.3	Who notifies whom of what?	232
12.4	Who has access to an accident scene and what of the wreckage?	235

CHAPTER 13: NIGHT FLYING ... 237

13.1	The Night Rating	237
13.2	What is night?	239
13.3	Are you fit to fly at night?	239
13.4	Is your aircraft equipped and are you ready?	241
	13.4.1 Cockpit equipment (A) sound and light	241
	13.4.2 Lights to be displayed by aircraft at night, in flight or on the movement area	242
	13.4.3 Taking a passenger at night?	243
13.5	Night flying is VFR but . . .	243
	13.5.1 Weather and wind	243
	13.5.2 Height and terrain	244
	13.5.3 Aerodrome lighting	244
	13.5.4 Tower, unauthorised entry and interception signals	247
	13.5.5 Encountering aircraft: lights	247

PART FOUR: FLYING DRONES

INTRODUCTION ... 251

CHAPTER 14: SOME KEY POINTS ... 254

14.1	Key points about licences	254
14.2	Key points about the operation of drones	254
14.3	Key points about the 'size' of drones	257

CHAPTER 15: DRONE PILOTS ... 260

15.1	The Remote Pilot Licence	260
15.2	Theoretical training and examination	261

15.3	Practical flight training	263
15.4	Maintaining a Remote Pilot Licence	265

CHAPTER 16: PILOTING DRONES 266

16.1	R-VLOS private operations	266
	16.1.1 Rules and restrictions for R-VLOS private operations	266
	16.1.2 Exemptions for R-VLOS private operations	269
	16.1.3 Visual representation of R-VLOS operational limits	270
16.2	Key points for pilots about ROC operations	271
	16.2.1 Operator vis-à-vis Pilot	272
	16.2.2 Pilot logbook and flight folio	273
16.3	VLOS, E-VLOS and B-VLOS operations	274
16.4	By way of conclusion	274

BIBLIOGRAPHY 275

ANNEXURE 1: Extracts of the Chicago Convention of 1944 279

ANNEXURE 2: IAIP organogram 280

ANNEXURE 3: Nomenclature of CARS and CATS 281

ANNEXURE 4: Example of NOTAM 283

ANNEXURE 5: Logbook rules and annual summary 285

ANNEXURE 6: Syllabus of theoretical knowledge (A) (H) 290

ANNEXURE 7: Practical syllabus for flight instruction PPL (A) 329

ANNEXURE 8: Progress Report Sheet 339

ANNEXURE 9: Duties of PIC regarding flight preparation 340

ANNEXURE 10: Aeronautical Chart Index and Classification of Airspace . 343

ANNEXURE 11: Flight Plan regulation 348

ANNEXURE 12: Fuel policy 351

ANNEXURE 13: Flight Authorisation Sheet 355

ANNEXURE 14: Duties of PIC regarding flight operations 356

ANNEXURE 15: Interception signals and phraseology 360

ANNEXURE 16: Search and Rescue (SAR) scenarios and procedures 365

ANNEXURE 17: Night Rating Training (A) (H) 368

ANNEXURE 18: Drone Operations 373

QUESTIONS: Part 1 Chapters 1, 2, 3 381

QUESTIONS: Part 2 Chapter 4 385

QUESTIONS: Part 2 Chapter 5 390

QUESTIONS: Part 3 Chapter 6 395

QUESTIONS: Part 3 Chapters 7 and 8 400

QUESTIONS: Part 3 Chapters 9, 10, 11, 12 406

QUESTIONS: Part 3 Chapter 13 412

ANSWERS: Chapters 1–13 416

INDEX 417

Abbreviations and Acronyms

ACARS	Aircraft Communications Addressing and Reporting System
AD	Aerodromes
ADA	Advisory area
ADM	Aeronautical decision making
ADR	Advisory route
ADS	Automatic Dependent Surveillance
ADS-B	Automatic Dependent Surveillance Broadcast
AFM	Aircraft flight manual
AFS	Aeronautical Fixed Service
AFTN	Aeronautical Fixed Telecommunication Network
AGL	Above ground level
AIC	Aeronautical Information Circular
AIID	Accident and Incident Investigations Division (SACAA)
AIM	Aeronautical information management
AIP	Aeronautical Information Publication
AIRAC	Aeronautical Information Regulation and Control
AIREP	Aircraft report
AIRMET	Information by MWO on specified en-route weather affecting safety of low level operations not included in forecast
AIS	Aeronautical Information Services
AMSL	Above mean sea level
AOM	Aerodrome operating minima
ASFC	Above surface
ASI	Airspeed indicator
ASL	Air Service Licence
ATA	Aerodrome traffic area
ATC	Air Traffic Controller
ATNS	Air Traffic & Navigation Services
ATO	Aviation Training Organisation
ATPL	Air Transport Pilot Licence
ATS	Air Traffic Services
ATSU	Air traffic services unit
ATZ	Aerodrome traffic zone
BARO VNAV	Barometric vertical navigation
BRLOS	Beyond radio-line-of-sight
B-VLOS, BVLOS	Beyond visual line-of-sight
C2	Command and control
C of R	Certificate of Registration

CAA	Civil Aviation Authority
CAHRS	Confidential aviation hazard report system
CARS	Civil Aviation Regulations
CATS	Civil Aviation Technical Standards
CFI	Certified flight instructor
CG/CofG	Centre of gravity
CofR	Certificate of Registration
CORSIA	Carbon Offsetting and Reduction Scheme for International Aviation
CPDLC	Controller Pilot Data Link Communications
CPL	Commercial Private Licence
CTA	Control area
CTR	Control zone
DAME	Designated aviation medical examiner
DFE	Designated flight examiner
DOF	Date of flight
DSAME	Senior designated aviation medical examiner
EASA	European Aviation Safety Agency
EET	Estimated elapsed time
EFIS	Electronic flight information system
ENR	En route
EOBT	Estimated off-block time
ETA	Estimated time of arrival
ETD	Estimated time of departure
E-VLOS, EVLOS	Extended visual line-of-sight
FA	Field Africa
FACA	Cape Town Flight Information Region
FAD	Danger area
FAJA	Johannesburg Flight Information Region
FAJO	Johannesburg Oceanic Flight Information Region
FAK	First aid kit
FAP	Prohibited area
FAR	Restricted area
FCL	Flight Crew Licence
FI	Flight instructor's rating
FIR	Flight Information Region
FL	Flight Level
FP	Flight plan
FPV	First person view
FSTD	Flight simulation training device
GNSS	Global navigation satellite systems

HDG	Heading
hPA	Hectopascals
IAS	Indicated air speed
ICAO	International Civil Aviation Organization
IF	Instrument flying
IFR	Instrument flight rules
IMC	Instrument meteorological conditions
I'M SAFE	Acronym for self-check of health issues before a flight
IR	Instrument rating
ISA	International Standard Atmosphere
KIAS	Knots indicated air speed
KTS IAS	Knots indicated air speed
LRNS	Long Range Navigation Systems
MCM	Maximum certificated mass
MCTOW	Maximum certificated takeoff weight
MEA	Multi-engine piston aeroplane and Minimum en-route altitude
MEL	Minimum equipment list
METAR	Aerodrome routine meteorological report in meteorological code
MHE	Multi-engine helicopter
MMEL	Master minimum equipment list
MORA	Minimum off-route altitude
MPI	Mandatory periodic inspection
MSA	Minimum safe altitude and Minimum sector altitude
MSL	Mean sea level
MT	Magnetic track
MTOW	Maximum takeoff weight
MWO	Meteorological Watch Office
NM	Nautical miles
NOTAM	Notice to airmen
NP	National park
NPL	National Pilot Licence
NR	Night rating
NTCA	Non-type certificated aircraft
OAT	Outside air pressure
ONC	Operational Navigation Charts
OPI	Oral Proficiency Interview
OPMET	Operational meteorological information
PAPI	Precision approach path indicator
PAX	Passengers
PIB	Pre-flight information bulletin
PIC	Pilot-in-command

PICUS	Pilot-in-command under supervision
POH	Pilot operating handbook
PPL	Private Pilot Licence
PPL (A)	Private Pilot Licence (aeroplane)
PPL (H)	Private Pilot Licence (helicopter)
QFE	Barometric at aerodrome level: altimeter indicates 'height'
QNE	Standard pressure altitude indicated by altimeter set on 1013.2hPa, 'flight level'
QNH	Barometric pressure at aerodrome level reduced to MSL using ISA formula: altimeter indicates 'altitude'
RCF	Radio communication failure
RLA	RPAS Letter of Approval
RLOS	Radio line-of-sight
RMK	Remark (in a Flight Plan)
RMT	RPAS Maintenance Technician
RNAV	Area navigation
ROC	RPAS Operators Certificate
RPA	Remotely Piloted Aircraft
RPAS	Remotely Piloted Aircraft Systems
RPL	Remote Pilot Licence
RPS	Remote Pilot Station
RTE	Radio telephony examiner
R-VLOS	Restricted visual line of sight
RVR	Runway visual range
RVSM	Reduced vertical separation minimum
SACAA	South African Civil Aviation Authority
SADC	Southern African Development Community
SAR, SR	Search and rescue
SARPs	Standards and Recommended Practices
SAWS	South African Weather Service
SEA	Single-engine piston aeroplane
SELCAL	Selective Calling System
SGWX	Significant weather chart
SHE	Single-engine helicopter
SIC	Second-in-command
SIGMET	Information by MWO on specified weather en-route and other phenomena affecting safety of aircraft operations
SITA	Société Internationale de Télécommunications Aéronautiques
SOP	Standard Operating Procedures
SPECI	Aerodrome special meteorological report in meteorological code
SPIC	Student Pilot-in-command

SPL	Student Pilot Licence
SRA	Special rules area
SRM	Single-Pilot Resource Management
SSR	Secondary surveillance radar (transponder)
STAR	Standard terminal arrival route
SWACAA	Swaziland Civil Aviation Authority
TAF	Terminal aerodrome forecast
TAS	True airspeed
TIBA	Traffic Information Broadcast by Aircraft
TIPAN	Position report (traffic, identity, position, altitude, next)
TMA	Terminal Control Areas
TOD	Top of descent
UAS	Unmanned Aircraft Systems
UAV	Unmanned Aerial Vehicle
UIR	Upper Information Regions
VFR	Visual flight rules
VIS	Visibility
VLOS	Visual line of sight
VMC	Visual Meteorological Conditions
VOR	VHF omnidirectional radar
VTOL	Vertical take-off and landing
WTC	Wake turbulence category

PART ONE
BEFORE FLYING

Chapter 1

· · · · · · · · · · ·

Introduction

> The fear is gone now. It is gone. Rain continues to fall. My altimeter says that the Atlantic is two thousand feet below me, my Sperry Artificial Horizon says that I am flying level. I judge my drift at three degrees more than my weather chart suggest, and fly accordingly. I am flying blind. A beam would help.
>
> <div align="right">Beryl Markham <i>West with the Night</i>[1]</div>

West with the Night is an aviation classic. This quote illustrates the role of a pilot: to follow rules, rules on a chart about terrain, rules about altitude, rules about situational awareness, rules about airmanship. But 'rules' in Markham's time, the 1930s, 'rules' were mainly eyes, and basic instruments. Women and men pioneers flew into the night over the deep growl of the ocean, opening air paths where no man nor woman had been before. Their airmanship kept many of them safe, and their eyes and 'feel' for the machine told them where to go—so that they could tell their story. Many perished.

Did they know about air law? Hardly. They knew their machines, they could read the stars, and they landed when and where they could. These were their rules.

At that time rules were often those of common sense, of airmanship, and of knowledge of the mechanics of flying. A pilot could land anywhere and be greeted by hurrahs. No 'cop', as Lindbergh said, would file a report: the pilot would be given a lift to the local hotel and served a warm meal. Still, those pilots applied rules by instinct or by knowledge, in order to fly safely. Air law came later; it formalised what pilots and operators had done mainly of their own accord, and what legislators, faced in their time with an invention as revolutionary as the Internet, tried to frame as best they could in the early Aviation Acts.

Indeed, before 1945, legal international rules were not uniformly codified, as they are today, and air law, as we know it, did not really exist. But slowly and surely air law was developed, to ensure real world safety in the skies, and beneath them.

What pilots call 'air law' is in fact a set of international and national statutes and regulations that pilots must follow in order to fly safely, ie to be—

- safe in relation to their own mental and physical abilities;
- safe in relation to their physical environment (aerodromes, sea and terrain, weather);

---

[1] Beryl Markham *West with the Night* (1983) 284–5.

- safe in relation to other pilots (while flying);
- safe in relation to their passengers and the people above whom they are flying; and
- safe in relation to the aircraft they are operating.

This does not mean that a pilot who knows air law can be a lawyer who specialises in aviation legislation, or engages in litigation regarding matters of liability or international treaties, for instance.

Air law sets out the legal rules that pilots must follow to be proficient pilots who do not endanger their own lives and the lives of others. These rules apply not only to pilots, but also to others, such as air traffic controllers. Flying is one of the safest modes of transport, but any air crash gets immediate publicity because flying remains one of the greatest achievements of humanity. Flying pushes our limits. Our bodies are not designed for flight; when a heavier than air contraption becomes, as it were, lighter than air, if some rules are not applied, it may just fall to the ground. Flying is made safe by observing rules, and there are many of them. Air crashes happen when a rule is ignored. This is why air law is so important and a crucial part of a pilot's training.

Air law is a compulsory subject to obtain the Private Pilot Licence (PPL) and the Commercial Pilot Licence (CPL), as well as mandatory for the Air Transport Pilot Licence (ATPL), in addition to the National Pilot Licence and also non-flying licences such as those for flight engineers and cabin crew—all personnel who play a crucial role in aviation safety. Examinations vary but they all refer to the same core knowledge. In some countries, student pilots are not allowed to do their first solo unless they have first passed the Air Law exam successfully, which is wise.

1.1 THIS BOOK HAS SIX TYPES OF READER IN MIND

Air Law: A comprehensive source book for Southern African pilots is the first book on air law published by Juta, a leading South African publisher with a proud record of legal publications going back to 1853. Juta's purpose reflects a tradition of service to the public, and, in this case, to Southern African aviation—a proud and century-old tradition on this continent. (The first recorded flight took place on 28 December 1909, although it was not the first flight on the continent.)[2] Remember that the prefix for airfield locators (such as FAOR for Johannesburg) and for some airspace is FA (called the 'nationality letters'), which stands simply for 'Field Africa'. South African airfields were the first to be coded on this continent.

---

[2] Mentioned in Philip Kent *Drone Law* (2017) 18. The first flight in Africa took place in Algiers in 1906—Monsieur Métrot flew his biplane Voisin for 70 minutes (Centre de Documentation Historique sur l'Algérie). On 3 December 1909, 25 000 spectators watched an exhibition by the same pilot (*Flight, First Aero Weekly in the World* (11 December 1909) 1(50) 784.

Who are our readers?

- **Student pilots** who are training for their PPL: *Air Law* offers clearly presented information and guidance about regulations that they must know to get a 75% pass in their examination. But much more than that, this book affords trainee commercial pilots who proceed to CPL the **core knowledge** of air law, which will carry them right through their career in aviation. As any instructor will tell you: what you study for a PPL is what you should always remember. It is the core knowledge of piloting. And that applies to air law.
- The large community of **private pilots** who fly for pleasure, mostly under VFR,[3] and who sustain general aviation in Southern Africa through flying clubs and training academies, however small—the role played by general aviation in the supply chain of professional pilots cannot be underestimated. General aviation is a national asset.
- **Aviation Training Organisations** (ATOs) and instructors: this book is a reference work they can reliably use for ground school. Its format lends itself to easier teaching. 'What does the law say?' is often heard when a student (or instructor) gets stuck. The sticky point, as we are going to see later, is *where* does the law say it? This book guides students or teachers towards answers.
- **The South African Civil Aviation Authority**, as well as the civil aviation authorities of the SADC region, when they set up examination guidelines.
- **The general public**, who are often fascinated by aviation: this book opens a window onto the art and joy of flying, and shows why legal regulations, which at first glance seem a tad austere or bizarre, are in reality enabling tools. After you have read through Part 3, where a flight is described phase by phase, you will head for your nearest aerodrome, ready to sign up.
- And last, learned members of **the legal profession**, who struggle at times to find their way in the labyrinth of regulations, standards, and aeronautical information that make up air law, which can be confusing if one is not intimately acquainted with the 'real world' of aviation and piloting. **Aviation medical examiners** will also find this book useful to better understand how their protocols fit in the larger framework of pilot training.

1.2 A SCENARIO-BASED BOOK

Air Law: A comprehensive source book for Southern African pilots contrasts with other material available on air law in South Africa and in the rest of the English-speaking market in Southern Africa. This book is not a copy and paste of the regulations, which are in any event available on the South African Civil Aviation Authority website, nor does it reflect the somewhat monstrously complex European Aviation Safety Agency regulations. This is not meant as a criticism of fellow South African authors and dedicated aviators who have introduced air law

---

[3] Visual flight rules, which are central to Student Pilot Licence (SPL) knowledge.

to student pilots, and have contributed to the development of 'fly safe', as we pilots say instead of 'best wishes'. The basic purpose of other titles is to help student pilots to pin down a 75% pass in the Private Pilot Licence (PPL) air law exam, after which new private pilots forget most of what they learnt by heart to clear the exam hurdle.

The purpose, size and shape of *Air Law: A comprehensive source book for Southern African pilots*, however, is quite different—of course it does take care of examination knowledge, but it goes much further, and follows a different format.

'Scenario-based training' of pilots, it has been proven, brings better results than what is called 'manoeuvres-based training'.[4] The book uses that concept and applies it to air law. Organised as a narrative, *Air Law* does not simply duplicate the way in which legislation is presented: legislation is always written in typical parliamentary and lawyerly language, with parts, sub-parts, sections, cross-references, indices and appendices, that are all necessary because it is the law, and a main preoccupation of legal experts is to stay, precisely, on the right side of the law.

But what about pilots and especially student pilots?

And what about aviation enthusiasts who want to know more about the art of flying, which like all arts is framed both by techniques (the manoeuvres) and rules (air law)?

Instead of duplicating long excerpts from legislative and regulatory texts, and leaving it to readers to work out what they mean, I have written *Air Law* as **an extended narrative.** The book is written in as plain and simple a style as the law allows, and includes some light-hearted moments.

Source references to current legislation are of course quoted and clearly marked, as they provide milestones along the way.[5] Sometimes references to legislative and regulatory texts can be puzzling or even intimidating. *Air Law* makes access to legislation easier.

The book guides readers from a basic question ('What is air law?') to more complex ones. It tells a story about flying safely by applying rules. It imparts knowledge as a story about pilots and piloting.

The learning advantage of what is also known as the 'cognitive' method[6] is to help pilots in training and private pilots to integrate two aims:

- first, understanding regulations leads to flying performances that pilots themselves value as their goal and can be proud of;

---

[4] Peter M Schumacher & Jered Lease *Evaluating the effectiveness of scenario based training in the collegiate flight training environment* Final Report to the FAA/Industry Training Standards (2007).

[5] When SACAA forms are mentioned to help students locate an important application form, it is advisable to check the SACAA website (at Forms) to establish if the said form has been discontinued, replaced or amended.

[6] As developed by Albert Bandura in *Social Foundations of Thought and Action* (1986).

- second, regulations have a deeper value that goes beyond just passing an exam: adopting and adapting to better, safer flying behaviours.

Reading this book like a narrative will enable trainee pilots and confirmed pilots for whom a licence is always licence to learn **to project themselves and to imagine themselves performing flying gestures and operations through the application of rules**. Just as athletes are often taught to visualise their performance before getting onto the field, flying performance and abilities improve dramatically when pilots imagine an actual flight ahead of the actual operations they have to perform.

This will help students apply the rules naturally and allow aviation enthusiasts to visualise what is involved in flying, besides being proficient and competent at handling an aircraft.

1.3 THE COMPONENTS

Air Law: A comprehensive source book for Southern African pilots has four parts, plus Annexures and PPL examination questionnaires with answers.

Part 1 covers all that precedes training: it takes the reader from this Introduction to a more precise presentation of how air law is structured in terms of its various components, all of which are essential for pilots and aviation professions, and it ends with the medical side—how one is declared fit to fly.

Part 2 makes you step right into the training of a pilot: readers will see how air law actually frames training towards a PPL, and then enables a confirmed pilot to fly legally, and to add to a licence.

Part 3 asks you to 'come aboard': this section tells the story of a cross-country flight. By far the longest part of the book, it follows a pilot through all the phases of preparation, pre-flight, flight, and after flight. If you are not (yet) a pilot just imagine that you are sitting in the right-hand seat, looking at what a pilot does. And what a pilot does is apply rules. Student pilots are able to see how each regulation applies in real life—instead of learning by heart chunks of rules that often seem disconnected from what they love to do: to fly. We dramatise a flight from the moment a pilot gets up in the morning and decides to fly for the day, to the return to base later that day. As the scenario, or story of a cross-country flight, unfolds, each phase of the flight, from preparation to completing forms after landing, is highlighted in terms of air law regulations. A cross-country scenario is the best way **to tell a story about the law and flying**, as it takes pilot and reader through everything that makes up a real flight.

Part 4 is about piloting drones, or Remotely Piloted Aircraft Systems (RPAS), which is the official name. The number of drone pilots has increased dramatically in recent years, and so has the registration of RPAS, which have now overtaken helicopters. Although legislation and regulations are still developing, *Air Law* provides the rules as they stand at the time of publication: they are already fairly comprehensive and will guide drone pilots.

In the course of the book, points of particular interest to students are placed in italics, as a warning or a reminder about examinations.

Annexures provide ample informational guidance. They are meant to illustrate complex rules. They are correct as at July 2019, but subject to change.

Questionnaires are intended for students sitting their PPL Air Law examination. However, seasoned pilots, at the recreational and private level, and CPLs, should use the questions to test their knowledge currency.

Should seasoned private pilots test their knowledge now and then? Possibly, yes. If statistics for communications retention rates are accurate,[7] 24 months after passing their PPL Air Law examination, pilots may have lost 26% of their knowledge—so someone who passed with 75% (the pass mark) now knows only half of the basic regulations. This, to quote the famous book by Paul Craig, places that pilot 'in the killing zone'.[8] Or, as a congenial radio telephony instructor from Cape Town used to say after warning students about yet another radio rule not having been observed: 'And then, he crashed . . . and we are still looking for the wreckage.'

What about updates?

The core law is pretty stable with regard to the fundamental Act of Parliament on Civil Aviation, with amendments now and then. Civil Aviation Regulations (CARS) and Civil Aviation Technical Standards (CATS) are regularly amended. Aeronautical Information Publications (AIPs) record updates (more later on CARS, CATS and AIP). These revisions are taken into account as at the end of **July 2019** by *Air Law: A comprehensive source book for Southern African pilots.*

Later changes of note will be made available in the e-book version, or in a second edition.

To round off this introduction: if anyone wants to know everything about flying, the best source is actually air law. It contains everything from detailed explanations about flying exercises to varieties of airspace, from marshalling signals to schedules of medical issues, and from types of aircraft to emergencies. It is all in there. Air law also explains why pilots make up 0,000000001% of the world population (this tongue-in-cheek figure is not so far from the truth). Why not join them?

To read this book on air law is to delve into the art and joy of flying.

---

[7] See Paul A Craig *The Killing Zone: How and Why Pilots Die* 2 ed (2013) 230; and Jerry M Childs, William D Spears & Wallace W Prophet *Private Pilot Skill Retention 8, 16, and 24 Months after Certification* (1983).

[8] See note 7 above.

Chapter 2

. . . .

What is air law?

> It is not very difficult to master the art of flying, and one can learn almost as easily as one can learn to drive a motor-car. Perhaps it is not looking too far ahead to see the time when people will think of planes just as they think of motor-cars now, and talk over their week-end flights just as they discuss their motor-trips to-day.
>
> William J Claxton *The Mastery of the Air*[1]

If flying was as simple as Claxton suggests there would be no traffic rules and traffic lights either. The dream of free wings evoked in this pre-World War One book for young boys has since met, like old fashioned 'motoring around', the real world of regulations.

As we get into air law, the first questions to ask are obvious: Who decides about it? Who lays down the law? What comprises air law? Where can I find it?

It is worth thinking first about a standard definition of 'law'. The law, any law for that matter, consists of 'the **principles and regulations** established **in a community** by some **authority** and **applicable to its people**, whether **in the form of legislation** or of custom and policies recognized and **enforced by judicial decision**'.[2]

Applying this definition to aviation, we can see that pilots and those who take part in aviation, from flight engineers to marshallers, all form a 'community' that follows 'principles and regulations' that are 'recognized' and 'enforced'.

All this sounds for now rather grand or abstract, but when, later on, we discuss, for instance, accidents, it will become startlingly clear and concrete.

However, air law is peculiar. There is no denying it. It is 'established' for, and applies to an **international community** that is quite unusual: a pilot cannot be asked to follow judicially enforced rules in South African airspace and then, as the aircraft crosses into Botswana, to follow entirely different rules. Right from the beginning of aviation, in spite of wars, there was a strong idea that pilots form a world community, follow the same rules of the air, and communicate with each other in codes they all understand, such as the typical 'pilot's speak'—even when they were in a dogfight. By comparison, drivers do not have common rules: cross the Channel from England to France and you have to drive on the other side of the road, and decipher French road signage. There is no uniformity.

---

[1] William J Claxton *The Mastery of the Air* 1 ed 1914 (1930) 243.
[2] https://www.dictionary.com/browse/lay--down--the--law.

8 *Air Law*

Indeed pilots are told from day one of their training that they must 'aviate, navigate, communicate'. To achieve those goals safely, and not fly into each other or crash, there must be **uniform rules**.

What are these uniform rules and where do they come from?

2.1 THE CONVENTION ON INTERNATIONAL CIVIL AVIATION

The primary source of air law is an international diplomatic text, known as the Chicago Convention of 7 December 1944, which is the Convention on International Civil Aviation,[3] governed by an international body, the International Civil Aviation Organization (ICAO), which came into existence on 4 April 1947.[4] ICAO is a specialised agency of the United Nations *(exam question!)*. The Convention is not the first international agreement on civil aviation but it is the one that, today, governs aviation, and of which trainees and pilots must be aware—at least in name.[5]

The original Convention was signed by 52 states, in three 'equally authentic' (diplomatically legal) languages (English, French, Spanish—Russian was added by the Montreal Protocol of 1977, effective 1999). The Union of South Africa was a proud founding signatory in 1944 (see annexure 1).

One can safely say that air law as we know it, and as we must know it to be safe pilots, was born in December 1944.

The Preamble of the Convention assigns an idealistic goal to aviation:

> International civil aviation can greatly help to create and preserve friendship and understanding among the nations and peoples of the world.

It is an ideal, forged in the final years of the Second World War, according to which, once peace was restored, aviation would serve the greater purpose of linking continents and nations. This ideal shows itself in small ways: a pilot who arrives at an airfield, anywhere in the world, will be greeted with warmth and comradeship by fellow pilots. Language is no barrier. Aviation provides.

In practical terms it follows that ICAO must set up rules to give effect to 'safety of navigation of civil aircraft'.[6] And to ensure safety there must be 'uniformity' in regulations:

---

[3] Document 7300/9 of ICAO, 9 ed (2006), available at https://www.icao.int.

[4] The Convention has added other conventions and protocols since, such as the aircraft protocol to the Convention on International Interests in Mobile Equipments or Cape Town Convention of 2001 (sale, lease, registration, etc of aircraft that can carry more than eight passengers etc), effective 2006.

[5] A legal framework for international civil aviation was first developed by the Paris Convention of 13 October 1919.

[6] Convention, article 3*(d)*.

Each contracting State undertakes to keep its own regulations in these respects [rules of the air] uniform, to the greatest possible extent, with those established from time to time under this Convention.[7]

This is why the current South African Civil Aviation Act quotes the full text of the Convention. South Africa gave effect to the Convention for the first time in 1946, with the Carriage by Air Act.[8]

The principle of 'uniformity' in standards

Anyone familiar with the National Geographic television series *Air Crash Investigation* will recall how, for instance, in radio communication, the lack of respect for uniformity by pilots and controllers who belong to different cultures can have disastrous results.[9] Another possible factor is issues arising from the use of drugs that were not considered a risk until an accident happened.[10]

This guiding principle—that there should be legal uniformity between countries fiercely opposed during the Second World War and then the Cold War—is something of a paradox. However, states agreed that, for the sake of safety, aviation legislation needed one single, agreed upon source for all aviation laws, regulations and standards worldwide.

Article 37 of the Convention therefore mandates states to achieve–

the highest practicable degree of uniformity in regulations, standards, procedures, and organization in relation to aircraft, personnel, airways and auxiliary services in all matters in which such uniformity will facilitate and improve air navigation.

For instance, article 29 lists the seven documents that must be carried on board an aircraft engaged in international navigation, in order to be legal. This is the minimum requirement.[11]

In spite of its length (96 articles), the Convention could not deal with detailed specifics or anticipate rapid changes in aviation and technology. Those specifics are therefore provided by the **Standards and Recommended Practices** (SARPs).

SARPs are extensive (in the thousands) and often expensive documents available from ICAO. They give effect to the general, uniform rules of the Convention. For instance, SARP Annex 1 deals with licensing; Annex 4 with aeronautical

---

[7] Convention, article 12.

[8] *Summary of national regulations and international agreements/conventions* can be found in AIP GEN 1.6–1 to 9 (see below about the meaning of AIP).

[9] (Collective) 'Use of standard phraseology by flight crew and air traffic controllers clarifies aircraft emergencies' (March–April 2000) 26(3) *Flight Safety Foundation, Airport Operations*.

[10] See the 2014 report by the United States National Transportation Safety Board *Drug Use Trends in Aviation: Assessing the Risk of Pilot Impairment* NTSB/SS-14/01, 2014.

[11] SA regulations list up to 17 documents that must be carried on board an international flight, as per CARS 91.03.1. On CARS, see below.

charts; and Annex 5 with units of measurements. They offer national legislative standards to follow. They are constantly revised, adapted, and amended.

National regulations concerning aviation are in turn entrusted to a country's dedicated agency, often called the Civil Aviation Authority.

The official name and acronym of a national CAA may vary: Japan has a Civil Aviation Bureau, France a General Directorate for Civil Aviation, the United States a Federal Aviation Administration, and Australia a Civil Aviation Safety Authority (note: 'safety').

ICAO is also the inspiration for another large, transnational regulatory body based in the European Union (EU), the **European Aviation Safety Agency** (EASA). The opening paragraph of its basic regulation restates the guiding principle behind the Chicago Convention: to ensure 'a high and uniform level of civil aviation safety'.[12] EASA has competence over all member states of the EU plus associate states, which has resulted in common European standards across aviation, and of course licences (called FCL, or Flight Crew Licences), sometimes different from American or South African practice (for instance there is no EASA student pilot licence, or certificate, which is aligned with ICAO).

Nonetheless, safety in the skies depends on uniform laws..

So, we already know that air law stems from the 1944 Convention and has been further developed and detailed in Annexes to the Convention or SARPs. But all this is at an international level, and is not binding (hence 'recommended'). It becomes binding through national legislation.

2.2 AVIATION LAW OR AIR LAW?

Before we move now to the next level, precisely what is the difference between 'aviation law' and 'air law'?

Many countries had aviation legislation on their statutes before ICAO. In South Africa the first Aviation Act dates back to 1923.

So, what is the difference between aviation law and air law?

Someone who specialises in aviation law is bound to be a trained lawyer working at a law firm,[13] whereas a pilot who has passed an examination on air law does not get an academic law credit, and has no legal qualification.

---

[12] Regulation (EU) 2018/1139 of the European Parliament and of the Council of 4 July 2018 on common rules in the field of civil aviation and establishing a European Union Aviation Safety Agency.

[13] ICLG *The International Comparative Legal Guide to: Aviation Law 2019* 7 ed (2019).

Aviation law[14] is complex and covers a wide range of legal matters related to aviation, specifically, in South Africa, the following Acts of Parliament[15]—not to mention aviation legislation embedded in other laws (a good example is protection of the environment, see page 180):

Carriage by Air Act 17 of 1946

Air Services Licensing Act 115 of 1990

Airports Company Act 44 of 1993

Air Traffic and Navigation Services Company Act 45 of 1993

Convention on the International Recognition of Rights in Aircraft Act 59 of 1993
International Air Services Act 60 of 1993

Space Affairs Act 84 of 1993

Shipping and Civil Aviation Laws Rationalisation Act 28 of 1994

Transport Advisory Council Abolition Act 9 of 1996

South African Civil Aviation Authority Levies Act 41 of 1998

South African Maritime and Aeronautical Search and Rescue Act 44 of 2002
Convention on International Interests in Mobile Equipment Act 4 of 2007

South African Airways Act 5 of 2007

South African Express Act 34 of 2007.

In addition to the above Acts of Parliament, there is a host of legal regulations (13 at the time of writing) that mostly regulate industry linked to aviation.

One Act is fundamental to air law as pilots understand it: the **Civil Aviation Act 13 of 2009**.[16] The Act provides for a regulatory body, whose role is to implement the Act: the South African Civil Aviation Authority (SACAA). In turn this state agency develops and imposes what is sometimes called 'secondary legislation', regulations and standards, that constitute the bulk of air law (section 2.4 below).

2.3 THE SOUTH AFRICAN CIVIL AVIATION AUTHORITY

(Some of the points below come up as exam questions).

The South African Civil Aviation Authority is often abbreviated as SACAA or just

---

[14] See Chris Christodoulou & Antonia Harrison 'South Africa' in ICLG *Aviation Law* (n 13 above).

[15] A Bill 'passes' through Parliament and once approved by a vote becomes an Act. It becomes law once the President has 'assented' to it. Acts are published in the *Government Gazette*.

[16] Civil Aviation Act 13 of 2009, *Government Gazette* 32266 GN 461 of 27 May 2009 updated by *Government Gazette* 35183 GN 561 of 27 March 2012.

12   Air Law

CAA.[17] Everyone in aviation refers to 'the CAA'—usually, on the part of pilots, in an aggrieved tone of complaint about 'bureaucracy'. (All over the world pilots have the same complaint.)

National CAAs ensure that legislation applicable to aviation replicates as uniformly as possible the rules agreed upon through ICAO, and adapts them as appropriate to local circumstances, or traditions. ICAO audits national CAAs regularly.

2.3.1 What does SACAA do?

Here is what the South African Civil Aviation Act of 2009 says about the mission entrusted by law to SACAA:[18]

> **The objects of the Civil Aviation Authority are to–**
> *(a)* control and regulate civil aviation safety and security;
> *(b)* oversee the implementation and compliance with the National Aviation Security Program;
> *(c)* oversee the functioning and development of the civil aviation industry;
> *(d)* promote civil aviation safety and security;
> *(e)* develop any regulations that are required in terms of this Act;
> *(f)* monitor and ensure compliance with this Act and the Convention [the Chicago Convention].

Item *(e)* above provides an important clue to understanding what comes next, and is important to pilots in terms of air law: SACAA must, by law, '**develop regulations**', and a secondary set of rules called '**standards**' (more on them below).

Yet, not all regulations or standards developed by SACAA concern pilots directly (for instance the Mortgaging of Aircraft Regulations, 1997). There is, nonetheless, a body of regulations and standards directly applicable to pilots, owners, operators and aviation personnel, and aerodromes. They are commonly known as Civil Aviation Regulations, abbreviated as CARS, and Civil Aviation Technical Standards, abbreviated as CATS. Taken together, CARS and CATS are what pilots call air law.

CARS and CATS are what a student has to master to pass the Air Law examination (PPL, CPL)

But there are differences between ICAO rules and national regulations and standards.

---

[17] In this book we use SACAA uniformly and not SA CAA or 'the SACAA' except when necessary.
[18] Civil Aviation Act Chapter 6 section 72.

2.3.2 Differences between ICAO and SACAA regulations and standards

Differences exist *(exam!)*.

The differences are called 'significant'[19] and are clearly listed in a SACAA document called AIP GEN.[20] They concern (among other matters) personnel licensing, rules of the air, operations, and certifications. You may be surprised to learn that in many cases SA regulations are 'more exacting' (that is to say, stricter) or 'less protective' (less strict) than ICAO's SARPs.

For instance:

> South Africa's regulation [for a night rating] is **more exacting** in that the South African Civil Aviation Regulations, 2011, 61.10.1(2) state that a **night rating** is required to exercise the privileges of a licence by night. The night rating includes theoretical knowledge and instrument instruction as well as a skills test to be completed and that a night rating issued.[21]

An opposite example *(and exam question)*, which was the object of some debate among student pilots, is the following (the regulation was **aligned on two minutes in 2015**):

> South Africa's Regulation [for being late at a reporting point] is **less protective** in that the **South African Civil Aviation Regulations**, 2011, Regulation 91.03.4 9(12) (c) **states** that **if the estimated time at the next applicable reporting point,** flight information regional boundary, or aerodrome of intended landing, whichever comes first, is found to be in error **in excess of three minutes** from that **notified to the responsible ATSU**, a revised estimated time shall be notified to such ATSU as soon as possible; or . . . **ICAO requires two minutes**.[22]

Discussion closed, for now, but probably not for all time.

At least you now have a taste of how a regulation is written.

2.3.3 Civil Aviation Regulations[23]

The Minister has the authority under section 155 of the Civil Aviation Act of 2009 to 'develop regulations', and for that purpose he appoints the Director of Civil Aviation who is 'the head of the Civil Aviation Authority's administration'.[24] What

---

[19] AIP GEN 0.1–1—see below about the meaning of AIP.

[20] AIP GEN 1.7.

[21] AIP GEN 1.7–3 Annex 1—Personnel Licensing *(note the spelling : 'licensing', not 'licencing')* 2.3.2.2— the sentence 'and that a night rating issued' is grammatically faulty, but so it is.

[22] AIP GEN 1.7–4 (section 3.6.2.2). Amendment 9 of SEPT 2015: two minutes. To date not corrected in AIP.

[23] Civil Aviation Regulations *Government Gazette* 35398 GN 564 of 1 June 2012, and subsequent gazetted amendments.

[24] Civil Aviation Act Chapter 6 section 85. The Amendment Bill of 8 October 2018, *Government Gazette* 41962 GN 640 that proposed to replace 'Director' by 'Commissioner' has lapsed. It may be reintroduced in Parliament at a later stage.

the Director and SACAA do is described in Civil Aviation Regulations (CARS) and Civil Aviation Technical Standards (CATS) Part 11.

In effect, the Director oversees CARS according to guidelines that are laid down in section 155 of the Civil Aviation Act.

Once CARS are in place (and they do change, being regularly 'developed'), the Director of Civil Aviation has a further function, which creates a second set of legal rules of direct interest to pilots: the CATS.

One can refer to a regulation as a 'CAR'[25] and to a technical standard as a 'TS'.

2.3.4 Civil Aviation Technical Standards[26]

The Civil Aviation Act of 2009 is clear:

> The Director may issue technical standards for civil aviation on such matters as may be prescribed by regulation.[27]

And the Act adds a provision that reflects what we have seen earlier regarding ICAO uniformity of standards:

> The Director may incorporate into a technical standard any international aviation standard or any amendment, without stating the text of such standard or amendment, by mere reference to the title, number and year of issue of such standard or amendment or to any other particulars by which such standard or amendment is sufficiently identified.[28]

Air law, as far as pilots and aviation personnel who have to sit an Air Law exam are concerned, is made up of those two impressive documents, CATS and CARS, running together into some 2 500 pages of tightly written regulations with a whole system of cross references.

Pilots and personnel are not expected to know the Civil Aviation Act of 2009, or its history,[29] but they must know CARS and CATS, as applicable to the type of Air Law exam or component relevant to them (NPL, PPL, CPL, in the case of pilots).

---

[25] The name and abbreviation vary. The SACAA website uses CAR or SACAR for Civil Aviation Regulation (in the singular). You will also find CARS or 'CARs'. The Eighth Amendment of 27 May 2015 specifically says: "CAR" means Civil Aviation Regulations', so here is a plural word with a singular acronym. This book uses CARS.

[26] South African Civil Aviation Technical Standards (SA CATS); effective on the date of commencement of the Civil Aviation Regulations, 2011, with subsequent amendments as issued. The SACAA website refers to CATS or SA-CATS, or SA CATS.

[27] Civil Aviation Act, section 163(1)(*a*).

[28] Civil Aviation Act, section 163(2).

[29] Its forerunners were the South African Civil Aviation Act of 1998, and the Aviation Act of 1962 (also valid in South West Africa, present day Namibia). As for the Union of South Africa, as mentioned already, the first Aviation Act dates back to 1923 (Act 16 of 1923).

Can users have their say?

SACAA does not work in isolation, and you can, as a private person, suggest regulations: 'Any interested person may submit to the committee referred to in regulation 11.02.1, a proposal on the introduction, amendment or withdrawal of a regulation or technical standard.'[30] The procedure is not simple, but is precisely described in CARS Part 11. It means that, if the flying community wants to be involved in drafting Regulations or Technical Standards, it certainly can. Anyhow, when a proposal is finally drafted, it is advertised (on the SACAA website) by inviting written comments within 30 days. CARS and CATS changes are often the result of public participation.

Now that we have identified and named the two core documents for air law, CARS and CATS, and understand how they fit in the larger picture of legislation, let us take a closer look at those two basic, voluminous documents themselves, CARS and CATS.

2.4 CARS AND CATS

The regulations are in the public domain, since 'ignorance of the law is no excuse', and can be downloaded from the SACAA website—together of course with their amendments, without which some sections will be out of date.

It takes some agility to read them. It is also time-consuming. And one has to check regularly whether new amendments have been introduced or are being announced.

2.4.1 How regulations are written

CARS sets the general rules, CATS details them—when necessary. CATS therefore follows the chaptering ('Parts') of CARS. In other words the division of CARS in what is called internationally 'Parts' and 'subparts' is replicated by CATS. They work in tandem.

Subparts consist of 'regulations' or 'standards', paragraphs if you wish, and are subdivided into an often dazzling cascade of sub-regulations and sub-standards (this last expression is rarely used, for obvious reasons . . .), many with their own sub-entries.

Sometimes it is enough to look at CARS to make sure one is flying legally. In that case there may not be an equivalent standard in CATS. It means that CARS are sufficiently explicit and detailed for a pilot to be legal (with regard to that specific regulation or sub-regulation of course). If in doubt, turn to CATS, and double check if the regulation is expanded in a standard.

---

[30] CARS 11.03.1(1). 11.02.1 itemises topics about which the Director, together with the Civil Aviation Regulations Committee, advises the Minister.

16   Air Law

Regulations and standards are presented in a set style.
Let us take an example:[31]

Psychoactive substances

91.01.16 (1) Subject to sub-regulation (2), no person shall act in the capacity of any crew member, ground support, servicing or maintenance personnel, or perform any function or participate in any decision-making process that could affect aviation safety, where such person is, or is likely to be impaired by any psychoactive substance.

(2) Where a medication that may be considered to be a psychoactive substance has been prescribed by a medical doctor, the duties in sub-regulation (1) may be undertaken provided an aviation medical examiner so designated in terms of Part 67 certifies what duties may be safely accomplished while taking such medication.

(3) A person who has been prescribed medication that may adversely affect performance or is otherwise of the opinion that his or her performance may be impaired through the use of medication or combinations of medication shall so inform the operator.

Now, let us look at its encoding:
- The title of the regulation is in bold letters, above the numbering: **Psychoactive substances**.
- The first two digits **91** indicate the Part to which the regulation belongs—here Part **91**.
- The next two digits **01** indicate the Subpart—here Subpart 1 of Part 91. Note that the regulator uses a zero before any single digit.
- The next two digits **16** indicate the regulation itself—reg 16 of Subpart 1 of Part 91.
- The bracketed number **(1)** indicates a sub-regulation—here sub-regulation 1 of regulation 16 of Subpart 1 of Part 91.

The regulation then reads:

In Part 91, Subpart 01, regulation 16 dealing with Psychoactive substances is divided into three sub-regulations. Sub-regulation (1) gives the rule but this rule is subject to what sub-regulation (2) states as an exception; sub-regulation (3) states how and why a pilot must advise the operator.

(Note: in the case of a student pilot the operator would be the flight school).

You have noted that the regulator prefers to write 'subject to' instead of 'except in the case of'. Get used to it now. And the regulator often prefers to use the negative ('no person') instead of phrasing regulations positively (in that case it could be: 'A person is allowed to act . . . unless . . .').

---

[31] CARS 91.01.16.

Reading CARS and CATS requires some mental gymnastics, quickly acquired.

What you have to learn is what main Parts of CARS and CATS are relevant to you as a student pilot—as you will discover in the course of this book. You must learn the numbering of those main Parts, as many exam questions, right up to advanced licences, are about them. The number also reveals the nomenclature of CARS and CATS (annexure 3). As a SPL or PPL: Part 12 accidents, Part 61 pilot licensing, Part 62 national pilot licensing, Part 67 medical certification.

You may well ask: Why can't CARS just begin with what matters to us, pilots: licensing? Why relegate what matters to us to Part 61?

CARS does not follow a pilot's training logic but a legal logic: a legal document (read your medical aid contract!) begins with a list of definitions, so that we all agree on what the document says. So does CARS when it provides a long list of definitions in Part 1. Once definitions are established, CARS proceeds with Part 11, which is about the authorities in charge and in charge of what. And then it segues into Part 12, Aviation accidents and incidents.

Then you may ask: Why begin the real 'meat' of CARS, that which pilots must know to fly legally, with crashes? Because, if you recall, ICAO was set up in the first place to provide 'safety' and to avoid accidents. So the third part of CARS is about non-safe flying, or crashes. And so on.

Alert as you are, you now ask: but why is CARS jumping from Part 1 to Part 11 and Part 12? Why not Part 2, Part 3 and so on? This allows for intermediate Parts to be added at some stage, such as Part 101 about 'drones', which was added recently.

We agree it does not make a pilot's life simpler, but it adds to the rich tapestry of life in the skies.

Doesn't it?

2.4.2 CARS and CATS are read in tandem

CARS and CATS work in tandem, as already mentioned. And they must be read in tandem too.

Let us take an example. Under Part 91 of CARS, entitled 'General aviation and operating flight rules' (a very important section, indeed), a diligent operator (say, a flight school manager) will realise straight away that CATS begin at 91.01.5, that is at sub-regulation 5. In other words the Director of Civil Aviation (who oversees CATS) decided that there was no need to give more details for items 1 to 4 of CARS, but to be more explicit about 5—until further notice.

> **CATS 91.01.5 deals with 'Information on emergency and survival equipment'**
>
> CATS 91.01.5 deals with 'Information on emergency and survival equipment carried' (CATS phrase in Table of Contents).

> Now, if the same operator compares regulation CAR 91.01.5 with TS 91.01.5, this is what the operator will learn if Cessna 172 ZS-MOO is to take off legally with a flight instructor and a student pilot as PIC:
>
> In CARS:
>
> (1) The owner or operator of an aircraft shall have available for immediate communication to rescue coordination centres, a list containing information regarding the emergency and survival equipment carried on board the aircraft.
>
> (2) The minimum information to be contained in the list referred to in sub-regulation (1) is prescribed in Document SA-CATS 91.
>
> As you can see CARS is directing you to CATS in order to expand what is meant in sub-regulation 91.01.5 (1).
>
> In CATS:
>
> An owner or operator shall have a list containing the following minimum information regarding the emergency and survival equipment carried on board:
>
> (1) the number, colour and type of life rafts and pyrotechnics;
>
> (2) details of emergency medical supplies;
>
> (3) water supplies; and
>
> (4) type and frequencies of emergency portable radio equipment.

You will note three points, and how much language matters if you need to understand the law, before you cry, 'CARS and CATS do not make sense!':

- First, the owner or the operator are legally responsible, in terms of CARS, for having available an emergency and survival equipment **list**, not the pilot (unless he is the owner or operator), in order to provide it 'immediately' to a search and rescue centre.
- Second, the owner or operator (typically your school if you are a student) must refer to CATS to make sure the list contains a minimum of four items of information, as stated in CATS.
- Third, does it mean that the operator must 'ensure' that **what is listed** is on board your Cessna? Yes (if applicable), but these two CARS and TS do not state that it is the PIC's duty to check that what is supposed to be on board is on board (see Part 3 of this book), as the onus to operate according to rules of safety is placed on the operator or owner, and the 'person' operating an aircraft.[32]

So, students, at this stage do not become despondent about the crossword puzzle intricacies of CARS and CATS. Simply be alert to the wording of regulations. When

---

[32] For instance, as to whether a specific type of aircraft should carry life rafts in case of a water landing, refer to CARS 91.04.26. Typically a light aircraft will not carry a life raft.

*you read a regulation or a standard do not jump to conclusions. Do not try to read what you think it should be, and then **confirm a bias** you have about the regulation. Read carefully.*

By the way, **confirmation bias** does not only apply to misreading regulations: it is a mental or cognitive risk in flying. Its danger applies right from the beginning of your training: you assume that the southerly wind indicated by the windsock at take off is still a southerly, and on finals you do not check it, with a quick glance, because you are too busy getting the last degree of flaps and speed right and making a call, and then you drift badly. The wind has changed. You had a bias: you assumed that the wind cannot possibly change during the time of a circuit. Well, it can. You confirmed your bias by failing to check the windsock.

To a freshly enrolled student this may look fussy—but at ground evaluation, before the final Skills Test that will place in your hands the coveted PPL, your examiner may well ask you to show if you understand a given regulation.

2.5 INTEGRATED AERONAUTICAL INFORMATION PACKAGE

CARS and CATS are only the tip of the iceberg.

A pilot has to be aware of another layer of regulatory information, both *for exams* and safe flying. Earlier on we alerted you to the fact that there is a mass of regulations a pilot cannot possibly memorise; he or she must rather know how to find a specific rule or pertinent information. It is now time to describe where to find this information. What you need is an Integrated Aeronautical Information Package. The main and lasting component of IAIP is the Aeronautical Information Publication (AIP)

2.5.1 What is the AIP and its related components?

There is a set of regulatory documents which, by law, must be made public. In part they reflect the Civil Aviation Act, CARS and CATS; in part they add new and detailed information about, among others, operating rules, airspace, traffic control, and aerodromes themselves:[33]

- Aeronautical Information Publication (AIP)[34] including 'amendment services' which are AIP Amendments (AMDT);
- Supplements to AIP (AIP SUP) (which include AIRAC SUP)
- Notice to airmen (NOTAM); and pre-flight information bulletins (PIB)
- Aeronautical Information Circulars (AIC);
- Checklists and lists of valid NOTAMs.[35]

---

[33] As defined in CARS 1.01.1. Also AIP GEN 3.1–2.

[34] When AIP is quoted, the page number is indicated, not the paragraphing (unless mentioned otherwise).

[35] One NOTAM, two NOTAMs—although usage is far from consistent, and NOTAM will do.

20 *Air Law*

Typically pilots refer to 'the AIP' as their source of information. The IAIP is 'a package in paper, electronic or digital form' which contains items listed above. The terminology can be confusing.[36]

These documents are under the authority of SACAA. They are for information and compliance.

Pilots are not expected to have all that complex information at their fingertips, but there must be an awareness of its importance. An ability to navigate the AIP volumes, and a readiness to access them to retrieve information when preparing a flight is crucial.

Checking these sources can be quite complicated and time-consuming at the beginning—a serious task, before being able to say 'let's go fly'. In fact, while CARS and CATS are rarely on the desks of instructors, it is impossible to miss the plastic blue bound volumes of the AIP while you prepare a flight at your school. All schools have them. Knowing how to handle AIP to source and decode a NOTAM placed on a notice board, is far closer to the flying life of a pilot than paging through CARS and CATS—rather check *Air Law: A comprehensive source book for Southern African pilots*.

But, while the blue AIP tomes are handily placed on a shelf at the training school or the clubhouse (or you have bought you own set from SACAA), where does one find AIP Amendments, AIP Supplements, NOTAM, AIC, and checklists? All these documents can be obtained on the SACAA website. It takes some agility and patience, but it is all there, and of course updated (see organogram in annexure 3).

As for a student pilot, a ground evaluation will, for a large part, test whether you are familiar with the volumes that make up AIP, whether you are familiar with NOTAM (where to find them and how to decode them) and if you can see that an AIC has been issued with particular relevance to your own flying area.

2.5.2 Definitions of types of aeronautical information

Let us now take a closer look at each of the various documents that make up and are added to the AIP.[37]

Definition of AIP

AIP is a matter of the **time validity** for regulations. AIP is:

> 'A publication containing aeronautical information of a **lasting character essential** to air navigation'. 'Information' here means 'information resulting from assembly, analysis and formatting of aeronautical data'.

Do not be confused by the word 'lasting' as it is not quite used in its conventional sense. There are at least three meanings for it in aviation, and each one defines a specific document in AIP:

---

[36] As defined (for the time being) in CARS 1.01.1.

[37] A quick way to get a handle on AIP and its various components is to look at the SACAA website (http://www.caa.co.za). Click on Public Frequently Asked Questions.

- a change that is permanent is called an Amendment to AIP;
- a temporary change of long duration or operational significance is called a Supplement to IAP;
- a temporary change of short duration (less than three months) **or** a change when operationally significant permanent changes or temporary changes of long duration **are made at short notice**—is called a NOTAM.

Definition of Amendment to AIP[38]

Amendments are **'permanent changes** to the information contained in the AIP which are published by means of special pages'.[39] They are usually issued on 15 January, 15 April, 15 July and 15 October.

Definition of Supplement to AIP[40]

'The purpose of the AIP SUP is to bring to the attention of the user any **temporary changes of long duration (three months or longer) and/or information of operational significance containing extensive text or graphics**, which affect one or more parts of the AIP'.[41]

As you can see when a change is substantial ('extensive', 'graphics') even though it may not be for three months or longer, it is subject to being listed as a Supplement. AIP GEN (see below) contains of course a Record of Supplements, regularly updated.

Definition of AIRAC Supplement

A special type is the AIRAC AIP SUP. Since 1964 it has ensured the international safety of operations which explains why AIRAC stands for Aeronautical Information Regulation and Control. This is how ICAO defines its purpose:[42]

'Airspace structures and routes are revised, navigation aids change, SIDs and STARs are amended, runway and taxiway information changes. It is essential, for both efficiency and safety, that Pilots, Air Traffic Controllers, Air Traffic Flow Managers, Flight Management Systems and Aviation Charts all have the same information working from the same information base. This can only be achieved by following the AIRAC system.'

---

[38] In AIP GEN record of Amendments, an amendment is coded AD followed by a serial number. However the usual abbreviation is AMDT.

[39] CARS 1.01.1. Also AIP GEN 3.1–2.

[40] In AIP GEN Record of Supplements, a supplement is coded S followed by a serial number.

[41] AIP GEN 3.1–3.

[42] See ICAO Annex 15 *Aeronautical Information Services* (AIS).

In practice this means that changes mentioned 'shall be distributed by the AIS unit at least 42 days in advance of the effective date with the objective of reaching recipients at least 28 days in advance of the effective date. Whenever major changes are planned and where additional notice is desirable and practicable, a publication date of at least 56 days in advance of the effective date should be used'. Publication adheres to a calendar of 'cycle of effective dates' (ie when a change becomes reality) at intervals of 28 days and always on a Thursday *(all this is unlikely to be an exam question at PPL level, but you never know)*.[43]

Definition of NOTAM and PIB

This is how AIP GEN defines NOTAM (Notice to Airmen):[44]

> A NOTAM is a notice distributed by means of the Aeronautical Fixed Service (AFS) containing information concerning **the establishment, withdrawal and significant changes in operational capability of radio navigation and air-ground communication services,** the **timely knowledge of which is essential** to personnel concerned with **flight operations.**
>
> A NOTAM shall be originated and issued promptly whenever the information to be disseminated is of a **temporary nature [less than three months] and of short duration or** when operationally significant permanent changes, or temporary changes of long duration are made **at short notice**, except for extensive text or graphics.

The stress is on 'promptly' issued and on 'temporary'. Yet a NOTAM 'containing permanent or temporary information of long duration shall carry appropriate AIP or AIP Supplement references'.[45]

Regarding PIB: 'Pre-flight Information Bulletins (PIB) contain recapitulation of current NOTAM and other information of urgent character for operator/ flight crews' and are 'available from the Aeronautical Management Services Centre' (see next section).[46] They are chiefly of interest to commercial or airline pilots and air service operators.

Who issues a NOTAM?

A NOTAM is issued by the area control centre concerned, ie, in South Africa, any of three FIRs: Cape Town Flight Information Region (FACA), Johannesburg Flight Information Region (FAJA), or Johannesburg Oceanic Flight Information Region (FAJO) ('oceanic' in the sense that it covers the Indian and South Atlantic oceans).

---

[43] ICAO Doc 8126 *Aeronautical Information Services Manual*, Table 2–1.
[44] AIP GEN 3.1–4.
[45] AIP GEN 3.1–5.
[46] AIP 3. 1–5.

How do I get a NOTAM?

NOTAMs in force are available 24 hours a day from the centralised Aeronautical Information Management (AIM) service centre at OR Tambo International Airport (tel: 0860 FLY NOW (0860 359 669) and +27 11 928 6518). They can also be obtained on the ATNS online service (File to Fly) at https://file2fly.atns.co.za. If you need assistance to obtain a NOTAM, the NOF (NOTAM Office) is contactable by email (JSNotam@atns.co.za), by fax (011 928 6576/011 928 6514), by telephone (emergency only (+27 11 928 6592)), or in person. Replies to emailed, faxed and telephonic requests will be emailed back to you by NOF. If you use a fax, you must telephone to confirm it has been received.

Summaries of NOTAM and PIB are posted on the SACAA website daily and are valid only at the time of being created. A monthly NOTAM summary with a checklist is published on the 1st of every month.

Who should read NOTAMs?

The NOTAMs are distributed in six series, identified as A, B and C. Each series is for a specific readership. *(Students, please take note, as this can be a ground evaluation question).*

Six types of NOTAMs

NOTAMs fall into six series.

Each NOTAM is allocated a serial number by the NOTAM Office in the relevant series. The serial number within each series is consecutive and based on the calendar year.

'A – "NOTAM containing information of concern to long- or medium-range flights, and given selected international distribution;"

B – "NOTAM containing full information on all aerodromes, facilities and procedures available for use in international civil aviation and given international distribution to adjacent States only;"

C – "NOTAM containing information of concern to aircraft other than those engaged in international civil aviation and given national distribution only;"

D – "NOTAM containing information of concern for military airports only and given selected international distribution;"

E – "NOTAM containing information of concern for heliports only and given international distribution to adjacent States only;"

F – "NOTAM containing information of an administrative nature (e.g.: Hand amendments Publications, Trigger NOTAM); and given selected international distribution." '[47]

---

[47] AIC Series D 006/2019 of 25 APR 2019, 1. This updated AIC contains all relevant information on how to obtain NOTAMs.

Some SPL or even PPL holders fall into the bad habit of not checking NOTAMS. If you were to cross, for argument's sake, from Alexanderbaai airfield to FYOG Oranjemund airport, located in Namibia, you may be concerned by a B NOTAM, as Namibia is an adjacent state.

Are NOTAMs easy to decode?

It varies. ICAO has been working on reducing the 'proliferation' of NOTAMs and the use of abbreviations in the NOTAM free text.[48] But what is called 'free text', or plain language, is often still obscure. It does happen, however, that a NOTAM says, without further ado, 'Beware of birds'.

See an example of NOTAM and how to decode it in annexure 4.

Definition of Aeronautical Information Circular

The Aeronautical Information Circular (AIC) is defined by what it is not:

> 'An AIC is a notice containing information that does not qualify for the origination of a NOTAM or for inclusion into the AIP, but which relates to flight safety, air navigation, technical, administrative or legislative matters ... [and] AICs are classified into the following subjects—General, Operation of Aircraft, Personnel Licensing, Air Navigation Services, Aerodromes and Airworthiness.'

Since they are not included in AIP, you will find AICs that are 'in force' on the SACAA website,[49] and not in a record of circulars inserted in AIP.

As the 'I' in AIC implies, it provides '**information**' that need to be 'circulated' (hence the 'C').

Definition of checklist
Not to be confused with the checklists you use for actually flying your aircraft!

These mentioned here are a 'monthly checklist of Aeronautical Information which includes a reference of the latest AIP AMDT, checklist of AlP SUP and AIC issued'.[50]

---

[48] ICAO, Doc 8400 *ICAO Abbreviations and Codes*. Includes the NOTAM Code. SACAA has filed a notice of difference with ICAO Annex 15, as it ' will no longer publish the (monthly) plain language NOTAM Summary' (www.caa.co.za Information for the Industry Aeronautical Information Checklist of Publications).

[49] A list of AICs in force is available on the SACAA website, at Aeronautical Information.

[50] AIP GEN 3.1–5.

CATS is again useful in understanding this regulation:[51]

> 'The NOTAM checklist shall be issued every month end and shall [=must]
> (a) refer to the latest AIP Amendments, AIP Supplements and AIC;
> (b) have the same distribution as the actual NOTAM series to which the checklist refers and shall be clearly identified as a checklist.
>
> A monthly printed plain language Summary of NOTAM in force including a reference to the latest AIP AMDT, checklist of AIP SUP and AIC issued, shall be prepared with a minimum delay and forwarded by the most expeditious means to the recipients of the IAIP.'

In addition *(but this concerns professional pilots)* 'Pre-flight Information Bulletins (PIB), which contain recapitulation of current NOTAM and other information of urgent character for the operator/flight crews', are also made available, in plain language.

BIRDTAM—the presence of birds in the vicinity of an airport—are frequent occurrences.

ASHTAM—refer to the presence of volcanic activity (ash) that can affect operations.

2.5.3 Understanding the AIP

Let us now examine AIP in more depth, as it is the main component, and the one that you, as a pilot, must learn to navigate.

AIP is a **complex document** since it covers all that is important to a pilot in terms of operations. As the definition mentioned above says: it is 'the assembly, the analysis and the formatting' of aeronautical data. This means that in AIP SACAA has put together all that information, providing explanations and following a consistent format of presentation.

This explains why the massive amount of information has been divided into three parts, each with a specific theme, running into several volumes.

A description of AIP follows.

Students: Learn to find your way in AIP. Fumbling along at a ground evaluation will not look good. As an instructor friend used to bellow out: 'Immediate fail!' Not quite, but watch out.

---

[51] CATS 175.03.3–3.4 (12–13).

Part 1 or AIP General (GEN)
comprising five sections numbered GEN 0 to GEN 4

- GEN 0 provides general information and the all-important Table of Contents of GEN (GEN 0.6);
- GEN 1 gives information on national regulations, important contact addresses, requirements for Entry, Transit and Departure, differences between ICAO standards and SACAA regulations;
- GEN 2 explains codes, abbreviations and chart symbols (and even has a list of public holidays);
- GEN 3 has information on services (from aeronautical information service to search and rescue service);
- GEN 4 (which is section 5 in reality) lists charges for airports and heliports, and navigation services.

GEN is a **mine of general information**. You will learn there, once and for all, that the correct aviation abbreviation for 'nautical mile' is NM and not nm. And, lest you forget, time is always UTC and to the 'nearest minute', so that 12:40:35 must also be written 1241, and not 12:41. Pernickety perhaps, but correct for aviation, surely.

Part 2 or AIP En route (ENR)
comprising seven sections numbered ENR 0 to ENR 6

ENR makes for less austere reading than GEN: it is the nitty-gritty of flying. It begins once more with ENR 0, with editorial stuff and the noteworthy Table of Contents Then follow:

- ENR 1 provides all the rules for safe flying, from VFR to altimeter setting procedures and air traffic incidents;
- ENR 2 describes the South African Flight Information Regions (FIR), Upper Information Regions (UIR), Terminal Control Areas (TMA), Control Areas (CTA), Special Rules Areas and their VFR routing *(very important for private pilots!)*, plus other regulated airspace including Swaziland, Windhoek and Gaborone;
- ENR 3 describes air traffic service (ATS) routes;
- ENR 4 provides radio navigation aids and systems, and significant points— those odd words you find on charts, such as EKBEV or TETAN.
- ENR 5 lists navigation warnings including prohibited (FAP), restricted (FAR), or danger (FAD) areas, aerial sporting, bird migrations.
- ENR 6 describes en-route charts (pilots do not speak of 'maps', but 'charts').

> **Part 3 or AIP Aerodromes (AD)**
>
> This part lists, with all specifications, rules and requirements, what cannot be avoided once you have made the decision to take off: where to land safely.
>
> Apart from the routine AD 0, AD 1 deals with typical information for aerodromes and heliports (for example, fire fighting services), while AD 2 offers in alpha order a complete list of licensed aerodromes (and helicopter landing areas at aerodromes), in minute detail—everything an aeroplane pilot has to know, has to observe, and has to obey when using an aerodrome. Helicopter pilots find the equivalent information on heliports in AD 3.

AIP is full of abbreviations. Refer to the list of abbreviations at the beginning of this book, extracted from AIP ENR and CARS—*they can crop up in exam questions*, and not only in air law. The most comprehensive source is ICAO.[52] Some technical standards have their own abbreviations (medical or radio telephony).

On a lighter note, reading the 24 subsections of AIP, AD 2 or those in AD 3 makes one dream of flying to unknown aerodromes, and landing at far-flung places. It is, for a pilot, 'an invitation to voyage'. Some information is quaint: helicopter pilots are told to avoid the Dragon Peaks Mountain Resort on certain days and at certain times while the Drakensberg Boys' Choir practises.[53]

Regard these massive volumes as a mine of information, as safeguards and as enablers, and half of the dread of opening them will vanish . . . into thin air, of course.

This rounds off **what a pilot needs to know about the law**.

It is now time to get one step closer to **what air law is actually made for**: to enable you to fly. But flying is preceded by testing if your own machine, your body, can cope.

---

[52] ICAO, Doc 8400 *ICAO Abbreviations and Codes*.
[53] AIP ENR 3.4–4.

Chapter 3

. . . .

Medically 'fit to fly'?

> I am convinced that a judicious participation in aeroplaning provides a man with a very fine mental tonic. I already foresee that, in the future, flying will come to be regarded as one of the greatest health-givers. It will not be long in my opinion, before doctors tell ailing men to go in for a course in aviation.
>
> Claude Grahame-White The Story of Aviation[1]

These were the hopes in 1911, expressed by a great pioneer, the first aviator to do a night flight, and the owner of possibly the first flying school in Britain, at the famous Hendon aerodrome. Today 'ailing men', and women, would be told not to fly until they are fit again.

Before you begin your flight training, there is one important hurdle: are you fit? Let's call it the Law of Nature. If Nature has not given you the physical and mental capacity to be a pilot, there is hardly anything the law, CARS and CATS, can do to remedy the situation. Conversely there are disabled pilots (or rather 'handiflight pilots') and even blind pilots who are fit to fly.[2] But without the certification you will not fly.

Now enters a person who plays a crucial role in a pilot's life: your DAME or **'designated aviation medical examiner'**.

Before we speak of the DAME in your life, let us look at what 'fitness' means, since your DAME will decide about it.

3.1 THE MEDICAL CERTIFICATE OF FITNESS

If you want to become a pilot, your first step is to be declared fit—mentally fit and physically fit. Whether you are 15 (minimum age of an applicant for a Student Pilot Licence)[3] or 95 years of age, the principle is simple: if you fail the prescribed medical examination, called a **'certificate of fitness'** or 'medical certificate', the Director of Civil Aviation will not issue your likely first licence, the SPL.

Unfit? No SPL, no training. No PPL. No Airbus A850 or Boeing 797 in 10 years' time.

All regulations concerning medical certification at all levels of licensing are minutely explained in CARS Part 67, 'Medical Certification'. Further regulations with precise schedules and protocols, appear in CATS Part 67, 'Medical requirements'.

---

[1] Claude Grahame-White *The Story of Aviation* 1 ed (1911) 102.
[2] Using the Soundflyer system developed by aerospace firm Thales.
[3] 16 years for a National Pilot Licence Learner's Certificate and 14 for a paraglider's.

Students, remember Part 67—it crops up in many examinations. You do not need to know its extensive content, but the examiners will check that you know that anything medical falls under Part 67 so that, should you have any doubt whether you are legit to fly, you will know where to find the information.

If you are training for your Private Pilot Licence, you cannot apply for a SPL if the medical certificate has not been issued. Why? Because it must accompany the SPL application form.[4] It is as simple as that.

Definition: '"certificate of fitness" means the document issued to certify the acceptance of the applicant as being regarded as medically fit for appropriate flight duties'.[5]

First, your 'medical' is called a 'certification' because the correct terminology, alongside the commonly used 'medical certificate', is a 'certificate of fitness'.

The key term is **fitness**, which is defined as '**fitness for appropriate flight duties**'. You may be fit to pump iron at the gym or do a three-hour spin class, but you may not be fit to fly. You may be fit to be cabin crew, but not fit to be an air traffic controller.

Second, only medical doctors who have been designated by SACAA may declare a pilot fit—they themselves need to be certified to do so.[6]

Your family GP is unlikely to be a DAME or **designated aviation medical examiner**. Read this sub-regulation carefully: 'Flying personnel must be declared fit by their DAME according to the circumstances and not by their medical practitioner.'[7] This is quite explicit *(and an exam question)*.

From here on we will use 'medical certificate' rather than 'certificate of fitness'.

3.2 THE DAME IN YOUR LIFE

The Class 4 and 5 certificates have slightly different rules, both in terms of the protocols of assessment and of the issuing of the certificate (see 3.3 below): it does not require a DAME to issue it, but a registered medical practitioner (typically, a GP).[8]

A DAME has to follow guidelines in the delivery of certificates, and they are worth reading *(not an exam question, but for information only)*:[9]

---

[4] CARS 61.02.2 (c).
[5] CARS 10.1.1.
[6] CATS 67.00.4–1.
[7] CATS 67.00.9–1(6).
[8] CARS 67.00.5.
[9] CATS 67.00.9–2.

> **Guidelines**
>
> (1) The medical condition is the primary concern, and **a clinical assessment of being unfit to** exercise aviation related task **will determine the period of unfitness.**
>
> (2) The class of medical fitness determines which medical conditions will be allowable for the exercise of the aviation license, or how it may be waivered.
>
> (3) Knowledge of existing criteria and protocols as produced by SACAA is mandatory for proper interpretation of aviation medical fitness.
>
> (4) All **drugs** not published in the SA-CATS 67 need to be verified by SACAA before prescribing.
>
> (5) **Central acting drugs generally are unacceptable and unsafe as medication for aviation personnel.**
>
> (6) The **side effect** profile needs careful attention to determine acceptability.
>
> (7) The applicant's **co-morbidities** may cause medical unfitness (plain English: if you suffer from a disease or disorder in addition to a principal one).
>
> (8) The applicant's possible **adverse reactions to the medication** must be monitored before a decision regarding fitness may be made [plain English: 'allergies to medication'].

The DAME follows precise protocols, applicable to each class of certificate, that are minutely detailed in a large collection of Schedules, which you are able to access if you wish to.[10] CATS provides a precise list of tests, detailed enough for a pilot to gauge the criteria, and the potential disqualifying problems, for a given class of application. You are encouraged to look at them before you make an appointment with a DAME or DSAME.[11] Those details give you a good sense of where you stand *(some disorders may come up in an exam question).* You can also familiarise yourself with the Aviation Medical Report and see for yourself what it covers by accessing Form Number: CA 67–02(a) on the SACAA website. Bear in mind that you have to disclose any medical issue. (The form will help you to identify them before you see a DAME.)

The SACAA website, at Information for the Industry > Aviation Medicine, provides detailed information.

Your DAME will then decide if you are fit for your class of certificate or if you must come back later for a new assessment or be referred to a specialist. Your DAME will send a yellow copy of the certification to SACAA, and you will retain a white copy, which you must keep with your licence (this is compulsory). Your clinical assessment or report is now captured online.[12] Here are the general rules:

---

[10] CATS 67 Schedules.
[11] CATS 67.00.2. A DSAME is a senior DAME.
[12] Using the EMPIC software.

> **General requirement**
>
> (1) Impairment or sudden or subtle incapacitation
>
> Applicants must be free from any risk factor, disease or disability which renders them either unable, or likely to become suddenly unable, to perform assigned duties safely. These may include effects and/or adverse effects from the treatment of any condition and drugs or substances of abuse.
>
> (2) Medical deficiency
>
> Applicants must be free from any of the following, if it results in a degree of functional incapacity likely to interfere with the safe operation of an aircraft or with the safe performance of their duties—
>
> *(a)* Congenital or acquired abnormality;
>
> *(b)* active, latent, acute or chronic disability, disease or illness;
>
> *(c)* wound, injury, or outcome of operation.

3.3 MEDICAL CERTIFICATES: FIVE CLASSES

There are five classes of medical certificates.[13] Each class corresponds to what is termed in the definition of the certificate of fitness as 'being regarded as medically fit for appropriate flight duties'. Appropriate for what? Appropriate for the duties attached to your type of licensed pilot, or non-pilot (for instance, flight engineer or cabin crew), as mentioned.

This is logical: one has to be fit for the type of flying or non-flying operation one performs in aviation. A private pilot does not have the same 'flight duties' as an airline pilot. Different psycho-physical demands are made on them, hence different levels of fitness are expected of them.

The five classes of medical certificates are as follows (*learn the specs of classes 1 and 2!*).

> **Class 1**
>
> – ATPL
> – CPL for aeroplane, airship and helicopter
> – Class I test pilot rating
> – instrument rating
>
> **Class 2**
>
> – SPL
> – PPL for aeroplane, airship and helicopter

---

[13] CARS 67.00.2 as per 20th Amendment *Government Gazette* 42362 GN 645 of 29 March 2019.

- flight engineer licence
- free balloon CPL
- Class II test pilot rating
- commercial glider pilot
- Part 96 authorisation issued under a Part 62 licence (commercial operation of non type-certificated aircraft)

Class 3

- ATC
- air traffic service assistant
- RPL

Class 4

- cabin crew member licence
- microlight (conventional microlight weight shift) aeroplane pilot licence
- gyroplane pilot licence
- free balloon pilot licence (non-commercial)
- light sport aeroplane pilot licence
- touring motor glider pilot licence
- glider pilot licence (non-commercial)
- tandem paraglider pilot licence
- powered tandem paraglider and para trike pilot licence
- tandem hang-glider pilot licence
- powered tandem hang glider pilot licence
- powered parachute pilot licence
- tandem parachutist or skydiver licence
- flight instructor for microlight, light sport aircraft, glider, touring motor glider, gyroplane, gyro-glider, tandem paraglider, powered paraglider, tandem hang-glider, powered hang-glider, and tandem powered parachute
- national test pilot rating
- SPL for licence categories mentioned above

Class 5

- paraglider licence
- powered paraglider licence
- powered paratrike licence
- weight shift or surface control hang-glider licence

> - powered hang-glider licence
> - parachute licence
> - powered parachute
> - solo instructor for para-gliding or hang-gliding and all powers versions of them
> - paragliding, hang gliding and parachuting student licence

Three items to note:

SPL: Although this Regulation does not mention it, it is implied that a SPL holder in the Integrated Training program may apply for, and hold a Class 1, in lieu of a Class 2.

Class 4 to Class 2: You hold a Class 4, you fly above 12 000 ft: you need to be tested for respiratory functions and lungs as for a Class 2.

Class 5: Pilots concerned by a Class 5 who provide a 'medical self-declaration' if under the age of 60, or a 'medical declaration' if above that age – self-declaration or declaration being done in both cases on the appropriate prescribed form and signed by a medical practitioner (registered under the Health Professions Act) – are considered holders of a Class 5.

3.4 MEDICAL CERTIFICATE VALIDITY

What is 'validity'?

'Validity' refers generally to the fact that a document has been issued legally and not cancelled by the authority that delivers it (in this case, the DAME), and all requirements have been complied with.[14]

But validity also refers to time factors that help one better understand how medical certificates are designed:

- First, validity means that the expiry date has not been exceeded. Certificates have an expiry date, which may or may not coincide with the expiry date of your licence. A PPL holder may have to do a revalidation check ride on 15 July, but must undergo a new medical examination on 30 May—if for some reason the medical examination has been skipped, the pilot cannot fly legally and the revalidation check ride will have to wait.
- Second, your DAME can reduce the period of validity of your certificate, and endorse it accordingly, if he or she thinks this is necessary.[15]
- Third, age plays a role in determining the period of validity of a certificate (see below) *(exam question)*. This is explained in detail in the next section.

Since we are dealing with time issues, there are also age limitations because SACAA believes, rightly or wrongly, that age plays a role in determining 'fitness'

---
[14] CARS 1.01.1.
[15] CARS 67.00.6(5).

34   *Air Law*

for certain 'flight duties'. This 'curtailment of privileges' does not affect the validity of certification itself but it means that pilots engaged in **international commercial air transport** aged 60 and above cannot 'act as pilot of an aircraft', while the limit is pushed back to 65 in case of a **multi-pilot crew** *(not an exam question)*.[16]

Age and validity

Age plays a determining role in terms of the validity of medical certificates.

Class 1 medical certificate validity

12 calendar months, calculated from the last day of the calendar month in which the medical certificate is issued, where the applicant is **less than 40 years of age** on the date on which the medical certificate is issued.

6 calendar months in the case of an airline transport pilot (aeroplane or helicopter), engaged in single-crew commercial air transport operations, calculated from the last day of the calendar month in which the medical certificate is issued, where the applicant is **40 years of age or more** on the date on which the medical certificate is issued.

6 calendar months in the case of an airline transport pilot (aeroplane or helicopter), engaged in multi-crew **commercial air transport operations or a commercial pilot** (aeroplane or helicopter), where the applicant is **60 years of age or more**.

12 calendar months in the case of an airline transport pilot (aeroplane or helicopter), engaged in multi-crew commercial air transport operations, calculated from the last day of the calendar month in which the medical certificate is issued, where the applicant is **40 years of age or more, but less than 60 years of age**, *on the date on which the medical certificate is issued.*

12 calendar months in the case of a commercial pilot (aeroplane or helicopter), calculated from the last day of the calendar month in which the medical certificate is issued, where the applicant is 40 years of age or more, but less than 60 years of age, on the date on which the medical certificate is issued.

A Class 1 medical certificate referred to in the two categories placed in italics will be *valid only if the pilot—*

- *submits a six (6)-monthly medical report, if he or she has a medical disease or risk factor for which he or she receives regular treatment by his or her treating physician or DAME; the report shall include:*
  - *nature of disease or risk factor;*
  - *information regarding control of risk factors or disease;*
  - *complications that have developed as a result of the disease or risk factor;*
  - *type of treatment and side-effects of treatment.*

---

[16] CARS 61.01.11, for precise details. This policy varies from country to country.

> - *submits an annual follow-up blood test where applicable;*
> - *adheres to the requirements of any Schedule or Protocol as detailed in Document SA-CATS 67, where applicable.*
>
> **Class 2 medical certificate validity**
>
> **60 months**, calculated from the last day of the calendar month in which the medical certificate is issued, where the applicant is less than 40 years of age on the date on which the medical certificate is issued—or **24 months if 40 years of age or older**, or **12 months if 50 or older**.
>
> **Class 3 medical certificate validity**
>
> **48 months**, calculated from the last day of the calendar month in which the medical certificate is issued, where the applicant is 40 years of age or less on the date on which the medical certificate is issued—or **24 months if 40 years of age or older**, or **12 months if 50 or older**.
>
> **Class 4 medical certificate validity**
>
> **60 calendar months,** calculated from the last day of the calendar month in which the medical certificate is issued, where the applicant is **less than 40 years of age on the date on which the medical certificate is issued**;
>
> **36 calendar months**, calculated from the last day of the calendar month in which the medical certificate is issued, where the applicant is **40 years of age or more on the date on which the medical certificate is issued**.
>
> CARS 67.00.6 lists more rules. If you are to memorise one, make it the following:
>
> 'The holder of a medical certificate shall, at least 15 days immediately preceding the date on which such medical certificate expires, **apply for the extension** of such medical certificate.' To whom? To SACAA. Not to your DAME. If SACAA (formally, the Director) agrees, you will get an extension 'not exceeding 30 days'.

Just memorise what is relevant to your own licence (SPL) and to the licence you are aiming at (PPL).

3.5 THE APPLICATION PROCEDURE

In practice, you make an appointment, well in advance, with a DAME recommended by your flying school or club. You bring your ID, your current licence, and your credit card. If there is any requirement such as 'nil by mouth' so many hours before in view of a blood test, the nurse or assistant will tell you when you book. Do not forget to be specific about the medical examination you want.

The tests

You submit yourself to extensive physical tests (you'd better be fit, in the usual sense of the word). For the past few years these tests have incorporated a mental assessment, which some doctors do while you are simply talking about yourself and your life, and your passion for flying, or the club's mascot cat; that casual chat may be an indirect assessment as to whether you are depressed, hyperactive, suffering from attention disorder, etc. Tests can last up to an hour and a half.

Tests follow protocols that DAMEs have to adhere to.

You must be ready to disclose any medical history, including surgical operations even if performed in the distant past. Have the details ready, as well as your GP's contact details. Since 2017 the data are captured directly online by your DAME. If there is a problem the DAME may require further tests. If you wear corrective spectacles (trendy sunglasses do not qualify) this will be endorsed on your certificate—and remember the rule of redundancy: always carry two pairs.

You are then issued with a small white original certificate that must go in your pilot licence holder whenever you fly PIC or solo.[17] The DAME will forward the yellow duplicate to SACAA. There is no fee to pay SACAA, but be aware that medical aid schemes usually do not cover aviation medicals.

3.6 DUTY TO REPORT BEING UNFIT

Certifying you as fit is not the sole responsibility of the DAME. It is also your responsibility *(exam!)*.

Why? Because the DAME tests you at a given time, taking into account a verifiable past medical history and how you fare on the day of examination.

But the minute you step out of the DAME's practice, **like a new car leaving the show room, you lose value.** You may not be fit the following day. This leads us to the next point: reporting health trouble.

Reporting medical issues

- First, should a medical condition appear, you must advise what is called 'the designated body' (your DAME).
- Second, whenever you fly, you must not break certain medical rules (more on this later, when we deal with getting ready to fly, in Part 3).

In short, you have to remain as you were when you submitted yourself to the medical examination. **This is why you must report any problem 'without undue delay'.**

All this is encapsulated in the following provisions, as they appear in CARS.[18] *Read these rules carefully; they are exam question material!*

---

[17] CARS 67.00.9 (a).
[18] CARS 67.00.9 (1) (b) (c) (2).

> **As the holder of a medical certificate you must**
>
> - **NOT under any circumstances act as a PIC**, or in any other capacity as a flight crew member, an air traffic service personnel member or a cabin crew member, as the case may be—
>   - (i) if you are aware of any **medical condition or medication** which could affect the validity of such medical certificate;
>   - (ii) if **pregnant** during periods and under circumstances as prescribed in Document SA-CATS 67;
>   - (iii) if you have **given birth** in the preceding six weeks; or
>   - (iv) after your medical **certificate has expired**;
> - **AND without undue delay** notify the designated body *[Note: your DAME]* or institution of any—
>   - (i) injury;
>   - (ii) hospitalisation;
>   - (iii) surgical operation or invasive procedure;
>   - (iv) regular use of medication;
>   - (v) pregnancy;
>   - (vi) absence due to illness for a period of more than 21 days; or
>   - (vii) psychiatric treatment, which renders such holder unable to comply with the appropriate medical requirements and standards referred to in regulation 67.00.2(6).
>
> And: The holder of a medical certificate must, **before such holder resumes the exercising of the privileges of the licence** held by him or her, furnish the designated body or institution with proof that he or she has fully recovered from the decrease in medical fitness.

Here is a simple example: if you are 'aware' that a drug prescribed by your GP to help you write your matric exams is impairing your judgment by making you restless or hyperactive, you must tell your instructor, 'Sorry I can't fly solo today' (you apply the first rule), and you must 'notify' your DAME if you have been taking this medication 'regularly' (another rule).

You want to fly today? Observe eight prohibitions or you may not fly[19]

'As a pilot (or a "crew member") **you must NOT fly** ("act as a crew member") **if**

(a) **using any psychoactive substance** that may affect your faculties in any manner that may jeopardise safety;

(b) **within 24 hours following scuba diving**;

(c) **within 72 hours following blood donation** *[by you]*;

(d) *if you know or suspect that you are suffering from or, having due regard to the circumstances of the flight to be undertaken, are* **likely to suffer from fatigue** to such an extent that it may endanger the safety of the aircraft or its occupants;

and if you

(a) **consume any alcohol less than eight hours prior** to the specified reporting time for operational duty or the commencement of a shift *[for a PPL 'operational duty' is your estimated time of departure]*;

(b) *commence an operational duty while the concentration of* **alcohol** in any specimen of blood taken from any part of your body is **more than 0,02 gram per 100 millilitres;**

(c) **consume alcohol during the operational duty** period or while on standby for operational duty; and

(d) *within* **eight hours after an accident** or reportable incident involving the aircraft, unless the accident or incident was not related to your duties.

In addition, and it is specifically cited in Part 67 Duties of holder of medical certificate:

anaesthetics. The rules oblige you to contact your DAME, and not simply wait the number of hours specified, that is:

- A minimum of 24 hours following local or regional (including dental) anaesthetics. (The condition for which the anaesthetic has been administered must also be considered **prior to returning** an individual to flying or controlling duties) *[read: you do not return yourself; you are returned by your DAME, and the occurrence is placed on file]*.

- A minimum of 72 hours following general, spinal or epidural anaesthetic. This proscription includes drug-induced sedation. (The condition for which the anaesthetic has been administered must also be considered before returning an individual to flying or controlling duties) *[read: same as above]*.

---

[19] CARS 91.02.3.

> **Anti-anxiety or anti-insomnia benzodiazepine** (temazepam: acceptable): you wait 72 hours, no requirement to advise your DAME.'
>
> *Exam questions!*

CATS, under the heading 'Flight crew health precautions', although in a different context, provides a handy list, which is a recap of what to watch out for if you want to remain legal on a day when the skies are clear and you are about to climb into the cockpit:[20]

> '(a) alcohol and other intoxicating liquor;
> (b) narcotics;
> (c) drugs;
> (d) sleeping tablets;
> (e) pharmaceutical preparations;
> (f) immunisation;
> (g) scuba diving;
> (h) blood donation;
> (i) meal precautions before and during flight;
> (j) sleep and rest;
> (k) surgical operations.'

Alcohol, scuba diving and blood donation are standard exam 'traps'.

Medical certification is essential to flying.

Losing one's medical can be heartbreaking. There is no need to lose it, or endanger it, through negligence. Follow the rules and stay fit. Don't drink, don't dive, don't bleed. Pleasantries aside, your medical certification is the **gatekeeper** of your pilot's licence—of any pilot's licence—and of your dreams. Upset the gatekeeper, and the gate will slam shut on your wings.

Time now to look at what comes next, at long last: your first licence itself, your SPL!

---

[20] CATS 127.04.2–2.1.8 Commercial Helicopters Operations.

PART TWO

BECOMING AND BEING A PILOT

Chapter 4

. . . .

Becoming a pilot

> The engine was panting. I gently lowered the nose of the aircraft. It was not easy to maintain the plane on a slight downward slope together with a low speed in a descending trajectory. At an altitude of 750 feet, it cut out altogether. Nothing to be done but glide.
>
> Ryuji Nagatsuka I Was a Kamikaze[1]

You want to become a pilot. You will be taught how to glide after a (simulated) engine failure. No need to be a kamikaze ('divine wind' in Japanese). But kamikaze pilots went through the same training as you are about to follow. Save for the final dive. Even kamikaze pilots obeyed the law—especially them.

Your aim is to get your Private Pilot Licence (called 'certificate' in the United States): it is the foundation. Future careers in aviation are built on the skills and the knowledge acquired while training towards it and after obtaining it. But you will begin by being a student pilot, and getting a Student Pilot Licence, the SPL.[2] You will be allowed to wear epaulettes with one gold strip on your neatly pressed white shirt. And you will be allowed to train towards a PPL. The difference between a SPL and a PPL is simple: to get a SPL you just have to enrol at a school, fill in an application, get a medical certificate, and start training. If all goes well you will get your PPL at the end of it.

A word of advice: choosing the right Aviation Training Organisation (ATO)[3], school or flight academy, is very important. It is not a legal choice, but you have to consider carefully the reputation of the instructors, the type of training aircraft the school uses, and the one you want to fly on: comfy high wing, sexy low wing?

Also consider the hourly rate (a light sport aeroplane is usually cheaper than a type-certified one); the distance you will have to travel to the flight school (you do not want to become stressed by the traffic before flying, and have to rush if you are late); whether the school provides good amenities (food, bathroom, free wifi); and if you feel comfortable there.

---

[1] Ryuji Nagatsuka *I Was a Kamikaze* translated from the French original (2014) 61 (slightly adapted).

[2] SPL: in EASA licensing SPL refers to a Sailplane Pilot Licence—glider pilot licence. The SPL student pilot licence is being phased out in countries outside the EASA area. Australia's CASA for instance no longer delivers the student licence (Civil Aviation Safety Regulations, Regulation 61.112, compilation date: 31 January 2018).

[3] As per CARS Part 141.

Nothing legal in all that? In fact, it is borderline: if you pick a school that is far away or stuck beyond traffic jams, you might become stressed and on occasion you will have to apply the I'M SAFE test (see page 109) and evaluate if you may fly legitimately once you reach base. You may not be able to.

So, how do you start, legally?

Here is an obvious statement: a SPL is a licence, and a licence is a legal document.

First you have to apply for your SPL, and the procedure falls under CARS Part 61 Pilot Licensing. *Students, note: you will be asked about what Part of CARS and CATS deal with your licensing*:

- SPL and PPL licensing falls under **Part 61**,
- But the National Pilot Learner's Certificate and the National Pilot Licence fall under **Part 62**.

Integrated training: Some schools offer full-time integrated training that leads *ab initio* ('from the start' in Latin, or with no previous training) to CPL (VFR) (visual flight rules), CPL (IR) (Instrument Rating) (A) (aeroplane) and ATPL (air transport pilot) (A). Students do not get a PPL while training, but receive a CPL/IR at the end of training.[4]

4.1 YOUR FIRST PAPERWORK: YOUR STUDENT LICENCE AND LOGBOOK

In South Africa (and in Swaziland, Namibia, and Botswana), before you can start training you need to apply for your SPL.

Be proud of it. In many countries there is no student licence: students just train until they get their PPL. Here, your SPL is a Pilot Licence, and your first Pilot Licence. There is of course an application procedure and rules in place to keep it valid.

This will be your first paperwork.

4.1.1 Applying for a Student Pilot Licence

There is one condition: an application for a SPL demands that you hold a 'valid medical certificate', as we have seen already.

---

[4] CARS 61.01.15(2) and a full description CATS Appendix 3.0 (training syllabus), Appendix 3.B (specific to CPL (A)/IR (training syllabus) and Appendix 20.0 (multi-crew co-operation).

How to apply for a SPL[5]

- be 15 years or older;[6]
- hold a valid medical certificate;[7]
- be registered with an approved aviation training organisation (ATO) for training;
- fill in the 'Application for initial issue' form[8]

and attach to it the following:
  - certified proof of ID
  - proof of age
  - valid medical certificate, for the appropriate aircraft you will train on—for helicopters, only two types
  - two recent photos
  - the appropriate fee—get used now to paying fees for every single document. Fees are revised regularly through an AIP Amendment: pay the old fee and you are not legal.

- Once you get it back from SACAA, sign it 'immediately',[9] in black indelible ink. Keep a certified copy, just in case. If you lose it, you can ask for a duplicate—with a fee attached.

CARS Part 187 deals with Fees and Charges. It is regularly updated (usually in March, effective in April) by way of an Amendment to CARS, and is available on the SACAA website. You must check it before paying any fees. As a pilot you will be mostly concerned with regulation 187.01.10.

What is the definition of 'date of application'?

Date of application 'when used in connection with the issuing, renewal or re-issuing of a licence, certificate or rating, means the date on which the application is received in the prescribed form by the Director'.[10] In short, it is not the date on which you signed, dated and presumably sent the form.

---

[5] CARS 61.02.1–6.

[6] CARS 62.02.1: NPL, 16, for the Learner's Certificate, 14 in paraglider category.

[7] CARS 61.02.1(b). CARS 67.00.2 only mentions a Class 2. However, if you are doing the Integrated Training, you can ask for a Class 1 as it is mandatory for the CPL or ATPL. But beware of the time validity rules, and costs relevant to a Class 1.

[8] SACAA Form Number: CA 61.01.0 Application for initial issue of SA-CAR Part 61 Pilot Licence or Rating (excluding class and type rating).

[9] CARS 61.02.3 (2).

[10] CARS 1.01.1.

4.1.2 How to maintain a valid SPL

The SPL is issued for two years but you have to maintain its validity. The following rules apply:

- **Pay annual 'currency fees'** by the anniversary of the date of issue, otherwise your licence is no longer valid. Your licence is valid for two years, but there is a yearly fee to be paid on time ('anniversary date') to remain legal, together with sending the application called 'annual submission for maintenance of pilot licence validity'.
- **Follow a standard procedure** (same for your PPL). You will need to fill in the **annual currency form**,[11] attach to this application a **certified copy of your logbook consisting of the last three pages** containing entries indicating a record of flight times, an **annual summary** (annexure 5) indicating flight time per category, class, type and total time, as well as certified copies of **any endorsements entered into the logbook** in the preceding 12 months.[12] And do not forget a proof of payment (always check on SACAA website for the latest schedule of fees, Public> Fees> 3 Pilot Licensing Fees).
- **If you lose your medical** or report a medical condition that suspends your certification, your SPL is still valid, but you cannot fly until the medical matter is resolved (see chapter 3).
- **If, for some reason, your training exceeds two years**, you will need to re-apply.

Schools keep a record of all of this on their management system, and you will see a FAIL flag when you try to green tag for a flight if your SPL is not valid. You will be grounded. However, what matters is what is endorsed in your logbook.

4.1.3 Your logbook matters!

By now you have purchased a logbook. It is essentially made of two parts: most of it is a record of your flight hours or logbook, and the last pages are a record of endorsements.

We will return later to the **recording of flight hours** as it is not straightforward, so do not write anything in your logbook until you are sure how to do it properly (see page 66 and annexure 5 for the logbook summary).

You will record flight hours yourself. But you will not enter endorsements yourself.

About endorsements

Throughout your flying career, each time you pass a check, a skills test, a competency check, a rating or a conversion has to be endorsed in your logbook.

---

[11] SACAA Form Number: CA 61.01 16 Annual submission for maintenance of pilot's licence validity.

[12] CARS 61.01.5 (13).

'Endorsed' means that it is recorded in the back of your logbook by whoever has examined you and is in authority to do so. This is usually your instructor or an examiner, who dates, signs and stamps the endorsement.

Application, endorsements and record keeping[13]

(1) An applicant for a **licence, rating, revalidation, class or type rating or any familiarisation or differences training must have the applicable endorsements** in his or her pilot logbook as described in Document SA-CATS 61.

(2) The endorsement must include, but is not limited to, the following details—

    (a) date of the skills test;

    (b) aircraft registration and type;

    (c) name and licence number of examiner;

    (d) name of the ATO.

(3) The flight examiner conducting a skills test or revalidation check shall stamp, sign, initial and date the applicable form for each candidate, as required, before forwarding to the Director for processing and record keeping: the stamp shall include the following details:

    (a) Initials and surname of flight instructor or examiner;

    (b) Pilot licence number of flight instructor or examiner;

    (c) Designation applicable to the flight instructor or examiner, such as Grade I or II flight instructor or DFE I (A), (H), DFE II (A), (H) or DFE III (A), (H) as the case may be.

(4) Incorrect information contained on the stamp referred to in sub-regulation (3) shall invalidate the form.

In addition: 'An examiner who conducted a skills test, competency check or revalidation check shall endorse the logbook of the candidate or pilot as prescribed in Document SA-CATS 61.'[14]

Once your application for a SPL is granted by the Director of SACAA, this legal document, like any other legal document, exists for two main reasons: it demands that you do certain things, and it forbids you to do others. If you fail to do what is requested or take upon yourself to do what is forbidden, you are no longer legally a pilot, and that carries sanctions (from a fine, to suspension and even criminal proceedings if you are involved in an accident, for instance, while 'flying on the sly').

---

[13] CARS 61.01.18.
[14] CARS 61.01.5 (6).

48   *Air Law*

So, with a SPL in your flight bag, you are legally allowed to train and fly, but only under certain positive conditions which the law calls 'privileges', and negative ones which are called 'limitations'.

4.2 PRIVILEGES AND LIMITATIONS

What the Student Private Licence allows are 'privileges', and what it forbids are 'limitations'[15]

Students, note! You will be examined on privileges and limitations.

'Privileges' are enabling rules.

The word itself is a legal term. Why are enabling rules called 'privileges'? The word 'privilege' comes from Latin (the original language of the law) and means 'private law'. The laws that apply to a SPL, PPL, CPL, or ATPL are 'private', or particular, in so far as they do not apply 'universally', to everyone, but to a particular group called pilots. The rest of the populace—99.99% of humanity—is unconcerned by pilots' laws.

Now that this point of history is clarified, do not get sidetracked by the word: **pilot licence privileges are enablers**; they enable you to use your licence legally.

What you can legally do, or 'privileges'

YES
- Fly solo, but only:
  - for training purposes (no sightseeing flights);
  - in the type of aircraft you are training on and endorsed in your logbook.

YES
- Do training flights:
  - as prescribed in the curriculum (called 'exercises');
  - with written authorisation, typically signed by an instructor (or the CFI or someone appointed by the CFI who holds at least a PPL) and entered into the authorisation book *(Part 141 describes the procedures your ATO must follow, but they are not relevant for your PPL exam)*. An authorisation sheet is generated by the school system once you have entered details of the intended flight, including the mass and balance computation. This sheet is printed and signed off by you and your instructor;
  - under personal supervision—that is your instructor will either sit on the right or, if you fly solo, listen to your radio calls from the ground and be at hand if, as it happens, there is a spot of trouble (oil pressure, ASI not working, flaps not retracting) to advise you.

---

[15] CARS 61.02.5.

YES • ONLY fly VMC by day.

What is illegal for you to do, or 'limitations'

NO
• Fly internationally, that is, cross a national border.
NO
• Carry a passenger (never take a passenger on a solo flight until you hold your PPL—during a dual flight, your instructor may allow you to take a passenger).
   Note that as a SPL doing Integrated Training you can carry student pilots also undergoing Integrated Training at the same ATO for the purpose of navigation training, provided that you have passed the navigation progress test and are authorised by a Grade I or II instructor.[16]
NO
• Fly in conditions other than VMC; and no VMC by night.
   Note that a SPL doing Integrated Training may fly VMC by night if holding a valid NR (night rating) and fly under IFR if holding a valid IR (Instrument rating).[17]
NO
• Take off or land other than at an aerodrome except in an emergency—and if you have had to do so in an emergency, you are not allowed to fly the aeroplane, and only a CPL, ATPL or pilot approved for that purpose by the Director of SACAA is allowed to.

Now, you must put all this knowledge and your SPL to good use—in other words, get your training going. The law frames what training towards a PPL consists of. As a student pilot you will have to demonstrate, via exams and tests, two aspects:
• your flying proficiency;
• your understanding of flying.

In short: practice and theory.

What comes first in your overall training is (not) an egg and a chicken question. The law wants you to be both the chicken that can fly and the egg that explains the chicken.

So let us look first at the egg: theory.

---

[16] CARS 61.02.5 (2) (c).
[17] CARS 61.02.5 (2).

4.3 THE LEGAL FRAMEWORK OF YOUR TRAINING

The first thing you can and should expect from your instructor or school is to give you **four schedules or notices**, to make you aware of what is in store. If the school does not, ask for them. CARS Part 141 (which deals with ATOs) is explicit in this regard: your ATO must ensure that you are 'aware of the most appropriate learning conditions'.[18]

- The **syllabus of theoretical knowledge** (annexure 6). This is for your theoretical examinations and for a good understanding of airmanship for as long as you are a pilot. This leads to the seven theoretical exam papers (plus Radio Telephony and possibly the English proficiency examination). This is your core knowledge as a pilot, for now and ever.
- The **practical syllabus for flight instruction**, or the sequence of 19 practical exercises; in short, what you really want to do: flying. This will culminate in the Skills Test, without which there is no PPL. What you learn here will remain with you for as long as you are a pilot. Refer to annexure 7.
- The **Radio Telephony syllabus**. Flying involves a lot of talking and the use of telecommunication devices. Hence you must be trained in and obtain a Restricted Radio Certificate.
- **English language certification,** if you require it. If you are unsure, check the rules (4.4.5 below), so that you do not have a nasty surprise a day before your Skills Test.

4.4 THE THEORETICAL SYLLABUS AND EXAMINATIONS

This is possibly what many SPL trainees find the least enjoyable part of their studies: reading large volumes (including of course this book!); learning by heart things one does not really understand fully; trying to see how a description fits an actual engine part; grappling with odd words like 'longeron' or 'katabatic', not to mention puzzling over lawyerly verbiage; losing one's way in immense sentences running into ten lines at a time; and wondering how all that can possibly help you fly better.

Some trainees take to it like a seaplane to water. Most try their best and suffer repeated fails. Some get so discouraged that they stop flying. The problem here is that theoretical notions are the basis for future exams, they are the core of your knowledge as an aviator, and they actually make you a better, safer pilot.

So, let us **look at these legally imposed examinations as enablers** rather than obstacles.

---

[18] CARS 141.02.5.

4.4.1 The 7 +1 examination papers

Below, in alphabetical order, are your **seven examination 'papers'** (plus 1) as they are called.[19]

The 7 +1 exam papers

- Aircraft General (duration: 45 min)
- Air Law (duration: 60 min)
- Flight Performance and Planning (duration: 90 min)
- General Navigation (duration: 90 min)
- Human Performance and Limitations (duration: 45 min)
- Aviation Meteorology (duration: 60 min)
- Principles of Flight (duration: 45 min)

plus

- Radiotelephony[20] (duration: 90 min). See below 4.4.4.

The pass mark is 75%. This is not a regional standard: for instance, the Swaziland Civil Aviation Authority (SWACAA) has set its pass mark at 70%.[21] That does not mean it is easier.

Questions are multiple choice (usually three or four choices), single select, or multi select (there may be two correct replies). The question format can also be a true/false or a fill-in-the-blank variation.[22]

An Air Law paper usually has a maximum of 30 questions. Flight Performance and Planning lasts 90 minutes for, often, 29 questions only—they are tough. You will book each exam in advance at your school, pay a fee, and then write it online. The result is immediate. You also receive a 'coaching report', which highlights the parts of the syllabus you failed (not the exact questions).

However, if you turn to the **Syllabus of Theoretical Knowledge** (annexure 6) you will see that it does not correlate with the 7 +1 exam papers.

---

[19] CATS 61.03.1–2.

[20] Both radiotelephony and radio telephony are used.

[21] SACAA-AC—PEL018A (Advisory Circular of 2011). There are no CATS in Swaziland but Technical Guidance Material by way of Advisory Circulars.

[22] Procedures for examinations are described in CATS 61.01.10 (last amended SACATS AMDT 3/18, effective 6 December 2018).

4.4.2 Syllabus vs exams

Indeed the scope of the syllabus is breathtaking and intimidating (annexure 6), and is the basis for SACAA's central question bank,[23] but you will not find it divided neatly into seven sections, one per exam paper.

Why? Here is what SACAA says:[24]

> 'An examinee is assumed to be competent in all aspects of the theoretical knowledge requirements of the licence.'[23]

And it goes further than cross-paper questioning: 'This means, for example, that a question requiring PPL-level meteorology knowledge may be asked in a CPL Flight Performance and Planning examination.'[25]

In short, **questions are quite often not paper specific**. They test **core knowledge**. It explains why **questions about air law come up in other exams**, such as the Navigation paper, and vice versa—much to the surprise of students. *Beware of this!*[26]

4.4.3 When should I study?

Schools' approaches vary in terms of how they combine practical training with theoretical learning. Some will want you to do nearly all your exams as soon as possible, even before your do your first flight. Some will mix and match. Some will favour one-on-one briefings. Others will have group 'ground school' sessions lasting up to eight hours each. There is no straightforward recipe.

Young pilots straight from matric will not mind sweating again over papers. Worldly types used to ordering secretaries around at work will balk at it. It is also a question of season: when it is not flying time (winter in the Cape, or thunderstorms in Gauteng, not to mention the irrepressible fog at FAGG[27]), do the reading and get the exams done. The main point is that you finish it all in good time—what defines 'good time' is explained later on (4.4.6 below).

Another consideration is that, contrary to the practical schedule of flying exercises whereby exercises have to follow a set sequence (you cannot do exercise 3 if you have not performed 2 correctly), theoretical acquisition does not follow a compulsory sequence. This is why the seven exams are given in a near alphabetical

---

[23] CATS 61, Appendix 1.0.
[24] CATS 61.01.10 (11) (d) (i).
[25] CATS 61.01.16 (11) (d) (ii).
[26] By comparison the PPL Syllabus of the Civil Aviation Authority of Zimbabwe (CAAZ) lists specifics under Air Law (2002) (http://www.caaz.co.zw/regulatory#).
[27] George airport.

order. It means that you study and sit the theoretical exams when you wish, or as you are told—or as best as you can manage. **You sit them in no specific order**.[28]

Any advice? Try to do Human Performance and Limitations first, Principles of Flight second, and Air Law third, since the others will be easier once you have flown for a while, and are familiar with your machine.

Examinations are online. Usually you will sit the exam at your school, which acts as an Accredited Examination Centre. The school will also advise you on booking, protocols, and fees.

4.4.4 Radiotelephony[29]

A private pilot must hold the entry-level Restricted Radio Certificate in order to be able to apply for a PPL.[30] To obtain this certificate you must satisfy the English Language Proficiency Requirement (see 4.4.5 below) and these specific requirements:

- pass a theoretical knowledge examination;
- pass a practical communication test; and
- complete a full ATC flight plan.

The syllabus is exhaustive.[31] Your instructor will provide you with all the details. Often schools arrange for a seasoned Air Traffic Controller who is a RTE (radio telephony examiner) to hold a two-day workshop. Once done, your RTE and ATO will fill in and sign the relevant parts of your application form, called Notification of Restricted Radiotelephony Proficiency, form CA 61–01.0c, which you will send to SACAA. You will then be issued with your Restricted Radio Certificate, which will be endorsed on your licence.

4.4.5 Do you speak English? The Language Proficiency Certificate

No licence above SPL can be issued if you 'have not demonstrated or provided proof of the ability to speak the English language' as per rules below.[32] Pilots (A and H) have to be **fully 'proficient' in English**. And so do glider and free balloons pilots, ATC personnel and aeronautical station operators.

Note that **the release of a SPL licence does not impose a proficiency test in English** (which may lead to training problems for students who are not fluent, especially in written English). PPL does.

Typically, **you will be granted proficiency certification—that is you will not have to undergo the test—if you provide certified evidence that—**

---

[28] CATS 61.01.10 (11) (d).
[29] CATS 61.03.1.
[30] CATS 61.03.1 (5).
[31] CATS 61, Appendix 1.5.
[32] CARS and CATS 61.01.7.

- you hold a foreign CAA language certification in English; or
- you hold a matric, O or M level, with a pass in English first language with a minimum symbol of D or its equivalent (you automatically meet the Language Proficiency Requirement as mandated by ICAO); or
- you hold a SAQA-recognised two-year tertiary qualification with English either as a subject or English as the language of tuition; or
- you are 'a present or past native of a nation where English is the first language, e.g. UK, USA, Australia or New Zealand'.[33]

If you do not fulfil at least one of these criteria, whether you are South African or a foreigner enjoying our southern skies, excellent schools and value-for-money rates, you need to submit yourself to a Language Proficiency test.

ICAO has established six proficiency levels with a rating scale: those who get a Level 6, 'Expert', need never be retested. But those at Level 5, 'Extended', need retesting every six years; and at Level 4, 'Operational (minimum level)', every three years. Below Level 4, the licence cannot be issued or maintained. If **you get a Level 4, you can fly legally for three years at a time.**

However **candidates who do not meet Level 4** can, and should undergo remedial language training as advised by the test results. Those who are vexed to get only Level 4 or 5 proficiency (and who do not want to be retested every few years) can apply for re-testing after a period of 90 days, to try to upgrade their rating.

NPL trainees need only 'demonstrate' an 'ability' to read, speak, and understand English for ground operations and for communicating during all phases of flight. In practice 'having graduated from a pilot licensing course conducted in English' is enough.[34]

What about the test itself?

The test or Oral Proficiency Interview

The OPI, or Oral Proficiency Interview (another name for the test) lasts up to one hour, sometimes more. Its aim is to evaluate speaking and listening proficiency only, and not the ability to read or write.

The OPI may be conducted by examiners at your own ATO if the ATO is accredited. Your ATO will tell you how to apply. Examiners charge a fee.

You will be jointly examined by two examiners, called Approved Language Proficiency Interviewers / Raters, who will sit in front of you, across a table:

- a subject matter expert (a pilot or ATC)—on aviation communication and phraseology;

---

[33] CATS 61.01.7 (12).
[34] CARS 62.01.11.

> - a linguistic expert (usually an English teacher)—to evaluate your spoken English in terms of clarity of pronunciation, ability to compose concise and unambiguous sentences, accuracy and scope of vocabulary, fluency in describing events and responding, ability to understand questions and follow instructions, and interactive ability to ask and answer questions and engage with ease in a two-way dialogue.
>
> The test is preceded by a **pre-interview** (completion of a bio-data questionnaire).

It is a nerve-racking examination, as both examiners will 'bombard' you from different angles, simulating situations where you have to interact while flying.

Since **your flying career can crash right there by failing that test** (failure = no licence), or have you living under the shadow of regular re-testing, I advise you to prepare thoroughly for the OPI and ask your instructor to stage a mock interview.

You should also do the OPI after you have completed your theoretical and radio telephony exams: it is the best way to know and show the subject matter expert that you can 'speak pilot' with ease and accuracy.

After all, this is legal English for pilots: one word badly pronounced or heard wrongly, and an air disaster may happen.

In fact, at the **Skills Test**, your proficiency in English will decide whether you are awarded your PPL or not. The examiner will observe and grade you in terms of your 'skills and knowledge to communicate with all stakeholders in the aviation environment using English language'; in short, how you make your calls, how you communicate with another aircraft, how good you are at using aviation language, and so on, in terms of your **fluency in spoken English**.[35]

4.4.6 Examination time-line issues

Time is of the essence when completing exams to get your PPL. SACAA's legal time-frames are stringent. The clock starts ticking at your first successful examination: you have 18 continuous months from the date of first passing an exam to complete all seven theoretical exams, plus Radio Telephony, plus, if applicable, the English Proficiency test.

Wasting time by failing exams: rewrite and re-mark

This is the main worry of any student: if I fail, when can I rewrite? The law is explicit and, unfortunately for newcomers to the freedom of the skies, since 2016 it is more stringent than before.

---

[35] Appendix 1.2 of CATS 61.

Rewrite after failure

CATS is worth quoting in full *(and some of it comes up in exams)*:[36]

> '(a) A candidate may not apply to rewrite an examination until he or she has received the official result notification *[in your case you will have it immediately after the exam]*;
>
> (b) A candidate **who has failed** an examination conducted by the Authority for the issue, re-issue, validation or conversion of a **PPL, Night Rating or a Restricted Radiotelephony Operator's Certificate**, as the case may be, **may not rewrite** the applicable examination subject **within a period of 7 calendar days after date of failure**;
>
> (c) A candidate **who has failed** an examination conducted by the Authority for the **issue, re-issue, validation or conversion of a flight crew licence or rating other** than those referred to in paragraph *(b)*, or a General Radiotelephony Operator's Certificate, **may not rewrite** the applicable examination subject—
>
>   (i) in the case of a first or second failure, within a period of 7 calendar days after date of failure;
>
>   (ii) in the case of a third or subsequent failure, within a period of 2 calendar months after date of failure;
>
>   (iii) in any case where a score of less than 50% was achieved, within a period of 2 calendar months after date of failure.
>
> (d) **If a score of less than 50%** is achieved for a subject in conjunction with a third or subsequent failure in that subject, the respective periods of 2 calendar months shall not be cumulative.
>
> (e) In exceptional circumstances and at the discretion of the Director, the period of 7 calendar days referred to in paragraphs *(b)* and *(c)* may be shortened, after written application by a candidate and with the written approval of the Director.
>
> (f) The period **of 2 calendar months** referred to in paragraph *(c)* is intended **to assist candidates to undergo remedial training** before they rewrite a failed subject and shall be referred to as a compulsory retraining period in this Technical Standard.
>
> (g) The administrative official responsible for the scheduling of an examination shall determine whether a candidate qualifies for a rewrite of a failed subject, taking into account paragraphs *(b)* and *(c)*, before scheduling such a candidate for the examination concerned.

---

[36] CATS 61.01.10 (9). Emphasis added.

(h) The compulsory retraining period referred to above shall not apply to candidates who hold credit for four (4) or more examination subjects on 2016–06–30. This exception shall remain applicable to such candidates as long as the credits held on that date remain valid. Candidates that qualify for this exception shall nevertheless be subject to the waiting period of seven (7) calendar days referred to in paragraph *(c)* for each failure of an examination subject.

(i) **Once credit is held for an examination subject, a candidate may not re-sit the applicable examination for any reason**, including an attempt to obtain higher marks. Examinations that have been passed may only be retaken when the credits previously achieved are no longer valid'.

Re-mark after failure[37]

Within 30 days after the date of notification (in your case it will be the day you failed, as you get the result right away) you can apply in writing to the Director for a re-mark of the **most recent** failed examination. Your application must include the applicable fee.

But you may apply only if you scored between 70% and 74%.

If the re-mark yields a pass, the fee is refunded.

Beware of re-marks unless you can clearly recall the phrasing of the question and clearly recall your answer, and then ask your instructor right away.

The report 'coaching' sheet you get after each exam does not list questions and answers, as already mentioned, but just areas of knowledge where you failed. So, do not challenge SACAA unnecessarily by second-guessing which question you think you answered correctly and failed because 'the system does not work'.

Set period in which to pass all your theoretical papers[38]

The applicant must have passed all seven theoretical knowledge examinations for a PPL **within a period of 18 months of obtaining the first credit** and must **have passed the final theoretical knowledge examination within the 36 months preceding the skills test for a PPL**.

If you have not obtained your (at least Restricted) Radiotelephony Operator's Certificate within 18 months of a first attempt you are allowed to rewrite the exam.[39] Remember that without it you cannot apply for a PPL. And also remember that you have to provide proof of English proficiency.

---

[37] CARS 61.01.10 (10) (as per AMDT 3/18).
[38] CARS 61.03.3 (A) and 61.04.3 (H).
[39] CARS 61.01.10 (12) (b) (as per AMDT 3/18).

58   Air Law

In plain language: you have a maximum of 18 months to do all your seven theoretical exams, and then a maximum of 36 months to complete your flight training. So, getting a PPL may well run into 54 months, or four and a half years. That is extensive, and expensive.

If you exceed the 18 months, you must rewrite all seven theoretical subjects. No credit is held from before.

This is the timeline:

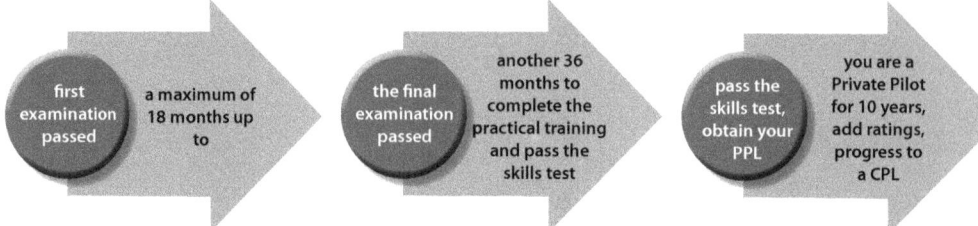

And now, what of the flying itself in terms of showing that you meet the legal requirements?

4.5   PRACTICAL FLIGHT INSTRUCTION

This is what you have been waiting for.

4.5.1   Flying exercises

The exercises you are being put through are standardised and strictly regulated. They are **sequential and cumulative**, meaning that you will move to the next exercise only when your instructor is satisfied you have proved proficiency in the previous exercise (and has recorded this in your file). Flying abilities accumulate as mind and body develop near automatic responses to situations in flight, in harmony with your machine—an alignment of mind, body, machine and flight conditions.

Your training is called *ab initio* (as noted earlier, Latin for 'from the start') as it refers to 'the practical training required towards the first issue of a national or PPL, issued in terms of Part 61 (= PPL) or Part 62 (= NPL)'.[40] On your school booking sheet, in the right hand top section, at 'Flight Type' you will see 'AbInitio' (often written as one word).

Your training *ab initio* comprises **19 exercises**.

You will not be allowed to fly solo unless you have met the requirements of exercises 1 to 13, after which you will be let loose in the general Flying Training Area and later on a cross-country navigation.

---

[40]   CARS 1.01.1.

For that reason, the law describes minutely legal requirements placed on dual flying, solo flying, and progress checks.[41] *You can expect exam questions on the more important regulations.*

The compulsory schedule and sequence of 19 exercises is called the **Practical Syllabus of Flight Instruction**.[42]

This syllabus is the detailed protocol according to which your instructor assesses you. You need to know what the actual, detailed content of each exercise is. This is your practical training (annexure 7).

The schedule of exercises detailed in the Syllabus is an international standard (with local variations), and is of course the basis of any pilot's flying handbooks or training manuals available commercially—or free of charge on the FAA website.[43]

4.5.2 Airmanship

You will notice that '**airmanship**' is a word your instructor may use quite often: 'You showed airmanship!' Or not. It is also an assessment value in many of the exercises mentioned, usually at the end of an exercise (refer to the Syllabus).

Airmanship is not a fancy word: it is a recurrent theme in CATS. For instance it is listed as one topic in the refresher seminars for a Flight Instructor ratings (many young pilots will proceed to an instructor rating, so take note).[44]

So, what is this thing called airmanship?

> Airmanship is 'the consistent use of good judgment and well-developed knowledge, skills and attitudes to accomplish flight objectives'.[45]

Do not dismiss airmanship as the relic of a bygone age of gentlemen flyers, when men flew in leather helmets and ladies in silk scarves. The key phrase is 'good judgment', based itself on 'well-developed knowledge': your instructor wants to see that, apart from performing the correct actions, you also apply your mind and are able to make the right choices, speedily and efficiently. And in doing so, your instructor is applying the law. It is subjective, and some instructors are known to be pernickety, but it is also an objective evaluation: if you misjudge an operation, and take too much time to correct it, and 'let the plane fly you', it is bad airmanship.

4.5.3 Making a call: student prefixes

Remember this: you are a student and when calling an ATS, you will want to let controllers know this. They will accommodate you and help you by being patient

---

[41] CATS (not CARS) 61.02.5, 1–2–3.
[42] Appendix 1.1 to SA-CATS 61.
[43] At www.faa.gov>Handbooks & Manuals. An unequalled resource.
[44] CATS 61.14.7 (2) (a) (v) (hh).
[45] CATS 1.01.1.

or, as the regulation says: 'ATC shall be aware that the flight has an ab-initio student on board and where applicable shall provide progressive instructions or clearances.'[46]

Consequently, on first contact when you identify your aircraft and greet Approach or Tower, always remember to prefix your call sign with 'Student' or 'Solo student', as in, eg:

- 'Student' ZS-WAM; or
- 'Solo student' ZU-BAM.

In fact, if you filed a flight plan those mentions should go at item 18 as a RMK (remark).

This will alert a controller—and other aircraft too—to your flying noviciate.

Note that prefixing ('helicopter') is recommended for helicopters, especially when the call sign does not make it clear it is a helicopter.

4.5.4 Debriefs

ATOs are legally compelled to make certain that straight after each flight **you are properly debriefed** by your instructor, that **the debrief is done on an appropriate form, called a Progress Report** (annexure 8), with relevant details following the sequence of flying, and that it is signed by you and your instructor, and placed in your file.

Debriefs are crucial: they help you understand why you have not met the requirements of a given exercise, hence the necessity of a debrief straight after each flight—to move on. If an instructor does not debrief you, request it. Don't be shy. SACAA may ask to see files during a school inspection, and it can lead to all sorts of trouble for you and the instructor, and the CFI, if your file is incomplete.

4.5.5 Endorsements

As already mentioned, your pilot logbook will be endorsed each time you achieve a benchmark in your training—your first solo for instance, and of course the Skills Test that concludes your training. You must make sure you get these endorsements.

4.6 TOWARDS YOUR FIRST SOLO

Your first solo (exercise 14) is really the point at which your instructor decides that you are ready for advanced exercises, that you have developed the mind–body–machine–flight conditions to fly alone.

Your first solo is framed by strong legal provisions.

Why? Because ICAO and SACAA are fully aware of the dangers involved, for you and others, in being a novice flyer. SACAA is also aware what a decisive

---

[46] AIP ENR 1.8–26, 27 Training flights.

benchmark it is to reach the solo stage and wants to ensure it is all done properly and according to ICAO standards. What are these safeguards?
- Your school should ask you to satisfy some basic theoretical knowledge **requirements** (separate from the theoretical exams) consisting of theoretical instruction and pre-solo examination (at the school):[47]
    - basic air law (for instance you should know which Part of CARS applies to a SPL, and know what your 'privileges' are); and
    - knowledge of your aircraft (make, model, and basic specs).

This short in-house exam should not be conducted by your own instructor. Some schools insist on 100% correct answers before they will consider letting you go solo (apart, of course, from being ready flying-wise).
- The instructor will also have to be satisfied that **you really understand the basic Principles of Flight**. Some students choose to write the PPL examination on that subject as they start flying. This is a good idea.

How does the law define a solo flight?

This definition is valid for the rest of your life as a student pilot, and only for the purpose of getting your PPL or in an integrated course.

Solo flight[48]

[F]light time during which the **student pilot** is the sole occupant of the aircraft and in which there is no other person present in the aircraft, be it an instructor, a safety pilot, another student pilot or any other passenger.

You are getting there! But as you will see, the law places in your way a series of precautionary requirements.

4.6.1 The path to solo

Once you have met the theoretical requirement described above, you may be allowed to go solo for the first time if you meet these requirements:

Legal requirements to go solo the first time[49]

As a SPL trainee student you cannot be released for your first solo flight unless you—
- have undergone a minimum of 10 hours of dual flight training;

---

[47] CATS 61.02.1 & 5.
[48] CARS 1.01.1 1st Amendment of 1 June 2012, published July 2013.
[49] CATS 61.02.5–1 (1) to (4).

62   *Air Law*

> - hold a student pilot licence;
> - prove that you possess adequate knowledge of the basic principles of flight *[see above]*
> - have undergone training in exercises 1 to 13;
> - have shown proficiency in handling the aircraft in the event of an engine failure during initial climb-out and from downwind position;
> - have shown proficiency in recovery from a balloon during landing and a bounced landing;
> - have shown proficiency in executing a go-around manoeuvre from a full flaps configuration; and
> - are at least 16 years of age.

You will notice that, apart from the obvious provision that you must have a valid SPL, these legal rules have to do with safe, good, competent flying. SACAA wants you to come back in one piece.

Let us put it in a story:

You are able to do the basic manoeuvres to fly the aircraft correctly and to fly the circuit. You are able to glide and land. You are able to recover when you mess up your landing, and you are decisive and competent ('proficient') with a go around—your instructor will be uncompromising in evaluating whether you are able to decide 'this is not good, I am going around' instead of wanting to land at all costs, that is: if you can without delay 'make the right decision'. Finally, if the law says 'full flaps' it is because, presumably, you have lowered all flaps for landing under normal conditions; if you have not, well, it is unlikely your instructor will let you do your first solo yet.

In sum, you have progressed steadily: you have added competent skills, one after the other up to the point you may be recommended for solo. It may take you just 10 hours (the legal minimum), or it may take you 30 hours, the legal maximum for aeroplane training, but progress there must be.

So, as you progress, you get checked on your path to solo.

4.6.2 Satisfactory progress: dual progress checks[50]

As you clock up hours of flying time, you will be checked by an instructor (not your own instructor) every 10 hours. This is called a 'dual progress check'. It applies **pre-solo and post-solo**. Remember the dual check so that you know when to expect it and are not startled when your instructor books you for it with another instructor—as you have now become used to flying with your own instructor or (after solo) on your own.

---

[50] CATS 61.02.5–2.

The legal principle is simple: you must make '**satisfactory progress**' before (and after) your solo, so that you reach the final Skills Test and obtain your PPL.

But what the law does is to provide for **a monitoring** in order **to avoid you becoming a 'potential safety risk'.**

If at a given dual check the dual check instructor believes that you are not as proficient at a particular exercise as it says in your file, your own instructor will be told to help you rectify this.

But as you clock up hours, this progress monitoring slowly but surely reaches a legal limit, at which point a major problem arises: are you a potential safety risk?

4.6.3 Failing to meet the standards for going solo

The law says that—

> A student pilot **who fails** to be recommended for solo flight after completing 30 (A) hours or 40 (H) hours of dual flight training **shall undergo a flight assessment by the CFI** of the ATO where he or she is receiving flight training.[51]

The issue here is one of potential risk, which is measured against the number of hours you have flown, performing exercises 1 to 13—yet, not being recommended to be ready for 14 (solo).

Regulations kick in if you have exceeded what the law believes to be the justifiable numbers of hours to prove you can fly safely alone.

Why? Because if you have exceeded these hours, while performing 1 to 13, and yet are still not ready, the law 'identifies' you as 'a **potential safety risk**' to yourself, and others.[52] And that is serious. A very common issue is that your instructor is not quite sure that, left alone, you can land safely—not perfectly, but safely, and more than once.

Now, what happens?

Can you rescue the situation?

Yes, you can.

There is a procedure and, one must say, SACAA is rather accommodating in trying to balance public safety with a pilot's dream.[53]

1. The CFI must notify you in writing and you must acknowledge receipt *(in writing)*. If you want to carry on, you must undergo up to '5 hours of dual flight instruction designed and implemented to address the knowledge, skills and attitude of the student' with an instructor (or the CFI).

---

[51] CATS 61.02.7–1 (1) as amended by SACATS 2/2016.
[52] CATS 61.02.7–1 (2) (a) as amended by SACATS 2/2016.
[53] CATS 61.02.7 as amended by SACATS 2/2016. This regulation is new, and absent in the 2011 version of CATS.

Mark those words: knowledge (theoretical), skills (flying), attitude (airmanship and psychological behaviour). Once done, your instructor will either recommend that you solo, or not.

2. If, having done 35 hours (A) or 45 hours (H) of dual training, you are not recommended by your instructor for solo, your case will be referred to the Director, who will appoint a DFE.

3. This DFE will conduct a flight assessment. If the DFE cannot recommend you, and you want to carry on, you must undergo up to another five hours (under the same conditions in item 1).

4. If the DFE then declares that you are still 'a potential safety risk', you will be notified in writing. You must acknowledge receipt, and you will then be able to undergo, again, up to five hours of training with your instructor.

5. If, having then done 40 hours (A) or 50 hours (H), you fail to be recommended by your instructor, your case will be referred to the Director, who will appoint a new DFE.

6. This new DFE will conduct a flight assessment. If you fail this assessment, the final procedure is complex.[54] First your training is **suspended,** you are informed in writing, and the Director is informed by your CFI. Second, your CFI compiles a full report for the Director's attention, which in essence is your file at the school. Then the Director decides on a course of action.

4.6.4 Dual competency check flight before first solo

However, this Armageddon scenario will not apply to you. You will reach solo in good time.

In preparation for the first solo flight (exercise 14), but before it can be done, the law needs to test in a formal way if you have the necessary competency.

Hence, the 'dual competency first solo check flight', which is nerve-racking for a trainee. The flight is called 'dual', because an instructor is in the right-hand seat. This check will decide if you may proceed to your first solo.

The law provides precise instructions as to what 'the dual competency first solo check' is.

How the law describes the dual competency first solo check flight[55]

- conducted by your CFI or Grade I or II instructor appointed by the CFI;

---

[54] CATS 61.02.7–3 (1) (2) as amended by SACATS 2/2016.
[55] CATS 61.02.5–2 (4).

- at least three take-offs and landings (instructor must not manipulate the controls);
- glide approach to a landing (instructor will close power, or ask you to, usually when you are on downwind);
- one simulated engine failure during climb-out (instructor will close power, but you can see it coming because it has to be during the climb-out; it is the reverse exercise of a glide approach: you will glide to land on a field ahead of you, which, by now, you know well);
- one go-around with full flaps (instructor will watch how you manage attitude, altitude and speed, and the correct retraction of flaps).

In practice, in many cases, on the day your instructor believes you may solo, you will be booked for a double slot of flying.

You will fly the circuit and show that you can competently complete the tasks set up by law just described above. If you have, it is a winner. Your sleepless night was not in vain.

Your instructor will call or ask you to call a full stop on the last circuit. But instead of taxiing back to the school's apron or hangar, you will probably vacate the runway and park on the side, engine running. You will know. 'Now I am at last free of him bugging me.' It is an emotional moment of trust: the instructor trusts you, and trusts that you will not kill yourself or land in the ostrich farm next door. You are ready. The instructor's reputation is also at stake—make no mistake, instructors are very proud of the training they provide, and quite naturally so. 'I don't want to hear about you one day in the papers' is a frequent remark. Instructor will disembark. You are on your own.

All you will have to do, being solo for the first time, is one take off and one landing.

And wait for the bucket of water.

Solo under you belt, you can now proceed with exercise 15.

But the law does not rest. It never does. You, however, do need rest after that flight.

4.6.5 Dual check after solo

During the first three hours of solo flying after your first solo an instructor will do a dual check before each solo flight. After those three hours of solo flights (that is, the dual flights before each solo are not being counted in), a dual check of at least one hour will take place for every five hours of solo flight time, until your get your PPL.

4.6.6 Unsatisfactory progress after solo

If, after your solo, the instructor believes your skills are not satisfactory, a remedy similar to the one described above (4.6.3) will be imposed, consisting of further training in two sets of three hours, leading possibly to the Director discontinuing your training permanently.[56]

4.6.7 Flying solo is being on a long leash: rules

But that will not happen.

So, once you have been cleared to leave the circuit area and fly solo in a general Flying Training Area and later on a 'nav' (cross-country flight), **your instructor will authorise each flight in accordance with training exercises** (that is: no pleasure flip, no flapping wings over mama's house), and will also **authorise where you may fly, and the route of the solo navigation flight.**

The **solo 'nav'** (exercise 18) must comply with the PPL (A) requirements before the Skills Test: it should be 'one triangular cross-country flight of at least 150 NM, on which at least one point must be not less than 50 NM from base and must include full-stop landings at two different aerodromes away from base'.[57]

In practice, schools have one or two favourite routes for that exercise, and you will be able to ask advanced trainees for advice and support—but, remember, your instructor is your first port of call. And you may not fly below 500 ft AGL unless an instructor is in the right-hand seat—or alone if you are practising exercise 17B (the precautionary landing exercise). Usually you will do a short nav with your instructor, then do it solo. Then you will do a long nav (the one just described), followed by the same solo.

4.7 LOGGING FLIGHT TIME

It is *your* flying life! Every hour counts. Log every minute. Your logbook is a legal document. There are rules, and the law is strict about the truthfulness of your logging, or recording of flight time.

Your instructor will show you how to log hours in your pilot logbook, by entering the correct information in the correct column. In black indelible ink. And no erasure, no strikethrough. No scribbles. Your entries must be neat. Refer to annexure 5.

4.7.1 Logging flight time: what, how, who

First, what is 'flight time'?

---

[56] CATS 61.02.7 (4).
[57] CARS 61.03.1 (2) (b).

> **What is flight time?**[58]
>
> - for the operation of aeroplanes, the total time from the moment an aeroplane first moves for the purpose of taking off until the moment it finally comes to rest at the end of the flight *(exam!)*
>
> Note—Flight time as defined here is synonymous with the term 'block to block' time or 'chock to chock' time in general usage, which is measured from the time an aeroplane first moves for the purpose of taking off until it finally stops at the end of the flight.
>
> - for the operation of helicopters, the total time from the moment a helicopter's rotor blades start turning until the moment the helicopter finally comes to rest at the end of the flight and the rotor blades are stopped.
>
> - for the operation of gliders, the total time occupied in flight, whether being towed or not, from the moment the glider first moves for the purpose of taking off until the moment it comes to rest at the end of the flight.

Read these regulations carefully:

> **How to log flight time?**[59]
>
> (1) **The holder of a pilot licence must maintain in a pilot logbook a record** of all his or her flight time, instrument time, FSTD time and instruction time. Where electronic logbooks are used, the electronic data must be printed on paper at least every 90 days and the printed pages filed sequentially in a binder.
>
> (2) The form of and information to be contained in the logbook, referred to in sub-regulation (1), and the manner in which such logbook must be maintained are as prescribed in Appendix A to Document SA-CATS 61.
>
> (3) Entries in pilot logbooks must be made within the following periods after the completion of the flight to be recorded—
>
> *(a)* **seven days in the case of flights not for hire and reward** (Part 91 operations), **flight training**, and domestic commercial air transport operations;
>
> *(b)* 14 days in the case of international commercial air transport operations;
>
> *(c)* **48 hours after return to base in the case where a pilot is engaged in flight operations away from the base where the pilot logbook is normally kept.**
>
> (4) All pilots must **retain their pilot logbooks for at least 60 months** calculated from the date they no longer hold a valid pilot licence.

---

[58] CARS 1.01.1.
[59] CARS 61.01.8.

> (5) If the holder of a pilot licence carries out a number of flights upon the same day and the **interval between successive flights** does not exceed one hundred and eighty minutes, such series of flights may be recorded as a single entry, provided that in the case of a cross-country flight the route and intermediate stops must be recorded.
>
> (6) The holder of a pilot licence **must make the logbook available for inspection** upon a reasonable request by the Director, an authorised officer, inspector or authorised person.

4.7.2 But, are you sure you are logging as the correct sort of pilot or as the legal PIC?

Let us break down what the law says, as some people become confused about students being, or not being pilot in command. First, who is a pilot, and then who is a pilot in command, and how do hours get logged in?

> #### Who is a pilot?[60]
>
> **'pilot-in-command' (PIC)** is the pilot designated by the operator (typically, your school) as being in command and charged with the safe conduct of a flight, regardless of whether or not he or she is manipulating the controls.
>
> **'student-pilot-in-command' (SPIC) or 'pilot-in-command under supervision' (PICUS)** means a co-pilot performing the duties and functions of a PIC under the supervision of the PIC who is appropriately rated and in an aircraft that is either certificated for multi-pilot operations (ie the aircraft has a type certification) or required to be operated by two pilots.[61]
>
> **'co-pilot'** means a licensed, type-rated pilot required by these regulations to serve in any piloting capacity other than as PIC, but excluding a pilot who is on board the aircraft for the purpose of receiving flight instruction.
>
> If you hold a valid PPL, you can **'act as co-pilot** of any aeroplane on which a co-pilot is not a requirement', provided that you are class- or type-rated for that aeroplane.[62] But **to log time** as a co-pilot an 'exacting' rule applies (see page 70).
>
> Note here that the EASA regulation is simpler: 'Student pilot-in-command' (SPIC) means a student pilot acting as pilot-in-command on a flight with an instructor where the latter will only observe the student pilot and shall not influence or control the flight of the aircraft'.

---

[60] CARS 1.01.1.
[61] CARS 1.01.1 1 CARS 1.01.1 states: 'student-pilot-in-command': See 'pilot-in-command-under-supervision'.
[62] CARS 61.03.5 (5) (a).

What about logging PIC flight time?

> **Who logs flight time as PIC?**[63]
>
> As the holder of a valid pilot licence you **log flight time as:**
>
> - **PIC if you are the designated PIC** of the aircraft; this is also the case if the designated PIC provides command supervision to another pilot;
> - **PIC if you are a student on a solo flight and as the sole occupant of the aircraft,** and **'SOLO'** is indicated in the remarks column;
> - **PICUS**, provided there is no intervention by the supervising PIC and 'PICUS' is indicated in the remarks column, with the entry certified by the supervising PIC. PICUS may, **irrespective of the licence held**, be flown from either the left-hand or the right-hand seat, **provided that the pilot is appropriately rated** and the aircraft is either certificated for **multi-pilot** operations **or** required to be operated **by two pilots;**[64]
> - **PIC if you give flight instruction** while occupying a pilot seat with access to the controls, provided that the time must also be logged as instructor time;
> - **PIC if you are a SPIC and acting as PIC** under the supervision of an appropriately rated flight instructor during flight training **on an approved course of CPL or CPL/IR training** and for a successful CPL or IR initial flight test—and note the following:[65]
>   - ➤ the SPIC time cannot be credited as PIC time if the flight instructor had reason to influence or control any part of the flight;
>   - ➤ a ground debriefing by the flight instructor does not affect the crediting as PIC;
>   - ➤ SPIC time will be logged in the PIC column with 'SPIC' indicated in the remarks column and certified by the supervising flight instructor.
>   - ➤ in the **Integrated Training**, PIC instrument time when flying under supervision, which must be certified by the instructor, with a maximum of 50 hours credited towards PIC time required for CPL or ATPL (A and H).[66] A minimum 15 hours of instrument flying logged in as SPICUS in addition to 5 hours SPICUS or dual.[67]

Now, as a student training toward a PPL on a single-engine, single-pilot aeroplane, what does that all mean in practice?
- you log PIC if you are alone in the cockpit, with your name or 'self' in column 4 of your logbook, and flight time in column 15, and note 'solo' in the remarks column of your logbook (column 32).

---

[63] CARS 61.01.8 (1) to (7).
[64] CARS 61.01.8 (7) (b).
[65] CARS 61.01.8 (e).
[66] CARS 61.01.9 (4).
[67] SPICUS logging specified in CATS, Appendix 3.0, 4, Table 1 (TS 61.01.22) and Appendix 3.B, 4, Table 1 (TS 61.01.22).

- you log 'dual' otherwise, with flight time in column 14 and your instructor's name in column 4 of your logbook.

Note: these are not all the entries you make in your logbook after a flight. What is indicated here relates only to PIC, solo, and dual matters.

- you do not log as co-pilot if for instance you sit on the right while the instructor is in the left seat because the definition of co-pilot, in South Africa, is unlikely to apply to your situation:

> South Africa's regulation is more exacting in that the South African Civil Aviation Regulations, 2011, Part 61 make no allowance for crediting of co-pilot flight time in an aircraft certified for single-pilot operation and flown with a co-pilot, unless this is in a part 121, 135 or 127 operation, which requires two pilots (at night or IFR).

Who says that? AIP GEN, of course.[68]

The definition in CARS is shorter but says the same: ' "co-pilot" means a licensed, type-rated pilot required by these Regulations to serve in any piloting capacity other than as PIC, but excluding a pilot who is on board the aircraft for the purpose of receiving flight instruction.'[69] Follow AIP GEN.

4.8 THE PRIVATE PILOT LICENCE SKILLS TEST

The big moment has arrived.

4.8.1 When am I allowed to test?

Assuming that your progress has been satisfactory and your instructor lets you test, and you are not ill on the appointed day, and you slept soundly, and the weather is on your side *(mind you: your examiner may ask you about weather minima if clouds are drifting low[70])*, here are the legal requirements without which you will not be allowed to apply for your licence if you pass the Skills Test:

> - You are at least 17 years of age.[71]
> - Your medical is valid.
> - Your SPL is valid.
> - Your last dual instruction flight was no more than 30 days ago.[72]

---

[68] AIP GEN 1–7.2 as per AMDT 3/6.
[69] CARS 1.01.1.
[70] On weather minima see page 114–118.
[71] One can imagine a scenario in which you test before you are 17, then wait until you are 17, and then send in the application within 30 days of testing as per CARS 61.03.2 (1).

> - You have completed the flying requirements of at least 45 hours' flight time in an aeroplane[73] (type-certificated or non type-certificated) with a MCM (maximum certified mass) in excess of 450 kg,[74] of which—
>   ➤ at least 25 hours was of dual instruction in aeroplanes;
>   ➤ and at least 15 hours was solo, which must **include**—
>   at least five hours' cross-country with 'one triangular cross-country flight of at least 150 NM, on which at least one point must be not less than 50 NM from base and must include full-stop landings at two different aerodromes away from base'.[75]

There are far too many 'at leasts', but the meaning is that these hours are minima, which you are allowed to exceed, up to a point (that of being declared a risk), and many do anyway.

Let us get a grip on these rules:

You may ask, '25 + 15 = 40: Where are the remaining 5 hours to make up the minimum of 45?' These are spent on a FSTD, of course, a flight simulator. The maximum allowed is 5 hours, which must be logged as dual.[76] In short: you can test once you have logged 30 hours dual, including 5 FSTD, and 15 hours solo, including 5 cross-country (with the said 150 NM nav). The rule of '5', as it were.

And do you remember the rule that 30 dual hours (A) may not be exceeded, under sanction of remedial action, before the first solo has to be performed?

If you want to test at 45 and you went solo at 30, you only have the minimum of 15 hours left to comply with solo hours (your first solo will be short, perhaps 20 minutes, but it does not give you much margin). These are the 15 minimum solo hours required to move onto the Skills Test. Contrary to the set numbers of dual hours allowed before your first solo, there is no limitation on the number of dual hours you can fly before you undergo your Skills Test.

---

[72] CARS 61.03.4 (1).

[73] Requirements for H are: 50 hours' flight time=25 hours dual+15 hours solo incl. 5 hours triangular cross-country 100 NM with two full-stop landings at two different aerodromes away from base, as per CARS 61.04.1 (2).

[74] CATS 1.01.1 states (and every word counts in this legal definition): maximum certificated mass 'means the maximum permissible mass shown in the AFM or other document associated with the certificate of airworthiness at which an aircraft may commence its take-off under standard atmospheric conditions at sea level'. (AFM refers to the aircraft flight manual.)

[75] CARS 61.03.1 (2) (a) amd (b).

[76] CATS 61.03.1 (4).

You cannot test before finishing your theoretical exams:

A candidate 'must have passed the final theoretical knowledge examination within the 36 months preceding the skills test for a PPL'.[77] The Skills Test (that validates your practical training) must be passed within 36 months from the date on which you successfully completed all your theoretical exams. And you cannot apply for the PPL if you have not received your (at least restricted) certificate of proficiency in radio telephony and have not proven your English proficiency, as applicable.

After 36 months, it all lapses—unless you are in Integrated Training, in which case you will have to rewrite only Air Law and Operational Procedures (other passed exams remain valid). Integrated Training is highly specialised and aims at training airline pilots, or at least commercial ones, *ab initio*, instead of going through a PPL first: your ATO will advise you on specifics, but as far as air law is concerned, you will need air law at CPL level—that is, have already absorbed core knowledge as presented here.[78]

4.8.2 Pre-test ground evaluation

The Skills Test is preceded by a ground evaluation.

This can take up to two hours. You will be handed a questionnaire that is in the format recommended by SACAA 'to achieve a uniform standard'.

This questionnaire comprises up to 100 questions drawn from CARS, CATS, AIP, POH, weather reports, and navigation (done when you prepare your nav plan). For instance: 'Which runway is uphill at FATZ?' Or: 'What is the maximum certified load factor in clean configuration?' (of your aircraft). Or: 'What would your take-off ground distance be at MTOW, ELV 5500' and 35°C OAT on a dry grass runway?' Or a local favourite: 'Discuss typical SA weather climatology.' In sum: it is heavy-going.

Of course, you will have access to all relevant documentation and reference material as the purpose is to place you in a real life situation when, if you want to fly, you have to prepare properly.

What is tested is your ability to **locate** information, **decode** information, and **apply** information. And in real life: decide to fly or not to fly.

The questionnaire can be done within 14 days of the practical test.[79] It has to be passed before you can move on to the Skills Test.[80]

The examiner will also note if you are dressed properly (pilot shirt, epaulettes if required, trousers, closed shoes), if your flight bag contains all that you need, and if

---

[77] CARS 61.03.3 (A) and 61.04.3 (H).
[78] As mentioned earlier, CARS 61.01.15 (2), in conjunction with Appendix 3.0, Syllabus for the CPL (VFR) CPL (IR) ATPL Aeroplane Integrated Training Course (TS 61.01.22) and Appendix 3.B, Syllabus for the CPL(A)/IR Integrated Training Course (TS 61.01.15).
[79] CARS 61.01.5 (9).
[80] CARS 61.01.5 (5).

you are mentally and physically fit—if you have a cold, you will not test that day. Most examiners are keen to put you at ease—but they will still do the checks nonetheless. They are fully aware that the **PPL is the core licence**.

4.8.3 The Skills Test can be split into two or more flights

Two provisions exist to split the Skills (flight) Test.
- If, due to 'unforeseen reasons' (bad weather, illness in flight, something wrong with the aircraft), a test (or revalidation check) cannot be completed in one flight, it can be completed on a different date, but within 14 days maximum and 'provided an examiner specifies the unforeseen reason on the applicable form'.[81]
- The 'navigation element' or cross country of the Skills Test can be done on a different day but within 14 days of the first flight.[82]

4.8.4 What does the Skills Test consist of?

The PPL Skills Test is strictly framed by law.[83]

Your examiner, a CFI, a Grade I or II instructor, will follow the form called Skills Test Report.[84]

You should acquaint yourself with two documents:

- the detailed Skills Test Standards (if you have the time),[85] and
- the Skills Test Report (absolutely essential).[86]

Skills Test Standards

SACAA produces these documents to help pilots and instructors, and to make sure standards are known by all and applied by ATOs 'uniformly'.

You need not read the voluminous Standards thoroughly, but do take note of the following:

---

[81] CARS 61.01.5 (10).
[82] CARS 61.01.5 (8).
[83] CARS and CATS 61.03.4 for (A) and 61.04.4 for (H). Fully developed by Appendix 1.2 CATS 61 (A) (H).
[84] SACAA Form Number: CA 61.03.4 Skills Test or Competency Check Report for Private Pilot Licence (aeroplane); SACAA Form Number: CA 61.04.4 Skills Test or Competency Check Report for Private Pilot Licence (helicopter).
[85] CATS 61 Appendix 1.2—a long document we cannot reproduce here. For (H): Appendix 1.4.
[86] Form CA 61–03.4 (A) and Form 61–04.4 (H).

> **Skills Test Standards**
>
> The primary purpose of this document is to assist Part 141 **Training Organisations to standardise the training and skills testing** for the Private Pilot Licence (PPL) in the aeroplane/helicopter category.
>
> Second, **it provides the trainee with a guide as to what the elements of training are** and what **performance criteria** will be assessed.
>
> Third, it provides **Flight Instructors and Designated Flight Examiners with a guide for the assessment of competency** and for the skills test assessment.

The Skills Test Report and why it is helpful

You must read the Skills Test Form carefully and make sure you fully understand what you will be examined on.

The Skills Test Report is a detailed protocol of all that you need to do 'competently'—the key word and the code your examiner will enter if you are competent (C). Download it and read it!

Do not hesitate to ask your instructor to go through the form with you ahead of the test. Make sure you understand the grading system (1 to 4). Do read the form carefully. It serves as recap of your training. You can also grade yourself to identify weak spots.

For instance, if you think you are borderline 2 to 3 for spin avoidance, keep practising to get yourself into the safe 3 range.

If, during the flight test, you get a 2 in any aspect (for example, fire/smoke in the cockpit (in-flight), you will get a second (and only) chance during the same flight. So, if you know the fire procedure is an aspect of your training that you have neglected, rehearse the procedure in the hangar the day before.

There will be no surprises, as all aspects to be tested are clearly listed in the protocol.

Use the form! SACAA has not produced it just to pass or fail you, and to have examiners tick boxes, but to help you gain a better and final awareness of what a competent pilot does.

Definition of the cross-country, navigation part of the Skills Test

The nav ('cross-country navigation flight of the skills test') should be 'not less than 200 nautical miles total distance and must include take-offs and landings at two aerodromes away from base. At least one of the aerodromes from which the aircraft takes off for this flight shall be an aerodrome at which an Air Traffic Services Unit (ATSU) is in operation'.[87]

---

[87] CATS 61.03.4 (1).

During the test, the examiner will remain silent, except for giving instructions (such as calling for a diversion), will not touch the controls, but will take notes. Do not get distracted by this note taking. The test begins at the preflight. And remember to treat the examiner as a passenger, showing that you know all the procedures related to carrying a passenger. If you notice the examiner has not fastened his or her seatbelt and harness when it has to be done, do not fail to remind him or her! All that is part of the test.

After the test, in the debriefing room, you will be given the form, with explanations about the grading, which you can query if you don't understand it. You and the examiner will sign the form and, if you were successful, you can prepare your dossier for the formal application to obtain your coveted licence. And get your logbook endorsed.

4.8.5 Should you fail . . .[88]

There is a remedy. You will be asked to 'refrain from' using your licence (SPL) and to undergo remedial ground and flight training; your ATO will then provide a letter certifying that you have now met the standards, and you will be retested by a 'DFE appointed by the Director'. Should you 'without reasonable cause' (bad weather during nav, for instance) fail again, the Director will cancel your licence (SPL) with immediate effect, and you may reapply for the initial licence (SPL) after a period of 24 months from the date of cancellation of this licence.

But none of this will happen, as you will have tested successfully.

4.9 At last! The 'brown book'

You now have your PPL licence.

Well, almost. First, you have to fill in the application.

Putting together the application dossier cannot be done on the back of an envelope, while sitting at the school cafeteria and narrating your aviating exploits. It takes time, attention, and care. Set aside a full day for it, and go through it twice to make sure everything is in order. Find a police station that can readily certify copies. Do not rush the compiling of this dossier. Once you have scribbled in your logbook, there is hardly any going back. SACAA does not like artistic impressions.

The law is explicit about the application procedure:[89]

---

[88] CARS 61.01.5 (14).
[89] CARS and CATS 61.03.1.

(1) **Within 30 days of the practical skills test** you must send your application to the Director, using Form CA 61–01.0[90] (the same you used for your SPL application).

(2) You must attach to the application itself:

- your flying logbook summarised in the prescribed format (see annexure 10); certified copy of your logbook consisting of the last three pages and pages with endorsements. You will draw up or paste the summary as a table as per the example in annexure 10) on the most recent page of your logbook, after the last Skills Test flight entry and the examiner's signed and the test stamped endorsement;
- a valid medical certificate;
- documentary evidence you hold a valid SPL (or have held one in the previous 60 months), a PPL issued by a Contracting State, or NPL issued under CARS Part 62;
- the original documentation proving that you have passed the theoretical knowledge examination (the law uses the singular, but in fact it refers to all your prescribed examinations, considered as a whole);
- the Skills Test Report;
- two recent passport-size photographs, unless you already hold another pilot licence issued in terms of Part 61 (you may already hold a PPL (H));
- the appropriate fee as prescribed in Part 187 (check the latest schedule of fees on the SACAA website; it will be an Amendment); and
- proof that you are 17 years of age or older.

Remember that without proof of English proficiency, your PPL cannot be issued.[91]

If the Director of SACAA approves all your paperwork, you (or your school) will receive within three weeks your brown book—your licence—which you must sign 'immediately' in permanent black ink in the space provided.

If you send the application after the 30-day prescribed period, written reasons that may be 'acceptable' to the Director must be attached.[92]

If you **lose your 'brown book'**, no problem: by law the Director has 'to maintain and to keep in a safe place a register of all pilot licences and ratings issued or validated' with pilot personal details (there is a fee attached to obtain a duplicate).

---

[90] SACAA Form Number: CA 61.01.0 Application for initial issue of SA-CAR Part 61 Pilot Licence or Rating (excluding class and type rating).

[91] CARS 61.01.7.

[92] CARS 61.01.5 (11) (c).

> This is also why **you must notify the Director within 14 days of any change** in name, date of birth (quite possible if registry was erroneous), postal or residential address (most common case), date of issuance or validation (in case there was a capturing error), ratings (same), or your nationality (it happens).[93]

You will always fly PIC with this licence in your flight bag. SPL time has ended. PPL time starts. Actually not: PPL flying will only start once you have received and signed the 'brown book'. **Until you receive it, you fly with your SPL**, in solo, each flight being authorised by an instructor. But SPL means **no passenger**![94] *(These points are exam question material).* Yet, whether you have the 'brown book' in hand or not, something else begins, right away: **maintenance of competency time**.

> 'The *initial* expiry date of the maintenance of competency of a licence (or validity of a rating) is calculated **from the last day of the month in which the skills test was conducted**'.[95] *If you test on 1 December, for example, expiry runs from 31 December.*

Do not treat the (rather ugly, we admit) 'brown book' lightly:[96] the SA PPL is fully recognised internationally and is known for certifying a training that is sometimes more exacting than elsewhere. South African pilots, those who proceed from PPL to professional licences, are in high demand abroad due to these standards. Hundreds of foreigners attend our ATOs every year, and not only for our more reasonable rates (which are not always more reasonable anyway), but also for the excellence of our training.

The 'brown book' may not to be as sexy as the FAA identity card type but, as the saying goes: never judge a book by its cover.

You can now slip the double golden epaulettes on your shoulder straps, and pin your wings on your left breast pocket. Congratulations, pilot!

And remember—a warning to students: regulations mentioned in the following chapter are extensive material for the PPL (and also CPL) Air Law examination.

---

[93] CARS 61.01.14.

[94] CARS 61.02.5 (1) (c).

[95] CARS 61.01.5 (11) (b) refers to the initial date, not to subsequent dates of revalidations as in CARS 61.01.5 (12). Do not get a headache from these Byzantine rules, just revalidate a few days before it is due and all will be fine.

[96] It seems that ID type pilot licence cards may be introduced in the coming years.

Chapter 5

. . . .

Being a pilot

> Evidently he lived in this vicinity for he told me that he had just bought a hydroplane and was going to try it out in the morning.
>
> F Scott Fitzgerald *The Great Gatsby*[1]

Like Gatsby, this is the sort of thing you can do once you have your PPL. But before you dock a seaplane on Hartbeespoort Dam, and look suave, remember the basics:

Your PPL is valid for 10 years from the date of issue by SACAA. (There is a debate about its de facto life validity, but *for exam purposes it is 10 years*).

You have to obey legal rules that give you 'privileges' and set 'limitations', just as your SPL did.

You must maintain your pilot logbook, according to the rules of logging flight time and ensure you have the legitimate endorsements.

You must retain 'competency' and pay 'currency fees'.

You must retain your medical certificate.

You may add 'ratings' to your licence, and of course you can proceed to CPL training.

All this sounds quite heavy-going. It is just a matter of keeping records.

This chapter provides detailed information on what has to be done to retain a legally compliant licence.

PPL and CPL Air Law examinations draw on these regulations.

5.1 KEEPING YOUR PPL VALID

To maintain your licence you have to observe a series of regulations. And remember them. This is easier if you still belong to a school or a flying club. For instance, their sign-in system will come up with a 'Fail' if your medical has expired. But it is not a foolproof safeguard, unless the operator keeps up-to-date records on clients.

If you are on your own, you must check the SACAA website regularly for amendments. You can also subscribe (free) to alerts (if operational), or buy the AIP, which will allow you to receive amendments.

---

[1] F Scott Fitzgerald *The Great Gatsby* (1925) 52.

But all this will not make you do what you have to do to **maintain competency**. You have to be proactive, and know the regulations.

In short: **your licence has to remain valid**.

5.1.1 What does 'valid' mean?

Here is the CARS definition:[2]

> 'valid' when used in connection with a **licence, rating, certificate, validation**, authority, approval or similar document means—
>
> (a) that the expiry date on the document, if any, has not been exceeded;
>
> (b) that the document has been issued legally and properly to its holder, and has not been suspended or cancelled by the issuing authority; and
>
> (c) that all requirements, prescribed by these Regulations in respect of the document, have been complied with.
>
> *If you are wondering how a 'validation' can also be made 'valid', don't bother: it refers to a specific rating at a specific ATSU or to a foreign licence. This is not likely to apply to you.*

You will notice that validity has to do with **a time line** (expiry), with **the legality** of its issuance and suspension or cancellation (in plain English: that it is done and undone by SACAA according to its own rules), and with the fact that **you do what is required** to comply with the law. If you comply after the expiry, SACAA may decide to suspend/withdraw your licence. If you do all that is required on time and truthfully, you will be fine.

One example: you may be late paying your annual currency fees (see 5.1.3 below). You settle them as soon as you realise it, and attach to your proof of payment a letter of apology addressed to the Director together with a good reason (family bereavement, absence from the country). If you make a reasonable case, it is unlikely SACAA will suspend your licence until the next annual payment.

5.1.2 How do you observe the 'period of validity'?[3]

By making sure that:

> (a) **currency fees** are paid in terms of regulation 61.01.16;
>
> (b) **competency** is maintained in terms of the regulations.
>
> (c) an **annual fee** is paid together with the relevant form, 'including certified copies of the last 3 pages of the logbook containing entries indicating a record of flight times, an annual summary indicating flight time per category, class, type and total time as well as certified copies of any endorsements entered into the logbook in the preceding 12 months' (see also annexure 10).

---

[2] CARS 1.01.1.
[3] CARS 61.03.6.

Now, let us go through the various regulations that govern the validity of your licence, starting with three basic reminders.

5.1.3 The three validity rules: competency, currency fee and medical

To keep your licence valid the law requires you to observe three basic rules: maintaining competency, fee currency, and your medical certification.

Competency or revalidation check[4]

Regarding your licence you maintain 'competency' if you undergo a first 'revalidation check' (called also 'competency check' on the relevant form, as mentioned page 73, note 86) **within 12 months of the date of initial issue** of your PPL and **thereafter every 24 months calculated from the date of reissue**.[5]

- If you do your revalidation (licence or rating) **within 90 days before the expiry date** of competency or a rating, the new expiry date is now calculated from the last day of the month of expiry.
- If you do your competency check, whether for a licence revalidation or for a rating, **more than 90 days before the expiry date** of competency or a rating, the new expiry date is now calculated from the last day of the month in which you did your check.
- You can also apply in writing, to the Director, for an extension not exceeding 30 days, with written reasons explaining the exceptional circumstances.[6]

You must also **submit the appropriate form** with documents to the Director within 30 days of the competency or revalidation check. Read section 5.1.4 carefully regarding time limits.

In addition, regarding your licence revalidation, a PPL (A) holder must have **flown 'a minimum of three hours as PIC in the six months** preceding a revalidation check' (meant to revalidate competency), and meet recency (see 5.2.3 below). This rule is not explicit under 'Maintenance of competency' but it is deduced from the mention of a 'revalidation check' which itself falls under a subregulation of Skills Test.[7] As for helicopter pilots, the rules are similar but fortunately brought under the single regulation dealing with maintenance of competency.[8]

---

[4] CARS 61.03.7 (A), 61.04.7 (H).
[5] CARS 61.01.5 (12) (a).
[6] CARS 61.01.5 (12) (b) (c) (d) as per 20th Amendment *Government Gazette* 42362 GN 645 of 29 March 2019.
[7] CARS 61.03.7 (Maintenance of competency), 61.03.4 (3) (Skills test).
[8] CARS 61.04.7.

Currency fee

You must maintain the 'currency fee': every year you must pay the 'annual currency fee as prescribed in Part 187 on or before the anniversary date of the licence'.[9] You must complete and send to SACAA your application form with certified copies of the last three pages of the logbook containing entries indicating a record of flight times, and an annual summary indicating flight time per category, class, type and total time. Do not forget certified copies of any endorsements entered into the logbook in the preceding 12 months.[10] Include proof of payment of the relevant fee. Electronic logbooks must be printed and bound sequentially at least every 90 days.

The schedule of fees is regularly updated on the SACAA site. Make sure you checked the latest Amendment regarding fees. *Part 187 refers to Fees and Charges. Make a note of it!*

Medical certification (A) and (H)

You must maintain 'medical certification' (see chapter 3).[11]

5.1.4 The Competency Check Report and rules for revalidation

The report is used by the examiner for your revalidation and is the same form as the Initial Skills Test (see 4.8.4 above) but with **fewer mandatory checks (A)**. For instance, cross-wind take-off (A) is not part of a competency check. And for (A) and (H), no navigation and en route procedures are retested.

Before a competency check, look at the form to see what is in store, and what you should practise. Read form CA 61-03.4 (A) or CA 61-04.4 (H) carefully.

Can the competency or revalidation check be done on different days?

Yes, if for some reason it cannot be completed, the same rule as for the Skills Test applies.[12]

Time limits to revalidate

Note that the 'initial' expiry date of your licence, that is the date at which **you must revalidate for the first time,** either for a licence or a rating, is calculated from the last day of the month when you passed your first skills test and got either your licence or rating.

---

[9] CARS 61.01.16 (1) (a).
[10] CARS 61.01.5 (13) and CARS 61.03.6 (c).
[11] (A): CARS 61.03.5 (1) (a) and (b) and (H): CARS 61.04.5 (1) (a) and (b).
[12] CARS 61.01.5 (11).

In short whether you test on the first or last day of a given month, it is the last day of that month that will determine the date at which you will have to revalidate for the first time (in case of a PPL, within 12 months, for the first revalidation).[13]

You have noted that, to maintain competency, **the second and later revalidations,** for a PPL, take place within 24 months calculated from the 'date of reissue', not from the initial date mentioned above.[14] Things do get a tad complicated.

Why? Because flying is weather dependent. This is why the regulator offers options: for a second or later revalidation (every 24 months), the rules provide for three scenarios to determine the new dates of reissue depending upon when you pass the revalidation test. The new date is calculated:
- from the date of reissue (ie when you did and passed your first revalidation) if you test within the normal 24 months; or
- from 'the beginning of the month following the date of expiry of the maintenance of competency' if this maintenance of competency is revalidated within 90 days immediately before expiry; or
- from 'the beginning of the month following the date of revalidation' of this maintenance of competency if revalidated before the period referred to above, that is before the 90 days period preceding expiry.[15]

Can you ask for an extension?

Yes, but only up to 30 days from the expiry date and by written application to the Director, providing for exceptional circumstances. This is specific to a revalidation check for maintenance of competency.[16]

What if you wait too long?[17]

You lose 'currency' (see the end of this section regarding this word).

If you let 24 months pass before revalidating competency and you are still below 36 months since competency lapsed (it lapsed the day you were supposed to be tested, and you were not), you must do ground and flight training at an ATO to reach the necessary standard and you must make sure you meet the recency requirements to act as PIC (see 5.2.3).[18] You must also do your revalidation check in the same aircraft category.

If you are beyond the 36 months, you have to rewrite the Air Law exam, retrain and become recent as above, and you must pass an initial licence Skills Test— which is heavier than a revalidation check.

---

[13] CARS 61.01.5 (11) (b). Regulations mentioned here take into account 20th Amendment to CARS, *Government Gazelle* 42362 GN 645 of 29 March 2019.

[14] CARS 61.03.7 51) (a).

[15] CARS 61.03.7 (b) (i), (ii).

[16] CARS 61.05.1 (12) (d).

[17] (H): CARS 61.04.7 (2) and (A): CARS 61.03.7 (2).

[18] CARS 91.02.4.

What happens if you fail the revalidation test?

You cry. But, to stay on course and get another chance:
- You should not use your licence: 'The Director shall require that the licence holder refrain from exercising the privileges.'[19]

    Why this civilised turn of phrase? Because it is impossible for SACAA to monitor every private pilot, except by fitting them with electronic bracelets—the risks, regulatory and criminal, are high if you 'fly rogue'. However, if you still belong to a school, your school will prevent you from flying anyway.

- You undergo (if you wish to regain your privileges) remedial actions in order to restore your privileges, that is, the right to fly legally—and these remedial actions are:[20]
    - remedial ground and flight training at an approved ATO;
    - the ATO must provide you a letter with the content of this remedial training and the assurance that you have now reached the standards required; and you forward this letter to the Director; and
    - you undergo the skills test with a DFE appointed by the Director, if the Director so decides.

If all fails, the general rule cited on page 75 and above kicks in, and then you are really allowed to have a good cry, because not only do you lose currency, but you also lose the use of your licence.

Another currency

This is where '**currency**' comes into play again, although you will not find it defined in the CARS glossary.

With reference to 5.1.2 above you are current if you have complied with competency, that is maintained your licence by undergoing a revalidation, or any test or check required for a rating within the time frame prescribed and paid the annual fee and submitted the form and documents required.

Put differently, with regard to your PPL, your licence 'runs' (the meaning behind 'current') so long as you remain competent, and to remain competent you have to be tested according to the law (time frame and type of check), and you comply with annual fee procedures.

If you fail a revalidation, you are no longer current.

Do not confuse this currency with the currency fee: you may be fine with regard to fee currency, but not fine with competency-related currency.

Enough with this terminology brainteaser. Let us move onto your 'privileges'.

---

[19] CARS 61.01.5 (14).
[20] CARS 61.05.1 (14) (a), (b) and (c).

84   *Air Law*

5.2 PRIVILEGES AND LIMITATIONS OF A PPL

You will be examined on privileges and limitations.

5.2.1 Privileges

As mentioned earlier in this book, **privileges are enabling rules**: they tell you what you can do.

Your privileges, as holder of a PPL, permit you:[21]

– **to act as PIC or co-pilot in any aeroplane for which you hold the appropriate valid class rating or type rating**—even if it is not a requirement for the aeroplane to have a co-pilot;[22]

– **to provide for special VFR, you may fly in IMC**, in sight of the surface and clear of cloud, fog or mist within a control zone, after being authorised to do so by the responsible air traffic services controller;

– **if you hold the appropriate valid rating,** to exercise the privileges of the licence for any of the special purposes (the ratings for special purposes, see below);[23]

– **to act as co-pilot of any aeroplane on which a co-pilot is not a requirement; and**

– to act as PIC in the course of your own or your employer's business, provided that the flight is only incidental to that business or employment; and the aeroplane does not carry passengers or freight for reward or hire.

All these are exam questions at PPL level and further.

However, privileges have a flip-side, called, as you are already aware, 'limitations'.

5.2.2 Limitations: general and human performance

Limitations fall into three categories, which are not presented in that order in CARS or CATS, because of the way in which legislation is put together. However, do take note of the following *(they come up as exam questions)*:
- general limitations,[24]
- human performance limitations,[25] and
- recency limitations.[26]

---

[21] CARS 61.03.5 5 (1) to (5).
[22] CARS 61.03.5 (5) (a).
[23] CARS 61.03.8.
[24] CARS 61.03.5. A and H are quite similar, but for details of limitations for PPL (H) please refer to CARS 61.04.5.
[25] CARS 91.02.3.
[26] CARS 91.02.4.

General limitations are plain and simple.

> General limitations forbid you, as holder of a PPL:
> - to act as PIC of an aeroplane that is carrying passengers or freight for reward or hire;
> - to be remunerated for acting in any pilot capacity;
> - to act as PIC or co-pilot in any aeroplane for which you do not hold the appropriate valid class rating or type rating; and
> - to exercise the privileges of the licence for any of the special purposes ratings if you do not hold the appropriate valid rating.

Human performance limitations are well known to pilots but the regulator has restated them:

> **Limitations linked to human performance as a PPL state that:**[27]
> - You cannot act as crew member if you are under the influence of a **psychoactive substance**, or have been **scuba diving** 24 hours before, **donated blood** 72 hours before, know that you **are fatigued or will be** during the flight, or **drank alcohol** 8 hours before and your blood concentration level is more than 0,02 g per 100 ml.
> - You are not allowed to fly if the accumulated flight time after your flight is completed exceeds, or is likely to exceed, the **permissible aggregate** of—
>   - (i) 10 hours within a 24-hour period for pilots not subject to an approved flight time and duty period scheme *(this is you!)*;
>   - (ii) 400 hours, during the preceding 90 days;
>   - (iii) 700 hours, during the preceding six months; or
>   - (iv) 1000 hours, during the preceding 12 months.
>
> This sub-regulation is valid for 'all flying'. Why these limitations? Because too much flying causes fatigue, which affects human performance, and so fatigue is a disqualifier. And bear in mind this regulation already mentioned:[28]

---

[27] Refer to CARS 91.02.3 (3) (a). However CARS 91.02.3 (3) (b), (c), (d) and (4) provides for different rules regarding flight instructors in ab initio training (six hours per calendar day), and pilots under IFR; although for pilots in non-commercial air transport aircraft with passenger seating capacity of over 19, rule (i) (10 hrs in 24 hrs) is discarded for reasons explained in the correlating sub-regulation, CARS 91.02.1 (2).

[28] CATS 67.00.9–2 Guidelines Table.

- **Anaesthetics**:
  - ➢ A minimum of 24 hours following local or regional (including dental) anaesthetics. You do not return to duty, or to flying: you tell your DAME who decides, and the occurrence is placed on file.
  - ➢ A minimum of 72 hours following general, spinal or epidural anaesthetic. This proscription includes drug-induced sedation: you tell your DAME who decides, and the occurrence is placed on file.
- **Anti-anxiety or anti-insomnia benzodiazepine** (temazepam alone is 'acceptable'):
  - ➢ you wait 72 hours: no requirement to advise your DAME.

Memorise this list. It is an exam question right up to CPL.

5.2.3 Limitations linked to 'recency'

Recency limitations are **stringent** because they are linked to how recently you have flown, hence being able to fly safely now **with passengers**—this is due to the often rapid decay of skill retention ('getting rusty'). It has to do with being still 'proficient' with certain requisite skills such as taking off at night.

A FAA study has shown that after eight months of not flying only 54% of pilots can meet the standards for steep turns. This could mean that after just three months of not flying, a skill designed to make you land safely is already quite impaired.[29] Do the maths. Mind the stall.

The difference between 'recency' and 'currency'

Take an example: you are current, that is, you have done your revalidation check. Now, you want to take a passenger on a night flight. But are you recent? If you have not complied with the regulation cited below (recency limitations), you are not. Is an instructor checking that you are recent and endorsing your pilot logbook accordingly? No, because it is not a competency check: it is up to you to apply the rule of recency.

---

[29] Jerry M Childs, William D Spears & Wallace W Prophet *Private Pilot Skill Retention 8, 16, and 24 months after Certification* (1983), cited by Paul A Craig *The Killing Zone* 2 ed (2013) 230.

Recency applies to licences and ratings.

The PPL limitations linked to recency are as follows:

> **Recency limitations (A) and (H)**
>
> The holder of a PPL (Aeroplane) and (Helicopter) must comply with the recency requirements of regulation 91.02.4.[30] That is:[31]
>
> - **You cannot act as PIC** of an **aircraft**, or second-in-command (SIC) of an aircraft required to be crewed by more than one pilot, **carrying passengers by day**,
>   - ➢ unless you have personally, **within the 90 days immediately preceding** the flight, carried out **either by day or by night at least three take-offs and three landings** in the same class or, if a type rating is required, type or variant of aeroplane,
> - and in the case of a **helicopter** three circuits including three take-offs and three landings in the same type of helicopter as that in which such flight is to be undertaken.
>
>   These landings may be completed in an **FSTD** approved for the purpose.
>
>   In the case of a **tail-wheel** aeroplane, each landing shall be carried out to a full stop.
>
> - **You cannot act as PIC** of an **aircraft**, or SIC of an aircraft required to be crewed by more than one pilot, **carrying passengers by night**,
>   - ➢ unless you have personally, within the **90 days immediately preceding the flight, carried out at least three take-offs and three landings by night** in the same class or, if a type rating is required, type or variant of aeroplane,
>   - ➢ and in the case of a **helicopter** three circuits including three take-offs and three landings in the same type of helicopter as that in which such flight is to be undertaken.
>
>   These landings may be completed in an **FSTD** approved for the purpose.
>
>   In the case of a **tail-wheel** aeroplane, each landing must be to a fullstop.
>
> - **If you are Instrument Rated** you cannot act as PIC or SIC of an aircraft on an instrument approach to an aerodrome in IMC unless you have, within the 90 days immediately preceding such approach procedure or procedures established by the Director or an appropriate authority, executed at least two approaches in an aircraft or an FSTD approved for the purpose or a combination of aircraft and FSTD approved for the purpose, either under actual or simulated conditions, with reference to flight instruments only; or undergone the appropriate skill test as prescribed in regulation 61.15 of CARS Part 61.

All this sounds rather limiting. But, far from limiting you, the law provides for pushing the limits of your PPL.

---

[30] CARS 61.03.9 (A) and 61.04.9 (H).
[31] CARS 91.02.4.

5.3 A PPL IS A LICENCE TO LEARN: ADD RATINGS

Ratings are not easy to grasp immediately and often are, to quote Churchill, 'a riddle wrapped in a mystery inside an enigma'. Let us try to find a key.

First, you will hear your ex-instructor say: 'Your PPL is a licence to learn'—not necessarily to train toward a CPL, and ultimately fly galactic. It is an opportunity to learn how to fly safer, fly better, and add 'ratings' to your licence. And that is in keeping with the original meaning of 'rate': 'value'. **A rating adds value to your PPL**.

Second, what about the definition of the first privilege of your licence?

'To act as PIC or co-pilot in any aeroplane **for which you hold the appropriate valid class rating or type rating**'.

And the reverse limitation?

'Not to act as PIC or co-pilot in any aeroplane for which you do not hold the appropriate valid class rating or type rating'.

Clearly, class and type are a legal issue, and this is why ratings are codified.

Third, you will also have noticed that your PPL, the 'brown book' itself, comes with a loose sheet, the Licence Details, a list of Class/Type Ratings. You have trained on a C172. But C150 is also listed, not to mention that Reims Rocket you did not know existed. To be able to fly all of those listed in the ratings legally—or fly very different ones—you will have to do some further training, moderate or extensive, which is the idea behind the 'rating', but it does not stop there, as we are going to see in this chapter.

All this leads to the following definition of rating:

> 'Rating' means an **authorisation entered on or associated with a licence** and forming part of such licence, **stating special conditions, privileges** or **limitations** relating to such licence.[32]

These below are PPL exam questions!

Ratings for pilots under CARS Part 61:

The whole schedule of ratings is based on pilot licences issued under **Part 61**, which are: SPL, PPL (A), PPL (H), CPL (A), CPL (H), ATPL (A), and ATPL (H).

Under Part 62, NPL, ratings are different.

So, under Part 61, there are four series of ratings:

---

[32] CARS 1.01.1.

- Category ratings
- Ratings for special purposes
- Class ratings
- Type ratings

Category, Class, Type, and Special Purposes ratings for pilots are itemised but not detailed in CARS 61.01.3.

Class and Types Ratings are detailed in CARS 61 Subpart 9.

Each rating has its own dedicated and detailed CARS Subpart (running from Subpart 10 to Subpart 27), including Instructor Ratings for instance.

Lastly, do not confuse a pilot category or class, or even type rating with an aircraft category or class. Turn to the last section of this chapter on categories of aircraft and aeroplanes. Aircraft 'categories' are, for the novice, another 'riddle wrapped in a mystery inside an enigma', until you get the key to it, which is one purpose of this chapter.

5.3.1 Category ratings[33]

The regulator identifies only two category ratings: Aeroplane and Helicopter.

If you hold a PPL (A) or (H) you have the relevant category rating.

In Australia a PPL falls into at least one of five category ratings: aeroplane (A), helicopter (H), powered-lift aircraft (P), gyroplane (G), and airship (AS).[34]

By contrast, if you have a South African National Pilot Licence (under Part 62) (*note!*), there are seven category ratings available to you.[35]

5.3.2 Class and Type ratings: definitions[36]

If you look up 'class' under Definitions in CARS 1.01.1 (which is always your first stop when you do not understand what the law refers to), you will be surprised to see that 'class' applies to a series of items that have nothing to do with licensing (in other words, with ratings). There is no mention of class ratings in the Definitions.

---

[33] CARS 61.01.3 (1) (a).

[34] Australian Civil Aviation Safety Authority as at February 2016.

[35] CARS 62.01.5: conventionally controlled microlight aeroplanes; weight-shift controlled microlight aeroplanes; gyroplanes and gyrogliders with a maximum all-up mass of 2 000 kg or less; hang-gliders, including powered hang-gliders; paragliders, including powered paragliders and powered paratrikes; light sport aeroplanes; and touring motor gliders.

[36] CARS 61.09.1 (4) (5) (A and H)—CARS 61.01.3 (1) (b) (c) reflects a list that predates the changes made to CARS 61.09.1 (4) (5).

There are six aeroplane and helicopter class ratings:[37]

> Class ratings (A) and (H), single pilot
> - SEA (L): single-engine piston aeroplanes (land) certificated for single pilot operation.
> - SEA (S): single-engine piston aeroplanes (sea) certificated for single pilot operation.
> - MEA (L): multi-engine piston aeroplanes (land) certificated for single pilot operation.
> - MEA (S): multi-engine piston aeroplanes (sea) certificated for single pilot operation.
> - SHE: single engine helicopters certificated for single pilot operation.
> - MHE: multi-engine certificated for single pilot operation.

Example: You hold a PPL (A). It is a category rating (Aeroplane) and the class rating is SEA (L). (Do not get confused by the acronym: 'SEA' as in single-engine aeroplane, not 'sea' as in 'seaplane'.)

Type ratings (A) and (H) apply to:[38]

> - **Aeroplanes** certificated for operation with **more than one pilot**.
> - **Turbojet and turbofan** powered aeroplanes.
> - **Helicopters certificated for multi-crew** operation.
> - **Any aircraft** *(meaning: aeroplane or helicopter)* **considered** necessary **by the Director.**
>
> Type ratings for helicopters issued in terms of this Part comprise a type rating by name for each type of helicopter.[39]

With regard to type ratings:
- We are now dealing with **multi-pilot or high performance** or (unconventional) aircraft at the Director's discretion.
- Type ratings are issued according to CARS together with a list published by SACAA.[40]

---

[37] CARS 61.09.1 (4) (a).
[38] CARS 61.09.1 (4) (b).
[39] CARS 61.01.3 (3).
[40] CARS 61.09.1 (5). SACAA Type Rating & License Endorsement List (as at 26 June 2017).

- Regarding warbird type rating: although no longer mentioned specifically,[41] Appendix 10.4 of CATS makes provision for a practical flying training syllabus.
- There is a type rating not falling under Part 61 but Part 62 that is both interesting and open to a PPL holder: you may be able to get a Touring Motor Glider (first type) rating with a 'relaxation' of requirements in terms of experience and theoretical knowledge.[42]

5.3.3 Class and Type ratings training prerequisites

If, for instance, you hold a single-pilot, single-engine SEA (L) and you want to obtain a single-pilot, multi-engine MEA (L) rating: that is a **class** rating. Or you hold a MEA (L) and you want a rating on a twin-engine, multi-pilot aircraft: this is a **type** rating. In both instances you do not already hold an initial class or type rating in the class or for the type you are applying for. You then have to meet prerequisites and undergo training.

Prerequisite for an initial training for a class rating

Before being able to undergo a class rating training you must have flown 100 hours as pilot-in-command of aeroplanes for the multi-engine class rating.[43]

Prerequisites for an initial training for a type rating

The prerequisites are tough:[44]
- at least a CPL or no less than 350 hours as pilot-in-command of aeroplanes for an aeroplane type rating
- at least a CPL or no less than 200 hours as pilot-in-command of helicopters for a helicopter type rating
- a valid instrument rating in the case of aeroplanes
- a multi-engine class rating in the case of multi-engine aeroplanes
- multi-pilot operation training and certificate in the case of multi-pilot aircraft. The multi-pilot operations training is only required for the first multi-pilot aircraft rating.

These are prerequisites, but what are the requirements in terms of the training itself?

The examination

Initial training is required and must be endorsed in the licence and it consists of:
- theoretical knowledge instruction

---

[41] In CARS 61 Subpart 9 Class and Ratings, 61.09.4 (b). But listed in CARS 61.01.3 (c) (v).
[42] CARS 62.17.2 (3) and 62.17.4 (2).
[43] CARS 61.09.3 (2) (b) (i).
[44] CARS 61.09.3 (2).

92 Air Law

- a theoretical knowledge examination
- flight training
- a skills test conducted by a DFE, in an aircraft or (only for a type rating) in a FSTD.[45]

Before you start flight training you must have passed the theoretical knowledge examination. Upon completion you must submit the required documents and pay the fee.

Revalidation

Each type of rating (in the case of a private pilot, the most likely ratings are for NR and IR) is validated by a Skills Test but **some ratings have a time-specific validity** (IR, 12 months),[46] which implies undergoing a **revalidation check** within a given time frame, both in compliance with general competency or revalidation rules (see 5.1.3 above) and specific ones.[47]

5.3.4 Conversion training[48]

Another way of obtaining a rating is when you already have endorsed in your licence an aircraft in a given class, or of a given type. You now want to fly legally on a different model in the same class or variant of the type you are allowed to fly. This is called a conversion. You want the model or variant to be endorsed in your licence.

A conversion is less demanding than the process described above since you already have experience in flying an aircraft close or reasonably close to the one you wish to fly.

Since experience varies, the regulator makes room for a conversion either by differences training or by familiarisation.

Conversion training 'consists of either differences or familiarisation training' in order to add
- a different manufacturer, model or variant of an aircraft within a particular class to a licence already endorsed with the relevant class; and
- a variant within a particular type to a licence already endorsed with the relevant type.

Conversion is compulsory when converting:
- from one aircraft manufacturer to another; or one model to another of the same manufacturer—for aircraft in the same class;

---

[45] CATS 61.09.4 to 61.09.6.
[46] CARS 61.11.6.
[47] CARS 61.11.7, IR.
[48] CARS 61.09.7. References to CATS in this section and the next follow Amendment SACATS 3/2016, which is current.

- from one variant to another variant of the same model—for aircraft in the same class; or
- from one variant to another—for aircraft of the same type.[49]

What is the difference in conversion between 'differences training' and 'familiarisation'?

In the case of differences training:[50]
- you must undergo theoretical knowledge instruction, a theoretical knowledge examination at your ATO (at least 100 questions for a type rating and 50 questions for a class rating; and achieve 75% pass in both cases);[51] and
- you must undergo flight training, but may do it in a FSTD.

In the case of familiarisation:[52]
- only theoretical instruction (no examination) is required;
- flight training is not mandatory—unless your instructor deems it necessary (and in this case alone familiarisation has to be done at an ATO, otherwise it is not mandatory).

5.3.5 Turbojet or turbofan mentor programme

The programme is relatively new and concerns only 'the initial training in the case of single pilot turbojet or turbofan aeroplane type ratings as well as single-engine and multi-engine turboprop aeroplanes within a class'.[53]

This is advanced training, and *it is unlikely that an exam question* will crop up at the PPL examination.[54]

5.3.6 Ratings for special purposes

As the name indicates each rating fulfils a special purpose, a set of skills that add value to your licence.
- PPL holders have access to 10 ratings for special purposes, some for A,[55] some for H.[56] The list (A) and (H) taken together is as follows:[57]

---

[49] CARS 61.09.7 (2).
[50] CARS 61.09.8 and CATS 61.09.7.
[51] CATS 61.09.4–2 (2).
[52] CARS 61.09.9; CATS 61.09.7 (2).
[53] CATS 61.09.3–1 (2).
[54] PPLs who are interested in this rating should consult CATS 61 and correlate the version online with the latest amendment to CATS to make sure that the online version does reflect the amended TS. See also note 47 above.
[55] CARS 61.03.8.
[56] CARS 61.04.8.
[57] CARS 61.01.3 (1) (d).

94 *Air Law*

> - night rating
> - instrument rating
> - post-maintenance test flight rating
> - tug pilot rating
> - touring glider rating
> - helicopter sling load rating
> - helicopter game or livestock cull rating
> - agricultural pilot rating
> - aerobatics rating
> - tow pilot rating
>
> *SPL students, note: you may be asked at the Air Law exam about these ratings!*

- Among them, two are available to a SPL holder who is doing the Integrated Training: the Night Rating (NR)[58] and the Instrument Rating (subject to requirements, such as holding a NR).[59]
- Ratings depend upon the licence you hold: as a PPL, some ratings are open to you, while some are not. For instance, to qualify for an instructor rating you must at least hold a CPL. Aerobatics rating is open only to PPL (A). An Instrument Rating is open to a SPL, if you already hold a Night Rating which is open to a SPL, as mentioned. A SPL also has access to an Agricultural Pilot Rating (subject to requirements).[60] Of course, some ratings are specific to helicopters.
- Together with ratings open to CPL and ATPL holders, you will find below a list with criteria summarised and coded A (aeroplane), H (helicopter), and SPL, PPL, CPL, according to the **lowest licence you must hold** to apply for the rating.

> **Ratings for special purposes (SPL to ATPL)**
> - Night rating[61]—PPL (A, H); SPL (A, H) (Integrated Training);
> - Instrument rating[62]—PPL (A, H); SPL with NR (A, H) (Integrated Training);
> - Flight instructor ratings[63]—CPL (A, H) [not listed under 'special purpose' A or H but listed under Ratings for pilots CARS 61.01.3];

---

[58] CARS 61.02.6.
[59] CARS 61.11.2.
[60] CARS 61.25.1.
[61] CARS Subpart 10: 61.10.1 to 5.
[62] CARS Subpart 11: 61.11.1 to 8.
[63] CARS 61 subparts 12 to 17.

- Post-maintenance test flight rating and test pilot rating[64] PPL (A or H, minimum 500 hrs flight time, including minimum 300 hrs PIC) [listed separately under CARS 61.01.3 (iv) (v)];
- Tug pilot rating[65]—PPL (A) (minimum 60 hrs PIC);
- Helicopter sling load rating—CPL (H) [not listed under 'special purpose' H];
- Helicopter game or livestock cull rating—PPL(H);
- Helicopter winching rating—CPL (H) [not listed under 'special purpose' H but listed under CARS 61.01.3];
- Agricultural pilot rating[66]—SPL (A, H) CPL (for commercial op);
- Aerobatics rating[67]—PPL (A) (membership of aerobatics sport controlled body);[68] divided into four classes of aerobatics rating;
- Tow rating[69]—PPL (A).

Let it be said that the most likely 'special purpose rating' a pilot might add first to a PPL is the NR. Not only is it the obligatory first step toward a CPL, but for general aviation pilots it is the best way to become more proficient at flying with instruments (as this is a large part of NR training) without embarking on a full IR.[70] Night Rating practical training is sometimes referred to as Exercise 20.

See chapter 13 and annexure 17 for more details on night flying.

5.3.7 Endorsement and validation of rating and conversion

There are two different procedures, both involving endorsement in your logbook, and a notification or application on a specific form.

Notification of conversion: The instructor who conducts the conversion, if satisfied, will endorse your logbook as per the rules[71] and 'complete a notification of differences or familiarisation', which you will submit to the Director within 30 days of completing the training.[72]

The form concerned is Notification of Aircraft Differences or Familiarisation Training CA 61–09.7.

---

[64] CARS Subpart 19: 61.19.1.
[65] CARS Subpart 20: 61.20.1–2.
[66] CARS Subpart 25: 61.25.1 to 4.
[67] CARS Subpart 27: 61.27.1 to 4.
[68] On acrobatic flight CARS 91.07.30. Note that one refers to an 'acrobatic flight', but to 'aerobatics' (always with an s) as the discipline.
[69] CARS Subpart 21: 61.21.1–2.
[70] Wouter Gous, Bob Ewing & Lee-Anne Dixon *Flight Instructor's Manual of Training and Procedures* (2009), on the SAA website.
[71] CATS 61.09.7 (3).
[72] CARS 61.09.7 (4).

Endorsement for Class or Type Rating: the general rule for endorsement applies, as mentioned earlier in this book (refer to page 47), that is to say, in abridged form:[73]

(1) An applicant for a licence, **rating,** revalidation, **class or type rating or any familiarisation or differences training must have the applicable endorsements** in his or her pilot logbook.
(2) The endorsement must include, but is not limited to, the following details—
   (a) Date of the skills test;
   (b) Aircraft registration and type;
   (c) Name and licence number of examiner;
   (d) Name of the ATO.

However, the Application form is not the standard CA 61–01.0[74] but a specific one: Application for Class or Type Rating (A) (H) CA 61–09.06.

Endorsement for other Ratings: they are endorsed as by the regulation mentioned and applied for on the standard Application for Initial Issue of SA-CAR Part 61 Pilot Licence or Rating CA 61–01.0.

Endorsement for Warbird Rating: Beside the endorsement, and according to SA-CATS Part 61 Appendix 10.4, upon completion of training the application must be made on form CA 61–13–9.1.

5.4 CATEGORIES OF AIRCRAFT AND AEROPLANES

Now that we have dealt with 'category ratings for pilots' it is worth clarifying what the 'categories' of aircraft or aeroplanes are to avoid any confusion with rating categories and types. *For information and CPL level.*

- **In terms of Regulations for Air Services**, domestic and international, there are six categories of **aircraft**. These are for the purpose of air service licences:[75]
  - category A1—any aircraft, excluding a helicopter, with a maximum certificated mass exceeding 20 000 kilograms
  - category A2—any aircraft, excluding a helicopter, with a maximum certificated mass exceeding 5 700 kilograms but not exceeding 20 000 kilograms
  - category A3—any aircraft, excluding a helicopter, with a maximum certificated mass exceeding 2 700 kilograms but not exceeding 5 700 kilograms
  - category A4—any aircraft, excluding a helicopter, with a maximum certificated mass of 2 700 kilograms or less

---

[73] CARS 61.01.18.

[74] SACAA Form Number: CA 61.01.0 Application for initial issue of SA-CAR Part 61 Pilot Licence or Rating (excluding class and type rating).

[75] Domestic Air Services Regulations, 1991, section 4; International Air Services Regulations, 1994, section 4.

- ➢ category H1—any multi-engine helicopter
- ➢ category H2—any single-engine helicopter.

- **In terms of type certification** (as in Type Certificated vs 'NTCA' Non-Type Certificated), under Part 21, the regulator has a list of nine 'types' of **aircraft**:[76]
  - ➢ gliders, power-assisted gliders, and touring gliders
  - ➢ very light aeroplanes
  - ➢ aeroplanes of normal, utility, acrobatic and commuter categories
  - ➢ aeroplanes of the transport category
  - ➢ rotorcraft of the normal category
  - ➢ rotorcraft of the transport category
  - ➢ manned free balloons
  - ➢ non-rigid airships
  - ➢ ornithopters (bird-like machine designs with flapping wings; these go back as far as Ancient Greece, and have been flown – with alarming results – even very recently).[77]

Certification takes the form of a 'type acceptance certificate', which is valid until surrendered, suspended, or cancelled.[78]

- **In terms of wake turbulence** (vortex effect) related to weight based on the maximum certificated take-off mass, there are three wake turbulence categories (WTC):
  - ➢ H—heavy, 136 000 kg and more
  - ➢ M—medium, less than 136 000 kg but more than 7 000 kg
  - ➢ L—light, 7 000 kg and less.

Also the Super Heavy category J: Airbus A388 and Antonov An225, 560 000 kg.

Remember this: 'An aircraft which is obliged ... to keep out of the way of another aircraft, shall avoid passing over or under the other aircraft, or crossing ahead of such aircraft, unless passing well clear, taking into account the effects of wake turbulence.'[79] WTC is valid on the ground as well, in terms of horizontal separation distance.

Super add a suffix to their call sign on first contact: 'Approach/Tower, Airline 326, Super.'[80]

H, M, L are the designators used on a Flight Plan at item 9 'Wake Turbulence Category' *(can be an exam question)*.

---

[76] CARS 21.01.2. Both 'certified' and 'certificated' are used. See for example CATS 47.01.3-2 and 2A which uses both.

[77] See Horst Räbiger *How ornithopters fly* (multi-lingual, comprehensive, and highly technical), available at www.ornithopter.de.

[78] CARS 21.04.6.

[79] CARS 91.06.7 (2).

[80] AIP ENR 1.8–25 (Oct 2016). AIC 005–2018, 21.1 (b) Note 1: 'Heavy'.

- **In terms of approach speed**—that is, the KIAS at the runway threshold (V_{AT}) itself being calculated as 1.3 times the stall speed in the landing configuration (V_{S0}) at maximum certificated landing mass—there are five categories of **aeroplanes**. These are used to determine minima in an **instrument** approach. They apply across operations: Part 121 (air transport, 20 or more passengers, or all cargo maximum certificated take-off weight more than 8 618 kg), 135 (air transport 19 or fewer pax, or all cargo maximum certificated take-off weight of 8 618 kg or less), 137 (aerial work operation), and 138 (air ambulance) *(CPL level)*.[81]
  - Category A—Less than 91 KTS IAS
  - Category B—91 KTS or more, but less than 121 KTS IAS
  - Category C—121 KTS or more, but less than 141 KTS IAS
  - Category D—141 KTS or more, but less than 166 KTS IAS
  - Category E (military)—166 KTS or more, but less than 211 KTS IAS.

- **In terms of performance**, aeroplanes are divided into four performance classes from A to D[82] (helicopters are in three classes from 1 to 3):[83]
  - Class A:
    - multi-engine aeroplanes powered by turbo-propeller engines with a maximum certificated mass exceeding 5 700 kg
    - multi-engine turbojet-powered aeroplanes
  - Class B: propeller-driven aeroplanes, other than single-engine aeroplanes, with a MCM of 5 700 kg or less
  - Class C aeroplanes: aeroplanes powered by two or more reciprocating engines with a MCM exceeding 5 700 kg
  - Class D: single-engine aeroplanes.

This classification has to do with the aircraft capacity (Class A and Class C), in case of a critical power-unit failure, to abort a take-off safely or clear obstacles; or at landing to clear obstacles and land within the distance available, in both cases by a safe or adequate margin.[84]

You will note that **a further classification** comes into play in terms of the number of passengers and all cargo MCTOW **in relation to the air transport Part** under which the aircraft is operating (121, 135). Finally, provision is made under CATS 47.10 for **'historic aircraft'**. The 'Classification of Aircraft' table at CATS 47.11 is the product of a fertile imagination and has no bearing on your training.

---

[81] AIP ENR 1.8–2.
[82] CARS 91.08.4.
[83] CARS 91.08.3.
[84] CARS 91.08.5.

Are you now ready 'to fly to the moon' (by day)? The law wants you to. The next part is the heart of this book. The Law or Justice may often be portrayed as blindfolded but she definitely does not want you to fly blind. Secure your harness and put on your Ray-Bans.

PART THREE

LET'S FLY!

> We flew close to the *Spirit of St. Louis* and noticed an unusual phenomenon. The colonel (Lindbergh) would select a tomato and toss it out from his window at a slightly forward angle. The tomato would be caught at once in the slipstream of the whirling propeller, so that its forward movement was quickly checked. For a fraction of a second it appeared to hang in space, as its hulk and smooth round surface prevented the wind blasts from hurling it backwards. Then it began to move to the rear, slowly and almost majestically, as though to show its disdain at being disposed of so summarily. Lindbergh continued this performance until the last tomato was gone.
>
> Donald E Keyhoe *Flying with Lindbergh* (1928) 204

You cannot drop tomatoes any longer from an aircraft 'en route', to relieve a long cross-country flight—except with the permission of the Director. This part will take you through each phase of a flight, seen from a legal perspective. Without dropping tomatoes.

Step by step you will see how legal requirements have to be implemented for you to (actually) fly in terms of the law, while also providing students about to sit examination papers—Air Law in particular—with the required knowledge and, even better, the necessary knowledge. Note the reference to 'papers' and not simply the Air Law paper: SACAA wants you to have a broad knowledge, across the subjects that make up the **core knowledge** required for a pilot.

The aim is to illustrate how the law applies continually throughout a flight, which should help you not to forget what regulations you have to observe in an actual flight. Rather than providing an abstract presentation of regulations and sub-regulations, and to-dos and not-to-dos the chapters dramatise them and make them more real. This will help you to better memorise legal procedures for each phase of a flight.

As for private pilots, including those moving onto advanced licences or ratings, this serves as a recap of the core knowledge.

The regulations are therefore correlated with each phase of a flight, and give both pilots and aviation enthusiasts a better sense of why regulation so and so has to be applied at such and such a time.

So, let us follow the natural progression of an actual flight, from getting up and getting ready to go to the airfield, to filling in your logbook after getting safely back to base, a dramatisation of a flight with all legal aspects being taken care of. Law (not) on the fly, as it were.

Chapter 6

. . . .

Before you call 'clear prop'

As we begin, a basic rule: **the law requires that your duty, as PIC, and no one else's, is to 'ensure' that actions to be undertaken to fly safely and legally are done, and done properly.**

Indeed, when air law requires a pilot 'to ensure' any action or operation, this pilot is **fully responsible** for carrying out the task and carrying it out according to what the regulations say.

> The definition of '**to ensure**' is not for the faint-hearted:[1]
>
> 'ensure' in relation to any person, body or institution and in respect of any matter, activity, process, condition, requirement or other person, or anything else, means to take, considering the nature and context of the provision requiring the ensuring, and any other appropriate legal provisions, in good faith, all necessary, and all reasonably incidental and practically executable preliminary, precedent and precautionary steps in order to be able and prepared to take, and afterwards to take, all necessary and reasonably incidental and practically executable steps, to substantially achieve the clear particular objectives of the provision requiring the ensuring and, in general, the promotion of civil aviation safety and the public interest.

All set?

Time is 0500B (that is 5 am local time). You have booked an aircraft of the class and type you are legally allowed to fly. From where you are it looks likes a clear, cool day with light wind and no significant weather change in view. Everything looks fine for that perfect nav flight you prepared yesterday. You took out the aeronautical chart, tracing the route, checking airspace and jotting down altitudes and frequencies—or did the same on your electronic device, hoping it would not go on the blink mid-air, leaving you to scramble for the chart you have hopefully not left at home. You have a rough idea of your route.

From now on you have to take a series of actions to get ready, and ready legally.

This chapter is divided into a succession of seven actions you should try to do in sequence.

---

[1] CARS 1.01.1.

6.1 ACTION 1: I'M SAFE?

It is 0600B. In plain English, 6 o'clock in the morning.

Your first assessment after breakfast is a quick self-evaluation. You evaluate yourself as a 'resource' for flying, and you do it as the law requires.

The evaluation is called I'M SAFE?[2]

Before you do the check, remember the regulations (under Part 67) **that forbid you to fly if you are unfit (see pages 30 and 31).**

The I'M SAFE checklist assumes that, as for the above, you are in the clear.

I'M SAFE ?

Do I feel **I**ll?

Am I taking **M**edication?

Am I **S**tressed (by work, family or money problems) or stressed by lack of **S**leep?

Any **A**lcohol eight hours before? (or more if your body is still under the influence)

Am I **F**atigued, or tired because of a lack of sleep?

Have I **E**aten a good breakfast and food that is not going to create gastric problems?

Each question in I'M SAFE points to a rule of safety:

- Ill? Feeling ill (eg, a running nose): don't fly.
- Medicating? Don't fly, as medication can have a 'psychoactive effect' (in plain English, prevent you from thinking clearly, applying good judgment and taking the right decision)—unless prescribed by a doctor and certified safe for flying by your DAME.[3]
- Stressed? 'Stress' is a vague notion but stress can be a medical condition, or be a nervous reaction to personal issues. In any event, if you 'suspect' stress will impair your airmanship, don't fly.

Stress can also be related to a **lack of sleep**, and the law is stringent in this regard. As a pilot of a single-pilot aircraft (not subject to an approved flight time and duty period schedule) **you cannot fly legally if your 'permissible aggregate' (or total hours in a given period) has been exceeded, as we seen before (see page 85).**

- Alcohol? You know the rule already: as a crew member you cannot 'consume any alcohol less than 8 hours prior to commencing standby for operational duty or commencing operational duty, which operational duty shall be deemed to

---

[2] Adapted from the neat flash-card type document produced by Rob Rhodes-Houghton, SACAA, Manager: Testing Standards, 'Teaching ADM/SRM' (November 2011) (on the SACAA website). ADM stands for Aeronautical Decision Making, SRM for Single-Pilot Resource Management. The document is intended for instructors but of great value to pilots.

[3] CARS 91.01.16 (1) and (2).

commence at the specified reporting time, if applicable' and 'commence an operational duty period while the concentration of alcohol in [your] blood, is more than 0,02 gram per 100 millilitres'[4]—beware of the rate of alcohol elimination if you binged the evening before.[5]

- Fatigue is a serious risk. It can be a condition you 'know' or 'suspect' you suffer from, and you want to brush it off ('it will pass', 'I am used to it'): hence fatigue is perverse. Think of the image of 'metal fatigue': tiny cracks in the exhaust, hard to see, and one day the perverted exhaust splits. Mind and body are the same. It may also be that you are likely to suffer from fatigue due to the type or circumstances of flight (for instance, a long nav over hazardous mountains or a long stretch to Graaff-Reinet over arid land with hardly any visual references on the ground). Fatigue risk management is very much at the forefront of aviation concerns, and this includes private pilots.[6]

If fatigue is such that 'it may endanger the safety of the aircraft or its occupants', you cannot fly.[7] Of course you can, but the consequences if anything goes wrong are serious (from losing your licence to criminal prosecution).

- **Eating properly** is common sense. But some food can cause acid reflux, diarrhoea, intestinal gas stomach cramps (onions, fizzy drinks). In fact CATS Part 64, which concerns Cabin Crew Licensing, requires training in dealing with an 'incapacitated flight crew member' and food poisoning.[8] It follows that you should, as a pilot, exercise caution. What is good for the Airbus 380 goose is good for the Cessna 150 gander.

If you are accompanied by a safety pilot or a fellow pilot with whom you are going to share flying and a very expensive sardine burger upon arrival at Margate FAMG, make sure she can also declare: I'M SAFE.

And by the way, do not forget to wear adequate clothing—always have something warm, just in case you do a forced landing near Putsonderwater at sunset. If you go for a nav take 5 litres of water, some nutritious bars, bananas or

---

[4] CARS 91.02.3 (2) (a) and (b).

[5] A blood alcohol content calculation based on two stiff glasses of liquor at 40% vol, plus half a bottle of pinotage at 14,5% vol drunk between 8 pm and 11 pm may put your blood alcohol concentration (BAC) well over the limit at 9 am the following day (see calculator at www.defencelaw.com).

[6] '"fatigue" means a physiological state of reduced mental or physical performance capability resulting from sleep loss, extended wakefulness, circadian phase, and /or workload (mental and/or physical activity) that can impair a person's alertness and ability to safely operate an aircraft or perform safety related operational duties.' As per 20th Amendment *Government Gazette* 42362 GN 645 of 29 March 2019.

[7] CARS 91.02.3 (b).

[8] CATS 64.02.2, 2.2.3.16 (2) (a).

chocolate (pioneer pilots ate chocolate while flying across the Sahara or the Andes). If you take off two hours after having breakfast, four hours later you will be hungry, which will lead to stress or fatigue, and you will no longer be able to pass I'M SAFE during the flight!

So you, personally, are safe to fly! You have done a risk management analysis of yourself.

Actions described in the following sections are termed in CARS '**Duties of PIC regarding flight preparation**' (annexure 9).[9]

6.2 ACTION 2: AIRSPACE

It is now 0700B and you are at the clubhouse or the school where you hire and fly.

You, personally, are good to go, but what are the skies up to?

It is pointless to pre-flight if the meteorological conditions for flying are not what they should be—regardless of the seemingly perfect flying weather over the departure aerodrome.

In this scenario you fly VFR ('R' for rules). So you must 'determine' the meteorological conditions, or VMC ('C' for conditions).

Airspace and weather are interrelated in many ways. The most important way is how bad weather prevents you from operating under VMC in a given airspace.

So the first logical step is to remind yourself what types of airspace there are in Southern Africa and in which ones you will operate during the coming flight that will place constraints on you, especially, but not exclusively, in terms of weather issues.

6.2.1 Check your airspace

This is a reminder of knowledge acquired in navigation, but again, questions about airspace will come up in the Air Law exam.

Use of charts and AIP

If your charts are up to date, when you draw a track on a chart it will intersect a variety of airspace classes and areas. Each one has its own size and shape, specifications, frequency, forming a multicoloured puzzle which looks like an alien code to non-pilots and which only you are able to decipher. In addition, charts carry a load of information about terrain, obstacles, navigation symbols and acronyms, all easily understood, provided that you have not cut off the bottom part of your chart where the symbols are decoded. *Some symbols may come up as exam questions.*

AIP ENR will provide you with the information you need apart from the charts.

What you should now do is to trace your **true track or course** by drawing on your chart the route, waypoints, and checkpoints, circling in red the highest terrain

---

[9] CARS 91.02.7.

within a 5 NM radius, 'little houses', blue arrows for wind direction, Top of Climb, Top of Descent, and calculate the data (if you already have wind direction and velocity) and then transfer them into your flight log, and use some of this data to file a flight plan.

Charting a route, filling in a flight log, and filing a flight plan take care and take time. Of course we have electronic devices, but if their batteries go flat, you had better have it all on paper. Even if you decide to fly a track on GPS like a bird on a wire, when you file the plan you have to know how to describe that wire to the officer on the telephone.

Airspace is no simple matter.

What is 'airspace'?

Keep it simple: 'your' airspace is that flying space between two aerodromes, the one you depart from and the one you land at. Or where you are forbidden by law to do just that (but others may—such as the military). The result is that when you prepare a flight and draw on a chart a track between those two points it will traverse zones the state has carved out into categories of airspace and areas.

Let us look at it step by step.

Southern African airspace is represented by a series of 16 world aeronautical charts, scale 1: 1 000 000.

South Africa has been tasked by ICAO to publish and maintain these 16 world aeronautical charts or WAC (the projection is Lambert Conformal Conic with two standard parallels—*this may be an exam question*), produced by the National Geo-spatial Information office or NGI (annexure 10).[10]

The NGI, whose proud history of surveying goes back to 1652, also maintains and publishes charts in 1: 500 000 (annexure 10). Charts in 1: 250 000, however useful, are no longer maintained. And do not say 'map', please: show respect, say 'chart'.

However, what flying is allowed in each of these 16 geographical spaces is a different matter, because an airspace is more than the upward projection of a terrain divided into sections measured in degrees.

How is the South African airspace divided?

To begin with, the Director of SACAA designates any portion of the airspace as:
- flight information region;
- advisory area;
- control area (CTA);
- control zone (CTR);
- special rules area (SRA);
- aerodrome traffic area (ATA);

---

[10] Offices in Cape Town (head office) and Pretoria.

- aerodrome traffic zone (ATZ);
- prohibited area (FAP);
- restricted area (FAR);
- danger area (FAD).
- Terminal Control Areas (TMA) at main airports;
- Airways (AWY), Upper Control Areas, RNAV Routes (not for GA private pilots, except AWY if considering a flight plan, see page 127).[11]

This is why South Africa's airspace is divided into three regions called FIR (as mentioned in the section on NOTAM earlier on) that 'cap' the rest: Cape Town Flight Information Region (FACA), Johannesburg Flight Information Region (FAJA), and Johannesburg Oceanic Flight Information Region (FAJO) ('oceanic' as it covers Indian and South Atlantic). Inside them SACAA has designated the areas and zones listed above.

The designations listed are in fact functional as they serve specific functions: 'other regulated airspace' which includes mainly the Special Rules areas (SRA) help the flow of VFR traffic in uncontrolled airspace near major airports by assigning to aircraft under VFR routings for arrival, departure, bypassing, altitudes, reporting points, frequencies and radio failure procedures, switching on of landing lights and maximum indicated airspeed. These rules have to be strictly respected by VFR pilots.[12]

Another case of airspace fitting a function is the designation of areas as prohibited (FAP), restricted (FAR) and dangerous (FAD).[13] Flying Training Areas are not listed as such because they are a case either of FAD (those used by training schools for instance) or FAR (military).

6.2.2 Airspace structure and classes

Regarding the type of **air traffic services**, airspace is divided into 'classes', either controlled (A, B, C, D, E) or uncontrolled (F, G).[14]

Controlled airspace

This airspace has defined dimensions within which an air traffic **control** service (ATS) is provided to IFR flights and to VFR flights in accordance with the airspace classes (A to E, see page 109 and Table page 110).

Uncontrolled airspace

Airspace of defined dimensions (Classes F and G), within which air traffic **advisory** service or flight information services are provided depending upon the Class (F or G, see page 109).

Advisory airspace is an airspace of defined dimensions, within which air traffic advisory service is available. It can be an area (ADA) or a route (ADR) within a FIR.

---

[11] CARS 172.02.1. Part 172, Subpart 2.
[12] AIP ENR 2.2 detailed.
[13] AIP ENR 5.1–1 to 33 describes and tabulates all FAPs, FARs and FADs in terms of 'lateral and vertical limits, the type of restriction or hazard involved, the times at which it applies and other pertinent information'.
[14] AIP ENR 1.4–1, 2, 3; 1.8–7, CATS 172.02.2.

All airspace fit then into **Classes, from A to G**, which are defined by seven parameters:
- IFR or VFR, permitted or mandatory;
- separation of aircraft;
- type of ATS offered;
- VMC minima applicable or not;
- speed limitations;
- radio contact;
- ATC clearance needed or not.

This results in the list below.

Controlled[15]

Class A. Airspace as designated, above FL145 (conventional air routes), 195 (continental FIRs), 245 (oceanic). *IFR ONLY.*

Class C. Below FL200 according to ICAO standard. Controlled airspace most used by private pilots. VFR flights separated from IFR ones and receive traffic information in respect of all other VFR flights. In an ATZ aerodrome separation applies. TMAs are C. *IFR, VFR.*

Class D. All controlled airspace below FL200 in the case of an ATZ. No separation provided for VFR flights but information on request. *IFR, VFR.*

(**Class D** is new in SA: FAGC.[16] **Classes B** and **E** are not in use.)

Uncontrolled

Class F. Advisory service is provided to IFR flights, traffic information to IFR and VRF flights on request. *IFR, VFR.*

Class G. All uncontrolled airspace in South Africa. Information provided to all flights if requested. *IFR, VFR.*

Things to remember about airspace and traffic services

Remember also that an ATZ is established at an aerodrome for the protection of controlled traffic, and extends from ground level to a specified upper limit, with variable lateral limits and can be Class C (traffic is separated),[17] Class D (information is provided) or Class G (information service provided on request to VFR and IFR flights; example: FAOH, Oudtshoorn). Remember also that a CTR (Class C) has lateral limits of at least 5 NM from the centre of the aerodrome in the direction from which approach is made, and extends also from the ground to a

---

[15] AIP ENR 1.4–1 in accordance with ICAO standards. CATS 172.02.2 and Table 1.
[16] AIP AD 2-FAGC-7, 2.17 (3).
[17] AIP ENR 1.4–1.

specified upper limit. Controlled traffic (IFR and VFR) is separated by radar (transponder).

This rather complex, multi-criteria, classification has been tabulated by the regulator as follows.[18]

ATS AIRSPACE CLASSIFICATIONS								
		CONTROLLED					UNCONTROLLED	
		A	B	C	D	E	F	G
I F R		SEPARATION: All aircraft	SEPARATION: All aircraft	SEPARATION: IFR from IFR IFR from VFR	SEPARATION: IFR from IFR	SEPARATION: IFR from IFR	SEPARATION: IFR from IFR as far as practical	SEPARATION: Not provided
		SERVICES: Air traffic control service	SERVICES: Air traffic control service	SERVICES: Air traffic control service	SERVICES: Air traffic control service including traffic information about VFR flights (and traffic avoidance advice on request)	SERVICES: Air traffic control service and traffic information about VFR flights as far as practical	SERVICES: Air traffic advisory service Flight information service	SERVICES: Flight information service
		VMC MINIMA: Not applicable	VMC MINIMA: Not applicable	VMC MINIMA: Not applicable	VMC MINIMA: Not applicable	VMC MINIMA: Not applicable	VMC MINIMA: Not applicable	VMC MINIMA: Not applicable
		SPEED LIMITATION: Not applicable	SPEED LIMITATION: As published for relevant airspace	SPEED LIMITATION: As published for relevant airspace	SPEED LIMITATION: As published for relevant airspace	SPEED LIMITATION: As published for relevant airspace	SPEED LIMITATION: As published for relevant airspace	SPEED LIMITATION: As published for relevant airspace
		RADIO: 🎧	RADIO: 🎧	RADIO: 🎧	RADIO: 🎧	RADIO: 🎧	RADIO: 🎧	RADIO: 🎧
		CLEARANCE: ATC	CLEARANCE: ATC	CLEARANCE: ATC	CLEARANCE: ATC	CLEARANCE: ATC	CLEARANCE: Not required	CLEARANCE: Not required
V F R	NO VFR OPERATIONS ALLOWED		SEPARATION: All aircraft	SEPARATION: VFR from IFR	SEPARATION: Not provided	SEPARATION: Not provided	SEPARATION: Not provided	SEPARATION: Not provided
			SERVICES: Air traffic control service	SERVICES: (1) Air traffic control service for separation from IFR (2) VFR traffic information (and traffic avoidance advice on request)	SERVICES: Traffic information between VFR and IFR flights (and traffic avoidance advice on request)	SERVICES: Traffic information as far as practical	SERVICES: Flght information service	SERVICES: Flght information service
			VMC MINIMA: As published in RSA - Part 91, Subpart 06	VMC MINIMA: As published in RSA - Part 91, Subpart 06	VMC MINIMA: As published in RSA - Part 91, Subpart 06	VMC MINIMA: As published in RSA - Part 91, Subpart 06	VMC MINIMA: As published in RSA - Part 91, Subpart 06	VMC MINIMA: As published in RSA - Part 91, Subpart 06
			SPEED LIMITATION: As published for relevant airspace	SPEED LIMITATION: As published for relevant airspace	SPEED LIMITATION: As published for relevant airspace	SPEED LIMITATION: As published for relevant airspace	SPEED LIMITATION: As published for relevant airspace	SPEED LIMITATION: As published for relevant airspace
			RADIO: 🎧	RADIO: 🎧	RADIO: 🎧	RADIO: Not required 🎧	RADIO: 🎧	RADIO: Not required
			CLEARANCE ATC	CLEARANCE ATC	CLEARANCE: ATC	CLEARANCE: Not required	CLEARANCE: Not required	CLEARANCE: Not required

Now that you have a better idea of the airspace ahead of you, and your chart will indicate, if it is up to date, the class of each airspace you are going to use, you should ask yourself how the weather is going to be en route.

Asking yourself that question will help you determine how the weather minima will impact on your operations. Why? Because controlled and uncontrolled airspace, in Classes C, F, G, CTR (Class C) and ATZ (Classes C, D or G) too, require you to respect minima, of forward visibility, of distance from clouds, of ground visibility and ceiling; and these are weather dependent. So they must be checked.

By the way, what is visibility? It can be two things:

'Visibility' is 'the ability, as determined by atmospheric conditions and expressed in units of distance, to see and identify prominent unlighted objects by day and prominent lighted objects by night'.[19]

'Forward Flight visibility' is 'the visibility forward from the cockpit of an aircraft in flight'.[20]

These questions lead us to the next action.

6.3 ACTION 3: CHECK YOUR WEATHER

So, what is to be done? It is called '**determination**'.

6.3.1 Determination of meteorological minima under VFR

Determination does not mean that you are determined to take off; it means quite the opposite: that whatever you are determined to do, you must check, or determine if you can fly at all, given the weather conditions.

You must determine if the meteorological conditions meet 'minima', that is the least acceptable conditions, below which you cannot fly legally.

What the law says about weather and VFR operating minima

1. 'The owner or operator of an aircraft shall ensure that

    (a) VFR flights are conducted in accordance with VFR prescribed in Subpart 6;

    (b) special VFR flights are not commenced when the visibility is less than the visibility prescribed in regulation 91.06.22 (1).'[21] *The regulation cross reference for aeroplanes is unpacked below. (Helicopters: 91.0622 (2))*

And it adds, just in case you did not get the message loud and clear — 5 out of 5 as pilots say:

---

[19] AIP ENR 1.8–6.
[20] AIP ENR 1.8–3.
[21] CARS 91.07.10 (a) and (b).

> 2. 'The PIC of an aircraft **operating outside a control zone or an aerodrome traffic zone** is responsible to ascertain [plain English: make absolutely sure] whether or not **weather conditions permit flight in accordance with VFR.**'[22]
>
> 3. And it insists: 'The PIC of an aircraft **shall not commence a flight unless** he or she is satisfied that the weather at the **departure** and **arrival** aerodromes and **en route**, including any possible **alternate** aerodromes or routes, will not preclude **safe completion of the flight.**'[23]
>
> *By the way, note again that Part 91 deals with operations for general aviation and flight rules, just in case.*

Simply put, you, the PIC, must check the weather in order to make sure the 'minima' are met, that is the minimal weather conditions under which your VFR flight will be operating are safe and legal.[24]

By the way, do you recall what 'ceiling' means? It refers to half of the sky covered, up to 20 000 ft or, to be precise: 'The height above the ground or water of the base of the lowest layer of cloud situated below 20 000 feet and covering more than half the sky.'[25]

Look at it this way: **minimal conditions are not the best** (optimal) conditions, they are **in fact the least** (minimal) conditions. So, if you think the weather meets the minima, it may still not be that safe to fly, but you would be flying legally. It is your choice and your responsibility. If you believe minimal meteorological conditions will **stress** you, do not fly.

You may hear about 'all weather operations': this refers to 'any take-off, en-route or landing operations in IMC and operated in accordance with IFR'.[26] It does not apply to a flight under VFR.

Determination is done methodically, as follows.

6.3.2 Weather at departure, en route, and at destination

This assumes that you have an idea of your estimated time of arrival (ETA). For the sake of this scenario we assume you did some prep the day before, at least tracing your route on a chart and a rough calculation of estimated elapsed time (EET).

As you must always anticipate a problem with the weather, check the weather at alternate[27] aerodromes, if the weather pattern looks untoward. Apart from the obvious thunderstorms, menacing fronts, high winds or mountain waves, it is

---

[22] CARS 91.06.23 (1).

[23] CARS 91.02.7 (1) (n) (ii).

[24] CARS 91.02.7 (mentioned) and specifically CARS 91.07.9 (2) for VFR, and 91.07.9 (1) (a) and (b) for IFR.

[25] AIP ENR 1.8–3.

[26] AIP ENR 1.8–1.

[27] Note that in aviation the word is 'alternate', never 'alternative'.

common sense to anticipate advection fog along the sea, if you intend to use a coastal airstrip, or upslope fog (when lifting air cools upslope, and then fog builds from higher downwards into a valley), if you are flying into mountainous areas.

In any event, your first port of call is the South African Weather Service's dedicated site for aviation (http://aviation.weathersa.co.za). SAWS is the only designated aeronautical meteorological authority for South Africa[28] *(exam)*. Print out the significant weather chart (SGWX) from SAWS, the local meteorological aerodrome report (METAR) and terminal aerodrome forecast (TAF). You have several other reliable websites to check aviation weather: the most comprehensive, at time of writing, is Windy.

Without going into details on how to check the weather, which does not fall under air law as such (checking does; *how* you check it is another matter), it is worth noting that if you hire and fly from a school or a club, the electronic operator's system will produce a **Flight authorisation** sheet for you to sign (and make you liable): what is useful is that, if you have forgotten to check local weather, the authorisation contains local METAR and TAF details—in small print, but they are there. Pilots who fly an aircraft they bought for hour building, or pilot-owners who do not have to produce an authorisation sheet, miss an opportunity of getting basic weather (see example in annexure 13).

The METAR may provide you with the runway visual range (RVR), that is the range over which the pilot of an aircraft on the centre line of a runway can see 'the runway surface markings or the lights delineating the runway or identifying its centre line'.[29] RVR is reported when required, usually when visibility is below 1 500 m, and if the aerodrome has the automated sensing equipment to determine it. The information is meant for larger aircraft, but to a general aviation pilot a RVR in a METAR will give a good idea whether you will be able to see the runway, or markings, or the lights (if any) on approach. You may then have to select an alternate aerodrome. (RVR is not PPL level).

As an aside (**not PPL level**): do not confuse this RVR with the Required Visual Reference (it is misleading because of the 'RVR' initials). The required visual reference denotes 'the runway environment, ie runway threshold, touch-down area, touch down zone lighting, or approach lighting which must be visible for sufficient time for the pilot to determine that the aircraft is in a position for a normal visual descent to land'.[30] To put it simply, it describes a situation on approach when a pilot transitions from instrument to external visual references.[31]

---

[28] As per CARS Part 174.
[29] AIP ENR 1.8–6. ICAO, Annex 6, *Operation of Aircraft*, Part I.
[30] AIP ENR 1.8–6.
[31] Refer to the excellent briefing on Skybrary (www.skybrary.aero) at Visual Rcfcrences.

You must also check SIGMET and AIRMET on the SAWS website. AIRMET is a forecast of particular relevance to **low level flying (below 10 000 ft)**, 'to cover a layer between the ground and flight level 100 or higher if necessary'; it contains 'information on en-route weather phenomena hazardous' at this level of flight either occurring or expected to occur; and it is issued every 6 hours with a validity of 6 hours at a time. (Observed and recorded AIRMET information is however valid for 4 hours maximum.) SIGMET will alert you to thunderstorms, severe turbulence, cyclone or volcanic ash (the last one goes into a NOTAM).[32]

6.3.3 Check VFR minima[33]

The law demands that you now apply your mind and follow certain rules to make sure the weather does not turn your aircraft into a news story.

In this scenario you fly VFR, not IFR.[34]

VFR absolute rule *(exam!)*:

> 'Every VFR flight shall be so conducted that the aircraft is flown with visual reference to the surface by day and to identifiable objects by night and at no time above more than three eighths of cloud within a radius of five nautical miles of such aircraft.'[35]

1) Next point to consider, under VFR, is if you have to approach, land, or take off in a control zone (CTR) or an aerodrome traffic zone (ATZ).

You are going to operate en route, during a cross country, but you do have to take off and land somewhere, and possibly more than once.

This is where an important set of rules come into play, regarding weather minima, in terms of **forward visibility and distance (horizontal and vertical) from cloud**, and the **airspace in which you are operating**. And what matters here is whether you will be operating in a control zone, CTR or an aerodrome traffic zone, ATZ (which does not comprise a CTR or part of a CTR). Why? Because there is bound to be traffic taking off and landing, and thus many safety issues.

---

[32] CARS 174.04.6 (2) and 174.04.8 AIRMET; CARS 174.04.7 (2) SIGMET.
[33] CARS 91.06.21 with 3 Tables and 22, CARS 91.07.10.
[34] IFR: see CARS 91.07.8 for 'Planning minima for IFR flights' as well as 'Instrument Flight Rules' 91.06.24-25–26-27.
[35] CARS 91.06.21 (1). It applies to night flying as it is under VFR (see chapter 8).

Chapter 6: Before you call 'clear prop' 115

2) Therefore, you have to make sure that your entire VFR flight will be conducted in VMC all the way and you need to know what the minima are outside CTR and ATZ:

- On a flight under VFR, you cannot commence take-off unless current meteorological reports, or a combination of current reports and forecasts, indicate that the meteorological conditions **along the route**, or that part of the route **at the appropriate time**, will comply with the rules, especially the one we mentioned at the beginning of this section, the 'absolute rule'.[36]
- Outside CTR and ATZ, you as PIC are 'responsible to ascertain whether or not weather conditions permit flight in accordance with VFR'.[37]

The VFR minima are not easily memorised. The entire regulation (A and H) is tabled and illustrated at the end of this section.

Students, for PPL or even CPL, please take note! This is core knowledge.[38] You will be tested on the minima. You can also expect your instructor to take a casual glance at the skies, and ask you, as if making conversation, 'So, how does it look to you?'

3) What happens if the weather deteriorates while you are in controlled airspace?

This scenario is different from the one mentioned in (1) (and illustrated in the Tables at the end of this section) because, here, you are not on approach, taking off or landing, but 'passing through', en route. Do not confuse the two. What do you do to remain legal?

Inside controlled airspace or a CTR and if weather deteriorates and therefore does not allow the PIC to maintain minimum distance from cloud and minimum visibility *(translation: both VFR minima are not met)*, the PIC must take the following actions to remain legal:[39]
- **in controlled airspace**, the PIC
    ➤ requests an amended clearance enabling the aircraft to continue in VMC to the nearest suitable aerodrome, or to leave the airspace within which an ATC clearance is required;
- if the PIC cannot 'obtain' a clearance in accordance with the rule above, continue to operate in **VMC and land at the nearest suitable aerodrome**, notifying the appropriate ATC unit of the action taken;

---

[36] CARS 91.07.9 (1).
[37] CARS 91.06.23 (1).
[38] CARS 91.06.2–22–23.
[39] CARS 91.06.23 (2).

116 Air Law

> - **within a CTR**, you either request
>   - ➢ authorisation to operate as a special VFR flight; or
>   - ➢ you request clearance to operate in accordance with **IFR** (if you have an Instrument Rating).

This leads us to another scenario: special VFR flights.

6.3.4 Check special VFR (SVFR) weather minima

> **Special VFR flights (A) (H)**[40]
>
> SVFR flights are permitted for:
>
> Aeroplanes within a CTR / (helicopters within) a CTR or ATZ (under the conditions stated in the tables at the end of this section)[41] only;
>
> - (A) and (H) under the terms of an air traffic control clearance;
> - (A) by day only/(H) by day or by night with a cloud ceiling of at least 300 ft;
> - (A) with a cloud ceiling of at least 600 ft and visibility of at least 1 500 m, measured from the aerodrome reference point (the aerodrome reference point 'means the designated geographical location of an aerodrome')[42]/ (H) clear of clouds and forward visibility of at least 800 m;
> - (H) if the helicopter will be operated at such a speed that the pilot has adequate opportunity to observe any obstructions or other traffic in sufficient time to avoid collisions;
> - (A) if your aeroplane is equipped with two-way radio equipment capable of communicating with an ATSU on the appropriate frequency;
> - (H) in accordance with minimum heights regulations;[43]
> - (A) (H) when your Special VFR flight will not unduly delay an IFR flight;
> - (A) if you are leaving the control zone, in accordance with instructions issued by an ATSU before departure.

---

[40] CARS 91.06.22 (1) applies to A. For H see CARS 91.06.22 (2).
[41] CARS 91.06.21: VFR tables.
[42] CATS 139, Definitions.
[43] CARS 91.06.32, especially (2).

Chapter 6: Before you call 'clear prop' 117

However, weather happens, by definition, in airspace, and aeronautical airspace is not simply 'the heavens' but a series of legally defined flying areas. You have to take this into account.

Combining what we have seen regarding the meteorological minima of the airspace in which you are flying with the definitions of classes, we can now bring everything together.

6.3.5 VFR weather and airspace operations[44]

Memorise this fundamental rule: In VFR, aircraft is to be flown—
- with visual reference to the surface by day
- with visual reference to identifiable objects by night,
- never above more than three eighths of cloud within a radius of five nautical miles of the aircraft, and
- with the forward visibility and the distance (vertical and horizontal) from cloud being equal to, or more than, the conditions set out in Tables 1 and 2 (A) and Tables 3 and 4 (H) below.

No transonic or supersonic or Class A airspace VFR flying is allowed (just in case you may wish to try), as mentioned earlier in this book.

The conditions set are minima, and as the word implies: below them you cannot fly VFR.

Remember also that in South Africa a CTR is Class C and that a Class C ATZ can also be established, so do read the categories below carefully.

Aeroplane (or aircraft excluding helicopters) VFR minima

Table 1

Airspace	Forward Flight visibility	Distance from clouds	Ground visibility and ceiling
Control zones	Five km	Horizontally: 600 metres Vertically: 500 ft	No aircraft shall take-off from, land at, or approach to land at an aerodrome or fly within the control zone when the ground visibility at the aerodrome concerned is less than 5 km and the ceiling is less than 1 500 ft.
Within an aerodrome traffic zone (which does not also comprise a control zone or part of a control zone)	Five km	Horizontally: 600 metres Vertically: 500 ft	No aircraft shall take-off from, land at, or approach to land at an aerodrome or fly within the aerodrome traffic zone when the ground visibility within such aerodrome traffic zone is less than 5 km and the ceiling is less than 1 500 ft.

---

[44] CARS 91.06.21.

Air Law

Table 2
In Airspace other than those specified in Table 1

Airspace class	Altitude band	Forward Flight visibility	Distance from cloud
C F G	At and above 10 000 ft above MSL	8 km	1 500 m horizontally 1 000 ft vertically
C F G	Below 10 000 ft AMSL and above 3 000 ft above MSL, or above 1 000 ft above terrain, whichever is the higher	5 km	1 500 m horizontally 1 000 ft vertically
C	At and below 3 000 ft above MSL, or 1 000 ft above terrain, whichever is the higher	5 km	1 500 m horizontally 1 000 ft vertically
F G		5 km	Clear of cloud and with the surface in sight

Pictorial of VFR Minima as per Tables 1 and 2 (A)

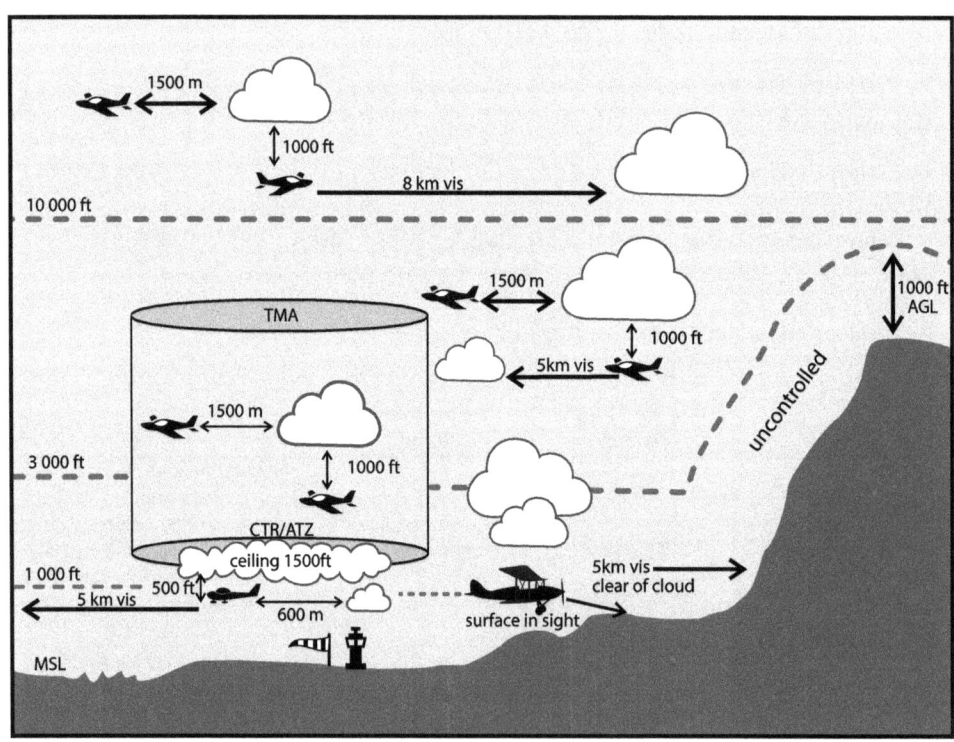

Chapter 6: Before you call 'clear prop' 119

A **quick recap:**
- ➤ visibility refers to forward visibility of the pilot (abbreviation VIS) (ICAO Annex 3 defines aeronautical visibility as 'as the greater of the greatest distance at which :a) a black object of suitable dimensions, situated near the ground, can be seen and recognized when observed against a bright background; and b) lights in the vicinity of 1 000 candelas can be seen and identified against an unlit background);
- ➤ vertical separation is both upward and downward;
- ➤ horizontal separation is both in a forward and a backward direction;
- ➤ clear of cloud means 'do not enter a cloud', 'stay clear of clouds';
- ➤ surface in sight means no cloud in between you and the ground: remember that legally you cannot fly VFR above more than 3/8 of cloud (within 5 NM radius of your aircraft).

The minima set in **Table 1 do not apply if** you—
- ➤ enter or leave a CTR and your flight has received clearance from an ATSU to operate under Special VFR minima (see 6.3.4); or
- ➤ enter or leave an ATZ on a cross-country flight; and
- ➤ maintain two-way radio communication with the aerodrome control tower or aerodrome flight information service unit, in which case you can leave or enter the aerodrome traffic zone when the ground visibility is equal to or greater than 5 km and the ceiling is equal to or higher than 500 ft.

Helicopter VFR minima

Table 3

Airspace	Flight visibility	Distance from clouds	Ground visibility and ceiling
Control zones	2 500 m	Horizontally: 300 metres Vertically: Clear of cloud	Except when operating under a SVFR clearance no helicopter shall take-off from, land at, or approach to land at an aerodrome or fly within the control zone when the ground visibility at the aerodrome concerned is less than 2 500 metres and the ceiling is less than 600 ft.
Within an aerodrome traffic zone (which does not also comprise a control zone or part of a control zone)	2 500 m	Horizontally: 300 metres Vertically: Clear of cloud	No helicopter shall take-off from, land at, or approach to land at an aerodrome or fly within the aerodrome traffic zone when the ground visibility at the aerodrome concerned is less than 2 500 m and the ceiling is less than 600 ft.

Table 4
In Airspace other than those specified in Table 3

Airspace class	Altitude band	Forward Flight visibility	Distance from cloud
C F G	At and above 10 000 ft above MSL	8 km	1 500 m horizontally 1 000 ft vertically
C F G	Below 10 000 ft AMSL and above 3 000 ft above MSL, or above 1 000 ft above terrain, whichever is the higher	5 km	1 500 m horizontally 1 000 ft vertically
C	At and below 3 000 ft above MSL, or 1 000 ft above terrain, whichever is the higher	2 500 m	1 500 m horizontally 1 000 ft vertically
F G		1 500 m unless in accordance with exception below	Clear of cloud and with the surface in sight

The minima set in **Table 3 do not apply if—**

➤ you want to conduct hover-in-ground-effect or hover-taxi operations within the confines of a controlled aerodrome or heliport, if the visibility is not less than 100 m;

➤ you are entering or leaving a CTR or ATZ and your flight has received clearance from an ATSU to operate under Special VFR minima as prescribed in regulation 91.06.22 *(refers to SFVR rules).*

And note the exception mentioned in row FG in Table 4: you are allowed to operate in less than 1 500 m flight visibility outside of controlled airspace, if you manoeuvre at a speed that will give adequate opportunity to observe other traffic or any obstacles in time to avoid collision.

6.3.6 Weather and aerodrome operating minima IFR

Not PPL level, only for information.

This section is of less concern to private pilots who are not instrument rated or, being so, are not flying IFR on a given flight. It deals with the minimal conditions under which an aircraft can operate in IMC. By minimal conditions the regulator means the minimal cloud base and minimal runway visibility conditions under which an approach and departure can be performed at a given aerodrome (as detailed in AIP ENR). For that reason they are called Aerodrome Operating Minima (AOM).

Aerodrome Operating Minima (AOM)

The following sub-regulations are worth pondering as they concern common sense and safety:

> In terms of a PIC's duties:
>
> 'The PIC of an aircraft shall not commence a flight unless he or she is satisfied that the **aerodrome operating minima** are not less than the operating minima of the aerodrome being operated to or from, established by the appropriate authority of the State in which the aerodrome is located, unless such appropriate authority approves lower aerodrome operating minima.'[45]
>
> In terms of an aerodrome operating minima:[46]
>
> 'No pilot of an aircraft shall use an aerodrome as a destination or alternate aerodrome, unless the operating *minima* for such aerodrome, established by the appropriate authority of the State in which the aerodrome is situated, can be complied with.'

The first regulation has a general purpose: it concerns all flights. The second one is more specialised: it concerns mainly the operations of air transport aircraft as AOM are related to instrument non-precision and precision approach procedures, in keeping with aircraft performance and specifications, and aerodrome equipment.[47] It does not concern you as a private pilot flying a light aircraft and not engaged (yet) in instrument approach.

However, the regulations are not without interest to a VFR pilot. The cloud base minimum is easy enough to understand, but what about the other minimum, the RVR, and why should you, as a VFR pilot, bother about it? If, as already noted, under VFR, you intend to take off or land at a major airport, you must check the METAR to see if there is a report on RVR, which is intended for instrument pilots, but will tell you about what you can expect if you are in any doubt about meeting the VFR minima explained earlier on.

How is a RVR, or runway visual range, determined? Special sensors determine 'the RVR or visibility in the take-off direction of the aircraft'. And the pilot has to determine if this RVR 'is equal to, or better than, the applicable minimum'.[48]

In short, not only pilots engaged in Air Transport Operations but also private ones under IFR have to comply with what is called 'preflight selection of aerodromes', both at destination and at alternate. It has to do mainly with weather deterioration or 'other reasons'. The rules are complex and are relevant to CPL air law.

This leads us now to the next action: checking the aerodromes you may have to use while en route.

---

[45] CARS 91.02.7 (1) (k).
[46] CARS 91.07.5 (1).
[47] Standards are in ICAO, Annex 6 and ICAO Doc 8168—*Procedures for Air Navigation Services (PANS-OPS)*. Also, AIP ENR 1.8–1 to 20.
[48] CARS 91.02.7 (1) (o).

6.4 ACTION 4: CHECK YOUR AERODROMES

Two aspects come into play: checking aerodromes against weather, particularly to determine their suitability, and then more general regulations.

6.4.1 Alternate, adequate and suitable aerodromes

As a pilot flying VFR, if you file a flight plan you will be asked for two alternates (at item 16 on your Flight Plan, 'Altn. Aerodrome and 2nd altn. aeodrome').[49]

The following list of regulations is an excellent example of how regulations form a chain of tight links, and why selection of aerodromes concerns you.

- Sub-regulation 91.02.7 (1) (q) states: 'The PIC of an aircraft shall not commence a flight unless he or she is satisfied that an adequate and suitable aerodrome is available for take-off, *en-route* and destination, should it become inadvisable to continue to or land at the destination aerodrome.' VFR applies.
- Sub-regulation 91.07.3 (1) enjoins: 'No pilot shall use, and no owner or operator shall authorise the use of, an aerodrome as a destination or alternate destination aerodrome, unless such aerodrome is adequate for the type of aircraft and operation concerned.' Now we learn that the chosen aerodrome(s) must be adequate for the aircraft you are flying, for landing and taking off in VFR. Will that grass airstrip be suitable?
- Sub-regulation 91.07.7 (3) adds: 'A take-off alternate aerodrome shall be selected and specified in the operational and ATS flight plan, as prescribed by regulation 91.03.4, if the meteorological conditions at the aerodrome of departure are at or below the applicable aerodrome operating minima, or it would not be possible to return to the aerodrome of departure for other reasons.' It becomes more complex and it does apply to you, on a VFR flight, because of the minima tabled earlier, whether in a CTR or ATZ, or not.
- Sub-regulation 91.03.4 cited above states: 'The ATS flight plan shall be filed in respect of

    (a) all flights to be conducted in **controlled or advisory** airspace: Provided that [ie except that] this requirement shall not apply in respect of

    (i) a local flight;
    (ii) a flight crossing an airway or advisory routes at right angles; or
    (iii) a VFR flight entering or departing from an aerodrome traffic zone or control zone, from or to an unmanned aerodrome and where no other controlled or advisory airspace will be entered during the flight.'

(Sections (b), (c), (d), and (e) of the regulation are not quoted as they should not concern you as a private pilot, apart from (b) if you pilot an international flight, which may well happen in VFR). Filing a plan is dealt with in the next section.

---

[49] Form CA 172–04 of 22 July 2015.

So, reading backwards through this sequence of regulations: if you must file a flight plan or if you want to (for Search and Rescue), you select alternates bearing in mind the weather minima and the suitability of the airfield. If you do all that you will satisfy the first requirement, and you will be able to take off with the law on your side, under VFR.

But, how do you evaluate whether an alternate is suitable, or adequate? This question is crucial for air transport and flights under IFR, but not without importance for you, under VFR.

The law wants to ensure that, apart from your departure aerodrome, the aerodrome you will have to land at, by choice (as planned) or by necessity (diversion to alternate), and presumably to take off from afterwards, is safe.

'Suitable aerodrome' means

an adequate aerodrome:

(a) with **weather reports or forecasts** or any combination thereof, indicating that the weather conditions are at or above operating minima, as specified in the operation specifications;

(b) the field condition reports indicate that **a safe landing** can be accomplished at the time of the intended operation; and

(c) the facilities necessary to complete an approach at such aerodrome are **operational**.

But then what does '**adequate aerodrome**' mean?

An aerodrome licensed in terms of **Part 139 or that is found to be equivalent** to the safety requirements prescribed in Part 139 and that meets the requirements of regulation **91.07.5** for the type of aircraft operating into it.

In that case **what is Part 139** of CARS and CATS? It is about the physical, technical, material fittings of an aerodrome or heliport, its construction if you wish, and therefore appears under the licensing and operations of **Aerodromes and Heliports.**

In short, although this applies in relation to operating minima for such aerodromes (CARS 91.07.5 as cited), it teaches the VFR private pilot, or even VFR commercial pilot, to better understand the sort of care that should go into selecting an aerodrome.

124 Air Law

Finally, as an illustration, this is **how to decode information given about an aerodrome on an aeronautical chart**—the example is Pietermaritzburg airport:[50]

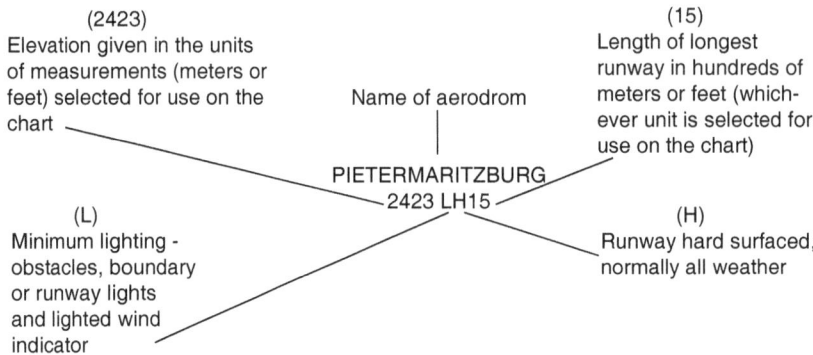

6.4.2 Where can you take off or land?

Where do you land? On airfields, preferably, but it is not that simple. In addition to checking alternate aerodromes, which is mainly weather dependent, you have to check the physical suitability of airfields while on a cross-country flight in particular.

Be 'satisfied' with conditions at airfields

The law is clear:

As PIC you must be 'satisfied' that 'the requirements in respect of ... weather, minimum safe altitudes, aerodrome operating minima and availability of alternate aerodromes for the route being flown and any likely alternates, whether flown under instrument or VFR, are complied with'[51]—meaning: *you* comply *(exam!)*.

Let us unpack this command.

In general terms 'to be satisfied' entails that you must check what the operational conditions are (runway orientation and surface, slope, obstacles, etc),[52] as well as refuelling, telephone, office hours, etc at your departure and destination aerodromes.

You will **look up the relevant AIP AD, NOTAMs, AICs** to find out. If in doubt about the serviceability of an aerodrome, of its navigational aids or communication facilities, you must call an ATSU or another reliable source (such as the owner or operator of an unlicensed airfield). If you notice en route that something is

---

[50] Aeronautical Chart 2928 Durban.
[51] CARS 91.02.7 (1) (j) (excerpted).
[52] CARS 91.02.7 (1) (n) (i).

inadequate at an aerodrome (refuelling facility closing earlier than noted in AIP), advise an ATSU in order to help others.[53]

Taking-off or landing on a road

Unless it is an emergency you cannot take off or land legally on a road: [54] this emergency must involve the safety of the aircraft or its occupants (you and your pax); or must be for the purpose of saving human lives (engine failure over a crowd, so you pick a road); or in civil defence or law-enforcement ops, must be provided that you take reasonable care for the safety of others under the prevailing circumstances (do not play cowboy).

Taking-off or landing at night

'Except in an emergency' you cannot legally 'take-off or land by night, unless the place of take-off or landing is equipped with night flying facilities.[55] That means: unless the aerodrome is night equipped, you cannot use it. But if it is not night equipped and it is an emergency, then you can. What are those night facilities? 'At least runway edge, threshold and runway end lights must be on.'[56]

And remember that if it is an emergency, then you have to declare an emergency (see chapter 9).

Operating at private-use airports

A 'private-use airport' is any aerodrome or airfield 'used exclusively by private persons for their own private aviation needs, or which can only be used by prior permission of the owner or licensee.'[57]

AIC 002/2019 re-states formally: 'Pilots must ensure that prior permission is obtained from the licensee for the operation of all aircraft to and from aerodromes published as PRIVATE.' Note that this AIC mentions 'licensee', not owner.[58]

Under normal circumstances (planning a flight) you need permission from the owner, otherwise you are trespassing. In the case of an accident, insurers will also want to know if you called the owner, got permission, enquired about the state of the strip and obstacles (hill, mast, windmill), and if you flew over first to check the actual conditions. Airport Regulations of 1982 noted that private aerodromes display a letter ℙ to indicate a private airfield but this sign is no longer part of the regulations *(although a question might crop up at the exam)*.[59]

---

[53] CARS 91.02.7 (2) (a) (b) (c).
[54] CARS 91.06.1.
[55] CARS 91.07.3 (2).
[56] AIP ENR 1.8–12 at 3.2.5.
[57] White Paper on National Civil Aviation Policy, *Government Gazette* 40847 of 19 May 2017, 503.
[58] AIC Series E 002/2019, 31 JAN 2019.
[59] Airport Regulations, 1982, Appendix A2.

Generally speaking, as a VFR pilot who is likely to land on unlicensed airfields, if not basic airstrips, you should make up, so to speak, operating minima by paying attention to a number of factors:

> the length and surface of the airstrip, possible slope, in relation to the performance of your aeroplane: a grass runway requires different performances at landing and (presumably thereafter) at take-off, with a different technique as well.

> the elevation of the airfield and the air temperature depending upon the season will result in a density altitude you may not expect, and quite a different performance from your aircraft, as the landing and the take-off run will be longer for instance: the higher the density altitude,[60] the lower the aircraft performance, and the vice versa.

> whether rain is expected at your destination airfield, before or at landing, that will affect your landing in particular: will the runway be wet (no significant area of standing water) or contaminated (more than 25% with more than 3.0 mm deep)? Is there a risk of aqua/hydroplaning?

Performance graph charts of your AFM should be looked at, if you are unsure.

At this stage you should be able to ask yourself the question: GO, or NO GO? And answer it unequivocally. Any serious doubt? Do not fly.

Now, how do you get from aerodrome A to aerodrome B? You fly along a track you have drawn on your chart. In any event the law requires you to carry on board charts and publications (typically copies of aerodrome details, or relevant en route information taken from AIP) related to your trip.[61]

It is now 0800B. Time to file a flight plan.

6.5 ACTION 5: FLIGHT PLAN—TO FILE OR NOT TO FILE?

A flight plan is tersely defined in CARS:[62]

> 'specified information provided to air traffic services units, relative to an intended flight or portion of a flight of an aircraft'.

Very helpful, isn't it?

You can find the Flight Plan form on the SACAA website[63] and the 'Air traffic service flight plan and associated procedures' in annexure 11.[64]

Or read what follows.

---

[60] Remember that 'high' density altitude means a **reduced** air density, which depends on altitude, temperature and marginally on humidity.

[61] CARS 91.2.07 (1) (l).

[62] CARS 01.1.1 and restated in great details by AIC 005/2019 of 25 April 2019.

[63] SACAA Form Number: CA 172–04 AFTN Flight Plan.

[64] CARS 91.03.4.

What is the point of a flight plan for a VFR flight?

A flight plan will ensure that air traffic services that are able to separate traffic, to control, to advise, to inform you, will possibly come to your rescue.

If you file an IFR flight plan the legal implications are that your aircraft is equipped for IFR, that you are qualified, and that as PIC you will conform to all IFR provisions.

6.5.1 To file or not to file for a VFR flight?

To file or not to file, that is (not) the question

- You **do not need to file** if your flight is
  - local;
  - crossing an airway or advisory routes at right angles; or
  - VFR entering or departing from an ATZ (aerodrome traffic zone) or CTR (control zone), from or to an unmanned aerodrome and where no other controlled or advisory airspace will be entered during the flight.[65]
- But **you must file** a flight plan in specific cases, which are:
  - all flights to be conducted in controlled or advisory airspace (**except cases above**);
  - all international flights (including flying across a neighbouring border);
  - all flights undertaken in terms of a Class I or Class II licence issued in terms of the Air Services Licensing Act 115 of 1990 or the International Air Services Act 60 of 1993[66] [in plain English: public air transport flights, scheduled or not];
  - all flights for which alerting and Search and Rescue, or to avoid military interception, is required by the appropriate ATS.[67]
  - all flights operating between aerodromes where an ATSU is operating.[68]
- And 'flight plans may be filed for any flight'.[69]

Students! Please take note of these updated rules!

---

[65] CARS 91.03.4 (4) (a) (iii).
[66] International Air Services Regulations, 1994 section 2.
[67] CARS 91.03.4 (d) and (e).
[68] AIC 005/2019, 2.2 (e).
[69] AIC 005/2019. Note.

6.5.2 How do I file?

Whatever the case may be (if you decide to file or are obliged to file), you have to abide by rules to fill in accurately all sections of the required document,[70] then to file with the Aeronautical Information Management Service Centre (AIM) by calling (SA share call) 0860 359 669 (0860 FLY NOW), (international only) +27 (0)11 928 6517/8,[71] or filing electronically (self briefing service) on ATNS File2Fly https://file2fly.atns.co.za (in this case the draft form will help you do the online self-briefing more easily). Or hand it in in person at your nearest ATSU, or even, in 'exceptional circumstances', over the radio channels. You can also fax it to +27 11 928 6514.

The advanced method of filing (professional) is to use the Aeronautical Fixed Telecommunication Network with the address FAORZPZX;[72] or SITA, code JNBXTYF.[73]

If, as a private pilot, you file by telephone or over the radio, prepare the flight plan in advance, and read it off in sequence, item by item. If you fax it, fill in the form in black ink, in legible upper case.

The good thing about having a live officer at the end of a telephone line is that, should you forget about semi-circular rules (see page 170), you will be put back on track. Officers are attentive to errors and helpful. And, in turn, you are helping to train aspirant ATCs by calling in.

6.5.3 When do I file?

120 hours before estimated time of departure (ETD): 'It is, however, encouraged that flight plans are filed as far in advance as possible, up to 120 hours'.[74] This is often shortened to '5 days', which is not actually accurate.

You file **at least 30 minutes** before departure if the flight[75] is to be conducted in controlled or advisory airspace (unless authorised otherwise). Updated regulation no longer distinguishes between a domestic and an international flight.[76]

In flight and while flying outside controlled or advisory airspace, you file **at least 10 minutes before** you estimate your point of entry into that airspace or of crossing an airway or advisory route.

---

[70] Dietlind Lempp, in her classic *The Pilot's Radio Handbook*, provides clear instructions on how to fill in a flight plan, item by item.

[71] AIP ENR 1.10–1 15 JAN 19 mentions only extension 6518.

[72] As per ICAO Annex 10, *Aeronautical Telecommunications*, II.

[73] SITA stands originally for Société Internationale de Télécommunications Aéronautiques.

[74] AIC 005/2019.

[75] See note 73 above.

[76] As was the case in CARS 91.03.4 (6). Current version: AIP ENR 1.01.1 paragraph 1.1.

Flight plans **filed more than 24 hours in advance** of estimated off-block time (EOBT) should preferably be amended within 24 hours of ETD.[77]

Flight plans **filed by fax** 'are to reach the AIM Service Centre **at least 60 minutes prior** to planned departure time'.[78] And you must confirm its successful receipt, and its acceptance, telephonically—failing which the flight plan will not be processed.[79]

If a flight is **delayed over the midnight period**, therefore with a change of DOF (date of flight), it is recommended that you cancel the original flight plan and re-file a new one.

A flight plan has to be 'accepted', that is, you must be told so by the officer in charge, or you must check that it is earmarked 'processed' in File2fly.

You will be issued with a **flight plan reference number**, which you should write down immediately on your flight log:[80] when you contact your ATSU to activate the plan you may be asked for it—normally the call sign is what they require.

6.5.4 When do I activate my flight plan?

You must activate the flight plan **within one hour of the departure time that you indicated** on the flight plan. Your first call to the relevant ATSU will activate it.

It is best to activate it as soon as you are leaving the circuit and heading for that long-awaited cross-country.

You can activate it on the ground by calling the relevant FIS. This is helpful if you are stuck out somewhere in a remote area without good radio contact. Enter the code but you will only switch your transponder to ALT before take-off.

In both cases you will be given what matters most: your squawk code.

A flight plan that has been filed with an ATSU and is not activated within one hour of ETD or amended ETD is actually cancelled.

If you are delayed, you can amend the plan before the one-hour slot lapses. Or you can file a new plan altogether.

6.5.5 What is a flight plan valid for?

A flight plan is valid for only one flight. If you stop at your destination, the flight back to base or the next leg needs another flight plan (if you wish to file or if it is mandatory).

---

[77] AIC 005/2019, 3.4.
[78] AIC 005/2019, 13 (c). Although not explicitly linked to a faxed filing, the context of the paragraph indicates that it does refer to that method.
[79] AIC 005/2019, 13 (d) and (e).
[80] CARS 91.02.7 (1) (f) if required as per CARS 91.03.4.

Rules are in place if you deviate from a filed flight plan and a plan can also be changed while in controlled airspace, but these are en route issues, so refer to section 9.2 later in this book.

6.5.6 What right does the flight plan give me?

The flight plan gives you the **right to be rescued** if you request it, or if you are overdue between two controlled aerodromes.

But it does **not give you the right to enter a controlled airspace,** even though this is implied by your routing on the flight plan: you have to 'request entry', and get clearance.

6.5.7 When do I close my flight plan?

A plan closes automatically when your wheels touch the ground at a controlled aerodrome.

If you filed to be able to have Search and Rescue and are landing at an uncontrolled airfield, once you have it in sight, close the plan and the SAR. Or wait until you land, and then cancel it by calling, but do not exceed the time given to trigger SAR (for instance ETA+1HR: 1 hour after ETA, SAR will trigger although you or your operator may get a call first).

You may also have to file an arrival report: see page 224.

When you cancel you will be given the time by ATSU; make a note of it.

Time is 0815B. You step out of the clubhouse or the operator's office. Your aircraft is waiting on the apron. Ready to fly? Not quite, as you know.

The law requires that you 'ensure' your flying machine is legal.

6.6 ACTION 6: AIRCRAFT INSPECTION: NINE CHECKS

Time now to attend to your aircraft.

But is it *your* aircraft? Are you the owner or are you renting it from an operator, or an owner? The answer is not straightforward.

Before we go any further, here is a reminder of the legal definitions of 'owner' and 'operator', since they will play a role later on.

Operator, owner[81]

'operator' means a natural or artificial entity, holding a valid licence and operating certificate or equivalent thereof, authorising such person to conduct scheduled or non-scheduled or general air services, and may be referred to as 'airline', 'air carrier', 'air service operator', or 'commercial air transport operator'.

---

[81] CARS 1.01.1.

> **'owner' in relation to an aircraft, means** the person in whose name the aircraft is registered, and includes—
>
> *(a)* any person who is or has been acting as agent in the Republic for a foreign owner, or any person by whom the aircraft is hired at the time;
>
> *(b)* a person who has the right of possession of an aircraft for 14 days or longer;
>
> *(c)* **for the purpose of Part 91 and Part 93, an operator of an aircraft engaged in non-commercial operations** (remember: 91: general aviation, 93: corporate and high performance).

These definitions may cause confusion when it comes to hiring an aircraft for a private flight. If you hire, the owner is actually responsible for a number of duties, and so are you as PIC (in case of an accident lawyers may argue differently). By contrast the FAA states that 'to operate an aircraft' includes 'the piloting of aircraft, with or without the right of legal control (as owner, lessee, or otherwise)'.[82]

This is why it is more sensible, when you fill in a flight plan, at item 18 you will enter: OPR/ name of operator—and not your name.

Regardless, your duty as PIC is to verify the aircraft's airworthiness.

The law says that the PIC 'shall not commence a flight' unless you are 'satisfied that the **aircraft is airworthy**'.[83] You must be personally satisfied with it: no one else can do it for you. It is your duty as PIC to ensure the aircraft is airworthy.

Just in case you are wondering, here is the legal definition of 'airworthy':[84]

> **'airworthy' means**
>
> *(a)* *when used in relation to an aircraft, that the* **aircraft is serviceable** and meets all the **requirements prescribed** for the issuing of a certificate of airworthiness and such other requirements as have been prescribed for the continuing validity of such a certificate;
>
> *(b)* when used in relation to the status of an engine, propeller or rotor, or part of an aircraft, it conforms to its approved design and is in a condition for safe operation.

In short, the aircraft must be as she was when the certificate of airworthiness was issued or revalidated. More specifically, in plain English: check that the engine, the propeller and all other parts are what they are supposed to be for serviceability.

Do not confuse this with the type certificate without which no aircraft is allowed to fly, and that is valid for five years (aeroplane type with a MCM exceeding

---

[82] *Code of Federal Regulations Title 14.*
[83] CARS 91.02.7 (1) (a).
[84] CARS 01.1.1.

5 700 kg) or three years (5 700 kg and less) (rotorcraft: 2 730 kg and more, and 2 730 kg and less respectively), which is obtained by the owner.[85]

What is meant here is that, regardless of that certificate, you must ensure your aircraft is safe to fly—worthy to take to the air. As PIC you must be personally 'satisfied' that the aircraft is. Records in a Flight Folio will help.

Pre-flight checks consist of a detailed inspection of your aircraft. They are mostly found in CARS Part 91. They are called **Duties of PIC regarding flight preparation**.[86]

So, imagine that you are now walking around your aircraft, bearing in mind the following two basics:

- 'The **external surfaces** are checked prior to take-off for any **deposit** which might adversely affect the **performance** or **controllability** of the aircraft, unless otherwise permitted in the AFM referred to in regulation 91.03.2, and if such deposit is found, to have it removed'.

  Think about it: smudged insects on a leading edge will affect the airflow and increase drag; ice changes the shape of a wing, and may reduce lift; a dirty windshield can indirectly affect how you control the aircraft by limiting your situational awareness; a static port may be covered by muck; the nose wheel may show an oleo problem; both sides of the elevator must work concurrently (connecting pin is in place); etc. These are the fundamental checks you have been trained to observe in order to decide whether you can fly with a plane whose mechanical and material components are serviceable.

- 'The requirements in respect of **fuel, oil, oxygen** are complied with.'[87]

That second basic rule sounds simple enough? It is not.

Surely you can check the oil of your Lycoming, as you know how many quarts that engine needs to run safely, and you can take along an extra can just in case. Oxygen? Not that straightforward. But what about fuel? It is getting slightly more complicated.

Let us now detail what the regulation cites (Duties of PIC regarding flight preparation), says or implies—beyond the routine sequence of pre-flight in your Standard Operating Procedures (SOP).

6.6.1 Fuel supply

The law has a lot to say and to prescribe about fuel quantities—this is not about fuel types or grades but about supply.

---

[85] CARS 21.02.2 (2).
[86] CARS 91.02.7.
[87] CARS 91.02.7 (1) (j) (excerpted).

So, you are perched on a ladder, or bent over a low wing, checking the tanks with a dipstick. What are you actually checking?

> **So many fuels, so little time!** *(and as many exam questions)*
>
> **#1, aeroplanes: 'an owner or operator must base the fuel policy including calculation of fuel ... on the following planning criteria':**[88]
>
> '(1) When the flight is conducted in accordance with the **instrument flight rules** and a **destination alternate aerodrome is not required** in accordance with regulation 91.07.7(6), flight to the aerodrome of intended landing and thereafter for **at least 45 minutes** at the normal cruising altitude consumption rate;
>
> (2) when the flight is conducted in accordance with **the instrument flight rules** and a **destination alternate aerodrome is required**, flight to the aerodrome of intended landing, thence from the aerodrome of intended landing to an alternate aerodrome and thereafter for **at least 45 minutes** at the normal cruising altitude consumption rate;
>
> (3) when the flight is conducted in accordance with the **visual flight rules by day**, **flight to the aerodrome of intended landing and thereafter** for **at least 30 minutes** at the normal cruising altitude consumption rate; or
>
> (4) When the flight is conducted in accordance with the **visual flight rules by night**, flight to the aerodrome of intended landing and thereafter for **at least 45 minutes** at the normal cruising altitude consumption rate'.
>
> Note : CARS 91.07.12–1 (e) states that 'when **no destination alternate aerodrome is required**' the **final reserve fuel** is 'for a reciprocating engine aeroplane, the amount of fuel required to fly for 45 minutes, under speed and altitude conditions specified by the Director; for a turbine engine aeroplane, the amount of fuel required to fly for 30 minutes at holding speed at 1 500 ft above aerodrome elevation in standard conditions'.
>
> **#2, helicopters:** there are specific rules regarding fuel and oil supply, depending upon meteorological forecast, expected traffic, IFR, loss of pressurization or engine failure, consideration of alternates in IFR flight or by night, over water destination and safe carriage of additional fuel.[89]
>
> **#3, 'usable fuel' is calculated by taking into account seven categories of fuel quantity**.
>
> The law now breaks down fuel into finer categories in order to **help you calculate how much usable fuel** you have in your tanks. And here they are:

---

[88] CATS 91.07.12–1 (1) to (4).
[89] CATS 91.07.12–2 (1) to (4).

> 'taxi fuel'
> 'trip fuel'
> 'contingency fuel'
> 'destination alternate fuel'
> 'final reserve fuel'
> 'additional fuel'
> and (as if that was not enough) 'discretionary fuel'.
>
> Taken together (whether you have calculated all of these or not, since the last one is at the pilot's discretion) they form the **'usable fuel'**.
>
> **Turn to annexure 12** for definitions of 'fuel' in the categories listed above and fuel policy.[90]
>
> *Students, note: Exam questions about fuel occur regularly from PPL onward. It is core knowledge.*

Do not forget to drain the tanks to check for water or solid contamination. And check that the tank caps are firmly closed. Always refuel on level ground.

Refuelling, and flammable gas and liquids

If you have refuelled and are on level ground, you must check the tank levels and test the fuel for impurities or water again.

By the way, if you refuel, bear in mind the regulation which states that an aircraft cannot be refuelled (or defuelled) with aviation gasoline (or highly flammable 'wide-cut' type fuel) while a passenger is on board,[91] and that, as PIC, you must take necessary precautions. (Corporate, air transport and commercial helicopter ops have their own rules.)

One such precaution would be to remind your friend who wants a quick, last fag, please, before climbing into the right-hand seat that:

'No person on a licensed aerodrome or heliport is allowed to smoke in, or bring an open flame into any place where such an act is prohibited by a notice displayed; or any place **within 15 metres of an aircraft** or of any vehicle used for the supply of fuel to an aircraft or a store or dump or liquid fuel or explosives.' For the same reason your friend, who is not too happy about it already, will not be allowed to take on board a cigarette lighter that stores a 'flammable liquid' or 'gas'. That is the law.[92]

Vaping: a vaporiser often contains propylene glycol, which is a liquid and is flammable. Not on board. Think liability.

---

[90] CARS 91.07.12 (3).
[91] CARS 91.07.13 (1).
[92] CARS 139.01.9.

Time to reach into the aircraft to switch on the master, and check the lights. But what lights?

6.6.2 Operating lights

Here is a reminder of what the regulations are in terms of compulsory aircraft operating lights *(exam!)*:

Lights to be displayed by your aircraft[93]

Unless your aircraft is initially type-certificated without these lights or a non-type certified approved without them,

- while operating **in flight** during **the day and at all times at night**, **anti-collision lights** intended to **attract attention** to the aircraft [these are 'non-steady' lights, beacon and strobes];
- while operating during **night, navigation lights** intended to indicate the **relative path** of the aircraft to an observer [these are steady lights, and sometimes called **position lights**]: **See picture on page 246D.**
- while operating **on the movement area** of an aerodrome, **lights intended to attract attention** to the aircraft;
- while operating with **engines running on the movement area** of an aerodrome, the **rotating beacon** is on;
- while moving on the **movement area** of an aerodrome during **night** you switch on your **navigation lights** to indicate the relative path of the aircraft [position] to an observer;
- unless stationary and otherwise adequately illuminated, **on the movement area** of an aerodrome during **night** you display lights intended to indicate the **extremities** of the plane.

Unsure of what 'movement area' means? See page 149 below. In the situations above it means that on the apron lights as applicable are switched on already.

Note: you are allowed to switch off or reduce the intensity of any flashing light (strobe) if it affects your performance or 'dazzles' an outside observer.

6.6.3 Oxygen

You now climb into the aircraft, and you check oxygen supply.

Oxygen is the second crucial check. It is actually called '**supplemental oxygen**' as we are not dealing here with the ambient air you are supposed to breathe, but the artificially added oxygen you and your passengers must breathe if ambient, breathable air just vanishes into . . . thin air.

Of course legal requirements vary, depending on whether your aircraft is pressurised or non-pressurised. For most PPL or even CPL pilots, before they

---

[93] CARS 91.06.10.

136   Air Law

move to higher planes, it will be the latter. If you fly a six-seater 'Boere Boeing' you had better read what follows carefully.

Remember this rule:

> An owner or operator **may not operate a non-pressurised aircraft**
> - at altitudes **between 10 000 feet and 12 000 feet for longer than 120 minutes** intended flight time,
>
>   or
> - above 12 000 feet
>
> **unless supplemental oxygen equipment,** capable of storing and dispensing the oxygen supplies required, **is provided.**[94]

The amount of supplemental oxygen therefore depends:[95]
- on flight altitudes and duration with reference to the flight manual.
- on how many 'flight deck crew' are on duty in the cockpit. If two, then both must have supplemental oxygen at the ready for the entire flight time at pressure altitudes above 12 000 ft and, if you are between 10 000 ft and 12 000 ft pressure altitude, for any period exceeding 120 minutes intended flight time. The same rule applies to cabin crew (larger aircraft). A passenger in the right-hand seat of a Cessna 172 is not flight deck crew.
- on passengers. If you are above 12 000 feet for the entire flight, all your passengers (including infants ie children under the age of two) must each have supplemental oxygen. But if you intend to fly between FL100 and FL120 for more than 120 minutes, only 10% of passengers need supply and only for the time beyond those 120 minutes.

Of course, in a smaller general aviation plane, you will have 'units of the portable type', as CATS quaintly puts it.[96]

And why 'FL'? Because we are dealing here with pressure altitude.[97]

6.6.4 Communication and navigation equipment

As you are now inside the aircraft, having checked the oxygen canisters, your next check is to ensure that:

---

[94] CATS 91.04.16 (1).
[95] CATS 91.04.16.
[96] CATS 91.04.14 2 (2).
[97] CATS 91.04.16 (3) for full details.

'**The instruments and navigation, communication and other equipment** required for the particular type of operation to be undertaken, are installed and are serviceable and functioning correctly, except as provided for in the MEL.'[98]

The 'minimum equipment list', MEL, 'provides for the operation of aircraft, subject to specified conditions, **with particular equipment inoperative**, prepared by an operator in conformity with, or more restrictive than, the MMEL established for the aircraft type'—and the "master minimum equipment list", MMEL, is compiled for a particular aircraft type by the **manufacturer** of the aircraft with the approval of the appropriate authority of the State of Manufacture containing items, one or more of which is permitted to be unserviceable at the commencement of a flight'.[99]

There are two legal points here which you, as a PIC, must comply with:
1) The general rules on communication and navigation equipment put in place in Subpart 5 of Part 91.
2) The specific rules on flight, navigation and 'associated equipment' put in place in Subpart 4 of Part 91.

Obscure? Complicated? At first sight. But let us look at it logically, by discussing communication equipment separately from navigation equipment.

6.6.4.1 Communication equipment capability

Communication[100]

(1) Except with prior written approval by the Director, no aircraft shall be operated in **designated airspace or under IFR** unless such aircraft is equipped with radio communication equipment capable of—[in other words, without special permission, you can only fly an aircraft in a designated airspace or under IFR if it is equipped for and capable of]

   (a) two-way communication at any time during the flight on such frequencies as may be prescribed by the appropriate authority;

   (b) receiving meteorological information at any time during flight.

(2) The radio communication equipment referred to in sub-regulation (1) shall be capable of providing for communication on the aeronautical emergency frequency 121.5 MHz.

(3) All flight crew members involved in large aeroplane operations and who are required to be on flight deck duty shall communicate through boom or throat microphones below the transition level/altitude.

---

[98] CARS 91.02.7 (1) (b).
[99] CARS 1.01.1.
[100] CARS 91.05.1.

> (4) The radio communication equipment in the aircraft shall be installed and be of a type as prescribed in Document SA-CATS 91.
>
> **Navigation**[101]
>
> The main rule reads: 'No person shall [= is allowed to] operate an aircraft unless such aircraft is equipped with navigation equipment enabling it to proceed in accordance with its flight plan, including approaches at the planned destination or any alternate aerodromes, and the appropriate ATS requirements.
>
> Provided that the provisions of this regulation shall not apply to [translation: Except for. . .] flights operated in accordance with VFR, if such flights can be accomplished by visual reference to landmarks. Such landmarks for helicopter operations shall be no further apart than 60 nautical miles'.
>
> In plain English: you can only operate an aircraft (A) if it is equipped with what the rule says but it does not apply to VFR flights as long as visual reference to ground landmarks exists (for H, the 60 NM rule). Landmarks are roads, lakes, cooling towers etc. They will be on your aeronautical chart but you must establish visual contact.

6.6.4.2 Flight plan communication and navigation capability

Your communication and navigation equipment has to be specified in your flight plan. There are special designators that you will input at item 10, in sequence (general, voice communication, data link communication and navigation/SSR and ADS).[102]

This is a reminder of what you studied for your Radiotelephony examination.[103] Here are the most common designators you may be asked about in the *PPL exam*:

- S: you have VHF (V), VOR (O) and ILS (L) (this is the standard equipment)
- Z: you have a GPS but it is non-certified (you will note it at item 18 as NAV/GPS)
- V: you have VHF voice communication over your normal radio
- D: you have a DME
- F: you have ADF
- O: you have VOR
- C: you have a transponder mode 'Charlie' that transmits your four identifying squawk code numbers and your altitude.

---

[101] CARS 91.05.2.
[102] Automatic Dependent Surveillance.
[103] Please refer to D Lempp *The Pilot's Radio Handbook* for details on how to enter the sequence of designators correctly. This is also comprehensively explained, item by item, in AIC 001/2019, Appendix.

This combination of designators, VFOZ/C, means that you are equipped with the standard general aviation two-way VHF radio, an ADF and a VOR, a non-certified GPS and your transponder is mode Charlie.

6.6.5 Compulsory instruments

Your head is still in the cockpit. You have looked at communication and navigation equipment, but keep your head in there and ask yourself: do I have, for this flight, all **compulsory** instruments, and are they serviceable?

So, what are the compulsory instruments? *(Exam!)*

Compulsory instruments and equipment under VFR[104]

(a) a magnetic compass;

(b) an accurate time-piece showing the time in hours, minutes, and seconds;

(c) a sensitive pressure altimeter with a subscale setting, calibrated in hectopascal, adjustable for any barometric pressure setting likely to be encountered during flight;

(d) an airspeed indicator;

(e) if so required for use in designated airspace, a pressure-altitude reporting transponder, unless authorised by the responsible ATSU; and

(f) if to be operated by night, a chart holder in an easily readable position that can be illuminated.

Compulsory instruments and equipment under IFR[105]

(a) a magnetic compass;

(b) an accurate time-piece showing the time in hours, minutes and seconds;

(c) for large aeroplanes, two independent sensitive pressure altimeter systems with subscale settings, calibrated in hectopascal, adjustable for any barometric pressure setting likely to be encountered during flight and for all other aircraft, one sensitive pressure altimeter with subscale settings, calibrated in hectopascal, adjustable for any barometric pressure setting likely to be encountered during flight;

(d) an airspeed indicator system with heated pitot tube or equivalent means for preventing malfunctioning due to either condensation or icing;

(e) a vertical-speed indicator;

(f) a stabilised direction indicator;

---

[104] CARS 91.04.4.
[105] CARS 91.04.5.

(g) a turn-and-bank indicator, or a turn co-ordinator incorporating a slip indicator;

(h) an attitude indicator and for large aeroplanes for which an individual certificate of airworthiness was first issued after 1 January 1975, an emergency power supply, independent of the main electrical generating system, for the purpose of operating and illuminating, for a minimum period of 30 minutes, an attitude indicator, clearly visible to the PIC. The emergency power supply shall be automatically operative after the total failure of the main electrical generating system and clear indication shall be given on the instrument panel that the attitude indicator(s) is being operated by emergency power;

(i) a means of indicating, in the cockpit or in the flight deck, the outside air temperature in degrees Celsius;

(j) a chart holder in an easily readable position which can be illuminated for operations by night;

(k) a means of measuring and displaying whether the supply of power to the gyroscopic instruments is adequate; and

(l) a pressure-altitude reporting transponder.

Compulsory instruments and equipment for single pilot in IMC or at night[106]

(a) the single pilot flying is equipped with a headset with boom microphone or equivalent and has a transmit button positioned in such a way that it may be operated without the pilot having to remove his or her hands from the control wheel, joy stick or cyclic stick;

(b) the aircraft is equipped with a means of displaying charts that enables them to be readable in all ambient light conditions;

(c) if the aircraft is flown in IMC, such aircraft has been certificated for single-pilot IFR operations and is equipped with a serviceable automatic flight control system with at least altitude hold and heading mode; or

(d) in the case of a helicopter, if it is flown at night under VMC, such helicopter is equipped with a serviceable automatic flight control system with at least altitude and heading mode or similar equipment: provided that this requirement shall not apply to a helicopter operated in the circuit of the aerodrome of departure or over densely populated, well-lit areas in accordance with the provisions of regulation 91.06.32(2), but not higher than 3 500 feet above the prescribed minimum height.

Some of this is discussed again in chapter 13, on Night Flying.

---

[106] CARS 91.04.6.

Chapter 6: Before you call 'clear prop' 141

And remember some instruments need power, and power means circuit breakers or **fuses**:[107] the rule is, you must have on board 10% spare fuses of the total number of fuses, or 3 spare fuses, whichever is greater (if there are 10 fuses, you need 3, as 3 is greater than 10% of 10, which is 1) *(exam question!)*. You can deactivate a circuit breaker in flight only in accordance with what your AFM says.[108]

While you are still inspecting the inside of the aircraft, check the fire extinguisher.

6.6.6 Fire extinguisher

At least one **hand-held fire extinguisher** is required on the flight deck (in your case, the cockpit), usually placed between the front seats in a small aircraft and not away in the back compartment ('conveniently located on the flight deck'), Halon 1211 or 'equivalent'.[109] In the passenger compartment, if applicable, 1 extinguisher is needed for 7 to 30 passengers, 2 for 31 to 60, and up to 8 for 601 plus passengers.[110]

6.6.7 Safety belts and harnesses

Are you done inside the cabin? Not quite.

Seat safety belts with or without a diagonal strap, or safety harnesses are required for each passenger older than two years of age (ie a child).

Safety harnesses with an automatic restraint are required for each flight crew seat, with a device that can automatically restrain the torso in case of rapid deceleration.

And, if you take an infant, ie a child of less than two years of age, you need a **child restraint device.**

All belts and harnesses must have a single point release.[111]

These are defined 'as applicable' to the type of aircraft you fly, but you must check them and possibly demonstrate to your passengers.

Ready to climb out? You may now do so. And one last check.

---

[107] CARS 91.04.12. Refer to J M Pratt, *PPL 4*, Gen 103 about fuses.
[108] CARS 91.04 .2 (3).
[109] CATS 91.04.18–2 (2). Typically Halon 1301 is installed in cargo hold.
[110] CATS 91.04.18 for precise details.
[111] CARS 91.04.11.

142   Air Law

6.6.8 Stowage, baggage and cargo

You climb out of the aircraft, but what about stowage, large or small?

Stowage, baggage and cargo

The PIC must ensure that they

- 'are placed in a manner which prevents movement likely to cause injury or damage [or stowed where it cannot happen] and does not obstruct aisle or exit [in your SEP Piper, a large bag on the right will obstruct your own exit],[112]
- or 'the load carried by the aircraft is properly secured, fit to be conveyed in accordance with Part 92[113] and is so distributed that the centre of gravity is within the limits prescribed in the AFM'.[114] If you place, neatly secured, 40 bottles of wine in the small hold of your Cessna 172, you had better be careful at take-off, even though the mass and balance says it is 'in the envelope' and just fine.

6.6.9 First aid kit, universal precaution kit and strips

The **first aid kit** is compulsory for any general aviation operation: you cannot operate an aircraft without having the FAK on board. As simple as that.[115]

Do not confuse it with the **universal precaution kit**: not one but at least two[116] of that type of kit is compulsory for 'general aviation operations for which the maximum certificated passenger seating is 20 or more and on which is carried a cabin attendant'. This is unlikely to be needed in your case.[117]

The FAK is often located in the storage compartment of a light aircraft. Make sure it is there. It must be on board, checked for condition, and readily accessible (which is not always the case in light aircraft, while in flight). Your duty as PIC, whether you are alone or with that keen friend who always wants to come along 'to take pictures' and then keeps talking, is to check it.

A FAK is no simple matter.

---

[112] CARS 91.04.12.

[113] CARS and CATS Part 92 deals with the conveyance of dangerous goods. The sub-regulation does not apply only to dangerous goods: it means that any load has to be secured (simply think of that case of beers you are taking to a bush fly-in, ready to topple over) and CofG distributed, and, if dangerous, in accordance with Part 92.

[114] CARS 92.02.7 (1) (e).

[115] CARS 91.04.13 (1).

[116] CATS 91.04.13–4 (1).

[117] CARS 91.04.13 (5) and (6).

A FAK contains a minimum of 15 items, plus a checklist. **From 1 to 100 passengers you need 1 kit**, from 101 to 200, 2 kits and so on, until 500. From 501 passengers, you need 6 kits.

Standard first aid kit

- bandage;
- burns dressings;
- wound dressings, large and small;
- adhesive tape, safety pins and scissors;
- small adhesive dressings;
- antiseptic wound cleaner;
- adhesive wound closures;
- adhesive tape;
- disposable resuscitation aid;
- temperature reading device (non-mercury);
- simple analgesic eg paracetamol;
- nasal decongestant (saline solution is best);
- gastrointestinal antacid (avoid bottles, use tablets);
- disposable glove;
- first aid handbook.

Universal precaution kit

- disposable gloves;
- dry powder that converts small liquid spill into sterile granulated gel;
- germicidal disinfectants for surface cleaning;
- skin wipes;
- face/eye mask;
- large absorbent towel;
- pick-up scoop with scraper; and
- bio-hazard disposal waste bag.

At the same time, check that the 'Strips' are there (to use as ground signals in a Search and Rescue, after you have crashed) (see page 202).

Inspection done.
Your watch reads 0845B.
Time to fly.
Not quite.
What about paperwork?

6.7 ACTION 7: PAPER PLANE!

Your aircraft is made up of mechanical parts, a fuselage, wings, empennage and, advisably, an engine, but it is also made out of paper. Lots of paper. Without it being in order, it cannot fly. It is also a paper plane.

You must check that all the legal papers (called 'documents and records') related to the aircraft are in good shape.

The best way to determine the legal paperwork involved is to look at the list of documents or their 'certified true copies' that you must carry **on board**.[118]

The list varies depending on whether your flight is domestic or international (for all you know your sight-seeing nav may take you across the Namibia or Botswana borders). *Students! You will get examined on this list!*

> **Up to 12 documents to be carried on board on each individual domestic flight:**[119]
>
> - the certificate of registration, or its 'certified true copy' in domestic operations only;[120] valid until cancelled or becomes invalid in terms of Part 47;
> - the certificate of airworthiness (or an Authority to Fly in case of a non-type certificated aircraft, NTCA);[121] valid for 12 months or until surrendered, suspended or cancelled (the most important: is your aircraft safe to fly?);[122]
> - the appropriate licence and medical certificate of each crew member;
> - the aircraft radio station licence;
> - the certificate of release to service; to be kept for 12 months calculated from the date of issue; plus a second copy where the aircraft is usually stationed; valid 12 months or 100 hours flight time since last Mandatory Periodic Inspection (MPI) whichever comes first;[123]
> - the AFM (aircraft flight manual) referred to in regulation 91.03.2 or an equivalent document;[124]
> - the mass and balance report; valid five years;[125]

---

[118] CARS 91.03.1.
[119] CARS 91.03.1 (a) (i) to (xii).
[120] CARS 47.02.3 (a) (international flight: the original) and (b) (domestic: a certified true copy).
[121] Under Part 24.
[122] CARS 21.08.12 (1).
[123] CARS 43.02.8 Section A, 2 (4) (a).
[124] CARS 91.02.2 : the owner or operator is responsible for ensuring that each aircraft has her own approved AFM, and for keeping it up to date. But it is the pilot's responsibility to take it on board.
[125] CARS 43.02.7 (1).

- the flight folio (which includes a record of oil and fuel);[126] to be retained five years calculated from date of last entry;[127]
- the MEL (operator's minimum equipment list), if applicable;
- the noise certificate, if such certificate has been issued for the type of aircraft;
- the list of visual signals and procedures for use by intercepting and intercepted aircraft;
- the licence to operate the service, if required.

You must add to this list current IFR and VFR charts and related publications (such as AIP aerodrome information or airspace specs) required to depart from your base, operate en route, divert and arrive at your destination.[128]

Up to 17 documents to be carried on each individual international flight:[129]

- the certificate of registration;
- the certificate of airworthiness or, for non-type certificated aircraft, an authority to fly;
- the appropriate licence and medical certificate of each crew member;
- the general declaration;
- the aircraft radio station licence;
- if passengers are carried, the passenger manifest, unless the information is included in the general declaration;
- if cargo is carried, a manifest and detailed declaration of the cargo;
- the certificate of release to service;
- the navigation log when a navigator is carried;
- the AFM, referred to in regulation 91.03.2, or an equivalent document, which document shall include the statements referred to in technical standard 91.07.31 5(5)(a) of Document SA-CATS 91, if flight in RVSM airspace is contemplated;[130]
- the mass and balance report;
- the flight folio;
- the MEL, if applicable;

---

[126] CARS 91.03.6 (2) and (3). Also, CARS 91.03.5 (5).
[127] CARS 91.03.5 (5).
[128] CARS 91.02.7 (1) (f).
[129] See page 171 about RVSM.
[130] In order to respect the legal limitations of the MCM of your aircraft for this specific flight as per CARS 91.02.7 (d).

146 Air Law

- the noise certificate, if such certificate has been issued for the type of aircraft; and
- a list of visual signals and procedures for use by intercepting and intercepted aircraft;
- if a flight in RVSM airspace is contemplated—
  - a valid RVSM licence endorsement issued by the Director; and
  - if applicable, a valid RVSM operational approval for the particular RVSM airspace; and
- where applicable, a licence to operate air services, FOP or equivalent document giving authority for the flight.

In addition:
- **mass and balance sheet**: you calculate it for each flight,[131] either manually or electronically—air transport operations under Part 121 and Part 135 make a load and trim sheet compulsory.[132] You need not have your mass and balance sheet on board.
- **aircraft checklists**: as PIC you must 'ensure the checklists used on board the aircraft are complied with'—so far it is easy to understand, but read the next sentence: 'and utilised having due regard to human factors principles'.[133]

Now, what does this last sentence mean?

You must turn to CATS, which says that **checklists must be easy to handle, easy to read, easy to follow, adapted to workload** in the cockpit and have each item intended to achieve a goal. This is directed mainly at larger aircraft but, in your case, make sure you have the checklist on board and easily accessible just in case.[134]

- **Authorisation sheet** if you hire and fly from an operator (example, annexure 13).
- **Waiver of liability or indemnity form** for passengers. Even if you take a good friend with you, you should have your pax (passenger) complete one. Schools usually have blank ones. The waiver offers pilot some protection in case of an accident, so long as you fulfil all your duties as a pilot. But if you are negligent, either in not having your pax complete one even for a 10-minute 'flip' or in

---

[131] In order to respect the legal limitations of the MCM of your aircraft for this specific flight as per CARS 91.02.7 (d).

[132] CARS 91.02.7 (3) for the general rule, and 121.04.9, 135.04.9.

[133] CARS 91.03.3 (2). But note that it is the 'owner or operator' who has, by law, 'to establish and make available' a system checklist 'for all phases of the operation under normal, abnormal and emergency conditions' (CARS 91.03.3 (1)). This is not the pilot's responsibility.

[134] CATS 91.03.3 2 (1).

ensuring you do what a PIC is supposed to do (which is basically what this book is about), you, or your family, will have your day in court. The matter is complex, and the best is to seek professional legal or insurance advice before 'flipping' (see example of waiver at annexure 13).

Usually, as you often fly the same aircraft, all this should be at the ready. You simply need to check every paper is up to date. Pay attention to the flight folio to verify that previous entries are correct and the aircraft is not, in fact, due for MPI. Most papers go in a folder, the folder in a flight bag, the flight bag in the aircraft, and of course the aircraft is on the apron, which leads to the next step: the pre-flight.

Placards? Your control panel is likely to have a few placards, indicating operating limitations, as prescribed. Check that they are clean, legible and have not come unstuck.[135]

Electronic devices? If you, PIC, think that 'any portable electronic device à may adversely affect the performance of the systems and equipment of the aircraft' you must disallow it (exceptions: heart pacemaker, hearing aid, *portable voice recorder*, *electric shaver*, electric portable equipment for pacing or resuscitation, *any other you decide to allow*—items in italics are not be used during critical phases of flight).[136]

The time is now 0855B. Time to freshen up, clean your windshield if you have forgotten, check that the pitot cover is off, make sure the luggage compartment door will not swing open, and check the windsock. You are in luck today, your passenger friend is on time and taking a selfie, unaware of the fact you have been up since dawn.

---

[135] CARS 91.04.1 (4) 'Placards and instrument markings, containing those operating limitations required by the type certificate or by regulation to be visible to the flight crew, shall be displayed in the aircraft'. Also CARS 91.08.1 (1) (b).

[136] CARS 91.01.9. A different wording is under consideration (*Regulation Gazette* 42581 of 17 July 2019).

Chapter 7

Ready to taxi!

Before you start up, the obvious: chocks.

This is what the law says:[1]

- 'Except when the brakes are serviceable and are fully applied, chocks must be placed in front of the wheels of an aeroplane before starting the engine or engines, and a competent person must be seated at the controls when the engine or engines are running.
- If the pilot of an aeroplane is the only person present and it has been necessary for chocks to be used, he or she must ensure that the chocks are removed prior to starting the engine, unless the aircraft is equipped with a parking brake, in which case the parking brake must be set before the pilot removes the chocks'.

And regarding the **switching on of aircraft lights**, here is a reminder,[2] meant to avoid the risks attached to runway incursions and to enhance situational awareness:

Before starting engines	Rotating beacon on
Before taxi/pushback	NAV lights on
Start of taxi	Taxi light on
Entering a runway for take off	Strobe light on
On receiving take off clearance	Landing light on
Crossing a runway	All above exterior lighting on (including strobe)

As you call 'clear prop', a new set of rules applies. From now on, your **'duties of PIC regarding flight operations'** come into play (annexure 13).[3] Pre-flighting is not an operation, it is an inspection. Operations start now.

And 'flight time' begins as you start moving.

---

[1] CARS 91.07.29 (1) and (2).
[2] AIP ENR 1.8-24.
[3] CARS 91.02.8.

- **Flight time (A) and (H)** 'Flight time for the operation of aeroplanes means the total time from the moment an aeroplane first moves under its own power for the purposes of taking off until the moment it finally comes to rest at the end of the flight' and is 'synonymous with the term "block to block" time or "chock to chock" time in general usage, which is measured from the time an aeroplane first moves for the purpose of taking off until it finally stops at the end of the flight'.
- For the operation of helicopters, flight time is the total time from the moment a helicopter's rotor blades start turning until the moment the helicopter finally comes to rest at the end of the flight and the rotor blades are stopped.[4]

As you know—but it is worth repeating since what is obvious is easily taken for granted, and what is taken for granted can fall on the wrong side of the law—from the moment you have done your radio check and then called 'taxiing' until you call 'taking off' you are on the ground.

Moving on the ground has all sorts of implications. Your aircraft is moving but moving **on what** actually?

7.1 WHERE ARE YOU TAXIING AND WHAT ARE THESE AREAS CALLED?

Remember the terminology below; it will be tested in PPL and CPL exams:[5]

Taxiing terminology[6]
- The '**manoeuvring area**' is that part of an aerodrome used for take-off, landing (including the runway strips), and taxiing. The apron is excluded.
- The '**movement area**' is manoeuvring area plus the apron: take-off, landing and taxiing, runway strips, and apron.
- **Taxiing refers 'to the movement of an aircraft on the surface of an aerodrome under its own power, excluding take-off and landing'.**
- And what about '**taxiways**'? A taxiway refers to 'a defined path on a land aerodrome' that 'provide[s] a link' between two parts of an aerodrome on which you can, and need, for that reason to taxi. There are **three types of taxiways:**
  - aircraft stand taxilane: a portion of an apron 'designated' to provide access to aircraft stands only.

---

[4] CARS 01.1.1 (a) and (b).
[5] CARS 1.01.1.
[6] CARS 1.01.1.

150   Air Law

> – apron taxiway: a portion of a taxiway located on an apron in order to provide a through taxi route across the apron.
> – rapid exit taxiway (*this definition comes up frequently at the CPL Air Law exam, with a picture*): it is 'connected to a runway at an acute angle' and is made 'to allow landing planes to turn off at higher speeds' than on other exit taxiways, 'minimizing runway occupancy time' [in plain English: avoiding congestion].
>
> - What is an **apron**? It is 'a defined area on a land aerodrome intended to accommodate aircraft for the purpose of loading or unloading passengers or cargo, refuelling, parking or maintenance'.[7]

Now that you know the 'lie of the land', you are ready to roll . . . if you are allowed to.

If you are interested in the fascinating physical or equipment characteristics of aerodromes, from lighting to runways, from measurements of windsocks to signalling devices and markings all sorts (under Part 139), refer to the most recent update (Amendment SA-CATS 1/2019, effective 21 June 2019).

7.2 LIGHT SIGNALS[8]

Indeed, if you are at a controlled aerodrome you cannot just leave the apron and start taxiing. Usually you first contact Apron (so they can charge you) then Ground for taxi clearance. But there may be light signals once you have started to taxi if you are at an aerodrome that uses light signals. It is rare but comes up often in *exam questions*.

Those signals are sent from the Tower by a so-called 'light gun' (a signal lamp, actually) and are directional: the beam will be focused on your aircraft.

First look at this well-known diagram[9] (it represents a horizontal surface!):

---

[7] CARS 1.01.1.
[8] CATS 91.06.13–4.
[9] CATS 91.06.13–4 (1) (a).

Chapter 7: Ready to taxi! 151

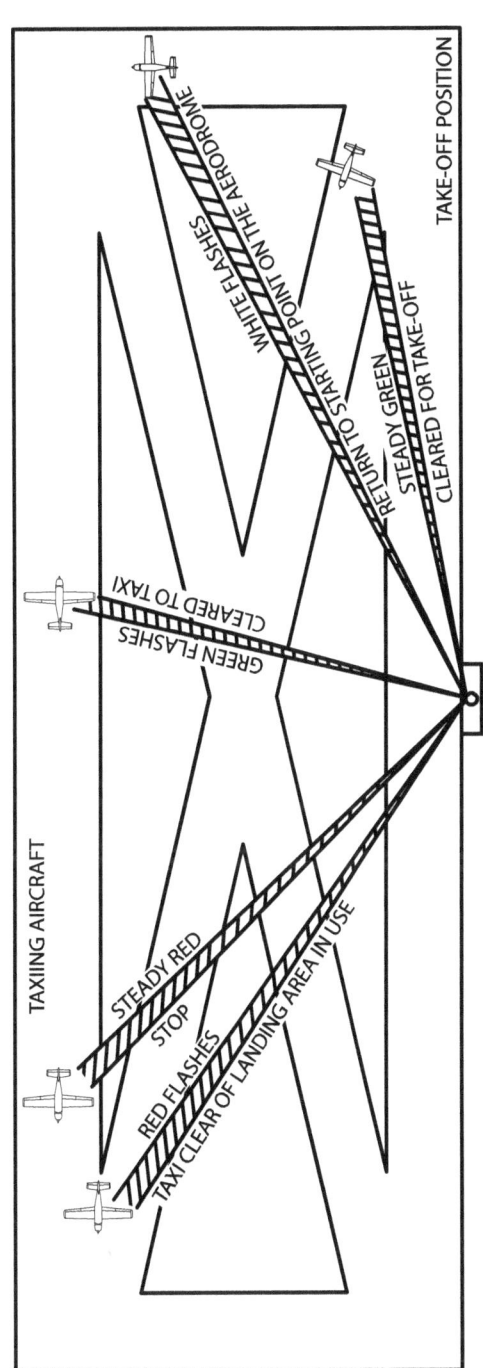

And now read the explanation, with mnemonics that may help:

> **Light signals directed at your aircraft taxiing** (*Students, please note!*)
>
> - series of green flashes = cleared to taxi
>   - ➤ you go you go you go you go
> - steady green = cleared for take off (no mnemonics needed)
> - series of white flashes = taxi back to starting point
>   - ➤ blank try!
> - series of red flashes = taxi clear of landing area
>   - ➤ get out get out get out get out
> - steady red = stop (no mnemonics needed)
>
> ... and **your acknowledgment** in all cases is:
>
> - day time: move ailerons or rudder as you wish
> - night time: flash on and off landing light, or switch the navigation lights on and off twice.

You are at long last moving on taxiway Alpha which, with a bit of luck, will lead you directly and without delay to the holding point.

Keep an eye out for signal lights from the Tower.

But more legal trouble lurks, so keep your eyes peeled, as a battery of safety rules come into action that you had better follow. **Taxi rules imply 'rights of way'**.

7.3 TAXI RULES AND RIGHT OF WAY ON THE GROUND

Before you read the details of taxi rules, consider this sub-regulation: 'Nothing in this regulation shall relieve the PIC of an aircraft or the person in charge of a vehicle, from the responsibility for taking such action as will best aid to avert collision.'[10]

This is the general risk avoidance idea. In short, do not cling to your legal right of way if the other pilot is clearly taking no notice and carries on taxiing regardless.

And for the specifics:

Taxi rules and right of way[11]

- A vehicle which is towing an aircraft is given right of way by vehicles and by other aircraft which are not taking off (or landing).
- An aircraft is given right of way by a vehicle which is not towing an aircraft.
- An aircraft or vehicle which is obliged by the provisions of this regulation to give right of way to another aircraft, must, if necessary in the circumstances in order to do so, reduce its speed or stop.
- If **danger of collision exists between an aircraft or vehicle and another aircraft or vehicle**, such of the following procedures as may be appropriate in the circumstances, must be applied [*students, take note of this entire sub-regulation, it comes up often in exam papers*];

    (a) When the two are **approaching head-on or nearly head-on**, each shall turn to the right;

    (b) when one is **overtaking** the other, the one which is overtaking shall keep out of the way of the other by turning to the right, and no subsequent change in the relative positions of the two shall absolve the one which is overtaking from this obligation [in plain English: the aircraft that is overtaking must stay out of the way of the other by going right, whatever happens when both are moving], until it is finally past and clear of the other;

    (c) when the two are **converging**, the one which has the other on its right, must give way to the other and must avoid crossing ahead of the other unless passing well clear of it.

    Students, please note that in these three cases it is not only aircraft-to-aircraft but also aircraft-to-vehicle—this is an exam trap.

- A vehicle moving along a runway or taxiway, shall as far as practicable keep to the right side of the runway or taxiway.

---

[10] CARS 91.06.11 (12).
[11] CARS 91.06.11.

- When an aircraft is being towed, the person in charge of the towing vehicle is responsible for compliance with the provisions of this regulation.
- An aircraft operated on a **controlled aerodrome** must not taxi on the manoeuvring area without clearance from the aerodrome control tower and shall comply with any instructions given by that unit. [Why? Because you are controlled, so you follow instructions.]
- An aircraft taxiing on the manoeuvring area of an **uncontrolled aerodrome** shall taxi in accordance with the ground control procedures which may be in force at such aerodrome.
- While taxiing at **controlled aerodromes**, you must
    (a) stop and hold at all runway-holding positions unless otherwise authorized by the aerodrome control tower [at uncontrolled, you stop, listen to the radio, check if anyone is on downwind or base by looking around, and move on if it is clear];
    (b) stop at all lighted stop bars and only proceed further when those lights are switched off.

Just in case you'd ask: **Can someone else taxi my aircraft** while I am having an espresso? **Yes, provided that, on the movement area,** all of these conditions are met:[12]
- the taxi person has a valid pilot licence (SPL will do), or has been declared 'competent' to taxi by the holder of a flight instructor rating or, in the case of a foreign aeroplane, a person authorised by an appropriate authority,
- the taxi person, if using the radio, is authorised to do so,
- the taxi person knows the aerodrome routes, signals, phraseology, etc, and is able to apply these rules.
- **BUT the aircraft cannot enter the manoeuvring area if radio is mandatory** (in that case the taxi person will move only on the apron, which is very exciting).

---

[12] CARS 91.01.3.

154   *Air Law*

7.4 RUNWAY MARKINGS AND DISPLACED THRESHOLDS

Do you recall the definition of 'threshold'? *(exam!)* It 'means the beginning of that portion of the runway usable for landing'.[13] Remember that if taxiway markings are in yellow, runway markings by contrast are white.

7.4.1 Various runway markings

You are likely to encounter these as a PPL pilot.[14]

   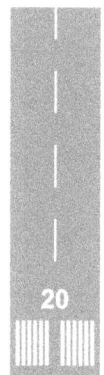   

Basic runway:
visual runway
hard surface
(or grass, gravel)
designator only
(on hard surface)
centreline
no threshold markings
(no stripes)

GA airfield type:
non-precision runway
hard surface
centreline
threshold markings
(stripes)
('piano keys')

Airport type:
precision runway
hard surface
centreline
touchdown zone
threshold markings
(stripes)
edge markings required

Note that the number of stripes help you determine the width of a runway:
4 stripes, 18 m; 6 stripes, 23 m; 8 stripes, 30 m; 12 stripes, 45 m; 16 stripes, 60 m.

---

[13] CARS 1.01.1.

[14] Graphics are inspired by the community website www.theairlinepilots.com, as well as the valuable FAA *Airfield Standards*, Southern Region Airports Division, 2018.

7.4.2 Displaced thresholds

Displaced thresholds are of four types *(and a favourite at examinations)*:

➢ In both cases below the white arrows indicate that the area is suitable only for ground movement, taxi, and for take off.

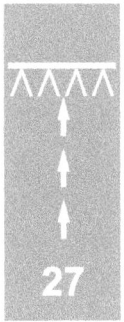

Permanently (> 6 months) displaced threshold with **pre-threshold area available for taxi and take off** but not for landing. **Being permanent the runway designator 27 has been moved up after the piano keys.**

Temporarily pre-threshold area available for taxi and take off but not for landing. Because it is temporary the runway designator stays where it is.

➢ In both cases below the white crosses indicate that the area is unfit for aircraft movement and unsuitable as a stop way.

Permanently (> 6 months) displaced threshold with **pre-threshold area unfit for movement and unsuitable as a stop way in case of a rejected take-off.**

Temporarily pre-threshold area unfit for movement.

156   *Air Law*

7.4.3 Pre-threshold area unfit for normal movement of aircraft (yellow chevron)

Refer to the picture on page 246B.

7.5 RUNWAY AND TAXIWAY MANDATORY AND INFORMATION SIGNS[15]

Refer to the picture on page 246B.

7.6 AERODROME SIGNALLING PANEL AND SIGNALLING AREA[16]

Signals are large movable panels displayed on the signalling area, or signal area[17] of 9 m² visible from all angles. Radio has made them nearly redundant. These panels are becoming a rarity—and highly collectable (refrain from taking them away).

Some of them are meant to communicate to you while you are above the airfield, rather than before take-off. Most are used for take-off and landing.

As quaint and jolly as they may look, they have to be known, *as quite a few questions about them do come up in the exam.*

Refer to pages 216 and 246B–C for a list (they have been listed in the landing part of the narrative because they are more likely to be seen from above).

You may also find, at or near the control tower, a number indicating the direction of **take-off** 'expressed **in unit of 10 degrees to the nearest degrees of the magnetic** compass' *(exam!)*:[18] |09|

You are now at the threshold, but before you call 'lining up' and come to rest on the 'piano keys', bear in mind these rules: if you are on the ground, and another aircraft is taking off, or about to land or landing, this aircraft has priority over your aircraft,[19] and you must not attempt to take off if there is an 'apparent' risk of collision.[20] How do you judge 'apparent'? By looking around you on the ground and above you in the air, and by listening to calls.

At last, ready to take off!

---

[15] Designs can be found at CATS 139.02.1 Aerodromes and Heliports—Physical characteristics (52). That long sub-regulation (65 sections) states how an aerodrome must be designed and equipped in terms of its physical characteristics, in order to be licensed.

[16] CATS 139.02.1 (22) Aerodromes and Heliports, while the panels are described at CATS 91.06.13–4 (2).

[17] 'Signalling' is the term used by CATS.

[18] 91.06.13–4 (2) (e) (ii).

[19] CARS 91.06.7 (6).

[20] CARS 91.06.7 (8).

Not quite. First a reminder of that little sing song before taking to the air, **'What To Do Last'**:

> **W**ind sock to make sure you are taking off into wind, and you realise there is a bad crosswind.
>
> **T**ransponder goes on Alt (altitude) and the numbers are set on 2000 (make sure of it, it is your last chance before you trigger an emergency by mistake . . .) unless you are at a controlled airfield; in which case Ground will have already given the squawk code, which you would have set on your transponder, and you will only switch it on Alt now, just before taking off.
>
> **D**irection indicator to compass to runway (reset your direction indicator if deviant).
>
> **L**anding light on and fue**L** pump on, if required.

And let us hope you did not forget to do your **passenger briefing,** 'verbally' and 'before take-off',[21] preferably after boarding but some schools teach students to do it after the run-ups, on how to brace and behave in case of an emergency ('don't touch the controls, don't grab me!'), how to get out ('to the back!' because of the propeller; do tell your pax), where the extinguisher is located, make sure harnesses are 'safe and secure', and do not simply trust that your two pax have buckled up. They possibly have not and are taking pictures. Cockpit should be 'sterile' at this stage: pax have to keep quiet. All of this is your PIC's duty to 'ensure'.

You are now saying the magic words, 'ready, runway 27'. Your flight log will read: t/o: 0705Z (always in Z).[22] You have been prepping since 0600B. You will get all that done more quickly in due course, but whatever your velocity, you had better make sure you do what has to be done.

---

[21] CARS 91.07.20.

[22] Z refers to Zulu time or Coordinated Universal Time. South Africa Bravo time, which is local time, is two hours ahead of Zulu time. 0800Z=1000B, or 10 am. The acronym UTC is a compromise between the French (TUC) and the English (CUT), the result being what it is. Remember that aviation time is Zulu time. It is not Durban time. A flight plan is in Zulu time.

Chapter 8

. . . .

Flying away, en route!

You take off. You climb. You are about to leave the circuit. From now on what are called '**Rules of the Air**' come into play. They are set by ICAO, to guide you and make the skies safe.[1]

You are effectively 'en route'.

How is en route defined? There are three useful definitions to remember, to avoid any confusion:

En route![2]

'**en-route phase**' means **that part of the flight from the end of the take-off and initial climb phase to the commencement of the approach and landing phase**.

'**en-route alternate aerodrome**' means an aerodrome at which an aircraft would be able to land after experiencing an abnormal or emergency condition while en-route.

'**en-route safe altitude**' means an altitude which will ensure a separation height of at least—

   (a)   1 000 feet above the highest terrain or obstacle where the height of such terrain or obstacle does not exceed 5 000 feet above sea level within five nautical miles of the aircraft in flight;

       or

   (b)   2 000 feet above the highest terrain or obstacle located within five nautical miles of the aircraft in flight where the height of such terrain or obstacle exceeds 5 000 feet above sea level.

However, **when you are en route, the law does not want you to collide with anything 'on the way'** (which is the translation of the French 'en route'), be it another aircraft in flight, a ground feature or extreme bad weather. It is as basic as that.

This is why the law provides you with safeguards: regulations made for collision avoidance while aloft.

How to avoid collision in flight?

---

[1] ICAO, Annex 2.
[2] CARS 1.01.1. En route, en-route, enroute—all three mean the same thing.

Collision avoidance in flight falls into eight sets of rules that are presented systematically below. This is a more rational and at the same time natural way to present a host of regulations.

8.1 COLLISION AVOIDANCE: 'RULES OF THE AIR'

The purpose of these rules is to ensure aircraft do not get into each other's way, and collide. The first risk of collision indeed is having aircraft getting into each other's way.

Aircraft can endanger one another either close to an aerodrome, or away from it. For that reason—but do not expect the legislator who drafted the regulations to spell it out loud and clear for you—rules of the air fall into two main categories:
- either you fly 'on and in the vicinity of an aerodrome',[3]
- or away from it—en route, if you wish.

'Vicinity' means 'neighbourhood' or 'proximity'. CARS does not define 'vicinity' directly. But it means: when you are within 5 NM of the airfield or above it, the rules apply.[4]

Now, how do you avoid collision? By 'observing', that is looking at traffic (and listening to calls) and observing rules.

8.1.1 The general rules

They are simple:
- As PIC you must 'observe other aerodrome traffic' to avoid collision and 'conform with or avoid the pattern of traffic formed by other aircraft in operation'.[5]
- You must comply with any ATC clearance (you can ask for an amended clearance), operate according to the ATSU instructions, and if you deviate from a clearance or an instruction, you must notify the ATSU as soon as practicable.[6]

8.1.2 The specific rules

The rules relate to three different situations:
- You are in **uncontrolled** airspace (typically at your local airfield).
- You are within an aerodrome traffic zone (ATZ) and **controlled** by ATC.
- You are within an aerodrome traffic zone with a **flight information service**.

Of course these rules apply at take off, approach and landing. Note also the location and service differences (italicised).

---

[3] CARS 91.06.12.
[4] AIP ENR 2.2–1. ICAO Annex 14 6.3.10 mentions 10 000 m (10 km), equivalent to 5.399 NM. This can also be inferred from CARS 91.06.5 (b).
[5] CARS 91.06.12 (1) (a) and (b).
[6] CARS 91.06.18.

> **Operating rules of the air *on or in the vicinity* of an aerodrome in uncontrolled airspace**[7]
>
> - Make all turns to the left when approaching for a landing and after taking off, unless otherwise instructed by an ATSU, or unless a right hand circuit is in force.
>
>   Warning: after taking off, do not climb out and turn right just because it is quicker.
>
>   Note: A helicopter may, 'with due regard to other factors and when it is in the interest of safety', execute a circuit to the opposite side.
>
> - 'Land and take off, as far as practicable, into the wind unless safety, the runway configuration or air traffic considerations dictate that a different direction is preferable, or unless otherwise instructed by an ATSU'.
>
> - Fly across the aerodrome or its environs[8] at a height of not less than [translation: at least] 2 000 feet above the level of such aerodrome.
>
> Note: If circumstances require that you fly at a height of less than [translation: below] 2 000 feet above the level of the aerodrome, you must conform with the traffic pattern at such aerodrome. Also, some aerodromes have specified altitudes.

> **Operating rules of the air *within* an aerodrome traffic zone *with a tower in operation*** [9]
>
> - You must 'maintain a continuous radio watch on the frequency of the aerodrome *control tower* responsible for providing aerodrome control service at the aerodrome'.
>
> - You must 'establish two-way radio communication as necessary for aerodrome control purposes and obtain such clearances for your movements as necessary for the protection of aerodrome traffic'.
>
> Note: In short, you listen carefully to what is on the radio (from the tower and other traffic), you establish contact with the tower, and you do as told by the tower.
>
> - And be on the watch out for visual signals (lights, flares, markings on the ground).

> **Operating rules of the air *within* an aerodrome traffic zone *with a flight information service*** [10]
>
> - You must 'maintain a continuous radio watch on the frequency of the aerodrome *flight information service* unit responsible for providing aerodrome flight information service at the aerodrome'.

---

[7] CARS 91.06.12 (1) (c), (d), (e).
[8] A French word meaning 'around here': the circuit area and over the airfield.
[9] CARS 91.06.12 (2) (a) and (b).
[10] CARS 91.06.12 (3).

> - You must 'establish two-way radio communication as necessary for aerodrome flight information service purposes . . .
> - . . . and obtain information in respect of *the surface wind, runway in use and altimeter setting and in respect of aerodrome traffic* on the manoeuvring area and in the aerodrome traffic zone'.
> - And watch out for visual signals either displayed or sent by the information service.

Remember here that the rules of the air exist for collision avoidance. Observing traffic, observing patterns, observing what tower or approach say, observing signals, taking note of a FIS human interface information or an ATIS recorded information is only one part of collision avoidance.

Now that you have observed what is happening, what do you do if another aircraft is not far from your aircraft? This is the second aspect of collision avoidance.

8.2 COLLISION AVOIDANCE: RIGHT OF WAY[11]

Aircraft rarely collide head-on (5% of reported cases), but mostly in overtaking (82%) with 35% of this last figure being from a 0° to 10° angle, in short, from behind.[12]

(Students, note! These are standard questions up to CPL.)

> **General rules about right of way in flight *between aircraft in the same category***
> - An aircraft in flight must give way to another aircraft taking off or about to land or landing, that is, the other aircraft has right of way.[13]
> - If you have right of way in flight you must maintain heading and speed, but can take action to avert collision, including avoidance manoeuvres. If you notice (listening on the radio for instance) that another aircraft is compelled to land, give way.[14]
> - If you are **approaching head-on**, or nearly so, another aircraft, each must change ('alter') heading to its right.[15]
> - If you are **converging** with another aircraft at approximately the same level (altitude) and if you have the other aircraft on your right, you must give way (right is right!), except in specific cases (see the picture on pages 163 and 164).[16]

---

[11] CARS 91.06.7, spelt right-of-way or right of way; also ICAO, Annex 2.
[12] FAA *How to Avoid a Mid Air Collision* document P-8740–51.
[13] CARS 91.06.7 (6).
[14] CARS 91.06.7 (9).
[15] CARS 91.06.7 (3).
[16] CARS 91.06.7 (4).

162 Air Law

- If you are being **overtaken**, you have right of way! The overtaking aircraft, whether climbing, descending or in horizontal flight, must keep out of your way (the overtaken aircraft), by changing its heading to the right (picture below). (If the aircraft overtaking you changes, heading to the left, there is a risk of collision.) In short: the overtaken aircraft should stay on course (except to take action to avert collision—first rule above—which makes sense).

Note 1: In a **right-hand circuit** the overtaking aircraft must change heading to the left (picture the situation: if going right, the overtaking will risk collision with the overtaken).

Note 2: How do you **define 'overtaking'**? The answer is somewhat convoluted: 'an overtaking aircraft is an aircraft which approaches another aircraft from the rear on a line forming an angle of less than 70 degrees with the plane of symmetry of the latter aircraft, and will therefore be in such position with reference to the other aircraft, that by night it should be unable to see either of the other aircraft's wingtip navigation lights'.[17] See the picture below.

- A general reminder: if you are compelled, due to this regulation, 'to keep out of the way of another aircraft', you must 'avoid passing over or under the other aircraft, or crossing ahead of such aircraft, unless passing well clear, taking into account the effects of wake turbulence'.[18]

- In an overtaking situation if there is a 'subsequent' change in the relative positions of your aircraft and the other, it is the duty of the overtaking pilot to apply the rules until entirely past and clear of you, the overtaken one. (Why is this? Because you have the right of way.) In plain language: if you do the overtaking, watch out for any change in the operation of the overtaken aircraft, and adapt to it.

Approaching head-on (each alters to its own right)

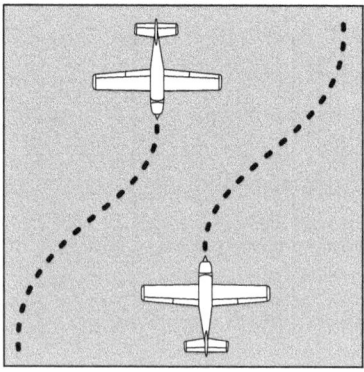

---

[17] CARS 91.06.7 (10).
[18] CARS 91.06.7 (2).

Chapter 8: Flying away, en route! 163

Converging aircraft at same altitude and category. An aircraft that has another aircraft on its right gives way to it **('on the right, in the right')**.

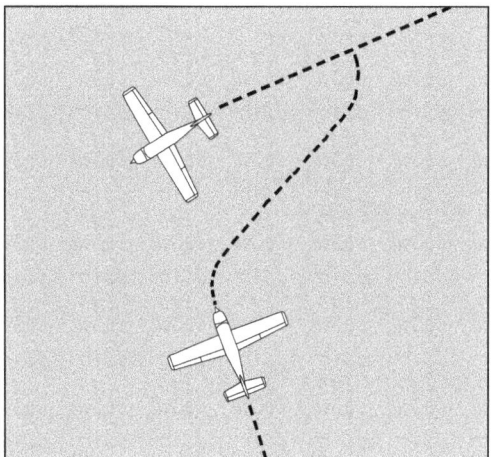

Overtaking in a left hand circuit and visualisation of what '70° angle' means (see note 2 above, in boxed text).

The overtaking aircraft is pictured changing course to its right.[19] In a right hand circuit the overtaking aircraft will alter to its left.

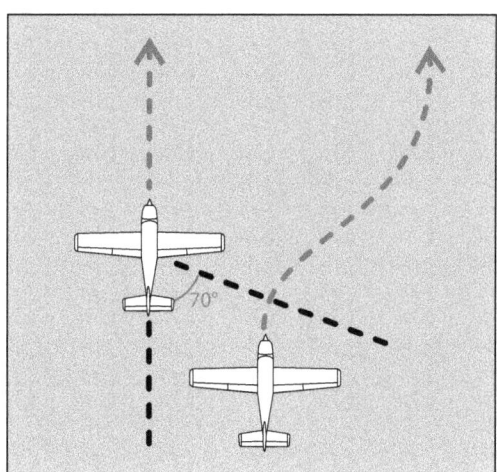

---

[19] CARS 91.06.7 (5).

164 Air Law

And now for a *frequent exam question* on situations you are likely to encounter while operating your aircraft:

> **Special rules applying to *converging* aircraft in different categories or in special operations**[20]
> - Power-driven, heavier-than-air aircraft (you!) give way to airships, gliders and balloons.
> - Airships shall give way to gliders and balloons.
> - Gliders shall give way to balloons.
> - Power-driven aircraft (you!) give way to aircraft that are—
>   – seen to be towing other aircraft (glider tow) or objects (banner),
>   – carrying an underslung load or are engaged in winching operations (helicopters),
>   – being towed (glider) or tethered (balloon).
>
> Note that it refers only to **converging**. You will note that balloons are at the top of the pecking order: they give right of way to no one, which is only fair since they started the great history of aviation.
>
> The picture below is somewhat misleading, as priority is not about altitude, as shown, but about two aircraft from a different category, or one engaged in a special operation, on a converging course.
>
> On approach for landing, power-driven, heavier-then-air aircraft give way to gliders.[21]

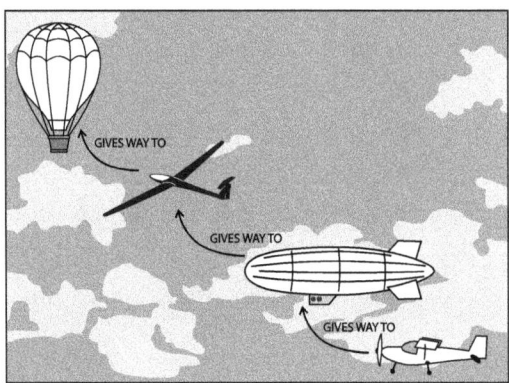

Note: This picture illustrates aircraft converging and does not illustrate the case of aircraft towing, carrying underslung loads, winching or being towed or tethered. Neither does it feature a RPA (drone).

---

[20] CARS 91.06.7 (4).

[21] CARS 91.06.7 (7) (b). As this is stipulated in the sub-regulation dealing with priority **at landing**, it is a way for the regulator to remind pilots that whether your aircraft is higher or lower than a glider, the glider goes first – which is an exception to the general rule of this sub-regulation, whereby an aircraft at lower level has right of way – and this applies only to heavier-than-air. In short: See a glider? Keep away. Let it land first.

8.3 COLLISION AVOIDANCE: FLYING UNDER PRESSURE AND FLIGHT LEVELS

Flying under pressure? Not a good idea (refer to I'M SAFE), but, scientifically speaking, pilots often fly under pressure, air pressure that is.

And here we meet a third aspect of collision avoidance: **setting your altimeter**—which relates directly to air pressure; that is ensuring that from a given altitude up all aircraft are operating at the standard pressure of 1013.2 hPa and at set flight levels. *Students, note! You will get questions on this!*

We are not dealing here with how to set an altimeter,[22] but where and when you have to attend to it: 'where' and 'when' because, remember, you are now aloft, flying, crossing the skies forwards and upwards and downwards, and rules apply to avoid collisions.

The **basic rule** is that you cannot fly if your aircraft (A, H) does not have 'a sensitive pressure altimeter with a subscale setting, calibrated in hectopascal, adjustable for any barometric pressure setting likely to be encountered during flight'. Here is an example set to Standard Setting:[23]

Note: 'adjustable for barometric pressure ... during flight'. This is what we are talking about.[24] (Under IFR: larger aeroplanes, and helicopters in commercial air transport, need two independent ones, as at least one will be set on QNH before take off).[25]

But what are we really talking about? We are talking about understanding, and applying, **altimeter settings and transition altitude**.[26]

---

[22] If you want to know the technical details regarding the testing of an altimeter, and therefore about what can go wrong with it, refer to CATS 43.02.9 (2) (b) (ii), where you will learn about scale error, hysteresis (not hysterics!) or lagging, friction, case leak and barometric scale error. Fascinating stuff.

[23] Image source: www.avionics.co.nz.

[24] CARS 910.4.4 (c).

[25] CARS 91.04.5 (c), 127.05.2 (1) (c) and AIP ENR 1.7–5.1.

[26] AIP ENR 1.7–1 and ICAO Doc 4444 *PANS-ATM, or Procedures for Navigation Services—Air Traffic Management.*

8.3.1 Altimeter setting, transition altitude and level

Do not be confused about transition **altitude** *and transition* **level:** *just remember the alpha order:* **A***ltitude comes before* **L***evel. And the transition layer is what lies ('lay-er') between them—what else? (exam!).*

Climbing out

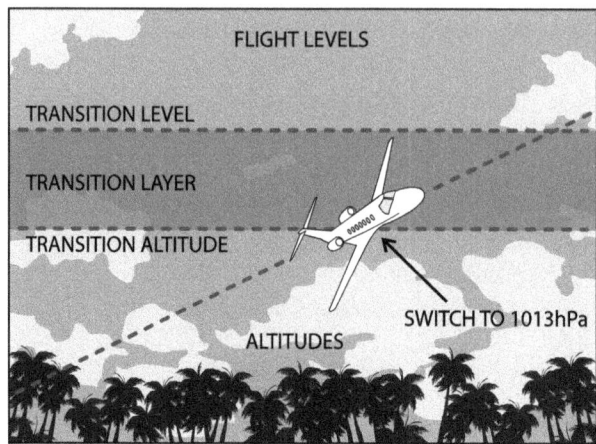

8.3.2 Altimeter setting scenarios

Let us imagine now that you have taken off at FARG (Rustenburg) for a cross-country to an airstrip called Krokodilnest. When you prepared your flight, you looked up in AIP GEN transition altitudes applicable in South Africa's airspace, and you found a table listing aerodromes (airports, if you prefer) with a declared transition altitude.

Indeed, aerodromes that are assigned a 25 NM radius within which specific altimetry for transition altitude applies are specifically listed in AIP GEN.[27] For instance, the transition altitude for Cape Town International Airport is 7 500 ft, Durban-King Shaka International Airport is 5 500 ft, and Johannesburg-O R Tambo International Airport is 8 000 ft.[28]

And don't get distracted by the word 'aerodrome'. It is generic for airports as well as unlicensed airfields. Like it or not, O R Tambo is an aerodrome.[29]

---

[27] AIP ENR 1.7–2, 3 for a full updated list.
[28] At time of publication.
[29] Civil Aviation Act of 2009, chapter 1, section 1(1). The word 'drome' comes from Ancient Greek 'dromos', meaning a race track which is preserved too in the word 'runway'.

Chapter 8: Flying away, en route! 167

Now let us see how this applies to your possible cross-country.

Transition altitude scenario

Looking at your chart and looking up the table in AIP ENR 1.7–2,3 you noted that FARG (elevation 3 700 ft) falls within a 25 NM radius of FAPN (Pilanesberg International). If you were staying in the vicinity of FARG, or were going en route below 1 500 ft AGL you would use the local QNH, or QFE, and not bother with what follows.

But you are leaving for a cross-country, so you are going to climb en route. Your track is magnetic east. In this case, this is what you have to do:

- You set the subscale of your altimeter to the local QNH before take-off,[30] for take-off and climb.
- You took off at 3 700 ft (FARG), and you are now passing 1 500 ft AGL (altitude 5 200 ft). You are on local QNH. But as you reach 7 400 ft (FAPN transition altitude) you change the subscale from local QNH to standard 1013.2 hPa. You are on FL.[31]

Why? Two reasons for it:

➤ First, having traced your track on a chart and checked in AIP ENR you know that where you are, at FARG, falls within a 25 NM radius of Pilanesberg International FAPN which has a listed transition altitude of 7400 ft.[32]

➤ Second, why 25 NM? The rule is that an aircraft departing from any airfield within a 25 NM radius of a given aerodrome or this reference aerodrome with a listed transition altitude (AIP ENR 1.7–2) must use the transition altitude specified for that aerodrome.[33] And FARG lies within the radius of FAPN—you know it because you have prepared your nav and have measured it on your chart.

In VMC, flights from or to points beyond 25 nm from a listed aerodrome use 2 000 ft as transition altitude.[34]

---

[30] AIP ENR 1.7–5.1 (c).

[31] AIP ENR 1.7–1 To quote: '**Flights required to comply with Altimeter setting procedures**. These altimeter setting procedures shall be observed by all aircraft operating in level flight at or above 1 500 feet above the ground or water irrespective of the weather conditions and irrespective of whether the flight is operating under VFR or IFR flight plan.' See also D Lempp, *Pilot's Radio Handbook*, chapter 4.

[32] AIP ENR 1.7–3 (c).

[33] AIP ENR 1.7–3 (c).

[34] AIP ENR 1.7–3 (d)

- You are now at FL75.[35] You no longer fly on altitude but on flight level. You are a grown up.
- But you have to climb to FL95, as per flight plan and as authorised by Approach.
  ➤ Why FL95? Because you are **flying east** (M) and the semi-circular rule applies, unless your ATSU instructs you differently—they have a clear picture of traffic vertical separation and may have to deal, for instance, with an emergency. What is the semi-circular rule? See section 8.4.

'In the bundu' scenario

If you take off (or land) somewhere in the bundu, **VMC**, or strictly speaking, **outside from any of those specified 25 NM aerodrome radiuses or these aerodromes themselves**,

➤ On climbing, the uniform transition altitude is 2 000 ft AGL, at which point you change from local QNH to standard 1013.2 hPa, and now you no longer fly ALT but you fly FL.[36]

➤ On descending, the uniform transition level is 3 000 ft AGL.[37]

And (it is a big 'and') remember that the **semi-circular rule** will apply for en route (see section 8.4 below).

If this happens to be in or close to a general Flying Training Area, you may decide to stay on local QNH as training aircraft usually do not fly FL, until you think it is safe to switch to standard and FL. If you do so you would have applied airmanship and placed safety above a strict application of the law. And this is fine indeed.

If in IMC:

- On departure or arrival outside a 25 NM area: The 'lowest safe cruising altitude' must be observed as 'transition altitude' *(exam!)*.[38]
- On intention to land outside a 25 NM area: 'Observe flight level 500 feet above the lowest safe altitude as the transition level.'[39]

---

[35] Note: In your flight plan do not write FL75, but F075.

[36] AIP ENR 1.7–3 note d. To quote : 'In VMC, flights departing from or arriving at points beyond 25 nautical miles from any of the aerodromes tabled above, shall observe a height of 2 000 feet above the ground or water as the transition **altitude**'.

[37] AIP ENR 1.7–4 note d. To quote: 'In VMC, flights intending to land at points beyond 25 nautical miles from any of the aerodromes, listed in paragraph 3 (b) [this is the list of 25 NM radius aerodromes], shall observe a height of 3 000 feet above the ground or water as the transition **level**'.

[38] AIP ENR 1.7–3 note e.

[39] AIP ENR 1.7–3 note e.

Do you have to request permission from, or inform, the ATC when you reset your altimeter? No, you do not.[40]

In sum:

- Above 1500 ft AGL you will fly an altitude or height, and climbing through the transition altitude of 2000 ft on a cross-country flight, operating 'in level flight' above ground or water, 'irrespective of weather conditions and irrespective of whether you are operating on a VFR or IFR flight plan' you operate at FL after changing your altimeter subscale to 1013.2 hPa.[41]
- If you prefer to operate VMC below 1500 ft, even on a cross-country, you are allowed to choose operating on local QNH (or QFE) and at any altitude (or height) 'irrespective of the aircraft's heading'[42]—which means: without respecting the semi-circular rule. You will fly on altitude.
- Apply the nearest 25 NM aerodrome transition altitude. If in the bundu, change to FL when in VMC you reach 2000 ft AGL or use 'lowest safe' in IMC.

This leads us to the other collision avoidance regulation: the semi-circular rule.

8.4 COLLISION AVOIDANCE: SEMI-CIRCULAR RULE, FLIGHT LEVELS[43]

Take note, there are many exam questions on this topic up to CPL!

Here is the governing regulation:[44]

- (1) Unless otherwise directed by an ATSU, the PIC of an aircraft in level flight shall fly at an altitude or flight level, as appropriate, selected according to magnetic track from the table as prescribed in Document SA-CATS 91. [See the graphic and table below.]
- (2) Aircraft flown in accordance with VFR at a height of less than 1 500 ft above the surface, shall not be required to comply with the provisions of sub-regulation (1), unless otherwise directed by an ATSU.
- (3) A flight conducted from flight level 200 and above, shall be flown in compliance with IFR'.

---

[40] AIP ENR 1.7–5.1 (Note).
[41] AIP ENR 1.7–1.1.
[42] AIP ENR 1.7–1.2.
[43] CARS and CATS 91.06.33. With tables.
[44] CARS 91.06.33.

8.4.1 Semi-circular rule and magnetic track[45]

- On a cruise the flyable skies are divided into two halves: 000° to 179° and 180° to 359°.
- These two halves are designed to avoid aircraft colliding with one another by imposing a vertical separation of **at least 500 ft** between IFR and VFR flights up to FL200, and of 1000 ft above that level (IFR flights airspace, see below). Note: 'at least'!
- Each half is assigned altitude or flight level according to your track in magnetic degrees:
  - ➢ From 000° to 179°, east, VFR starts at FL15, ends at FL195 (odd number + 500), IFR starts at FL30, up to FL490 etc.
    IFR starts at FL30, up to FL 490 and above
  - ➢ From 180° to 359°, west, VFR starts at FL25, ends at FL185 (even number +500) IFR at FL20, up to FL510 etc.

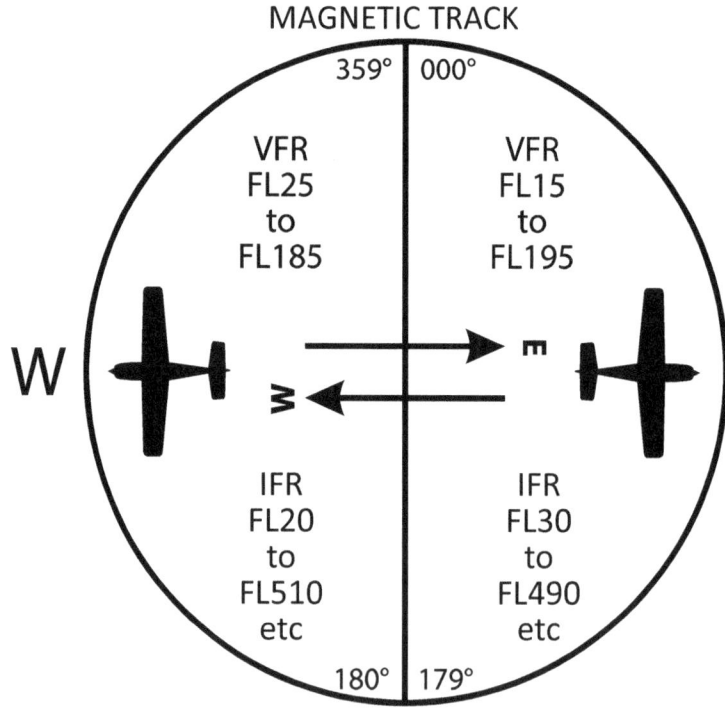

---

[45] AIP ENR 1.7–7 and CATS 91.06.33 (1).

The graphic above is a visual representation of the Magnetic Track table that follows.

MAGNETIC TRACK			
Flight Level			
From 000° to 179°		From 180° to 359°	
IFR	VFR	IFR	VFR
	15	20	25
30	35	40	45
50	55	60	65
70	75	80	85
90	95	100	105
110	115	120	125
130	135	140	145
150	155	160	165
170	175	180	185
190	195	200	
210		220	
230		240	
250		260	
270		280	
290		300	
310		320	
330		340	
350		360	
370		380	
390		400	
410		430	
450		470	
490 etc.		510 etc.	

To better understand the illustration and table, from FL290, see the next section.

8.4.2 About operations with RVSM, FL290–FL410

Although it is unlikely to be of concern to a private pilot (*and not for the PPL exam*), unless you fly a high performance aircraft, take note of the implications of RVSM on FL. RVSM denotes 'the vertical separation of aircraft by 1000 ft above Flight Level (FL) 290'.[46] 'Reduced' refers to the ICAO-aligned reduction from a previous 2000 ft separation.

---

[46] AIP ENR 1.8–22 and 23. See also D Lempp, *Pilot's Radio Handbook*, chapter 5.

- Above FL290 only state-approved RVSM aircraft are allowed to operate in FAJA, FACA and FAJO, these being the South African Area of Responsibility as established by ICAO (by state the regulator means the South African state; it does not refer to aircraft flown with state officials on board). Non-RVSM state aircraft (military police, customs) are permitted, with a 2000 ft vertical separation.
- FL420 is no longer a valid FL. The next available is FL430.
- If a 2000 ft separation is applied, appropriate RVSM FLs will also apply.
- Non-RVSM aircraft are permitted above FL410 if they are able to operate at that level. Clearance is needed and climb and descent are without interruption. A flight plan is compulsory.
- Non-RVSM flights are permanently excluded between FL290 and FL410 (except military police, customs), and must plan for operations at FL280 or below, alternatively above FL410.
- And why all this? Because these are operations in High Level Airspace (FL290 to FL410), which obliges operators to equip aircraft with two independent Long Range Navigation Systems (LRNS). In the same band (FL290 to FL 410) aircraft must be certified airworthy for RVSM, which implies two independent altitude measurement systems, an altitude altering system, an automatic altitude control system, a secondary surveillance radar transponder that can be connected to the altitude measurement system; and having provided training to the flight crew. RVSM approval is noted on a flight plan at item 10 'W'.

8.4.3 Flight level and magnetic track

A *common but understandable mistake of SPL trainees* is to think that the rule, hence the FL applies to where you are. No! **The rule applies to the direction in which you are flying, that is your magnetic track (MT).**

If your MT is 270, you are going west toward the 180° to 359° half, so you have to fly VFR FL25, 45, 65, etc (bearing in mind that you will decide on FL depending upon airspace and en route safe altitude—see 8.5—or as otherwise instructed by an ATSU) *(exam!)*.

Note these phraseology quirks in transmission of numbers[47]
FL180 is said 'one eight zero' but FL200 is said 'two hundred'
ALT800 is said 'eight hundred', ALT3400 'three thousand four hundred' but ALT12000 is said 'one two thousand' ('th' pronounced 't')
HDG100 degrees is said 'one zero zero', and 80 degrees 'zero eight zero'
QNH1010 is said 'one zero one zero', 1000 is said 'one thousand'

---

[47] AIC 005/2018.

And to understand how this works in real life you will notice that:

- For 'operations'[48] up to FL195/185 VFR and FL190/FL200 IFR the semi-circular rule ensures a vertical separation of 500 ft between VFR and IFR aircraft (FL30 IFR is between FL25 VFR and FL35 VFR).
- VFR level stops at FL195. Why? Because from FL200, you must fly IFR, not VFR.[49]
- From FL210 IFR (MT east) to FL280 IFR (MT west) (no VFR left at that level), separation is 1000 ft (FL 230 on an easterly MT is in between FL220 and FL240 on a westerly MT). From FL290, RVSM airspace, 1000 ft separation

Why these differences in separation? It is . . . in the air.

As you go higher, the air becomes more and more rarefied. It no longer reflects the standard loss of 1 hPa per 30 ft going up, which your reliable Cessna barometric altimeter usually measures (baro-meter means 'pressure-measure; 'alti-meter', altitude-measure, 'thermo-meter', heat-measure, etc).

At higher altitudes (from FL210) the differences in pressure per 1000 ft are less significant, so the altimeter becomes less accurate, hence the necessity for larger separation to make up for the altimeter's approximations.[50]

In sum:
- In **uncontrolled air space** (imagine you do a low-flying cross-country, outside any controlled airspace) if you are at or above 1500 ft AGL, you apply the semi-circular rule, and you watch out for traffic.
- In **controlled airspace**, you apply the rule (in your flight plan, for instance) but be ready to obey different instructions from an ATSU.

8.5 COLLISION AVOIDANCE: AND THE GROUND BELOW?

Of course, you are flying above ground. This physics phenomenon has a name: it is called flying.

An aircraft that can fly below solid ground has yet to be invented. Basically: you don't want to collide with terrain. The law sees to it.

---

[48] In ICAO terminology your flight is an 'operation'.
[49] CARS 91.06.24.
[50] See D Lempp *Pilot's Radio Handbook* 54.

So, imagine that you are en route for Krokodilnest, that you are safely separated vertically from various aircraft, and are respecting rules of right of way vis à vis more aircraft, but you also have to mind the ground below—be safely separated from the ground.

However, to be at a 'safe altitude' from the ground has different meanings. The terminology can be confusing to a SPL trainee and, unless a private pilot progresses to advanced licences, and is instrument rated, some of the notions below are just for noting.

8.5.1 General regulation

A general regulation designed to cover all scenarios is called 'Minimum flight altitudes'.

Minimum flight altitudes[51]

(1) No pilot shall operate an aircraft at altitudes below—

  (a) altitudes, established by the owner or operator, which provide the required terrain clearance, taking into account the operating limitations referred to in Subpart 8; and

  (b) the minimum altitudes referred to in Subpart 6;

except when necessary for take-off and landing.

(2) The method of establishing minimum flight altitudes referred to in sub-regulation (1) (a) is prescribed in Document SA-CATS 91.

(3) Where the minimum flight altitudes established by the appropriate authority of a foreign State are higher than the minimum flight altitudes prescribed in this regulation, the minimum flight altitudes established by such appropriate authority shall apply in respect of a South African registered aircraft flying in the airspace of the foreign State concerned.

Let us dissect the regulation to understand if or how it is important to a SPL or PPL VFR pilot:

> Sub-regulation (1) (a) refers to Subpart 8.

What is Subpart 8?

It deals with performance operating limitations for each class of aeroplane (A, B, C, D) or helicopter (1, 2, 3) (see page 98), which are determined first by regulations, and second by what the pilot needs to do to have the aircraft perform legally. So, although, or because you cannot influence the legal limitations, you can and must adapt your aircraft by knowing your AFM and your aircraft performance specifications, by observing mass and balance.

---

[51] CARS 91.07.2.

➢ Sub-regulation (1) (b) refers bluntly to Subpart 6.

What is Subpart 6?

It deals with Rules of the Air, among which are the minima (see pages 111–114, 117–121),[52] and instrument flight rules,[53] but also a host of regulations dealing with safe altitudes in a variety of situations, such as following line features (see page 178), operating in the vicinity of an aerodrome (see page 213), proximity and formation flights (see page xxx), the semi-circular rule, altimetry and flight levels (see page 169), and the important en route safe altitude procedure (see page 158). All those (except IFR) are of direct concern to SPL and PPL pilots.

➢ Sub-regulation 3 is a legal disclaimer that is self-evident: you obey the minima rules of the country where you fly even though you fly an aircraft registered in South Africa.

➢ Sub-regulation (2) cross-references a brief TS about Minimum Off-Route Altitude (MORA), which is a case of minimum flight altitude (see 8.5.3 below).[54]

8.5.2 En-route safe altitude, minimum safe altitude

This one is of particular interest to VFR pilots, SPL and PPL.

As you traced your track, or as you look now, in flight, at your chart, circled in red, on either side of your track and within a 5 NM distance are mountains or obstacles from which you must keep a safe distance. You will achieve safe separation from the highest obstacle by adding 1 000 ft or 2 000 ft to your altitude, calculated from the highest obstacle on either side of your track and depending upon the height of it, <or> 5 000 ft MSL (again, 5 NM each side, and make sure you are not measuring distances on a 1:1 000 000 chart with a 1:500 000 ruler . . . it happens). This is called en-route safe altitude and is of crucial importance to VFR flying *(exam!)*.

Two remarks:
- Think wind and turbulence. The regulation says 'at least 1 000 ft or 2 000 ft'. As always safety is the main concern. Bear in mind for instance that, having planned for adjusting your altitude, a downdraft might push you down as you try to clear a peak top? Or a wave might push you fast against a cliff? These possibilities can be anticipated by checking the weather en route. In that case, rather apply a higher quantum instead of sticking to 1 000 ft or 2 000 ft minima.
- Think flight level. You are flying VFR east at FL075. There is a mountain top en route culminating at 6 700 ft. The terrain is such that you have no choice but

---

[52] In Division Two of Subpart 6 Visual Flight Rules.
[53] In Division Three of Subpart 6.
[54] CATS 91.07.2 and AIP GEN 3.3–3 and 4.

to track near the mountain. Let us assume you fly at 7 500 ft, east. You add 6 700+2 000 (the clearance quantum). You should now fly at 8 700 ft. But you are flying east, and flying according to the semi-circular rule. There is no FL87 (either east or west for that matter). You must now climb to the next available level in an easterly direction: FL95. Unless being controlled, ATSU orders you otherwise. You will burn fuel and add time. Which means: plan that segment of your cross-country flight well.

Sometimes this en route safe altitude is referred to casually as MSA, **'minimum safe altitude'**. The acronym can lead to a confusion with what is properly called 'minimum sector altitude', which is the next point.

8.5.3 Minimum Sector Altitude, Minimum En-route Altitude, Minimum Off-route Altitude[55]

This section is for **advanced** pilots.[56]

Minimum Sector Altitude (MSA)

This is **advanced** training and flying information. MSA is defined as 'the lowest altitude which may be used which will provide a minimum clearance of 1 500 ft (457.2 m) above all objects located in an area contained within a sector of a circle of 25 NM (46 km) radius centred on a radio aid to navigation significant point, the Aerodrome Reference Point (ARP) or the Heliport Reference Point (HRP)'.[57]

Minimum En-route Altitude (MEA)

Again, this is relevant to **advanced** training and flying. The minimum en-route altitude (MEA) is the minimum altitude that provides adequate reception of navigational aids and ATS communications, in compliance with airspace regulations and traffic rules, while providing obstacle clearance—all that for each segment of a flight en-route.[58]

Minimum Off-Route Altitude (MORA)[59]

Using current Operational Navigation Charts (ONC) and World Aeronautical Charts (WAC) a computation is made to determine—

1) an area extending 10 NM on both sides of a route centreline and including a 10 NM radius beyond the radio fix or reporting point, or mileage break that defines this segment of the route mentioned;

---

[55] Words capitalised because of their acronyms.
[56] See D Lempp *Pilot's Radio Handbook* 149–168 for a clear and detailed explanation of IFR procedures without which the advanced notions described in 8.5.2 will not make sense.
[57] AIP ENR 1.8–4.
[58] ICAO, Doc 8168 *Procedures for Air Navigation Services (PANS-OPS)*.
[59] CATS 91.07.2.

Chapter 8: Flying away, en route! 177

2) in order to clear all terrain and man-made obstacles by 1 000 ft in areas where the highest terrain elevation or obstacles are up to 5 000 ft; while a clearance of 2 000 ft is provided above all terrain or obstacles that are 5 001 ft and above.

There are two types of MORAs, route and grid. But unless you avail yourself of IFR charts you will not have access to that information on your VFR aeronautical chart. MORA is therefore relevant only to IFR flights on a non-ATS or random route in order to clear terrain. This is how CATS illustrate it:

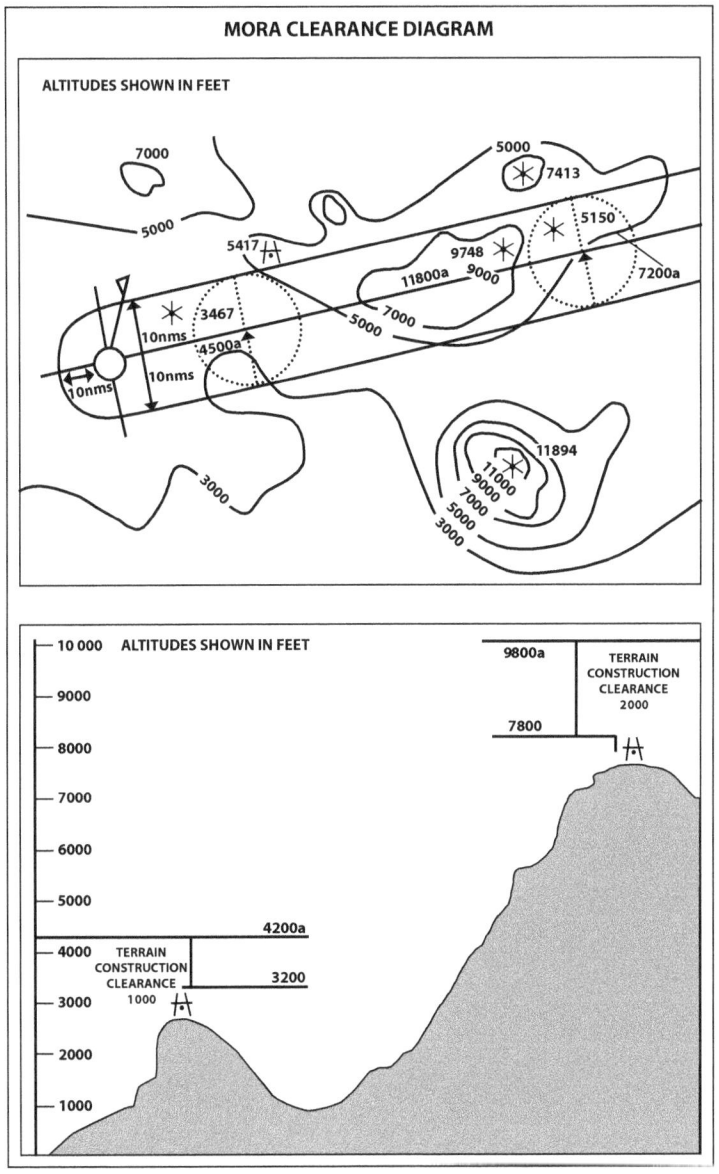

Page 193 – Minimum flight altitude

8.5.4 Minimum heights[60]

This regulation is of concern to **IFR flights, or in IMC, or VFR night flights**. This regulation is identical to the en-route safe altitude regulation (see page 244).

- fly 'at a height of at least 1 000 ft above the highest terrain or obstacle where the height of such terrain or obstacle **does not exceed 5 000 ft above sea level** within 5 NM of the aircraft in flight';

or

- fly 'at a height of at least 2 000 ft above the highest terrain or obstacle located within 5 NM of the aircraft in flight where the height of **such terrain or obstacle exceeds 5 000 ft above sea level**'.

And there is a proviso: 'Provided that within areas determined by the Director the minimum height may be reduced to 1 000 ft above the highest terrain or obstacle located within 5 NM of the aircraft in flight, and the aircraft is flown in accordance with such procedures as the Director may determine'. You should find this information in AIP.

(Students, note: sections that follow are exam questions.)

8.5.5 Line features

To find your way while flying VFR often consists of looking for visual references on the ground (that correlate with your chart), that is, to look for and identify areas, points or line features on your chart.

An aeronautical chart contains ground 'line features'—a power line, a road, a railway track, a canal, a coastline or any other (could be a long ridge of inland sand), a levee. If unsure, brush up on your **aeronautical chart symbols** that are at the bottom of any chart—some pilots cut it off to make the chart handier, but is this safer? This remains to be seen. At any rate, when you prepare a nav, make sure you understand the symbols along the way.[61]

Here are a few examples:[62]

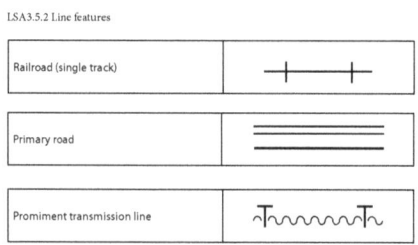

LSA3.5.2 Line features

---

[60] CARS 91.06.32 (3).
[61] Many symbols, but not all cartographic ones, are found in AIP GEN.
[62] AIP GEN 2.3–8 and 11.

Flying along line features has rules

If you decide to follow any of those (which may help you find your way home) by flying **at or below 1 500 ft and staying within 1 NM of the line feature, then you must stay on the right hand side of the line** (which means that flying from Durban to Margate along the coast, you will not be able to fly low and close over the Sardine Run because you will be overland). By implication you will have the line feature on your left, pilot side where you can see it—thus, ensuring separation and collision avoidance, and that is probably the reason for this regulation: that you can see the line feature. Of course an ATSU can direct you otherwise.[63]

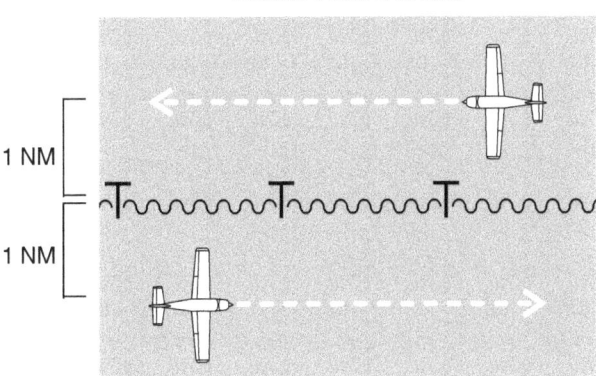

8.5.6 Minimum height over people

Flying over ground also means flying over people, as they tend to inhabit land. So over a 'congested' area (usually marked in yellow on your aeronautical chart, with a neat black contour; but a harbour full of boats with revellers on them would apply) or an open air assembly of people (and this can include an assembly on water), you must fly at least 1 000 ft above the highest obstacle (a tall building for instance) and maintain a clear radius of 2 000 ft from your aircraft.[64] This does not apply if you are taking off or landing, or have received 'prior written approval' from SACAA.

This sub-regulation is adapted in two cases:
- You can fly over sparsely populated land or water or loose groups of people at 500 ft, but not lower than that, and provided the flight is 'without hazard or nuisance to persons or property' and you ensure it will be safe in case of engine failure.[65]

---

[63] CARS 91.06.8.
[64] CARS 91.06.32 (a).
[65] CARS 91.06.32 (b).

180   *Air Law*

– You can circle over or do repeated overflights over an open air assembly but only at or above 3 000 ft ASFC (above surface—terrain or water).[66]

8.5.7 National Parks (NP) and World Heritage Sites

You must have a clearance of at least 2 500 ft above the highest point, which may result in your aircraft flying into controlled airspace, so watch out. On the SACAA website you will find a schedule by name (NP+serial number) with the highest point (ft), the NEMPAA[67] clearance (ft) and the MNM ALT (ft).

For instance, if you fly from Agulhas in a north-westerly direction, you will encounter the Agulhas National Park, highest point 1 020 ft, clearance 2 500 ft, minimum altitude 3 520 ft. That will make your top of descent to the nearby Oystercatcher airstrip a bit of a challenge if you want to fly straight down.

The point is still hotly debated among pilots: whether the 1978 National Parks Act that forbade flying below 500 m (metres, not feet) over a so-called proclaimed ('gazetted' or officially published by government) **reserve** (unless for take-off, landing, and being an authorised employee or officer) applies. No, the 1978 Act does not apply. Do not look for a regulation in CARS or CATS either. There is none.

But the **Protected Areas Act of 2003**[68] makes no distinction regarding what exists in reserves, protected areas and special areas, be they stones, animals (including high sounding 'game'), people, trees, or rivers—whether they contain fynbos or giraffes or catfish is immaterial. So-called (official) 'game reserves' fall under the Act mentioned. What matters to the law is 'protection'. And a plane flying, landing, taking off, hovering, or circling over these areas may infringe upon such protection.

In sum: a generic 2 500 ft rule applies. Heavy fines can be imposed for violation. If in doubt, check the list of areas on the SACAA website for minimum altitude and highest point. You can download charts from the site as well.[69]

Note: In AIP ENR 5.5.27 two Game Reserve areas (Entabeni, Mabula) are mentioned but they refer to Hot Air Ballooning areas, while two more in AIP GEN 2.4–5 and 11 refer to airfield location indicators (FATW for Tswalu).

8.6 COLLISION AVOIDANCE: WHAT ABOUT SPEED?

Speed is a major collision factor: an aircraft flying at 250 knots will catch up quickly with one puttering along at 90 knots—do the maths!

---

[66] CARS 91.06.32 (c).
[67] Acronym for National Environmental Management Protected Areas.
[68] National Environmental Management: Protected Areas Act 57 of 2003, section 47.
[69] SACAA website: Information for the Industry > Aeronautical Information > VFR Charts > Flight Restrictions Over National Parks and World Heritage Sites.

The law is clear regarding speed limits,[70] and *students please note, this is standard exam material*:

Speed limits
- **in uncontrolled airspace and below FL100:**
  - ➣ 250 KIAS maximum (SACAA Director can authorise more).
- **in a CTR or ATZ:**
  - ➣ 160 KIAS maximum reciprocating engine (you, probably)
  - ➣ 200 KIAS maximum turbine-powered aircraft (your rich friend) (ATSU can authorise or request more)
- **in Cape Town and Johannesburg SRA (Special Rules Area):**
  - ➣ maximum 180 KIAS[71]
- Adhere to **minimum safe IAS** if, for a particular flight, it is greater than those mentioned above.

8.7 COLLISION AVOIDANCE: FUN STUFF YOU CAN OR CANNOT DO

Exam question!
- You **cannot drop objects,** unless in an emergency, or with special permission from the SACAA Director, or unless it is 'fine sand or clean water used as ballast', or chemicals for 'spraying, dusting and cloud seeding'.[72]
- The reverse applies: **no picking up of objects** 'in flight' (unless granted permission by SACAA).[73]
- If you cannot drop and you cannot pick up, then **you cannot drag** either: as PIC you 'shall not permit anything to be towed by the aircraft' (except with prior approval from SACAA).[74]
- **Formation flight** is fun and is allowed provided that:[75]
  - ➣ the flight is not with passengers for commercial purposes (translation: private flight with passengers is fine);
  - ➣ the PIC of the other aircraft agree;
  - ➣ in controlled airspace formation flight can be approved by an ATSU if:
    - o all aircraft in formation operate as a single aircraft for navigation and position reporting (you do not want each aircraft to make calls, thus clogging and confusing communications); the flight leader will make the calls;

---

[70] CARS 91.06.9.
[71] AIP ENR 2.2–33 and 2.2–6.
[72] CARS 91.06.2.
[73] CARS 91.06.3.
[74] CARS 91.06.4.
[75] CARS 91.06.6.

182 Air Law

- o the flight leader is, together with the other PICs, responsible for separation, with periods of transition for separation, joining up and breakaway;
- o aircraft(s) must maintain at most 1 km/0.5 NM laterally and 30 m/100 ft vertically from the flight leader.
➢ it is for display purposes, as authorised by SACAA.
• **Acrobatic flight** is better left to those who have mastered that art,[76] and acrobatic flights near your base are restricted (you can apply to SACAA for permission otherwise and there are exemptions as per AIC 18.45):[77]
  ➢ an acrobatic flight must not endanger traffic,
  ➢ the manoeuvre must be concluded and the aircraft brought on an even keel at a height of not less than 2 000 ft above the ground or water,
  ➢ the aircraft must not be flown within a 5 NM distance of an aerodrome reference point[78] of an aerodrome licensed and approved in terms of Part 139, unless at a height not less than 4 000 ft above ground level,
  ➢ the flight must not be in the vicinity of air traffic services routes,
  ➢ the flight must not be over any populous area or public gathering.

8.8 RULES FOR COLLISION AVOIDANCE: COMMUNICATE!

Other anti-collision features that one does not always think of as anti-collision features relate to communication, some recommended, some compulsory as communication depends upon flying in contact with an ATSU or not, or being controlled by an ATSU. [79] Communication rules are part of the rules of the air.[80]

In essence, if you say who you are, and where and how high you are, and what your next move is, and you listen to other pilots or talk to ATC, you are less likely to collide.

This is regardless of being identified and tracked by an ATC Secondary Surveillance Radar (SSR), with your **transponder**. A transponder minimises the need for personal radio communication between you and the controller.[81] But talk you must.

Remember: **your transponder is always set on 2000 in South Africa**, from the moment you do your What To Do Last check, **until such time as an ATSU assigns you your own** four-digit squawk code.

---

[76] And hold an Aerobatics Rating as per CARS 61 Subpart 27 (note that the word is, in that case, not acrobatic but aerobatics).

[77] CARS 91.07.30.

[78] As defined on page xxx.

[79] For examples of RT talk, refer to D Lempp's *Pilot's Radio Handbook*, or Dylan Kemlo *VFR Fixed Wing RT* (2006).

[80] CARS 91.06.15 to 17.

[81] See Lempp *Pilot's Radio Handbook* 124–5 for a neat explanation. In mode A, which is quite rare today, altitude is not transmitted.

Regulations concerning communication vary, depending on whether you are in uncontrolled airspace or not.

These notes are **reminders** of your training in radio telephony and navigation: they are not meant to replace that specific expertise. It is also worth checking AIC 005/2018, an updated, comprehensive circular about radio telephony procedures (and be on the alert for later changes).

Here is the governing regulation:[82]

> '(1) The PIC of an aircraft—
>
> *(a)* flying in controlled airspace;
>
> *(b)* flying in advisory airspace;
>
> or
>
> *(c)* on a flight for which **alerting action is being provided** [*you, if you requested it in your flight plan!*]
>
> shall [must] ensure that reports are made to the responsible ATSU, as soon as possible, **of the time and level of passing each compulsory reporting point, together with any other required information,** and he or she shall further ensure that position reports are similarly made in relation to additional reporting points, if so requested by the responsible air traffic service unit and that, in the absence of designated reporting points, position reports are made at the intervals specified by the responsible air traffic service unit or published by the Director in terms of Part 175 for that area.
>
> (2) Controlled flights providing position information to the appropriate ATSU via data link communications shall only provide voice position reports when requested'.

8.8.1 In uncontrolled and information airspace

The law describes **three possible situations** in which, as a private pilot engaged in in VFR general flying, you must obey regulations concerning communication.

> **In uncontrolled airspace *at or below 1 500 ft*, or Special Rules Areas or Flying Training Areas or the circuits at uncontrolled airfields: TIBA**
>
> - You must **'broadcast TIBA'** (Traffic Information Broadcast by Aircraft). TIBA allows you to communicate with other aircraft so that they can identify who you are, where you are, and where you are going. It allows you to obtain information from fellow pilots and also to relay information.

---

[82] CARS 91.06.15.

- You do so on the **appropriate frequency**; if there is none, then use the default 124.8 MHz. The default for General Flying Training Areas without a specific listed frequency is 124.4 MHz.
- When you are en route, you broadcast **every 10 minutes** if safe (do not do it if you are caught in a mountain wave; just wait), when crossing a significant feature, or when you encounter traffic.

Be quick and do not interrupt broadcasts.

In addition, still at or below 1 500 ft:

- If you are **outside the lateral limits** of Johannesburg, Port Elizabeth, East London, Hoedspruit SRAs (a list of all SRAs is found in AIP ENR 2.2) or outside the lateral limits of a promulgated/established General Flying Training Area, you must maintain a **listening watch** and **broadcast** regular **position reports** (TIBA) on default frequency **124.8 MHz**.
- If you are **within 5 NM of an aerodrome without an ATSU and without a dedicated frequency,** make **regular position reports** on **124.8 MHz** but not if the aerodrome is in a General Flying Training Area, in which case you will broadcast on the standard 124.4 MHz (unless those areas with their aerodromes have their own frequency, such as Parys or Welkom).[83]

Example of a simple TIBA broadcast in the TIPAN format

Traffic: name the location, either 'Traffic in the Paternoster area' (no airfield), or 'Bethlehem Traffic' (there is an airfield and within 5 NM);

Identify:[84] aircraft type and call sign, 'Mooney ZS-MOO';

Position: 15 NM north (known place) or overhead (known place);

Altitude: FL or ALT (and/or passing, climbing, descending . . .);

Next (your 'routing'): estimate (known place) at (time) or in (x) minutes.

---

[83] AIP ENR 2.2–50 and 51 for a list of these aerodromes.
[84] Usually 'I' stands for 'Information' but it is about **identifying** your aircraft hence '**I**dentify'. If you get an exam question, rather answer 'Information'.

And remember: to avoid clogging TIBA frequencies with chatter not essential to traffic information, use the air-to-air frequency: 123.45 MHz.

In uncontrolled, information airspace *above 1 500 ft*:

You contact the **Information** Service of that area on the correct frequency (Johannesburg Central 120.3). This **ATSU will not control you but will inform you** and other pilots of reported traffic and possibly other information.

If you are TIBA do not forget to make a call saying that you are going to switch to the relevant information station frequency.

Once you have established first contact ('Johannesburg Central, ZS-MOO, good day') and Information has acknowledged and given you the go-ahead, the format of your report (AIREP, see insert below) is nearly identical to a TIPAN report (drop 'Traffic' and 'ZS') but

P becomes a narrative report:
- you describe where you come from, or where airborne,
- where you are en route to,
- your current FL,
- as you are in all probability climbing, to what FL,
- your estimate at a given known point and estimate time there,
- your destination and ETA there.

Information will tell you if there is 'reported traffic' and can tell you to report at a given point en route such as 'report ready to descend' next position, which you must do. Information can also provide you with weather and with a local QNH at your arrival airfield.

Note: on first contact always give the full call sign, 'ZS-MAC'; then only the abbreviated call sign, 'MAC', but only if the controller has abbreviated it.

8.8.2 In controlled and advisory airspace

The law is complex yet precise. Key points are in bold. They are particularly important for reports en route. CARS provides a neat definition of an 'air-report':

'A report from an aircraft in flight prepared to conform with requirements for position, operational and meteorological reporting.'[85]

To begin with, the general framework[86]

As PIC

- flying in **controlled** airspace;
- flying in **advisory** airspace;
- on a flight for which **alerting action** is being provided (this may be flying in uncontrolled airspace)

  ➢ you must ensure that you make **reports to the responsible ATSU, as soon as possible, of the time and level of passing each compulsory reporting point**, together with any other required information,

  ➢ you must further ensure that your position reports are similarly made in relation to additional reporting points, if so requested by the responsible ATSU and that, in the absence of designated reporting points, position reports are made at the intervals specified by the responsible ATSU or published by the Director in terms of Part 175 for that area.

  ➢ If you are on a controlled flight providing position information to the appropriate ATSU, **you will only provide voice position reports when you are asked to**. Simply put: as a private pilot flying a small aircraft, you have a transponder (=*trans*mitter+res*ponder*) mode A/C (possibly the advanced S). ATSU knows therefore where you are, so you do not report until you are asked to or at the position where you have been told to report. Then you call, for instance,'MOO zone outbound'– and once ATSU has responded and let you go, always thank ATSU for 'accommodating'.

In controlled airspace[87]

As PIC you must ensure that **before you enter a controlled airspace**,

➢ you establish a **two-way radio contact** with the responsible ATSU on the designated radio frequency (see next insert on AIREP)

➢ you ensure, **while in that controlled airspace and until you leave it**, that you maintain a **continuous radio watch**

➢ you ensure that further **two-way radio communication, as the ATSU may require, is established**

---

[85] As per 20th Amendment *Government Gazette* 42362 GN 645 of 29 March 2019.
[86] CARS 91.06.15.
[87] CARS 91.06.16 Mandatory radio communication in controlled airspace.

Provided that (in plain English: what follows are exceptions to the regulation just mentioned):

(a) the **ATSU may permit an aircraft not capable of maintaining continuous two-way radio communication** to fly in the control area, TMA, control zone or aerodrome traffic zone for which it is responsible, if traffic conditions permit, in which case the flight shall be subject to such conditions as such ATSU deems necessary to ensure the safety of other air traffic; and

(b) **in the case of radio failure, a flight for which an air traffic service flight plan was filed and activated by the ATSU on receipt of a departure time may continue in controlled airspace if the communication failure procedures specified in Document SA-CATS 91 are complied with.**

What are these procedures? Refer to 9.9 for mandatory Radio Communication Failure (RCF) procedures in controlled airspace.

AIREP

Station called: XXX

Identify: full call sign and 'Good day'

After Tower/Approach acknowledges and go ahead given

Identity: type of aircraft, call sign (no need to repeat aircraft type and ZS, ZU)

Position: overhead YYY

Time: 0510

Altitude: FL or ALT

Next position and time: estimating ZZZ 0540

Destination and ETA: destination AAA 0555

Endurance: 3 hours

In advisory airspace[88]

As PIC you must ensure that **before the aircraft approaches or enters an advisory airspace—**

➤ you establish two-way radio communication with the responsible ATSU on the designated radio frequency;

➤ if such communication is not possible, establish two-way radio communication with any ATSU that is capable of relaying messages to and from the responsible ATSU;

➤ if such communication is not possible, you must broadcast on the designated radio frequency, giving information on your intention to enter the airspace, and you must ensure, while you are within the advisory airspace and until you depart from it, that you maintain a continuous radio watch on the designated radio frequency and that (here is the actual text of the regulation):

 (i) such further two-way radio communication, as the responsible ATSU may require, is established with any other ATSU that is capable of relaying messages to and from such responsible ATSU;

 (ii) if such communication is not possible, such further two-way radio communication is established with any other ATSU that is capable of relaying messages to and from the responsible ATSU, as such responsible ATSU may require; or

 (iii) if such communication is not possible, broadcasts are made on the designated radio frequency giving information on passing reporting points and when leaving the airspace concerned: Provided that [plain English: except in the following cases]:

  (aa) **an aircraft maintaining a Selcal**[89] watch while operating within an advisory route in the Johannesburg flight information region and whose Selcal call-sign has been communicated to the Johannesburg flight information centre, shall be deemed to be maintaining a continuous radio watch [in plain English: ATC assumes you are alert and will notice the cockpit call system warning when ATC wants to talk to you].

  (bb) **in the case of a radio failure**, a flight for which an air traffic service flight plan was filed and activated by an ATSU on receipt of a departure time, may continue in advisory airspace if the communication failure procedures specified in technical standard 91.06.16 of Document SA-CATS 91 are complied with.

Refer to section 9.9.

---

[88] CARS 91.06.17 Mandatory radio communication in advisory airspace.
[89] SELCAL= Selective Calling System. See D Lempp *Pilot's Radio Handbook* 155.

> **Reporting for aircraft with VHF only**[90]
>
> Where an aircraft is equipped with VHF only and continuous radio contact cannot be maintained with an ATSU throughout the flight, the PIC should state before departure the reporting point(s) at which overdue action must be taken in the event of non-receipt of the position report, or whether overdue action is required only at destination.
>
> Use the AIREP format.
>
> Overdue action means triggering Search and Rescue.

A final point: when you call an aeronautical station, remember to let 10 seconds elapse before you make a second call.[91]

---

[90] AIC 40.2 2.1 (ii) Note.
[91] As AIC 005/2018 reminds us right at the beginning.

Chapter 9

Unplanned events en route and what you should do about them

> Two or three hours later, when again about to rise,[1] an unfortunate dog, annoyed by the persistently revolving propeller, tried to bite it. The dog was cut in two, the propeller broken, and the biplane simply turned over, not hurting the pilot or his passenger. So ended this attempt.[2]

That is the sort of en route trouble you are unlikely to suffer, as we have never seen a dog annoyed or not, fly up to an aircraft. However, en route there are a few unplanned and possibly dangerous scenarios that can disrupt a carefully prepared VFR flight.

In order of seriousness (except the last one), here are ten likely scenarios, each one triggering legal regulations:

- You may have to fly **from VFR to IFR**.
- You may have to **change your flight plan**.
- You may **stray** into an airspace where no civilian aircraft should be.
- You may have to declare **an urgency**.
- You may have to declare **an emergency**.
- You are **intercepted.**
- You are subject to **Search and Rescue.**
- You do a **forced landing, or you crash.**
- Your **radio fails but you land safely.**

And you may arrive late and be **flying at night**! See chapter 13: Night Flying.

9.1 FROM VFR TO IFR

Assuming you do hold an Instrument Rating, **can you fly from VFR to IFR**?

Yes, you can, provided that the regulation regarding 'flight determination and weather deterioration' is applicable (see above page 121).[3]

---

[1] Ie take off.
[2] *Flight, First Aero Weekly in the World*, No 92 (1 October 1910) 799.
[3] CARS 91.06.23.

Chapter 9: Unplanned events en route and what you should do about them

Let us re-state it:

> (1) The PIC of an aircraft operating **outside a control zone or an aerodrome traffic zone** is responsible for ascertaining whether or not weather conditions permit flight in accordance with VFR.
>
> (2) Whenever **weather conditions do not allow a pilot to maintain the minimum distance from cloud and the minimum visibility required by VFR**, the pilot—
>
> *(a)* if in controlled airspace, must request an amended clearance enabling the aircraft to continue in VMC to the nearest suitable aerodrome, or to leave the airspace within which an ATC clearance is required;
>
> *(b)* if no clearance in accordance with paragraph (a) can be obtained, must continue to operate in VMC and land at the nearest suitable aerodrome, notifying the appropriate ATC unit of the action taken;
>
> *(c)* if operating within a control zone, must request authorisation to operate as a special VFR flight; or
>
> *(d)* must **request clearance to operate in accordance with IFR**.

In short, if the conditions are met, you can change from VFR to SVFR (day time only), or IFR (if you hold an IR or a relevant licence).

If ATSU denies clearance you must comply with (b) or (c) sub-regulations.

In addition, minimum heights change in IMC or under IFR:[4]

> '**Except when necessary for take-off or landing**, or with the express permission of the Director, an aircraft shall **at night, in IMC or when operated in accordance with IFR**, be flown—
>
> *(a)* at a height of **at least 1 000 ft above the highest terrain or obstacle** where the height of such terrain or obstacle does not exceed 5 000 ft above sea level **within 5 NM of the aircraft in flight**; or
>
> *(b)* at a height of at least **2 000 ft above the highest terrain or obstacle located within 5 NM of the aircraft in flight where the height of such terrain or obstacle exceeds 5 000 ft above sea level**: Provided that within areas determined by the Director the minimum height may be reduced to 1 000 ft above the highest terrain or obstacle located within 5 NM of the aircraft in flight, and the aircraft is flown in accordance with such procedures as the Director may determine.'

Note: the regulation mentions 'aircraft'; not aeroplane or helicopter, but 'aircraft'.

---

[4] CARS 91.06.32 (3).

Conversely, if you are flying IFR and want to change to VFR, you can—but pay attention to the exact wording of the sub-regulations:[5]

> (1) The PIC of an aircraft who elects to change the conduct of flight of the aircraft from compliance with IFR to compliance with VFR shall, **if a flight plan was submitted for the flight**, notify the ATSU concerned that the IFR flight is cancelled and communicate to such ATSU the intended changes to be made to the current flight plan.
>
> (2) When an aircraft operating **under IFR is flown in or encounters VMC**, the PIC **shall not cancel its IFR flight unless** it is anticipated, and intended, that **the flight will be continued for a reasonable period in uninterrupted VMC**.

Beware here of an error of judgment called 'press-on-itis', which is a form of goal fixation: you want to get there and will do so even if it means flying IFR without having a rating, or, if you have one, without getting clearance in the conditions enumerated above.

9.2 CAN I CHANGE MY FLIGHT PLAN EN ROUTE?

For clarity's sake we must distinguish here between **two types of changes to a flight plan** you have filed with an ATSU—this assumes that 1) you have filed a plan, of course, and 2) that **you are in controlled airspace**.

9.2.1 Deviations from a flight plan

First, let us look at non-intentional causes for a deviation from your flight plan that do **not result in a change** of your filed flight plan.
- You are **'inadvertently' off track**:
  ➢ no need to change the flight plan. Just get back on your track 'as soon as practicable'.[6]
- Your **altitude** deviates:
  ➢ 'action be taken forthwith', immediately, to return to correct altitude. (Why? Risk of collision!)[7] You **need not contact your ATSU**.
- **Your average true airspeed (TAS) at cruising level between two reporting points 'inadvertently' varies, or is expected to vary by 5% or more**:
  ➢ you **must 'inform' your ATSU**.[8]
- You are 'in error in excess of 2 minutes' **at the next applicable reporting**

---

[5] CARS 91.06.26 (1) and (2). *This is not in the PPL syllabus.*
[6] CARS 91.03.4 (12) (a).
[7] CARS 91.03.4 (12) (d).
[8] CARS 91.03.4 (12) (b).

Chapter 9: Unplanned events en route and what you should do about them 193

point, flight information regional boundary, or aerodrome of intended landing, whichever comes first:

➢ you **must 'notify' your responsible ATSU** 'as soon as possible'.[9]

Note the word 'inadvertently': you did not intend such deviations or changes.

9.2.2 Changes to a flight plan

Now let us look at intentional changes that result in an amended flight plan:

- **You decide to amend your flight plan** while in controlled airspace (maybe due to the weather). In that case the change is no longer 'inadvertent' but a decision you take:
  ➢ **you contact the ATSU, you request the changes, and, if they are approved, you implement them.**
- And then there are **cases of urgency and emergency**, which are dealt with in sections 9.4, 9.5 and 9.6 below.

In short, when one talks of 'flight change', the expression covers a variety of situations.

9.3 BEING WARNED OFF AN AREA THAT IS OFF LIMITS

If **you happen to stray into a restricted or prohibited area or find yourself in a danger area** where there may be far more serious risks than those usually associated with a Flying Training Area, and you have not read a NOTAM about them, you should be prepared for warning action (although it is a rare occurrence).

You will be warned off by visual signals from the ground, and the wording of the sub-regulation is enough to make you think twice before straying over a 'deep state' facility:

> By day and by night, **a series of projectiles discharged from the ground at intervals of 10 seconds, each showing, on bursting, red and green lights or stars** will indicate to an unauthorised aircraft that it is flying in or about to enter **restricted, prohibited or danger area**, and that the aircraft is to take such remedial action as may be necessary.[10]

What is meant by remedial action? If you stray inadvertently, you leave the area promptly while broadcasting your intention; or, if you are in trouble, you declare an emergency.

---

[9] CARS 91.03.4 (12) (c).
[10] CATS 91.06.13-3.

9.4 DECLARING AN URGENCY

First, a question of vocabulary arises, as three words come into play:
- urgency
- emergency
- distress.

An urgency is not an emergency. And an emergency is declared when there is 'distress'.

An urgency is also called a PAN situation.[11] But you will be hard-pressed to find a direct, explicit definition of PAN in CARS, or for that matter in ICAO regulations.

The Search and Rescue Procedures regulations cut to the chase when they define 'Emergency communications from aircraft':

> **Emergency communications from aircraft are divided into two categories:**[12]
> (a) **distress** covers aircraft threatened by **grave and imminent danger** and in need of immediate assistance;
> (b) **urgency** identifies a **very urgent message concerning the safety** of a ship, aircraft or other vehicle, or some person on board or within sight.

Note also that distress and urgency signals are part of what is called 'Rules of the Air'.[13]

9.4.1 What is an urgency?

First, if you look up CARS, you will read that an urgency **must be declared by a PIC**

> 'when the calculated usable fuel predicted to be available upon landing at the nearest suitable aerodrome where a safe landing can be made is less than the planned final reserve fuel'.[14]

This sub-regulation appears in Part 121 and Part 135, and is concerned with Air Transport Operations.

But, to you as a PPL pilot it is relevant too, as a reminder of what is meant by 'planned final reserve'. Go back to the section above where fuel is discussed (page

---

[11] CARS 91.06.31 (2) (b) 'PAN' does not refer to 'panic' (although it could) but to the French 'panne' (pronounced 'pan') for 'breakdown'.
[12] AIC 40.2, 3.2.2.
[13] CATS 2.1.14 (l).
[14] CARS 121.07.23 (4) (b) and 135.07.22 (4) (b).

132). It means: 30 minutes for an aeroplane under VFR by day and 45 minutes for an aeroplane under VFR by night.

Practically, you will declare an urgency, to the responsible ATSU, or on the frequency in use, or on 121.5 MhZ, when you are

> 'concerned with the safety of your aircraft or other vehicle, or of some person on board or within sight, but which does not require immediate assistance'
>
> or if there are: 'difficulties which compel to land without requiring immediate assistance'.[15]

AIC 005/2018 implies that a medical condition or a situation where the aircraft is required to carry out a precautionary landing qualifies as an urgency.[16]

9.4.2 How to declare an urgency

But the law becomes more detailed about declaring an urgency.

> **Urgency signals**[17]
>
> (1) The following signals, used either together or separately, mean that an aircraft wishes to give notice of difficulties that compel [you] to land without requiring immediate assistance—
>
>   *(a)* the repeated switching on and off of the landing lights; or
>
>   *(b)* the repeated switching on and off of the navigation lights in such manner as to be distinct from flashing navigation lights.
>
> (2) The following signals, used either together or separately, mean that an aircraft has a very urgent message to transmit **concerning the safety of a ship, aircraft or other vehicle, or of some person on board or within sight** *[note that, stuck in here, we find a complementary definition of an urgency]*
>
>   *(a)* a signal made by radiotelegraphy or by any other signalling method consisting of the group XXX.
>
>   *(b)* 'a signal sent by radiotelephony consisting of the spoken words "PAN, PAN, PAN"'.[18]

---

[15] CATS 91.06.13-2 (1).
[16] AIC 0005/2018 24.1.
[17] CATS 91.06.13–2.
[18] As per CATS 91.06.13–2 (2) (b) (concerning Signals). This agrees with AIC 40.2 dated 01-12-15 (concerning Search and Rescue Procedures), item 3.2.2.2 which mentions a 'radiotelephony urgency signal PAN, preferably spoken three times'. But is not in

196   Air Law

> None of the provisions in this paragraph prevent the use, by an aircraft in distress, of any means at its disposal to attract attention, make known its position and obtain help.

You will also note that the law is silent on **what frequency to use**: again, airmanship comes into play as you decide which one to broadcast on, either the nearest ATSU, the latest frequency you used, or the international emergency frequency 121.5 MHz.

Now, you are supposed to say more than 'PAN-PAN' three times, otherwise who ever listens to your panic call will have no idea as to why you are declaring an urgency.

A referenced description of what is to be said is found in a Federal Aviation Administration document:[19]

> a. If distress, MAYDAY, MAYDAY, MAYDAY;
>   if urgency, PAN-PAN, PAN-PAN, PAN-PAN.
> b. Name of station addressed.
> c. Aircraft identification and type.
> d. Nature of distress or urgency.
> e. *Weather.*
> f. Pilot's intentions and request.
> g. Present position, and heading, or if lost, last known position, time, and heading since that position.
> h. Altitude or flight level.
> i. *Fuel remaining in hours and minutes.*
> j. *Number of people on board.*
> k. Any other useful information.
>
> *If time and circumstances permit you should also provide:*
>   *a. ELT (Electronic Locator Transmitter) status,*
>   *b. Visible landmarks,*
>   *c. Aircraft colour,*
>   *d. Emergency equipment on board.*

---

agreement with AIC 005/2018 of 16 AUG 2018 (concerning Radiotelephony Procedures), item 24.2, which mentions a 'radiotelephony urgency signal PAN-PAN (transmitted three times).

[19] FAA *Basic Survival Skills for Aviation* no date, available at http://www.faa.gov/pilots/training/airman_education. There is a similar list in AIC 005/2018, 26.1. (The items in italics are not mentioned by AIC.)

Of course this is a comprehensive list. It depends how much time you have, the navigation issues, and the emotional or physical state you are in.

9.4.3 Priority over other aircraft

Your ATSU will give you priority in accordance with this sub-regulation (*what refers to an urgency is in bold*):[20]

> **An ATSU shall give priority to certain flights regardless** of whether such flight is operating on an ATS flight plan or not, **if the PIC has notified** the ATSU that—
>
> *(a)* the aircraft is in a state of emergency, or the PIC has declared a distress or MAYDAY situation; or
>
> *(b)* **the PIC has declared an urgency or PAN situation**; or
>
> *(c)* **the PIC has stated that there is a critically ill person on board** the aircraft, or the flight is operated as an emergency air ambulance flight and the type of flight has been annotated accordingly in the flight plan; or
>
> *(d)* **the PIC has declared that the aircraft is in a state of minimum fuel**.
>
> An ATSU will give priority to urgency calls, but not above distress ones.

And we now seem to be able to piece together, from one mention in CARS and two mentions in CATS, a definition of an urgency:

> Difficulties concerning the safety of a ship, aircraft or other vehicle, or of some person on board or within sight that compel the aircraft to land without requiring immediate assistance, or when the calculated usable fuel predicted to be available upon landing at the nearest suitable aerodrome where a safe landing can be made is less than the planned final reserve fuel.

9.5 DECLARING AN EMERGENCY

What we are dealing with here is **properly called 'distress'**:

> a condition of being threatened by serious and/or imminent danger and of requiring immediate assistance; i.e—That of a possible/actual structural damage to the aircraft.[21]

So, we have three words: emergency, distress, MAYDAY. And they are not always used in the same context. For example:

---

[20] CARS 91.06.31 (2).

[21] AIC 005/2018, 24.1 (a), aligned on ICAO, Annex 10, *Aeronautical Telecommunications*. Services. Air TrafficManagement (abbreviated PANS-ATM)16 ed (2016) 1–8.

- ICAO speaks of: '**Emergency phase**. A generic term meaning, as the case may be, uncertainty phase, alert phase or distress phase'.[22] This has to do with Search and Rescue as it does not refer to you declaring an emergency but to actions initiated by an ATSU to come to your rescue.
- A typical emergency situation is a '**fuel emergency**': a PIC may declare '**minimum fuel**', which is **not an emergency** but **an indication to ATC that an emergency situation is possible** if any delay prevents landing, in which case the pilot must then broadcast **MAYDAY MAYDAY MAYDAY FUEL**.[23]

Now, having explained the terminology, ICAO lists a **distress situation particularly relevant to VFR flying**:[24]

VFR aircraft in distress

'A VFR flight reporting that it is uncertain of its position or lost, or encountering adverse meteorological conditions, should be considered to be in a state of emergency and handled as such. The controller shall, under such circumstances, communicate in a clear, concise and calm manner and care shall be taken, at this stage, not to question any fault or negligence that the pilot may have committed in the preparation or conduct of the flight. Depending on the circumstances, the pilot should be requested to provide any of the following information considered pertinent so as to better provide assistance:

a) aircraft flight conditions;

b) position (if known) and level;

c) airspeed and heading since last known position, if pertinent;

d) pilot experience *[if you are a student say 'Student ZS-PUC']*

e) navigation equipment carried and if any navigation aid signals are being received;

f) SSR mode and code selected if relevant *[that is your transponder]*

g) ADS-B capability;[25]

h) departure and destination aerodromes;

i) number of persons on board;

j) endurance'.

---

[22] ICAO, Doc 4444 *Procedures for Air Navigation Management Services. Air Traffic Management* (abbreviated PANS-ATM)16 ed (2016) 1–8.

[23] PANS-ATM, 15.5.4. CARS 91.07.12 (8) and (9).

[24] PANS-ATM, 15.4.1.1.

[25] Automatic dependant surveillance-broadcast.

Chapter 9: Unplanned events en route and what you should do about them 199

What is the correct procedure to 'signal distress'?

To declare an emergency due to a distress you send signals of distress, which can be verbal (radio telephony), electronic (transponder code on 7700), or visual.

Distress signals[26]

1) The following signals, used either together or separately, mean that **grave and imminent danger threatens and immediate assistance is requested**—

   (a) a signal made by radiotelegraphy or by any other signalling method consisting of the group SOS (... _ _ _ ... in Morse code);

   (b) a signal sent by radiotelephony consisting of the spoken word 'MAY-DAY' three times;

   (c) rockets or shells throwing red lights, fired one at a time at short intervals;

   (d) a parachute flare showing a red light.

(3) None of the provisions in this paragraph prevent the use, by an aircraft in distress, of any means at its disposal to attract attention, make known its position and obtain help.

You will transmit on the last frequency you have used or on the international frequency 121.5 MHz, by first saying 'MAYDAY MAYDAY MAYDAY' and then providing the same sequence of information as in a PAN call (see above).

A **distress call has complete priority** over all other communications until it is cancelled or transferred to another frequency. Silence from other pilots is the rule.

You can **impose silence** to all stations or one only by saying the words: 'ALL STATION STOP TRANSMITTING' together with the triple MAYDAY. Other aircraft will stop transmitting. The station handling your emergency will terminate the distress communications and silence conditions after the station has received a message from you cancelling distress (in the best of cases).

Set your transponder on emergency code 7700.

Note that if you are intercepted, one of the actions you take is to select 7700.[27] Interception is considered an emergency.

This leads us to the situation that you are least likely to encounter: being intercepted by a combat plane.

9.6 INTERCEPTION!

As a PPL pilot, interception is more likely to happen in the course of a cross-border flight if you have not taken a close look at charts. It may happen that you **stray** into

---

[26] CATS 91.06.13–1 (1) and (3).
[27] CATS 91.06.29–2 (1) *(d)*.

prohibited airspace outside our borders. Interception can also occur if you have declared (using transponder code 7500) or are believed to be subjected to 'unlawful interference', or if you have lost communication with ATSU or are unidentified.

All of this is part of the 'Rules of the Air'.[28]

Interception of a civilian aircraft is strictly regulated, in terms of who authorises it (typically the Minister), who performs it (typically air force personnel), and why ('public interest').

Here is what the law says:[29]

'Identification and interception of aircraft

(1) No person shall institute **in-flight surveillance** against, **give an interception signal** in connection with or **give an instruction to land** to a civilian aircraft suspected to be in contravention of the Act except—

    (a) on instruction by the Minister, the Director, an authorized officer or authorized person; or

    (b) if the person is a member of the South African Police Services or South African National Defence Force, acting within the course and scope of his or her duties; and

    (c) the in-flight surveillance, interception signal or instruction to land is in the public interest.

(2) The in-flight surveillance, interception signal or instruction to land must be executed in a manner that does not unduly affect aviation safety.

(3) The intercepted aircraft must follow out the instructions of the intercepting aircraft as prescribed in Document SA-CATS 91.[30]

(4) When the aircraft is intercepted, the pilot-in command (PIC) must immediately establish radio contact with the intercepting aircraft on 121.5 MHz.

(5) If the intercepting aircraft cannot establish radio contact with or contact in any other practical way the intercepted aircraft, visual signals as prescribed in Document SA-CATS 91 must be used.

(6) The PIC of an aircraft flying in South African airspace when intercepted shall comply with the procedures specified in this regulation.

(7) The PIC of an aircraft flying in foreign airspace when intercepted shall comply with the interception procedures of that country.'

---

[28] As per ICAO Annex 2.
[29] CARS 91.06.29.
[30] CARS 91.06.29 1-4.

Chapter 9: Unplanned events en route and what you should do about them 201

The three key elements are '**in-flight surveillance**', '**giving signals**', and '**instruct to land**'.

In plain language, there are three situations:
- a military plane flies alongside you, surveys you, and then goes away;
- the intercepting pilot sends you signals that you are supposed to understand and respond to;
- you are ordered to land.

One level need not lead to the next.

In any event, you may not notice immediately that you are going to be intercepted by a French Air Force Rafale above one of the French Scattered Islands that lie in the middle of the Mozambique Channel until you see the fighter jet materialise on the left hand-side, ahead and above your Tomahawk.

By 'signals' the law means '**visual signals**' sent by the intercepting aircraft to you, the intercepted one. It is best described as a visual dialogue between the two aircraft by using visual signals. The intercepting aircraft initiates it, not you.

These visual signals use the **wings, the landing gear, or the lights**. Each signal by wing, gear, or light has a specific meaning.

If you have established **radio communication on 121.5 MHz or 243 MHz** and if English is not thought to be understood by the intercepting pilot (pronunciation can get in the way, as many air crashes testify), you must stick to basic international phraseology and elocution to avoid confusion. For instance, you are indicating to the intercepting aircraft that you understand a visual signal and you will comply: you say '**Vill**-co' (not 'willco'). Intercepting aircraft may instruct: 'Dee-**send**'. Bold part is what is said louder or 'emphasised' (annexure 15).

If visual signals conflict with verbal messages, you must ask for clarification by radio while you **continue to obey visual signals**.

And, the moment you are intercepted, you **switch your transponder on 7700** because an interception represents an emergency.

In applying transponder codes, think of the mnemonics ICE

I: unlawful interference 7500 (hijack)

C: radio communication failure 7600

E: emergency 7700

Do not assign **I** to 'interception' and 7500—just think that **being intercepted is very much lawful** (although it may be the result of you doing an unlawful operation). Hence: 7700 for Interception.

202   Air Law

Students! Read Annexure 15 in this book for a full description by CATS of 'principles to be observed during interception', 'action by intercepted aircraft', 'radio communication during interception', and 'visual interception signals'.[31] *They are complex and difficult to memorise. Exams now and then contain one or two questions on interception signals. Remember: a list of interception signals must be carried on board (see page 145)!*

9.7 SEARCH AND RESCUE (SAR)[32]

This is the best place to mention Search and Rescue Procedures as they are related to urgency or emergency, and *are found in exam questionnaires.*

If you have declared an urgency you have in effect declared that the safety of your aircraft or passengers is at risk, even more so if it is an emergency. You vanish from the ATSU's radar screen, and alerting is triggered (see annexure 16).

9.7.1 The five golden rules[33]

Once SAR is triggered or is about to be (after you declared an emergency or an urgency), a pilot should observe the so-called five golden rules. They are not regulations or standards, but are nonetheless important, common sense reminders.

The five golden rules
They all begin with a 'c'

1. **confess** your predicament to any ATSU to enable the organisation to assist while there is still time;
2. **communicate** with the ATSU, passing on as much of the pertinent information as possible in the first message;
3. **climb**, if possible, for improved direction-finding and radar coverage;
4. **comply** with instructions and advice given and assist the ATSU with controlling communication on the frequency in use. Do not change frequency unless it is absolutely necessary; and
5. **conserve**—slow down and select power for maximum endurance.

---

[31] CATS 91.06.29.
[32] AIP uses the abbreviation SR; AIC 40.2 of 01–12–15 uses SAR—both are fine.
[33] AIC 40.2–3.2.1.

9.7.2 SAR procedures[34]

There are three phases in SAR:[35]

The three phases of SAR
1 Uncertainty Phase (abbreviation **INCERFA**)—a situation wherein **uncertainty** exists as to the safety of an aircraft and its occupants.
2 Alert Phase (abbreviation **ALERFA**)—a situation wherein **apprehension** exists as to the safety of an aircraft and its occupants.
3 Distress Phase (abbreviation **DETRESFA**)—a situation wherein there is **reasonable certainty** that an aircraft and its occupants are **threatened by grave and imminent** danger or require immediate assistance.

Each phase triggers its own procedures that are 'declared by the appropriate authority', **not by you**. You may declare an urgency or an emergency—or not declare anything at all if you have forgotten to cancel SAR! but it is the relevant ATSU that will decide on the SAR phase and procedures to put into action.

Possibly the most important thing to note for a private pilot are the **three main reasons for INCERFA** to be declared (for full details see annexure 16):[36]

- an aircraft that is operating on an 'overdue at destination only' flight plan is not in contact with the destination aerodrome within one hour after ETA;
- an aircraft that is operating on a flight plan stipulating alerting action after a specified time fails to arrive or is not in contact with the ATSU by the time specified in the flight plan, and preliminary checks fail to reveal the whereabouts of the aircraft;
- an aircraft that is proceeding to an unmanned aerodrome but which is operating on an 'overdue action' flight plan fails to report arrival by the time specified in the flight plan, and preliminary checks fail to reveal the whereabouts of the aircraft.

As for DETRESFA, take note of this as it has a direct bearing on what we have seen earlier in this book regarding **fuel**: 'if the fuel on board, as stated on the flight plan, is considered to be exhausted or to be insufficient to enable the aircraft to reach safety' DETRESFA will be declared.[37]

Unfortunately SAR is likely to be linked to a forced landing or a crash.

---

[34] AIP GEN 3.6–12, AIC 40.2 of 01–12–2015.
[35] AIP GEN 3.6–12 to 15.
[36] AIP GEN 3.6–13 and 14.
[37] AIP GEN 3.6–14.

9.8 WHAT TO DO AFTER A CRASH

These are occurrences you must prepare yourself for, and the law expects you to do what you can to save yourself and your passengers after you have crashed.

There are procedures you should attempt to follow **after crashing**. The regulations are phrased with sensitivity and common sense.

Action after crash or forced landing[38]

The pilot of an aircraft which has crashed or force landed shall use own discretion on whether to remain at the aircraft or to attempt to reach help.

Factors which could influence the pilot's decision are—

(a) if the aircraft was operating on an 'SAR action' flight plan and the aircraft has crashed or force landed in a desert area, a swamp area or a very sparsely populated area, it is advisable to remain at the aircraft and take such of the following action as may be appropriate or possible—

　(i) take steps to conserve the strength of survivors, e.g. avoid unnecessary exertion in the sun;

　(ii) conserve available water and food supplies;

　(iii) if a useable radio transmitter is available, make transmissions using the distress procedure, giving the aircraft's position and any other pertinent data, at H + 15 and H + 45. These transmissions should be kept as short as possible to conserve battery power. (H+15 and H+45 mean at times which are 15 and 45 minutes past the hour, e.g. 0715, 0745, 1215, 1245 etc.);

　(iv) if automatic SAR beacons are available one should be switched on for 5 minutes from H+15 and H+45. If however, aircraft are seen or heard a beacon should be left on continuously.

　(v) if flares are carried they should be conserved for use when search aircraft, ships or ground search parties are known to be in the vicinity. The danger of falling flares starting veld and bush fires must be borne in mind before using flares;

　(vi) if possible place the aircraft in a conspicuous position. Engine cowls, doors or other removable parts of the aircraft should be removed, polished-up and placed where they will reflect the rays of the sun. Fine sand can be used to remove paint from metal surfaces;

　(vii) lay out the appropriate emergency ground/air emergency signalling strips in a conspicuous place *[make sure the strips are on board! There are often questions about their 'signalling codes'—see the pictures below]*;[39]

---

[38] AIC 40.2, 3.3 and AIC GEN 3.6–14 and 15.

Chapter 9: Unplanned events en route and what you should do about them

> (viii) light smoke fires.
>
> *(b)* if the aircraft has crashed or **force landed in a settled area** where help is near at hand it is better to leave the aircraft to look for help. In such cases SAP stations, telephone exchanges, railway station masters, etc. will render such assistance as they can. The pilot should inform the unit he has called upon for help that he or she is operating on an 'SAR action' flight plan and ask them to advise the nearest ATSU of his whereabouts.
>
> [Note the text in bold: if you force land, or execute a precautionary landing, pick a location where you can get help from people; such areas are sometimes called 'civilisation' in aviation language. It is counterproductive to execute a precautionary where you cannot get help.]

Emergency ground/air signalling codes[40]

These codes are used to signal from the ground to air rescue by laying down the 'strips' according to pattern and meaning, that is, you or someone else who is not incapacitated must arrange them on the ground where they can be seen from the air. The strips are white, although shown in black in the picture below.

No.	Message	Code symbol
1	Require assistance	V
2	Require medical assistance	X
3	No or Negative	N
4	Yes or affirmative	Y
5	Proceeding in this direction	↑

The rescue team will use their own system of coding with strips if they have no other means to communicate with aircraft rescue.

---

[39] AIP GEN 3.6–11 Search and rescue signals.
[40] Ground–air visual signal code for use by survivors, ICAO, Annex 12, Appendix.

9.9 RADIO FAILURE IN CONTROLLED AIRSPACE, AND ARRIVING SAFELY UNDER VFR

But let us close this chapter with a less dramatic scenario. Imagine you suffer radio communication failure (RCF) under VFR while in controlled space.[41] The airfield is near. You cannot establish a two-way communication with your ATSU. What do you do?[42]

You try a series of remedies:

- You try another frequency (if Approach frequency fails, try Tower, try another Approach/Tower nearby), or you try to contact aircraft on a general frequency.
- If that fails, 'transmit blind', that is, continue reporting on the frequency you were supposed to be on initially: you say 'Transmitting blind, Durban Approach, etc.' Say each transmission twice.
- If you get no response, set your transponder code to 7600 and follow procedures:
  ➢ continue to fly in VMC and land at the nearest aerodrome, which leads to—
  ➢ arrival procedures which are:[43]
    1. Maintain squawk of 7600.
    2. Make a relevant blind broadcast to traffic in the area advising of the probability of a radio communication failure, position and intentions.
    3. Select landing lights on.
    4. Approaching the aerodrome, make a relevant blind broadcast to traffic on the controlled airfields frequency to indicate the probability of a radio communication failure, position and intentions.
    5. Join the aerodrome overhead at a height of 1 000 ft above circuit altitude to ascertain which runway is in use.
    6. Conform to the circuit pattern while joining, preferably on the downwind leg.
    7. Continue to make blind broadcasts on the controlled airfields frequency to indicate the position in the circuit pattern.
    8. Land and vacate the runway expeditiously and safely.
    9. Taxi to the nearest parking area and shutdown.
    10. Inform the owner or operator and ATC.
    11. Make the relevant entry in the aircraft's flight folio.

---

[41] RCF procedures under IFR are described in CATS 91.06.16–3. They fall into two scenarios: 1) if operating IFR and VMC, continue in VMC, and land at nearest aerodrome, apply the VFR procedures above, or procedures prescribed for the landing aerodrome, and report expeditiously to ATSU on arrival; 2) if operating IFR in IMC, or VMC but VMC cannot be maintained, the procedures are more complex (CPL level) and described in CATS 91.06.16–3 (2) *(a)* to *(g)*.

[42] CATS 91.06.16 with Appendix 1.

[43] Appendix 1 Standard Radio Communication Failure Procedure—VFR Arrivals.

By the way, if you are rescued by air ambulance and you are in a state to listen to calls, you may be interested to know that medical flights have their own call signs: Mercy flights add the suffix MERCY and Halo flights add the prefix HALO. Halo flight is of lesser medical urgency than a Mercy flight, which has 'utmost priority'.[44] Air ambulance operations are in Part 138.

However, you are still on a trouble-free cross-country and you are now approaching your planned, final destination. And your friend has woken up, and you tell her: yes, tell me quickly—because a sterile cockpit will soon be required.

You are not flying an airliner (yet), but the general rules of a '**sterile flight deck**' or cockpit should be observed during the 'critical phases of a flight', which include 'all ground operations involving **taxi, take-off, climb to cruise** up to 10 000 feet and **approach from cruise** below 10 000 feet'.[45] It is a bit tough on your sole passenger who would like to know 'what that little switch is for', but it is a safety rule that is in place to prevent the PIC from being distracted.

---

[44] AIP ENR 1.8–25 and 26.
[45] CARS 1.01.1.

Chapter 10

. . . .

At your final destination

> After circling down, which brought us quite close to Lion's Head, we flew at low altitude over Cape Town and her harbour. At 17:25, at last, the Switzerland landed softly on the ocean, not far from Adderley Pier, watched by hundreds of townsfolk who had waited to welcome that strange bird from far away.
>
> Walter Mittelolzer, René Gouzy and Arnold Heim *R-A-S-T*[1]

You are not flying a seaplane from Switzerland (of all maritime places!) to Cape Town, but at this stage of your cross-country flight you have negotiated several airspace smartly, you have done proficient radio work, you have met your reporting points on time, you have not been obliged to divert or declare urgency or emergency, and you have not been shot down by a military craft or ordered to land in Zanzibar.

You are now looking at your flight log and at your aeronautical chart, and you realise that you are approaching your destination. You will soon be on approach.

10.1 HOW DOES THE LAW DEFINE 'APPROACH'?

Here is what the law says, as already mentioned: 'the "en-route phase" means that part of the flight from the end of the take-off and initial climb phase to the commencement of the approach and landing phase'.[2]

Read it backwards: approach begins when en route ends. And en route ends when after having reached your TOD (top of descent), you are ready to descend and enter the zone 5 NM within the landing field, or you will first pass through transition level on your way down, and then change to local QNH (more on this below).

First, let us despatch an instrument approach as, by contrast, the law provides ample regulations for the management of instrument approach procedures that are essential to safe air traffic, and fill an entire ICAO document.

---

[1] Walter Mittelolzer, René Gouzy & Arnold Heim *R-A-S-T. En hydravion de Zurich au Cap de Bonne Espérance* (1927) (my translation). This is the story of the never before attempted flight by seaplane from Switzerland to Cape Town, via Alexandria, Lake Victoria, Lake Nyasa (nowadays Malawi), Beira and (then) Lourenço-Marques. The airplane was a Dornier Merkur.

[2] CARS 1.01.1.

Instrument approach procedures

Not for PPL students, but worth noting

For that reason, CARS does provide a clear-cut definition:[3]

"**instrument approach procedure'** means a series of predetermined manoeuvres by reference to flight instruments with specified protection from obstacles from the initial approach fix, or where applicable, from the beginning of a defined arrival route, to a point from which a landing can be completed and thereafter, if a landing is not completed, to a position at which holding or en route obstacle criteria apply.'

Instrument approach procedures are classified as follows—

(a) non-precision approach procedure. An instrument approach procedure which utilizes lateral guidance but does not utilize vertical guidance;

(b) approach procedure with vertical guidance. An instrument approach procedure which utilizes lateral and vertical guidance but does not meet the requirements established for precision approach and landing operations; or

(c) precision approach procedure. An instrument approach procedure using precision lateral and vertical guidance with minima as determined by the category of operation;

Note—Lateral and vertical guidance refers to the guidance provided either by—

(a) a ground- or space-based navigation aid; or

(b) computer-generated navigation data.

Then let us go back to VFR, of greater interest to a private pilot (or SPL trainee . . . *exam!*) Here are the basic procedures that the law asks you to comply with.

10.2 APPLY TRANSITION LEVEL AND RESET ALTIMETER

It is the reverse procedure of what you have done when reaching Transition Altitude (see page 166).

The rules:[4]

Transition level[5]

In all scenarios below you will change your barometric altimeter from standard 1013.2 hPa to local QNH as supplied by ATSU when you are at transition level.

---

[3] CARS 1.01.1.
[4] AIP ENR 1.7–4.
[5] AIP ENR 1.7–4.

> **The key is the list of aerodromes and their 25 NM radius area that have a specified transition altitude (mentioned on page 166), now used for transition level rules** (refer to AIP GEN 1.7–2, 3).
>
> a) The change in reference from flight level used while en route to altitude used in the vicinity of an aerodrome shall be made at **a horizontal plane located above the transition altitude called the transition level.**
>
> b) Transition levels vary with variations in barometric pressure in such a way that **no transition level will be less than 1 000 feet above the transition altitude within 25 nautical miles of an aerodrome with an Air Traffic Service Unit** (ATSU).
>
> c) If an ATSU is in existence at the aerodromes *(listed, 25 NM radius)* the current transition level for each aerodrome and for points within 25 nautical miles thereof shall be included in the approach and landing instructions.
>
> d) In VMC, flights intending to land at points beyond 25 nautical miles from any of the aerodromes listed *(in the table mentioned already)* must observe a height of 3 000 feet above the ground or water as the transition level.
>
> e) In IMC, flights intending to land at points beyond 25 nautical miles from any of the aerodromes *(those listed and already mentioned)* must observe the flight level 500 feet above the lowest safe altitude as the transition level.

10.3 RADIO CALLS ON APPROACH TO AN UNCONTROLLED AIRFIELD

If you are approaching an uncontrolled airfield, tune into the correct frequency within 20 NM from the airfield, and at 5 NM broadcast TIBA using the TIPAN model (see page 184) and make clear your intention to land in so many minutes, 'xxmn'.[6]

10.4 CANCEL SEARCH AND RESCUE AND CLOSE YOUR FLIGHT PLAN

Now is the time.

Your destination is an uncontrolled airfield
- If your flight plan includes SAR under item 18 (eg: RMK/SAR FACT EAT+1hr), you can already close it while on descent, if you feel everything looks fine. You will radio the relevant ATSU, and request to close FP, which will cancel SAR, and you **note down the time** of cancellation on your flight log for the record. Be extra careful: request specifically to cancel SAR. It may sound redundant, but better be on the safe side.
- Or you can close your flight plan shortly after landing by phoning FLYNOW.

---

[6] Refer to D Lempp *Pilot's Radio Handbook* for controlled and IFR approach.

If you do not cancel, SAR emergency procedures will kick in at Cape Town (as per example) one hour after your stated EAT has elapsed (see page 203).

Sometimes you or the operator will get a call (on the phone number provided on the FP, at item 18—so, it is not a bad idea to give both the operator's and your cell phone numbers) if ATSU is concerned about SAR closing time being up—before SAR itself is triggered.

Your destination is a controlled airfield

When you land at a controlled airfield, FP and SAR close automatically.

Facilities inadequate for closing and cancelling SAR

Refer to Arrival report on page 224.

10.5 OBSERVE RIGHT OF WAY AND RULES OF OPERATION

It is worth quoting again the two regulations regarding **right of way**[7] and **operation in the vicinity** of an aerodrome, which are particularly relevant to this last phase of a flight.[8]

These are particularly important if you are in an uncontrolled area and it is left to your own judgment to operate safely.

Right of way

All text in bold is important.

'(1) An aircraft which has the right-of-way, shall **maintain its heading and speed**, but nothing in these provisions shall relieve the PIC of an aircraft from the responsibility of taking such action as will best avert collision, including collision avoidance manoeuvres based on resolution advisories provided by ACAS equipment.

(2) An aircraft which is obliged, by the provisions of this Subpart, to keep out of the way of another aircraft, shall avoid passing over or under the other aircraft, or crossing ahead of such aircraft, unless passing well clear, taking into account the effects of **wake turbulence**.

(3) When two aircraft are **approaching head-on** or approximately so and there is danger of collision, each aircraft shall alter its heading to the right.

(4) When two aircraft are **converging** at approximately the same level, the aircraft which has the other aircraft on its right, must give way, except in the following circumstances—

---

[7] CARS 91.06.7.
[8] CARS 91.06.12.

(a) power-driven heavier-than-air aircraft shall give way to airships, gliders and balloons;

(b) airships shall give way to gliders and balloons;

(c) gliders shall give way to balloons;

(d) power-driven aircraft shall give way to aircraft which are—

(i) seen to be towing other aircraft or objects;

(ii) carrying an underslung load or are engaged in winching operations; and

(iii) being towed or tethered.

(5) An aircraft which is being **overtaken has the right-of-way** and the overtaking aircraft whether climbing, **descending** or in horizontal flight, shall keep out of the way of the overtaken aircraft by altering its heading to the right, and no subsequent change in the relative positions of the two aircraft shall absolve the overtaking aircraft from its obligation until such aircraft is entirely past and clear: Provided that where a right-hand circuit is being followed at an aerodrome, the overtaking aircraft shall alter its heading to the left.

(6) **An aircraft in flight or operating on the ground or water, shall give way to other aircraft landing or on final approach to land.**

(7) When **two or more heavier-than-air aircraft are approaching an aerodrome** for the purpose of landing, the aircraft at the higher level shall give way to the aircraft at the lower level, but—

(a) **the latter aircraft (at the lower level) shall not take advantage of this provision to cut in front** of another aircraft which is on final approach to land, or to overtake such aircraft;

(b) power-driven heavier-than air aircraft shall **give way to gliders** in all circumstances.

(8) An aircraft about to take-off, shall not attempt to do so until there is no apparent risk of collision with other aircraft [*translation: if you are landing, watch out for any aircraft that is taking off without looking around, and do not be obstinate in asserting your right of way at all costs, just go around, because your duty is to avoid a collision*].

(9) An aircraft which is aware that another aircraft is **compelled to land**, shall give way to such aircraft.'

Operation on and in vicinity of aerodrome

'(1) The PIC of an aircraft operated on or in the vicinity of an aerodrome, shall be responsible for compliance with the following rules—

  (a) observe other aerodrome traffic for the purpose of avoiding collision;

  (b) conform with or avoid the pattern of traffic formed by other aircraft in operation;

  (c) make all turns to the left when approaching for a landing and after taking off, unless otherwise instructed by an ATSU, or unless a right hand circuit is in force: Provided [*read:* except] that a helicopter may, with due regard to other factors and when it is in the interest of safety, execute a circuit to the opposite side;

  (d) land and take off, as far as practicable, into the wind unless safety, the runway configuration or air traffic considerations dictate that a different direction is preferable, or unless otherwise instructed by an ATSU; and

  (e) fly across the aerodrome or its environs at a height of not less than 2 000 feet above the level of such aerodrome: Provided [*read:* except] that if circumstances require such PIC to fly at a height of less than 2 000 feet above the level of the aerodrome, he or she shall conform with the traffic pattern at such aerodrome.

(2) If an aerodrome control tower is in operation, the PIC shall also, whilst the aircraft is within the aerodrome traffic zone—

  (a) maintain a continuous radio watch on the frequency of the aerodrome control tower responsible for providing aerodrome control service at the aerodrome, establish two way radio communication as necessary for aerodrome control purposes and obtain such clearances for his or her movements as may be necessary for the protection of aerodrome traffic; or

  (b) if this is not possible, keep a watch for and comply with such clearances and instructions as may be issued by visual means.

(3) If an aerodrome flight information service unit is in operation, the PIC shall also, whilst the aircraft is within the aerodrome traffic zone—

  (a) maintain a continuous radio watch on the frequency of the aerodrome flight information service unit responsible for providing aerodrome flight information service at the aerodrome, establish two-way radio communication as necessary for aerodrome flight information service purposes and obtain information in respect of the surface wind, runway in use and altimeter setting and in respect of aerodrome traffic on the manoeuvring area and in the aerodrome traffic zone; or

> (b) if this is not possible, keep a watch for visual signals which may be displayed or may be issued by the aerodrome flight information service unit.
>
> (4) An aircraft which is unable to communicate by radio shall, before landing at an aerodrome, make a circuit of the aerodrome for the purpose of observing the traffic, and reading such ground markings and signals as may be displayed thereon, unless it has the consent of the appropriate ATSU to do otherwise.'

10.6 Observe lights, signals and markings

As you approach and are now overhead the airfield or in its vicinity, you have to observe any lights, signals and markings from the ground or on the ground, usually sent from tower or displayed at a signal area near the tower—and at or on or close to the runways.

These signals fall into six categories.

10.6.1 Precision approach path indicator (PAPI)

Larger airports have a system of four lights, in a row, positioned perpendicular to, and most of the time on the left of the runway, and 300 m further than the threshold. (Always check in AIP AD for the specs of an airport you intend to land at, as it may be located on the right, or on both sides.) It is called a PAPI.

In ICAO terminology this four-lights device is a 'wing bar': 'The PAPI system shall consist of a wing bar of four sharp transition multi-lamp (or paired single-lamp) units equally spaced. The system shall be located on the left side of the runway unless it is physically impracticable to do so.'[9]

This row of four lights is visible up to 3 NM by day and 20 NM at night. It tells you if you are on the correct slope.

The lights will illuminate red or white depending on your position on the glide slope. Red ones are always closer to the runway because, logically, danger is closer to the ground.

---

[9] ICAO Annex 14 to the Convention on International Civil Aviation, Volume 1, Chapter 5, 5.3.5.23.

In the pictorials below red lights are represented in black.

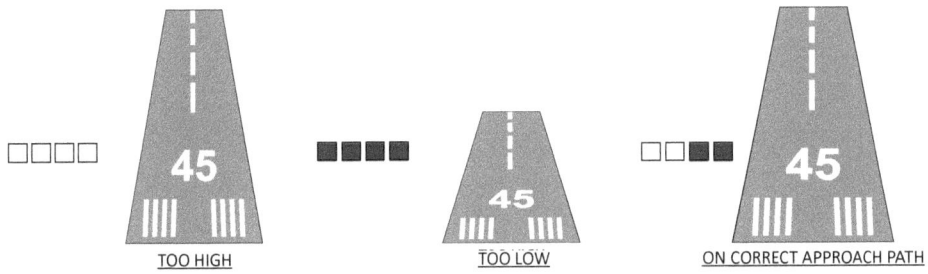

      'all white, too light'   **'all red you're dead'**   **'two two, to landing'**

You can also see how the angle of the slope, as you should see it from the cockpit, varies with the lights. You can of course get 3 red (always from runway, outward) and 1 white on the left: you are slightly low. Or 1 red and 3 white to its left: you are slightly too high. But KISS (keep it simple, sailor), and learn those three pictures by heart (*exam questions*).

Since VASI systems are nearly discontinued we will not mention them.

Regarding lights at larger airports, see pages 244 and 246A.

10.6.2 Aeronautical light beacons

Aeronautical light beacons are part of an aerodrome's lighting equipment (if provided) and are expected to be switched on at night or by day in bad visibility:
- white flashes or white-and-green flashes for a civil aerodrome
- green flashing of a two-letter Morse group every 12 seconds ('identification' beacon)
- red flashes from a military identification beacon.

10.6.3 Runway markings and runway and taxiway mandatory and information signs

Runway markings and displaced threshold

Runway markings are always white. Observe them from aloft!

Refer to pages 155–6 and 246B but the two below are of direct interest in the final phase of your flight, as they forbid the use of the pre-thresold area for landing.

216 *Air Law*

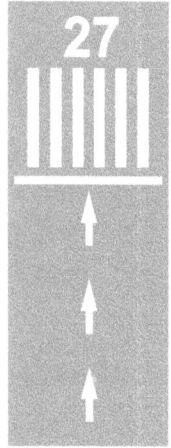
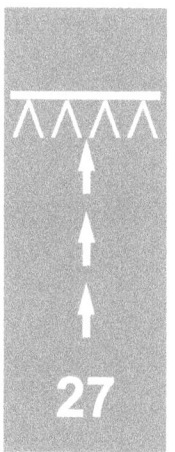

Permanently (> 6 months) displaced threshold with **pre-threshold area** available for taxi and take off but **not for landing.**

Temporarily **pre-threshold area** available for taxi and take off but **not for landing.**

Runway and taxiway mandatory and information signs

Refer to page 246B.

10.6.4 Visual ground signals and markings[10]

At or near a control tower

Pilots to report at air traffic office after landing: black C on yellow (C is for 'cash', as you have to settle your landing fees). See 246C for the colour version.

On the signalling area

A series of panels displayed on the signalling area.

Landing prohibited and prohibition likely to be prolonged: yellow diagonal cross on red. See page 246C.

Owing to the bad state of the manoeuvring area, or for any other reason, **special precautions** must be observed in approaching to land or in landing: diagonal yellow bar on red. See page 246C.

---

[10] CATS 139.02.1 (22) Aerodromes and Heliports (as per AMDT SA-CATS 2/18), while the panels are described at CATS 91.06.13–4 (2).

Chapter 10: At your final destination 217

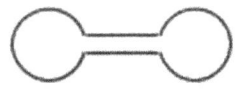 Called 'white dumbbell': aircraft must **take off or land or taxi** on runways and taxiways only. *How does one memorise it, as many get confused at exam time? Circles = runways (early runways were round fields, which was nice as you could decide the direction in which it was best to land but it probably confused everyone when calling a 'go around'). Strip in between = taxiway(s). All clear, all usable.*

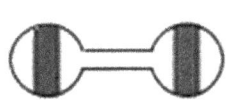 What happened to the dumbbells? The convenient round fields now have tarred runways, in black! And that is where you must **take off or land**. But 'other manoeuvres' need not be confined to those runways and the taxiway(s).

 Runway or taxiway is closed—white (or yellow).

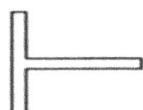 You **take off or land** toward the crossbar or 'cross arm' (that is where the runway, or 'shaft' as CATS put it, ends)—the T can be orange and at night illuminated or outlined by white lights. Cross arm is not a taxiway.

 Can be yellow and red, but in a 'conspicuous colour', displayed in the signalling area or near the runway. Indicates right and/or left hand circuit, that is the direction of turns after taking off and therefore, of the circuit itself. See page 246C.

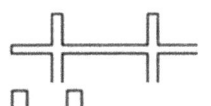 Beware, gliders are operating. *(If you are confused at the exam, just remember that gliders have very long wings.)*

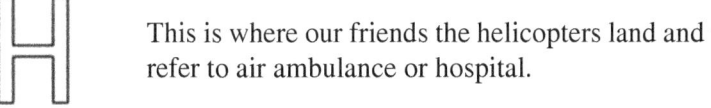

This is where our friends the helicopters land and take off. H does not refer to air ambulance or hospital.

 Very important in rural areas: agricultural flights in operation.

 Private aerodrome—but it appears nowhere in current regulations, as noted earlier (page 125)—although it could pop up as a rogue *exam question*. Just make a note of it.

10.6.5 Pyrotechnical signals (flares) sent from tower[11]

Flares are shot with a signal pistol or Very pistol (from the name of its inventor). They are **not directional** so can be seen from all directions, and for that reason are not meant for you in particular. They can be either—

Green = cleared to land
or
Red = do not land, wait for permission; overrides any previous instruction.

10.6.6 Light signals from tower[12]

So-called light guns send a **directional** beam, which is meant for you in particular. They emit red, green or white signals.

The pictorial on the next page best illustrates and summarises light signals from the tower *(exam questions aplenty)*:

---

[11] CATS 91.06.13–4.
[12] CATS 91.06.13–4.

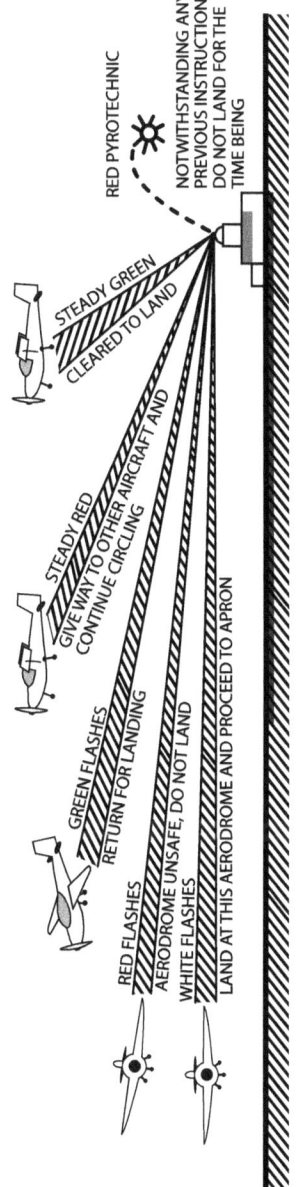

And explained, with mnemonics:

- steady red beam = do not land, give way to other aircraft, continue circling
  STeady= STandby
- flashing red beam = aerodrome unsafe, do not land, go to another aerodrome
  go away go away go away go away
- flashing green beam = return for landing (and you must ask for permission)
  come back come back come back come back
- steady green beam = cleared to land
  the grass (land) is green
- white flashes = cleared to land and proceed to apron
  clean kitchen-aprons are usually white

Of course be mindful of other traffic—if tower gives you a 'cleared to land' steady green beam it does not mean you fly blind. You must still ensure there is no danger of collision.

You have landed. Bravo! Your 'timepiece' (as the law calls it) reads 1700B.

Chapter 11

. . . .

Runway vacated!

You are on the ground, you have passed the holding point, you have called 'runway vacated', you have 'cleaned up' your aircraft, and are about to taxi. The law stands at the ready.

And now for the last regulations to bring you safely to where your aircraft 'finally comes to rest at the end of the flight', as CARS puts it, and to the end of your 'flight time':[1]

- Taxi rules that are general or of specific interest to a landing aircraft;
- Signals from or on the tower;
- Marshalling signals at aerodromes that provide the service;
- Paperwork.

11.1 TAXI RULES OF INTEREST TO A LANDING AIRCRAFT

> **Taxi rules**[2]
>
> '(1) Aircraft which are **landing** or taking off, shall be given right of way by other aircraft and by vehicles *[translation: you have right of way, but don't be adamant about it if some pushcart insists on driving on, just do what is necessary to avoid collision, as per sub-regulation (12) below]*.
>
> (2) An aircraft shall, **after landing**, unless otherwise authorised or instructed by an ATSU, **be moved clear of the runway in use,** as soon as it is safely possible to do so.
>
> (3) A vehicle which is towing an aircraft shall be given right of way by vehicles and **by other aircraft which are not landing** or taking off *[translation: you have right of way on the said vehicle]*.
>
> (4) An aircraft shall be given right of way by a vehicle which is not towing an aircraft.
>
> (5) An aircraft or vehicle which is obliged by the provisions of this regulation to give right of way to another aircraft, shall, if necessary in the circumstances in order to do so, reduce its speed or stop.

---

[1] CARS 1.01.1.
[2] CARS 91.06.11.

(6) If **danger of collision** exists between an aircraft or vehicle and another aircraft or vehicle, such of the following procedures as may be appropriate in the circumstances, shall be applied:

    (a) When the two are approaching head-on or nearly head-on, each shall turn to the right;

    (b) when one is overtaking the other, the one which is overtaking shall keep out of the way of the other by turning to the right, and no subsequent change in the relative positions of the two shall absolve the one which is overtaking from this obligation, until it is finally past and clear of the other;

    (c) when the two are converging, the one which has the other on its right, must give way to the other and must avoid crossing ahead of the other unless passing well clear of it.

(7) A vehicle moving along a runway or taxiway, shall as far as practicable keep to the **right side** of the runway or taxiway *[do not be confused here as this can be a trick exam question: your aircraft is an aircraft, not a vehicle]*.

(8) When an aircraft is being towed, the person in charge of the towing vehicle shall be responsible for compliance with the provisions of this regulation.

(9) **An aircraft operated on a controlled aerodrome shall not taxi on the manoeuvring area without clearance** from the aerodrome control tower and shall comply with any instructions given by that unit.

(10) **An aircraft taxiing on the manoeuvring area of an uncontrolled aerodrome** shall taxi in accordance with the ground control procedures which may be in force at such aerodrome *[translation: do your homework before selecting it as a destination, and get all the information needed]*.

(11) **While taxiing, an aircraft shall [ie must]** *[this applies to aerodromes that are fully equipped]*

    (a) stop and hold at all runway-holding positions unless otherwise authorised by the aerodrome control tower; and

    (b) stop at all lighted stop bars and may proceed further when the lights are switched off.

(12) **Nothing in this regulation shall relieve the PIC of an aircraft** or the person in charge of a vehicle, **from the responsibility** for taking such action as will best aid **to avert collision.**'

11.2 Signals from or on the tower

Refer to the pictorial on page 219.

11.3 MARSHALLING SIGNALS (A)

You will have to obey marshals when they are present—and learn the basic signals (A) and (H) reproduced below.[3]

As a PPL you must remember these basics for an arrival:[4]

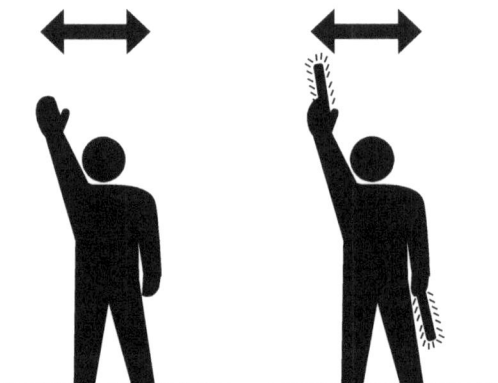

I am directing, follow instructions.

This bay!

Move ahead!

---

[3] CATS 91.06.10–5.
[4] CATS 91.06.13–5 .

Chapter 11: Runway vacated! 223

Turn to your left (= pilot's left).

Turn to your right (= pilot's right).

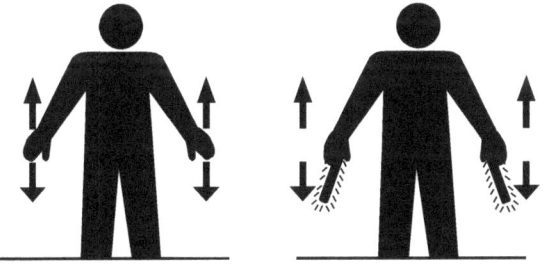
Slow down!

Stop!

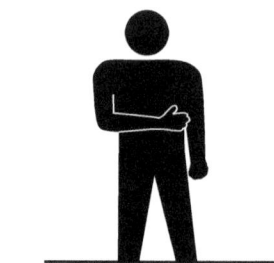

Engage brakes! (fingers extended, clenched fist)

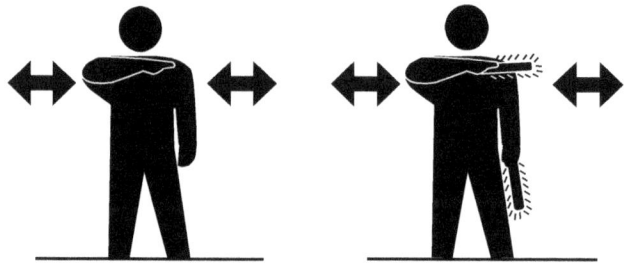

Cut engine(s)!

You are now stationed at the apron. It is 1705B.

Think of cancelling SAR if not already done! Note the time of cancellation.

What is left to be done, after securing the aircraft? Paperwork, of course. Back to your paper plane.

11.4 BACK TO PAPER PLANE

There are three vital actions; they are vital for this flight, vital for your aircraft maintenance record, and vital for your own logging of hours to reach the magic number of 1000:
- Filing an arrival report;
- Filling in the aircraft flight folio as per regulations; and
- Filling in your pilot logbook.

Bear in mind that the flight folio's main purpose is safety, through the **maintenance** of the aircraft, and not to prove that you have clocked up so many hours.

11.4.1 Arrival report in case of a flight plan

There are cases where you will have to file a report of arrival, or arrival report:

> **Arrival report rules**[5]
>
> - Where an ATSU is not in operation at the aerodrome of intended landing, a report of arrival as prescribed must be submitted to an ATSU, by the quickest means of communication available, **immediately after landing, in respect of a flight for which an ATS flight plan was submitted and not as yet closed or for which search and rescue notification was requested and designated with a particular ATSU.**
> - When **communication facilities at the arrival aerodrome are inadequate** and alternative arrangements for the handling of arrival reports on the ground are not available, the PIC must, **prior to landing the aircraft or immediately thereafter**, if practicable, **transmit to the appropriate ATSU a message comparable to an arrival report, in respect of a flight for which an ATS flight plan was submitted and not as yet closed or for which a search and rescue notification was requested with a nominated ATSU.**

The first case is a frequent one for private pilots who fly to aerodromes without an ATSU. Both cases apply only if a flight plan has been filed.

The arrival report follows a set format:

> **Format of an arrival report**[6]
>
> - aircraft identification
> - departure aerodrome
> - destination aerodrome (only in the case of a diversionary landing)
> - arrival aerodrome
> - time of arrival.

11.4.2 Filling in the aircraft flight folio

Here is a reminder of the purpose of a flight folio:

> **Flight folio**[7]
>
> '(1) The owner or operator of a South African registered aircraft shall ensure that the aircraft carries a flight folio or any other similar document which meets the requirements of and contains the information as prescribed in Document SA-CATS 91, at all times.

---

[5] CARS 91.03.4 (9) and (10).
[6] CARS 91.03.4–2.
[7] CARS 91.03.5.

> (2) **The flight folio shall be kept up-to-date and maintained in a legible manner by the PIC.**
>
> (3) All entries shall be made immediately upon completion of the occurrence to which they refer.
>
> (4) In the case of maintenance being undertaken on the aircraft, the entry shall be certified by the person taking responsibility for the maintenance performed.
>
> (5) The owner or operator shall retain the flight folio for a period of five years calculated from the date of the last entry therein.'

Specific information contained in a flight folio:

> **Information to be contained in a flight folio[8]**
>
> '(1) An owner or operator must retain the following information for each flight in the form of a flight folio—
>
> (a) aircraft registration;
>
> (b) date;
>
> (c) name(s) of flight crew member(s);
>
> (d) duty assignment of flight crew member(s);
>
> (e) place of departure;
>
> (f) place of arrival;
>
> (g) time of departure (off-block time);
>
> (h) time of arrival (on-block time);
>
> (i) hours of flight;
>
> (j) nature of flight;
>
> (k) incidents, observations (if any);
>
> (l) **signature of pilot-in-command;**
>
> (m) the current maintenance statement giving the aeroplane maintenance status of what maintenance, scheduled or out of phase, is next due;
>
> (n) all outstanding deferred defects which affect the operation of the aeroplane;
>
> (o) fuel and oil used; and
>
> (p) fuel and oil uplift.
>
> (2) The owner or operator need not keep a flight folio or parts thereof, if the relevant information is available in other documentation.

---

[8] CARS 91.03.5.

> (3) The owner or operator must ensure that all entries are made concurrently and that they are made in **ink or other permanent marking** *[as the PIC fills in the flight folio, the PIC has to use ink or permanent marking]*.'
>
> And remember this mandatory report as listed in 'Duties of PIC regarding flight operations' which restates item (m) above:
>
> 'The PIC of an aircraft shall **record any technical defect and the exceeding of any technical limitation** which occurred while he or she was responsible for the flight, in the flight folio.'[9] *[This can come up an exam question.]* Why is this so? Because the main purpose of the flight folio is good maintenance of the aircraft.

The PIC's duty with regard to the flight folio

In addition to the three items in bold in the two regulations above, you should note the following:

> 'It is the duty and responsibility of the pilot-in-command to ensure that unusual occurrences, defects or suspected faults, coming to his or her notice during operations and which affect or may affect the serviceability and safety of the aircraft, are recorded in the aircraft's flight folio as and when they occur and are reported to the appropriate maintenance personnel for investigation or rectification.'[10]

And note this, often overlooked, as it is buried in the Maintenance standards:

> 'Entries in the aircraft flight folio must be accompanied by the pilot's signature, licence number and the date of entry.'[11] *(This is an exam question, CPL included.)*

11.4.3 Logging of flight time in your pilot logbook

This is the most precious legal and personal requirement for a pilot's career. The law gives precise instructions on format, information contained, recording and maintenance.

Here are the **rules** *(exam questions!)*:[12]

---

[9] CARS 91.02.8 (4) (j).
[10] CATS 43.02.8 Section A 1(4).
[11] CATS 43.02.2–1 (3).
[12] CARS 61.01.8.

> '(1) The holder of a pilot licence must maintain in a pilot logbook **a record of all his or her flight time, instrument time, FSTD time and instruction time.** Where **electronic logbooks** are used, the electronic data **must be printed on paper at least every 90 days** and the printed pages filed sequentially in a binder.
>
> (2) The form of and information to be contained in the logbook, referred to in sub-regulation (1), and the manner in which such logbook must be maintained are as prescribed in Appendix A to Document SA-CATS 61 [see annexure 5 in this book].
>
> (3) Entries in pilot logbooks must be **made within the following periods** after the completion of the flight to be recorded—
>
> *(a)* **7 days in the case of flights not for hire and reward** (Part 91 operations), **flight training, and domestic commercial air transport operations;**
>
> *(b)* **14 days in the case of international commercial** air transport operations;
>
> *(c)* **48 hours after return to base** in the case where a pilot is engaged **in flight operations away from the base** where the pilot logbook is normally kept.
>
> (4) All pilots must **retain their pilot logbooks for at least 60 months** calculated from the date they no longer hold a valid pilot licence.
>
> (5) If the holder of a pilot licence carries out **a number of flights upon the same day** and the **interval between successive flights does not exceed 180 minutes**, such series of flights **may be recorded as a single entry**, provided that in the case of a cross-country flight the route and intermediate stops must be recorded.
>
> (6) The holder of a pilot licence must make the **logbook available for inspection** upon a reasonable request by the Director, an authorised officer, inspector or authorised person.'

You have now really landed back in the real world, made of paper and red tape, but you have flown legally, and flown beautifully—literally 'by the book'. You can sit on the stoep of the clubhouse, watch the sun set . . . and plan the next flight.

Alas, there may have been a problem or two.

Chapter 12

How to report an incident or an accident

In the course of your flight you may have been involved in an incident or an accident. What is to be done?

Two Parts of CARS and CATS are relevant here *(exam questions!)*:
- mainly Part 12, which deals with 'Aviation accidents and incidents';[1]
- and also Part 92, which deals with Conveyance of dangerous goods (more applicable to advanced pilots).

12.1 THE PIC MUST REPORT INCIDENTS AND ACCIDENTS

It is one of your listed duties and here is the governing rule:[2]

> 'The PIC of an aircraft shall [ie must]
> - report any accident or incident involving the aircraft in accordance with Part 12, unless the PIC is incapacitated or an operator has established another means of reporting accidents or incidents, in which case the operator shall initiate the report;
> - report any dangerous goods accident or incident involving the aircraft in accordance with Part 92;
> - if the aircraft is endangered in flight by a near collision with any other aircraft or object, faulty air traffic procedure or lack of compliance with applicable procedures by an ATSU or a flight crew member or a failure of ATS facilities, submit an ATS incident report as prescribed by regulation 12.02.2';
> - The PIC must report the accident or incident within 24 hours;[3]
> - **If it is an ATS related incident** someone, from pilot to ATS personnel, who witnessed it must **report** the incident **'as soon as possible'**.[4]

There is a fair amount of confusion about how 'notification' and 'report' are used, informally or formally. A **Report, as such**, termed either 'Preliminary' or 'Final',

---

[1] CATS 12 Part uses the singular in its title, 'Aviation Accident and Incident', but it does not change anything.
[2] CARS 91.02.8 (4) (g) (h) (i).
[3] CARS 12.02.2 (1) for accidents and (2) for incidents.
[4] CARS 12.02.2 (3): then the ATSU that has received the report will 'immediately on receipt of the notification, notify the Executive responsible for aircraft accident and incident investigation in the appropriate form'.

can be established only **by the Investigator-in-charge** and follows a strict format laid down in CATS and aligned with procedures defined by ICAO.[5] But it is your initial—on the spot, as it were—'report' that 'notifies' whoever is to be told of an incident or accident and that triggers a formal notification and an investigation leading to the Report itself.[6]

Below you will find more on who notifies whom exactly and of what.

First, what is the difference between accident and incident, and hazard?

12.2 DEFINITIONS: INCIDENT, ACCIDENT, HAZARD[7]

What is an incident?

> ' "Incident" means an occurrence, other than an accident, **associated with the operation of an aircraft,** which affects or could affect the safety of aircraft operations.'

What is an accident?

> ' "Accident" includes an **occurrence associated with the operation of** an aircraft which, in the case of **a manned aircraft takes place between the time any person boards the aircraft with the intention of flight until such time as all such persons have disembarked,** or in the case of an unmanned aircraft, takes place between the time the aircraft is ready to move with the purpose of flight until such time it comes to rest at the end of the flight and the primary propulsion system is shut down, during which—
>
> *(a)* **a person is fatally or seriously injured** as a result of—
>
>   (i) being in the aircraft;
>
>   (ii) direct contact with any part of the aircraft, including parts which have become detached or are released from the aircraft; or
>
>   (iii) direct exposure to jet blast, rotor or propeller wake, except when the injuries are from natural causes, self-inflicted or inflicted by other persons, or when the injuries are to stowaways hiding outside the areas normally available to passengers and flight crew; or

---

[5] CATS 12.05.1.
[6] The format of the report is at 12.05.1.
[7] CARS 1.01.1.

> *(b)* **the aircraft sustains damage or structural failure** which—
>
> > (i) adversely affects the structural strength, performance or flight characteristics of the aircraft; and
> >
> > (ii) would normally require major repair or replacement of the affected component, except for engine failure or damage when the damage is limited to a single engine, (including its cowlings or accessories), to propellers, wing tips, antennae, probes, vanes, tyres, brakes, wheels, fairings, panels, landing gear doors, windscreens, the aircraft skin (such as small dents or puncture holes), or for minor damages to main rotor blades, tail rotor blades, landing gear, and hose resulting from hail or bird strike (including holes in the radome); or
>
> *(c)* the **aircraft is still missing** after an official search has been terminated and the wreckage has not been located;
>
> or
>
> *(d)* the **aircraft is in a place** where it is completely **inaccessible**.'

In other words, to determine if something that happened (termed an 'occurrence') is an accident or an incident, you see if it matches the criteria for an accident. If not, it is an incident.

For example: as you were about to land at FA** an airfield worker, who was standing motionless and clear of the runway, suddenly starts running across the runway, and you have to power up to avoid him—that is an incident.

What is a 'hazard'?[8]

> '(1) Hazards are **negative indications of a safety trend, or a possibility** for an **incident or accident.**
>
> (2) Hazards include, but are not confined to, human factor errors, inadequate fire and rescue services, bird sighting at aerodromes or in migration, issues such as runway markings that are difficult to see, lack of diligence given to aeronautical information circulars, poor communications, ignorance about dangerous goods, incorrect perceptions of ATC or pilots, ergonomics, confusion about which frequency to use, visual illusions, medical problems, lack of or misunderstanding of legislation, prevalence for near collisions, passenger behaviour, and poor ramp standards.

---

[8] CATS 12.01.10.

(3) Many **incidents** are reportable to the Executive Manager: Aircraft Accident and Incident Investigation in terms of Part 12 of CARS. These incidents must not be sent as a CAHRS report *[CAHRS is the acronym for Confidential aviation hazard report system]*.[9] In such cases, if this is reported to the designated body or institution, the reporter must be advised of the correct method for such reporting. The designated body or institution will still maintain the confidentiality of such a report and will not forward the report to the Executive Manager: Aircraft Accident and Incident Investigation. However, **the nature of the hazard may be used for awareness purposes**.

(4) **Confidential aviation hazard reporting is a tool for accident prevention** in that hazards are identified before there is loss of life, injury or damage, ie loss. It is not a statistical tool. **It is non-punitive.**

(5) For further information on identification of hazards and confidential reporting refer to the ICAO Technical Publication 'Accident prevention manual' (Doc 9422).'

So, to go back to the airfield worker running across the runway: on second thoughts, you may decide to re-qualify it as a 'hazard' that is a trend of negligence at a poorly managed airfield, and report it using the CAHRS form. Hazard reporting is 'non-punitive'. The operator will get a letter telling them to get their act together or risk having the airfield closed.

12.3 WHO NOTIFIES WHOM OF WHAT?

Exam questions!

Notification of incidents[10]

'(1) The PIC, and any other flight crew member, operator or owner, as the case may be, of an aircraft involved in an incident (including a serious incident), **other than an ATS incident**, within the Republic, shall *[ie must]*, **as soon as possible but at least within 24 hours** since the time of such incident, notify of such incident—

(a) the Executive Manager: Aircraft Accident and Incident Investigation;

or

(b) an ATSU;

or

(c) the nearest Police Station.

---

[9] SACAA Form Number: CA 12–37 Confidential Aviation Hazard Reporting (CAHRS).
[10] CARS 12.02.2.

(2) If an ATSU is notified of an incident in terms of sub-regulation (1) *[read: other than an ATS incident]*, such ATSU shall, immediately on receipt of the notification and as prescribed in Document SA-CATS 12, notify—

   (a) the Executive Manager: Aircraft Accident and Incident Investigation; and

   (b) where such incident occurs on an aerodrome, the aerodrome manager.

(3) The PIC, any other flight crew member, operator or owner, as the case may be, of **an aircraft involved in an ATS incident** within the Republic, or any ATS personnel witnessing an ATS incident, shall, as soon as possible, notify an ATSU of such ATS incident, and such ATSU shall immediately on receipt of the notification, notify the Executive Manager: Aircraft Accident and Incident Investigation in the appropriate form.'

Notification of accidents[11]

'(1) **The PIC of an aircraft involved** in an accident within the Republic, **or if he or she is killed or incapacitated,** a flight crew member, or if there are no surviving flight crew members or if they are incapacitated, the operator or owner, as the case may be, shall, **as soon as possible but at least within 24 hours** since the time of the accident, notify—

   (a) the Executive Manager: Aircraft Accident and Incident Investigation;

   (b) an ATSU; or

   (c) the nearest police station,

   of such accident.

(2) If an air traffic service unit (ATSU) or police station is notified of an accident in terms of sub-regulation (1), such ATSU or police station shall, immediately on receipt of the notification, notify—

   (a) the Executive Manager: Aircraft Accident and Incident Investigation; and

   (b) where such accident occurs on an aerodrome, the aerodrome manager.'

Outside the Republic of South Africa, for instance an accident occurred in Botswana, the PIC—or, if killed or incapacitated, whoever is able to do so (crew, owner, operator)— must report it to the appropriate authority in the state or territory where the accident or incident occurred, directly or through any ATSU, and to the SACAA Executive Manager: Aircraft Accident and Incident Investigation.

The SACAA website provides contact details for the Accident and Incident Investigations Division (AIID): 24/7 telephone line: +27 (0) 60 991 9915. Email: AIIDInbox@SACAA.co.za.

---

[11] CARS 12.02.1.

Here is a list of 'particulars' you should try to provide ('submit') to the AIID officer in charge, who will then fill in the appropriate form (the form is an internal reporting form).[12]

> **Particulars of notification**[13]
>
> 'Any notification of an accident or incident referred to in regulation 12.02.1, 12.02.2 or 12.02.3 *[see inserts above]* other than an ATS incident, shall *[ie must]*
>
> (a) include the following particulars:
>
>   (i) type, model, nationality and registration marks of the aircraft;
>
>   (ii) name of the owner or operator, as applicable;
>
>   (iii) qualification of flight crew members;
>
>   (iv) the date and time of the accident or incident, specified in Co-ordinated Universal Time or local time *[Bravo time in South Africa]*;
>
>   (v) last point of departure and point of intended landing of the aircraft;
>
>   (vi) location of accident or incident with reference to an easily identifiable geographical point and, if known, with reference to latitude and longitude;
>
> number of—
>
>   *(aa)* flight crew members and passengers aboard, killed or seriously injured; and
>
>   *(bb)* other persons killed or seriously injured *[meaning people on the ground or in another aircraft or vehicle]*;
>
>   (vii) nature of the accident or incident and extent of damage to aircraft as far as is known;
>
>   (viii) terrain characteristics of the area where the accident or incident occurred;
>
>   (ix) details of any dangerous goods or hazardous substances known to be on board the aircraft; and
>
>   (x) any other relevant information; and
>
> (b) be submitted forthwith to the Executive responsible for aircraft accident and incident investigation, and any information which is not immediately available shall be submitted in writing as soon as it becomes available.'

In short you call or email, provide details, and later you can give more information in writing to the case officer.

---

[12] Personal communication to the writer from the Senior Manager, AIID of 28 November 2018.

[13] CARS 12.02.4.

12.4 WHO HAS ACCESS TO AN ACCIDENT SCENE AND WHAT OF THE WRECKAGE?

(Frequent exam questions)

Access to the scene of an accident[14]

'(1) No person other than *[translation: only the following are permitted]*
- *(a)* a member of the rescue service;
- *(b)* a pro tem investigator *[plain English: temporary]*
- *(c)* an investigator;
- *(d)* an accredited representative;
- *(e)* an advisor;
- *(f)* a member of the South African Police Service; or
- *(g)* any other person authorised by the Executive Manager: Aircraft Accident and Incident Investigation, after consultation with the investigator-in-charge, shall, until such time as the investigator-in-charge otherwise determines, have access to an aircraft which has been involved in an accident or to the wreck or wreckage and any marks resulting from the accident which may be of assistance in an investigation.

(2) Every person permitted by the provisions of sub-regulation (1) or authorised in terms thereof to have access to an aircraft which has been involved in an accident or to the wreck or wreckage or to places where marks resulting from the accident occur which may be of assistance in an investigation, shall be subject to the direction of the investigator-in-charge until the investigation has been completed.'

Guarding of wreckage[15]

'Where an accident occurs within the Republic, the PIC of the aircraft involved in the accident, or if he or she is killed or incapacitated, a flight crew member, or if there are no surviving flight crew members, or if they are incapacitated, the operator or owner of such aircraft or where the accident occurs on an aerodrome, the aerodrome manager, shall—

- *(a)* pending the arrival of a police guard, take such steps which may be necessary to prevent any interference with the aircraft, the wreck or wreckage and anything transported therein and any marks resulting from the accident which may be of assistance in an investigation;

---

[14] CARS 12.04.2.
[15] CARS 12.04.1.

(b) forthwith arrange with a member of the South African Police Service to guard the aircraft, the wreck or wreckage and anything transported therein and any marks resulting from the accident which may be of assistance in an investigation.'

Interfering with wreckage[16]

'(1) Subject to the provisions of this part, no person shall interfere with an aircraft which has been involved in an accident, the wreck or wreckage, a part or component thereof or anything transported therein or any marks resulting from the accident which may be of assistance in an investigation–

  (a) until authorised to do so by the investigator-in-charge; and

  (b) until, in the case of an aircraft which must be cleared by a customs officer by virtue of the provisions of the Customs and Excise Act, 1964 (Act No. 91 of 1964), clearance has been issued or permission granted by such officer.

(2) The provisions of sub-regulation (1) shall not prevent any action necessary for—

  (a) the rescue or extrication of persons or animals from the aircraft or the wreck;

  (b) the reasonable protection of the aircraft, the wreck or wreckage from destruction by fire or other causes;

  (c) the safeguarding by the owner, operator or police guard of precious metals, jewellery or valuables;

  (d) the prevention of danger or removal of an obstruction to other aircraft, other means of transport or to the public; and

  (e) the removal of the aircraft, any part or component thereof or anything transported therein to a safe place, when in water or otherwise endangered.'

Let's leave this grim reality, and let's fly into the magic of the night . . . if you were late and may now be in a spot of trouble without a night rating.

---

[16] CARS 12.04.4.

Chapter 13

. . . .

Night flying

> Now the Patagonia mail plane was entering the storm. He read his altitude, five thousand five hundred feet, and pressed the controls with his palms to bring it down. He corrected the gliding angle approximately, verifying on the chart the height of the Andes foothills. To keep a safety margin he determined to fly at a trifle above two thousand, staking his altitude as a gambler risks his fortune.
>
> Antoine de Saint Exupéry *Night Flight*[1]

Perhaps, as you are enjoying a leisurely flight back to base, you lose track of time and you realise that the sun is about to drop below the horizon. You will soon be flying at night if your aerodrome is 10 or so minutes away—hopefully you hold a Night Rating and your airfield destination has lights, and there is no fog, and you are not flying into the Golden Gate Highlands, like the famed aviator flew into the Andes.

In this scenario we assume you hold a Night Rating (NR).

If you do not have a NR and night is falling, what do you do? You declare an emergency, as you are at very serious risk, you and even more your passenger, who signed the waiver of liability with the understanding you would fly legally.

For that reason this chapter is meant to achieve two purposes:
- to provide information about the Night Rating to SPL or PPL pilots who are proceeding to advanced training, and need the NR;
- to be a refresher for the few private pilots who hold a NR and entice others to get that further training, for safety's sake.

Some PPL exam questions may relate to night flying. They are generally about the definitions of day and night, VFR rules, privileges, lights and signals.

13.1 THE NIGHT RATING

Students (A, H) interested in or preparing for a Night Rating are directed to annexure 17 where they will find all of the usual documentation: exam syllabus and training, test, licensing, privileges and limitations, as well as a copy of the Skills Test. There is little one can add to it except this piece of advice: passing the Skills Test revalidates your PPL licence, so think about it when you send in your application, and pay the fee.

---

[1] Antoine de Saint Exupéry *Night Flight* translated by Stuart Gilbert (slightly adapted) 1 ed (1932) 109.

238   Air Law

As far as the theoretical exam is concerned, it is (much too) short and mixes questions about air law, meteorology, human performance and limitations, and lighting systems.

The air law component deals with aspects that have already been covered in this book, and are covered again in this chapter as a recap or refresher, further on.

- the definition of night flying;
- the privileges and limitations associated with the night rating;
- the PIC's responsibilities;
- the equipment to be carried on board for night flying;
- aircraft lighting, including navigation lights;
- VFR differences from day flying;
- aerodrome requirements for night flying.

As for **human performance,** it is more about limitations due to night sensory activities: visual illusions, vertigo, hypoxia and autokinesis. These have been covered in your PPL HP&L syllabus. Turn to annexure 17 for a list.

As for **meteorology**, night flying has its own problems and the syllabus highlights fog (advection, radiation, katabatic), wind veering, ice and frost, and night thunderstorms. Remember that night flying is VFR. Go back to your notes for that PPL examination.

As for **lights,** they are of course essential, both in and on your aircraft and on the ground. These are covered already in this book, and are recapped below.

The NR examination should not pose any problem for you as it is by and large a reprise of what you studied for your PPL theoretical examinations.

Possibly the most important and valuable part of the NR training is to learn how to fly on **instruments** (10 hours minimum), and accurately so. It is also the most riveting part. At night, the margin for error is limited. Flying at night also sharpens your awareness of weather conditions. Fog can form suddenly and there is little you can do if you are not prepared, except to lock on a beacon and fly to the nearest airport, where the chances are better that you will be able to touch down than at your base airfield with minimal lighting set up during a seemingly perfect moonlit night, which has turned foggy.

An incidental aspect of NR practical training is using a **simulator**: 5 out of the 10 hours of instrument training may be done in a FSTD (A and H requirements vary: see annexure 17). They may be done before you actually sit 'under the hood' (a device that prevents you, while flying, from seeing anything other than the six main flying instruments or the EFIS display). But nothing replaces the feeling of flying and scanning instruments in flight, and recovering from unusual altitudes (a wing drop for instance) in an actual aircraft while nearly blindfolded.

All NR training, including the fantastic nav at night, is done dual at PPL level. No solo.

Read annexure 17 carefully. Your instructor, as mandated by law, will take you through it in the five hours of compulsory instruction.

Let us now refresh or recap.

13.2 WHAT IS NIGHT?

To fly at night legally you need to have and to do a number of things, starting with the obvious: recognise that night is falling. But, what is night?

> **'night'** means the period from 15 minutes after sunset to 15 minutes before sunrise, sunset and sunrise being as given in the publication 'Times of Sunrise, Sunset and Local Apparent Noon of the South African Astronomical Observatory' or a similar publication issued by a recognised astronomical observatory.[2]

Check the accurate time when you prepare for your flight and make sure your watch is more than a retro display with 50 illegible dials. An accurate time-piece is compulsory anyway.

And day?

> **'day'** means the period of time from 15 minutes before sunrise to 15 minutes after sunset, sunrise and sunset being as given in the publication 'Times of Sunrise, Sunset and Local Apparent Noon of the South African Astronomical Observatory' or in a similar publication issued by a recognised astronomical observatory.[3]

Although it does not apply to pilots who fly for pleasure, make a note of this *(as it can pop up in examinations later)*:

'night duty' means a period of not less than four hours between 20h00 and 06h00 of the next day.[4]

So, if the Observatory (local) time for sunset is 19h10 and you are on final approach at 19h30 although it still looks sort of clear and you can see the runway, you are in fact night flying—with all that goes with it, from procedures, and equipment, to risks and liabilities.

13.3 ARE YOU FIT TO FLY AT NIGHT?

Of course you are since you hold a valid medical certificate. But remember that night is fertile with illusions and sensory errors.

---

[2] CARS 1.01.1.
[3] CARS 1.01.1.
[4] CARS 1.01.1.

'It has been estimated that 80 percent of our total information intake is through the eyes' says a FAA document.[5] Why is this so important? Because night flying is VFR and V means visual, and the governing rule applies:

> **'Every VFR flight shall be so conducted that the aircraft is flown with visual reference to the surface by day and to identifiable objects by night and at no time above more than three eighths of cloud within a radius of five nautical miles of such aircraft.'[6]**

As a result, since you must fly under specific weather minima (= visibility) and by being able to see and identify correctly objects at night that will 'reference' your ability to judge position and distances, **visual issues** are crucial to flying at night. You must be fit to make calls of judgment, and that fitness depends upon physiological conditions, mainly visual.

When you transition from day flying to night flying, your vision has to adapt to the change in luminosity and depth perception (the rods come into operation). If you look straight into a gorgeous sunset, your eyes will take more time to adjust. Do not stare into the last rays of the sun, in any event.[7] As you know from your Human Performance and Limitations training, it can take up to 30 minutes for eyes to adapt.

Also, instruct your passenger not to play with his torch: a ray of light will blind you temporarily, as will a strobe.

Always look slightly off centre of a bright light in the distance. Do not rest your eyes for too long on what is close (your panel) to avoid empty field myopia, that is, evaluate distances by what you can see well, ie the instruments.

Night vision can also deteriorate at cabin altitudes as low as 5 000 ft due to oxygen depletion (hypoxia).

Eye–inner ear relation plays a role. Move your eyes slowly and do not move your head quickly as it will result in disorientation, and vertigo.

You will also begin to evaluate vertical and horizontal distances less accurately as you approach the runway, especially on a moonless or overcast night, over a terrain with only a few lights, resulting in what is called a 'black hole'. You may think the airfield is closer than in reality, that you are too high, and then correct with a too low approach, leading to a possible crash.

The rule is: **trust your instruments**, and trust the PAPI. Your body is not made to be in the air to begin with, and to be up there at night even less. Aircraft instruments and ground equipment exist to supplement and complement and

---

[5] *How to Avoid a Mid Air Collision*, document P-8740–51.
[6] CARS 91.06.21 (1). It applies to night flying as it is under VFR.
[7] These remarks are borrowed from FFA *Airplane Flying Handbook* chapter 10.

correct the wrong sensory input your body is giving you when you fly at night, without a natural horizon.

But you have a NR and all this will kick in. The main point here is to be aware of the transition from day to night, and not to carry on flying as you would do by daylight. Your eyes must now scan the instruments as you prepare for the circuit and anticipate your headings.

13.4 IS YOUR AIRCRAFT EQUIPPED AND ARE YOU READY?

Of course you did not inspect your aircraft in the morning of your departure as you would for a night flight—such as switching on the pitot and touching it to make sure it gets warm, something NR pilots always do. Let us assume you did.

What do you need to be legal at night? And this implies how you pre-flight by checking that all that is required for night flying is on board, or fitted, and serviceable.

13.4.1 Cockpit equipment (A) sound and light

General requirements
- Since night flying is VFR, you need '**a chart holder** in an easily readable position which can be **illuminated**'.[8]
- You need 'a **serviceable electrical torch** for each required crew member' (which is you), 'readily accessible to such crew member when seated at his or her designated station'.[9] Why? If the electrical system fails, at least you can use a torch. Redundancy is recommended for yourself: have an extra torch (or even better a forehead headlight, with a red filter functionality). And take batteries on a long night nav.
- The power supplied by the **electrical system** must have 'adequate **illumination for all instruments and equipment**, used by the flight crew and essential for the safe operation of the aircraft' and passenger compartment.[10]

Single-pilot extra requirements
- Your aircraft must be certificated for single-pilot operations at night if you conduct single-pilot flying.[11]
- In a single-pilot operation the aircraft must be 'equipped with a means of **displaying charts** that enables them to be readable in all ambient light conditions'.[12]
- In single-pilot operation, you must be 'equipped with **a headset with boom microphone or equivalent and have a transmit button** positioned in such a

---
[8] CARS 91.04.4 (f).
[9] CARS 91.04.3 (1) (d).
[10] CARS 91.04.3 (2).
[11] CARS 91.04.6 (1).
[12] CARS 91.04.6 (1) (b).

way that it may be operated without the pilot having to remove his or her hands from the control wheel, joy stick or cyclic stick'.[13]

13.4.2 Lights to be displayed by aircraft at night, in flight or on the movement area

Here are the rules:
- Serviceable **navigation lights**[14] 'intended **to indicate the relative path of the aircraft** to an observer', must 'be displayed in the air'[15] and on the movement area;[16] they can also be used to comply with the regulation that 'aircraft on the movement area of an aerodrome during night shall display lights intended **to indicate the extremities** of their structure'.[17] **See the picture on page 246D.**
- **In relation to the risk of collision at night** and with regard to the position of your navigation lights, you must consider the following:
  'An overtaking aircraft is an aircraft which approaches another aircraft from the rear on a line forming an angle of less than **70 degrees** with the plane of symmetry of the latter aircraft, and will therefore be in such position with reference to the other aircraft, that **by night it should be unable to see either of the other aircraft's wingtip navigation lights**'.[18] **Refer to the picture in section 8.2.**
- Two serviceable **landing lights**, or **one single serviceable** landing light housing with **two separately energised** filaments, are required.[19]
- A serviceable **rotating beacon or strobe lights** are needed.[20] The rotating beacon must be on when the aircraft is operating on **the movement area** with engines running.[21]
- **While in flight** '(during the day and) **at all times** at night, **(strobe) lights** intended **to attract attention** to the aircraft' must be used.[22]
- You may **reduce the intensity or switch off any 'flashing lights'** if they affect you or 'dazzle' someone outside, in the air or on the ground.[23]

---

[13] CARS 91.04.6 (1) (a).
[14] CARS 91.04.3.
[15] CATS 91.06.10–2.
[16] CARS 91.06.10 (1) (b) and (2) (a).
[17] CARS 91.06.10 (2) (b).
[18] CARS 91.06.7 (10).
[19] CARS 91.04.3.
[20] CARS 91.04.3.
[21] CARS 91.06.10 (1) (d).
[22] CARS 91.06.10 (1) (a).
[23] CARS 91.06. 10 (4) (b).

> **Helicopter**[24]
>
> You need to have:
>
> '(a) in the case of a flight by night within 10 nautical miles, a light or lights providing adequate illumination both forward and downward to facilitate safe approaches, landings and take-offs; or
>
> (b) in the case of a flight by night of more than 10 nautical miles, two landing lights or a single light having two separately energised filaments that are capable of providing adequate illumination both forwards and downwards to facilitate safe approaches, landings and take-offs.'

13.4.3 Taking a passenger at night?

You must be recent, that is, you must have '**personally**, within the 90 days immediately preceding the flight, carried out at least three take-offs and three landings by night in the same class'.[25] Day-time take-offs and landings do not count.

13.5 NIGHT FLYING IS VFR BUT . . .

. . . it has its own peculiar problems, and regulations, as follows:

13.5.1 Weather and wind

Weather: Refer back to page 117 for full details on applicable VFR weather minima.

Special VFR does not exist in night flying *(exam!)*, except for helicopters.[26]

Fog: Radiation fog is a common occurrence at night. There is valley fog or upslope fog in mountainous regions. Advection fog occurs near the coast.

Wind velocity: Night flying is supposed to be in 'smooth air'. If the surface wind (30 ft) can drop to nothing compared with daytime, the difference between it and aloft will be greater. You can experience **wind shear**.

Wind direction: Also remember that, in our hemisphere, the surface wind compared with wind at or above 2 000 ft veers at night, that is, changes direction counter clockwise, as you descend.

Katabatic wind: This is strong wind flowing downslope in mountains. It can also result in fog at the bottom.

Land breeze: Also, after sunset, near a coast, expect a land breeze, blowing from your inland airfield towards the nearby sea. This may result in a drift if your airfield is parallel to a coast: scan your direction indicator, and correct.

(These points tend to come up at examinations.)

---

[24] CARS 91.03.3 (4).
[25] CARS 91.02.4 (2).
[26] Refer to CARS 91.06.22.

13.5.2 Height and terrain

Here is the full regulation to avoid collision with terrain.[27]

> '**Except when necessary for take-off or landing**, or with the express permission of the Director, an aircraft shall **at night**, in IMC or when operated in accordance with IFR, be flown—
>
> (a) at a height of **at least 1 000 ft above the highest terrain or obstacle** where the height of such terrain or obstacle does not exceed 5 000 ft above sea level **within 5 NM of the aircraft in flight**; or
>
> (b) at a height of at least **2 000 ft above the highest terrain or obstacle located within 5 NM of the aircraft in flight where the height of such terrain or obstacle exceeds 5 000 ft above sea level**: Provided that within areas determined by the Director the minimum height may be reduced to 1 000 ft above the highest terrain or obstacle located within 5 NM of the aircraft in flight, and the aircraft is flown in accordance with such procedures as the Director may determine.'
>
> Note: the regulation mentions 'aircraft'; not aeroplane or helicopter, but 'aircraft'.

13.5.3 Aerodrome lighting[28]

Do not assume that a day time airfield suddenly becomes a night time one by magic. The airfield has to be properly equipped or on a terrain that does not pose a risk. AIP AD will give you the information you need.

> 'The Director may prohibit flights by night from or at any aerodrome or any heliport at which adequate facilities for night flights are lacking or where the terrain or other objects in the vicinity of the aerodrome or the heliport are such as to endanger operators of aircraft used in night flights.'[29]

So, unless the Director prohibits night flights from or to an aerodrome, you may use it on your VRF flight even with minimal 'facilities'. A sensible way to define such facilities is the next regulation (which concerns Instrument Approach Procedure).[30]

---

[27] CARS 91.06.32 (3).
[28] Aerodrome facilities are described in ICAO Annex 14 *Aerodrome Design and Operations*.
[29] CARS 139.01.5.
[30] CARS 91.07.3.

Minimum lighting facilities: 'For night operations at least runway edge, threshold and runway end lights must be on'.[31] *(exam question!)*

Elaborate lighting facilities for approach, runway and taxiway: refer to the picture on page 246A.

Illuminated signs

Mandatory and information signage for the runway and taxiway follow the same colour coding as in the day time, and are illuminated (refer to the colour picture on page 246A). You may also encounter this sign:

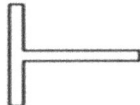

It is illuminated or outlined by white lights at night and, as already mentioned, means that you will take off or land on the longer bar ('shaft') and toward the crossbar ('cross arm', that is, where the runway ends). The cross arm is not a taxiway.

Other lighting

What you need to find out in AIP AD for a given airfield:
- Has it an identification **lit beacon** (for instance FAPM, Pietermaritzburg has a rotating beacon atop the tower)?[32]
- Is its **wind indicator** illuminated (white light)?[33]
- Is there any **obstacle** and is it lit (usually steady red, or flashing red)?
- If it has runway lighting, **how are lights serviced**? Many local airfields, even larger ones have pilot-operated lighting: when you are in the 5 NM radius you switch them on by clicking your PTT, on the airfield frequency as per AIP instructions. Do not make a call just before or after you click or it will confuse the system. Risky.

---

[31] AIP ENR 1.8–12 at 3.2.5 (Non-Precision Approach) Night Operations-12, and same ENR 1.8–14 at 3.3.6 (Precision Approach Category I) Night Operations. SACAA can prohibit flights by night if an aerodrome/heliport lacks 'adequate facilities' as per CARS 139.01.5.

[32] AIP AD2-FAPM-6 as at 15 January 2018.

[33] Licensed aerodromes are supposed to have an illuminated wind indicator (wind sock) and a beacon under certain conditions, such as mainly used for VFR, as in CATS 139.02.1 Physical characteristics (20) and (34).

Here is an artist's rendition of the chart insert explaining **pilot-operated lighting** at George Dick Montshioa Airport (FAMM):[34]

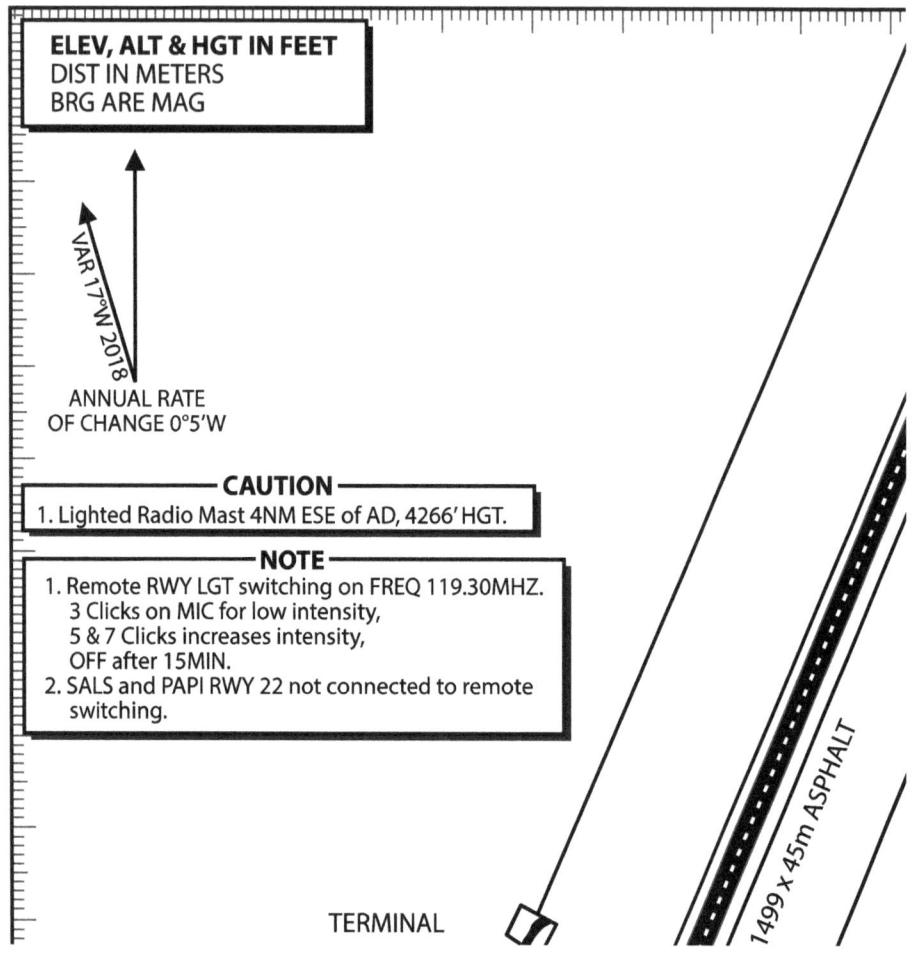

---

[34] For the actual chart, refer to Chart number AD-01 EFF: 08 NOV 18.

Runway and taxiway lights

(see operations on page 245)

This an artist's rendering of a taxiway and a runway with lights at a well equipped airport. It is not to scale in terms of relative distances between the various sections of the runway and their specific lighting systems (that are strictly set by ICAO) but it gives an accurate idea of what to expect.

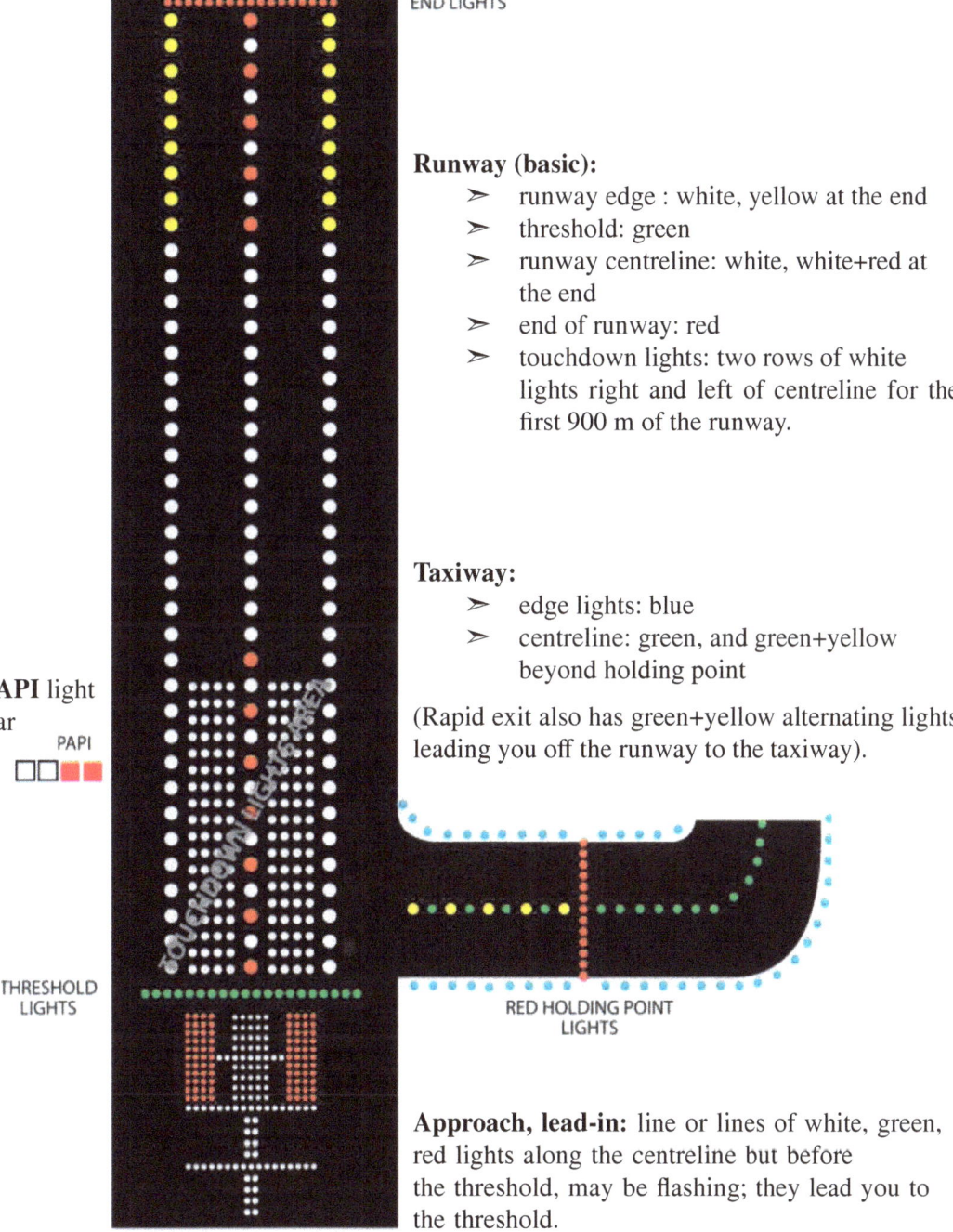

Runway (basic):
- runway edge : white, yellow at the end
- threshold: green
- runway centreline: white, white+red at the end
- end of runway: red
- touchdown lights: two rows of white lights right and left of centreline for the first 900 m of the runway.

Taxiway:
- edge lights: blue
- centreline: green, and green+yellow beyond holding point

(Rapid exit also has green+yellow alternating lights leading you off the runway to the taxiway).

Approach, lead-in: line or lines of white, green, red lights along the centreline but before the threshold, may be flashing; they lead you to the threshold.

Pre-threshold area unfit for normal movement of aircraft

(see operations on page 156)

The pre-threshold area is fit for use as a stopway only.

Runway and taxiway mandatory and information signs

(see operations on page 156)

Mandatory signs have white letters on a red background. Red means caution.

For instance, a sign placed on each side of the holding position will show the runway designator in white on red, while a yellow letter on a black background will indicate the taxiway that you are on. (The runway designator is also marked in white on the runway itself, indicating the direction in which you are taking off.)

At night they illuminate.

You are on taxiway E holding short of runway 25.

Information signs have two meanings:

Location: a black background signifies location

A yellow number on a black background = the runway you are on:

You are on runway 15.

A yellow letter on a black background = the taxiway you are on:

You are on taxiway A.

Direction: a yellow background means direction

A black letter (with or without a number) on a yellow background with a black arrow = your direction, the taxiway ahead or a runway exit (placed on the same side as the exit):

This is the direction to taxiway A.

Black numbers on a yellow background with a black arrow = direction to runway:

This is the direction to runway 27.

Visual ground signals and markings

(see operations on pages 156 and 216.)

At or near a control tower

 Pilots to report at air traffic office after landing

On the signalling area

A series of panels is displayed on the signalling area.

 **Landing prohibited** and prohibition likely to be prolonged.

 Owing to the bad state of the manoeuvring area, or for any other reason, **special precautions** must be observed when approaching to land or landing.

 Right hand circuit

 Left hand circuit

Navigation lights and angle of coverage

(see operations on pages 135, 195 and 242.)

Note the angle of coverage—exam question!

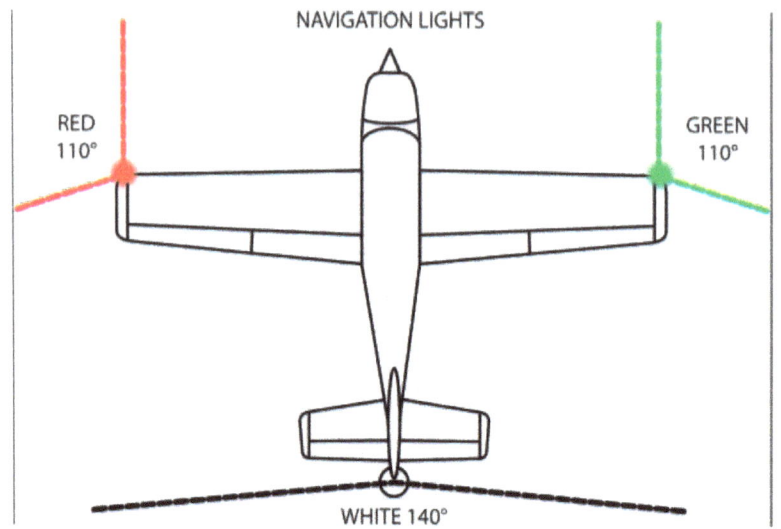

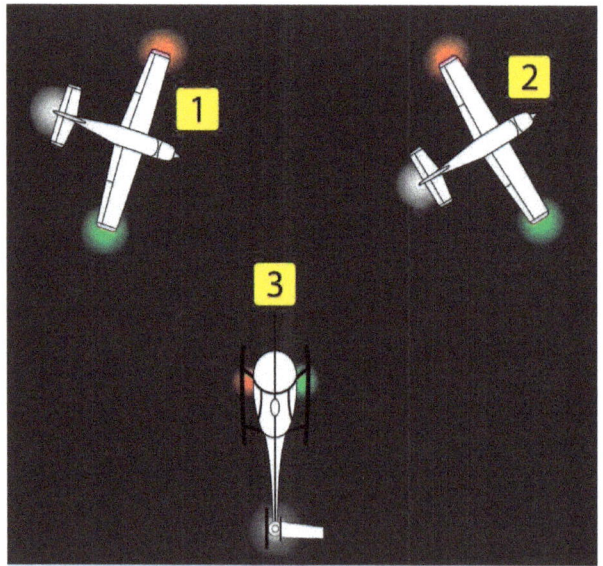

'Here we have an example of aircraft lighting. By interpreting the position lights on other aircraft, the pilot in aircraft 3 can determine whether the aircraft is flying in the opposite direction or is on a collision course. If a red position light is seen to the right of a green light, such as shown by aircraft 1, it is flying toward aircraft 3. A pilot should watch this aircraft closely and be ready to change course. Aircraft 2, on the other hand, is flying away from aircraft 3, as indicated by the white position light'.

Source: http://www.cockpitchatter.com/shedding-light-on-night-flying/ by Ivan Paredes. Well understood this smart pictorial illustrates the saying: green to red, red to green= unsafe; red to red, green to green= safe. Seeing both red and green right in front of you means a head-on! Look also at Saul-Pooley *Air Law* 25.

13.5.4 Tower, unauthorised entry and interception signals

Light signals from tower

Refer to page 218 about those signals **from tower**. Here is how you should respond 'in the hours of darkness':[35]
- in flight 'by flashing on and off twice the aircraft's landing lights, or if not so equipped, by switching on and off twice its navigation lights'.
- on the ground 'by flashing on and off twice the aircraft's landing lights or, if not so equipped, by switching on and off twice its navigation lights'.

Unauthorised entry

Visual signals that are used to warn an unauthorised aircraft flying in, or about to enter, a **restricted, prohibited or danger** area consist of 'a series of projectiles discharged from the ground at intervals of 10 seconds, each showing, on bursting, **red and green lights or stars**' *(exam!)*. You are to take 'such remedial action as may be necessary'. The projectiles are rockets or shells, not beams of light.[36]

Interception

This can happen if you stray off course at night into a prohibited or restricted area. Check Annexure 15 for those signals and how to respond to them at night.

13.5.5 Encountering aircraft: lights

And finally, you have to be able, in flight and by looking at the navigation lights of other aircraft, to determine whether you are on a collision course. See picture on page 246D.

If you do not hold a Night Rating yet, it is hoped that these pages have whetted your appetite for what is actually the next, natural step to take after a PPL, and that you will soon fly off into the night *(not an exam question!)*. Or, better yet, it is hoped that this chapter has helped you to pass your NR examination.

---

[35] CATS 91.06.13–4 (b).
[36] CARS 91.06.13–3.

PART FOUR
FLYING DRONES

Introduction

. . . .

'The modern aileron is no kitchen door.'

Wolfgang Langewiesche *Stick and Rudder*[1]

A drone is not a spinning top. And that is the reason why the legal name for drones is Remotely Piloted Aircraft Systems (RPAS).[2] In fact, the law makes the point quite clearly that RPAS regulations[3] do not apply to:
- autonomous unmanned aircraft, unmanned free balloons and their operations or other types of aircraft that cannot be managed on a real-time basis during flight;
- an aircraft operated in terms of Part 94, that is a Non-Type Certified Aircraft (NTCA)—commonly known as a 'microlight', even when they are more sophisticated than certified types;
- a model aircraft;
- a toy aircraft.

SACAA's regulations adhere to those of ICAO where RPAS are a subset of UAS,[4] 'Unmanned Aircraft Systems': the word 'RPAS' itself was formally added to the lexicon of ICAO in 2015. (The work on developing a new framework for regulations and practices began in 2003 and a first exploratory meeting on UAS was held in 2006.)[5]

In terms of the Convention on International Civil Aviation (1944) the concept is not at all new, and was already part of a 1929 Protocol amending the Paris Convention of 1919 (a forerunner of the 1944 Convention): 'pilotless aircraft' is the object of article 8 of the current Convention:

> No aircraft capable of being flown without a pilot shall be flown without a pilot over the territory of a contracting State without special authorization by that State and in accordance with the terms of such authorization. Each contracting State undertakes to insure that the flight of such aircraft without a pilot in regions open to civil aircraft shall be so controlled as to obviate danger to civil aircraft.

What was amiss then was a complex definition of 'pilotless' (it may have been inspired or made topical by a 1929 Royal Air Force, 400 miles-long flight on

---

[1] Wolfgang Langewiesche *Stick and Rudder* 1 ed 1944 (1972) 170.
[2] Terminology is still hesitant: RPA or RPAS (singular), and RPAS or RPASs (plural). It does not matter. Yet. ICAO does refer to a RPA. We use 'drone' here as well.
[3] CARS 101.01. 1 (3).
[4] ICAO, Circular 328 AN/190 *Unmanned Aircraft Systems (UAS)* (2011).
[5] ICAO *Manual on Remotely Piloted Aircraft Systems (RPAS)* Doc 10019, 1.1 and 1.2.

auto-pilot, or 'pilot's assister') that would fit today's rapid development of technology. This is now taken care of by ICAO.[6]

ICAO therefore provides a suite of legal definitions for RPAS, which also serves as a summary of the various acronyms used in the legislation, and a handy overview of the basics:[7]

Remotely piloted aircraft: 'An aircraft is defined as any machine that can derive support in the atmosphere from the reactions of the air other than the reactions of the air against the earth's surface. An aircraft which is intended to be operated with no pilot on board is classified as unmanned. An unmanned aircraft which is piloted from a remote pilot station [RPS] is an RPA.'

Associated components: 'RPA[8] are piloted from RPS utilizing a command and control (C2) link. Together with other components such as launch and recovery equipment, if utilized, the RPA, RPS and C2 link comprise an RPAS.

An RPA can be piloted from one of many RPS during a flight; however, only one RPS should be in control of the RPA at a given moment in time.'

Remote pilot station (RPS): 'The RPS is the component of the RPAS containing the equipment used to pilot the RPA. The RPS can range from a hand-held device up to a multi-console station. It may be located inside or outside; it may be stationary or mobile (installed in a vehicle/ship/aircraft).'

RPA observer: 'A trained and competent person designated by the operator who, by visual observation of the remotely piloted aircraft, assists the remote pilot in the safe conduct of the flight.'

An observer is used in E-VLOS operations (see chapter 14 and the illustration on page 259).

C2 link: 'The C2 link connects the RPS and the RPA for the purpose of managing the flight. The link may be simplex or duplex. It may be in direct radio line-of-sight (RLOS) or beyond radio line-of-sight (BRLOS) as described in (a) and (b).

(a) *RLOS:* refers to the situation in which the transmitter(s) and receiver(s) are within mutual radio link coverage and thus able to communicate directly or through a ground network provided that the remote transmitter has RLOS to the RPA and transmissions are completed in a comparable timeframe; and

(b) *BRLOS*: refers to any configuration in which the transmitters and receivers are not in RLOS. BRLOS thus includes all satellite systems and possibly any system where an RPS communicates with one or more ground stations via a terrestrial network which cannot complete transmissions in a timeframe comparable to that of an RLOS system.

---

[6] In addition to the ICAO documents mentioned, see the extremely valuable *Remotely piloted aircraft system (RPAS) Concept of Operations (CONOPS) for international IFR operations* (unedited version), abbreviated as RPAS CONOPS (not dated).

[7] Definitions quoted are from the *Manual on Remotely Piloted Aircraft Systems*.

[8] Spelling in the original text.

Introduction 253

The distinction between RLOS and BRLOS mainly concerns whether any part of the communications link introduces appreciable or variable delay into the communications than the architecture of the link.'[9]

In plain English, if controlling a RPA involves a relay via a satellite it is BRLOS. At present SACAA does not provide for BRLOS.

ICAO plans to begin full integration of RPAS in civil avation in terms of standards and practices by 2025 and will possibly not reach 'a mature and complete set of technologies, standards, regulations, guidance and procedures' until 2031.[10]

ICAO adopted a whole set of standards and recommended practices (SARPs) regarding remote pilot licensing in March 2018 to be phased in up to 2022.[11]

Since this final Part of *Air Law* is designed to help RPAS pilots, and because there is a fair amount of confusion about who can fly what sort of drone, we shall begin with some key points.

---

[9] *Manual on Remotely Piloted Aircraft Systems* 2–2.
[10] RPAS CONOPS 6.
[11] ICAO, Amendment 175 to the *International Standards and Recommended Practices, Personnel Licensing* (Annex 1 to the Convention on International Civil Aviation), March 2018.

Chapter 14

. . . .

Some key points

14.1 KEY POINTS ABOUT LICENCES[1]

Pilot licence

To pilot a drone in a **commercial, corporate or non-profit operation** you must have the appropriate pilot licence, called a Remote Pilot Licence or RPL.

A **private** drone operation does not require a RPL.[2] However, whoever operates a drone privately is required to observe a great number of regulations in terms of operating it, as we shall see later in this Part. And, you cannot call yourself a RPA 'pilot' if you do not hold a RPL. Of course you can **hold a RPL and operate privately**.

Operator licence or certificate

This is not to be confused with a RPL. An individual or a legal entity that operates a drone for a commercial, corporate or non-profit organisation needs to hold a Remote Operator Certificate (ROC) (it is not termed a 'licence', to avoid any confusion). However, and in addition to a ROC, a ROC holder who operates commercially needs to hold an Air Services licence issued in terms of the Air Services Licensing Act 115 of 1990 (see the next section).

14.2 KEY POINTS ABOUT THE OPERATION OF DRONES

What is a private drone operation?

'Private' means: operations for 'an individual's personal and private purposes where there is no commercial outcome, interest or gain'.[3]

Note the key words: individual (not an organisation of any sort); personal (not on behalf of your best friend or your club); private (not you as, for instance, owner

---

[1] As at July 2019, a slate of proposed changes was pending, in an effort to align SACAA's regulations and standards regarding RPAS on ICAO Amendment 175 as noted. Current Part 101 would be split between a new Part 71, Licensing, and a Part 101 more concerned with Operations, *Government Gazette* 42228 GN 644 of 15 February 2019. RPL medical certification has been aligned already on ICAO (see below section 15.1).

[2] The provision in CARS 101.05.10 (1) (a) that imposes an obligation to hold a RPL in order to fly a drone does not apply to private operations, in terms of an exemption in CARS 101.01.2 (2). But private ops are strictly regulated (see below chapter 16).

[3] AIC 009/2015, 4.

of a business); no commercial outcome; no interest (no 'quid pro quo' arrangement, whereby you operate a drone privately but in exchange you get something that brings you a tangible benefit); gain (a gain need not be cash in hand). The regulation is stringent, admittedly, and possibly hard to police. But it is there to prevent abuses and to ensure the safe operation of drones—which is, as we saw at the beginning of *Air Law*, the central focus of international aviation regulations. Say you crash your drone on a neighbour's house that is going on sale, while you are helping her to advertise it with a neat aerial video, and getting a small commission. You may find yourself in deep trouble as it would be a case of a non-private, non-personal, for gain operation—apart from her suing you, of course, for damage caused to the property and possible loss of value.

What is a commercial drone operation?

A commercial operation is an 'air service' as defined by the Air Licensing Act of 1990, the Domestic Air Services Regulations of 1991 and the International Air Services Regulations of 1994.[4] Unless you are also an operator, and are licensed as an operator (see chapter 16), what you need **as a pilot** is a Remote Pilot Licence.

What is an air service? Here is the dauntingly worded definition provided by the Air Licensing Act:

> 'Any service operated by means of an aircraft for reward, but shall not include—*(a)* the hiring out of an aircraft together with the crew to a licensee; *(b)* a service operated solely for the benefit of a company or a group of companies, or any subsidiary thereof, in its commercial activities by a person who is a member or in the employ of such company or group of companies or subsidiary, and which is not offered for reward to the public in general; *(c)* the conducting of flight testing or assessment of skills in respect of flying an aircraft; *(d))* any type of training or instruction in respect of flying an aircraft.'[5]

As a remote pilot you will operate your drone commercially as an air service, if you get a reward for flying it, unless you fly it as a corporate operation (see below), or unless you test a new drone for certification (and are certified to do so), or unless you provide instruction (and are approved to do so, and at an Aviation Training Organisation (ATO) as regulated by CARS Part 141—with some small adjustments).[6]

What is a corporate drone operation?

A corporate drone operation is a non-commercial operation or use of an aircraft by a company to aid company business and—here is the crunch—'flown by a

---

[4] As defined by the White Paper on National Civil Aviation Policy, *Government Gazette* 40847 of 19 May 2017.

[5] CARS 1.01.1, where all definitions are to be found, refers to this quoted definition in the Air Licensing Act (which has been somewhat modified since 1990).

[6] AIC 008/2015.

256 *Air Law*

professional pilot employed to fly the aircraft'. In short: if you own a company but you are not employed by it to fly a drone to 'aid' your business, then you cannot fly the drone as a corporate operation.[7]

What about a non-profit drone operation?

Do not be confused by 'non-profit'. The expression refers to non-profit organisations as defined by the Nonprofit Organisations Act of 1997,[8] that is 'a trust, company or other association of persons—*(a)* established for a public purpose and *(b)* the income and property of which are not distributable to its members or office-bearers except as reasonable compensation for services rendered'. In short: you may operate a drone for a nonprofit organisation and obtain a reasonable compensation, provided that you belong to the said organisation (and hold a RPL, of course).

Note that the definitions given above (private, commercial, corporate, non-profit) are not specific to RPAS. They apply across aviation.

The four types of operation and relevant regulations

The regulations and levels of approval needed are summarised in the table below.[9] Note the acronyms.

ASL—Air Service Licence
ROC—RPAS Operators Certificate
RLA—RPAS Letter of Approval
RPL—Remote Pilot Licence
C of R—Certificate of Registration
RMT—RPAS Maintenance Technician

Required approval	Type of Operation	Commercial	Corporate	Non-profit	Private
ASL		YES	N/A	N/A	N/A
ROC		YES	YES	YES	N/A
RLA		YES	YES	YES	N/A
RPL		YES	YES	YES	N/A
C of R		YES	YES	YES	N/A
NOTE: RMT is required for maintenance on RPAS classified as class 3 and higher					

---

[7] White Paper. CARS 1.01.1 provides a shorter, hence more ambiguous, definition.
[8] *Government Gazette* 18487 of 3 December 1997. The White Paper mentioned above wrongly terms it 'Not-for-Profit' Organisations Act (page 56).
[9] As per the SACAA website.

14.3 KEY POINTS ABOUT THE 'SIZE' OF DRONES

'It is all about size' is short hand for more technical specifications.

Indeed, as for 'size', RPAs are classified in terms of the energy they deliver at impact (expressed in units of energy or kiloJoule, kJ), and weight when loaded, called Maximum Take-Off Mass (expressed in kilograms).

The regulator has added two more criteria: the type of electronic and mechanical operation, called **line-of-sight**, and the **height** at which a RPA is allowed to fly. Do not confuse 'operation' as in private or commercial, with 'operation' as defined here and illustrated in the table below.

What is a line-of-sight? It refers to the actual physics and electronics of flying the machine, which involves two factors or 'lines':

- a visual line, that is, for the pilot to have a visual of the drone, to see it at all times, or have a physical, ocular relay or observer; this is called the visual line-of-sight (VLOS);
- a line of propagation of the electronic signal sent by the source to the receiver aboard the drone, enabling the pilot to control it at all times; this is called the radio line-of-sight (RLOS).

The **visual line-of-sight** (VLOS) can be **restricted** (R-VLOS), **extended** (E-VLOS), or the operation can be **beyond** it—no physical visual of the drone (B-VLOS). Both 'B-VLOS' and 'BVLOS' as well as 'E-VLOS' and 'EVLOS' are used by SACAA.

The **radio line-of-sight** (RLOS) can also have operations beyond it (BRLOS), but SACAA does not permit this at present.

For the time being, the combination of the four parameters (line-of-sight, energy, weight, height) produces the table below, which is a classification of RPAs (not in terms of the legal definition of private use or commercial/corporate/non-profit, but in terms of the material operation of a drone):[10]

---

[10] It is noteworthy that the Civil Aviation Authority of Zimbabwe (CAAZ) has established 8 classes that are sensibly different (Statutory Instrument 271 of 2018).

Remotely Piloted Aircraft Systems classification[11]

CLASS	TABLE 1: RPAS CLASSIFICATION			
	Line-of-Sight	Energy (kJ)	Height (ft)	MTOM (kg)
Class 1A	R-VLOS/VLOS	E < 15	h < 400	m < 1.5
Class 1B	R-VLOS/VLOS/EVLOS	E < 15	h < 400	m < 7
Class 1C	VLOS/EVLOS	E < 34	h < 400	m < 20
Class 2A	VLOS/EVLOS	E > 34	h < 400	m < 20
Class 2B	Experimental/Research			
Class 3A	BVLOS	E > 34	h < 400	m < 150
Class 3B	VLOS/EVLOS	Any	h > 400	m < 150
Class 4A	BVLOS	Any	h > 400	m < 150
Class 4B	Any	Any	Any	m > 150
Class 5	Reserved	Reserved	Reserved	Reserved

Reserved – means to be defined in the future
h – means height above the surface
E – means energy at impact
Note: All operations are limited to radio line-of-sight

What does this table imply, at this stage, for a pilot?

All operations are limited to RLOS. There is no provision yet for Beyond radio line-of-sight (BRLOS), as already mentioned.

A 'private' drone pilot (that is a pilot who flies a drone for private use, as there is no such thing as a 'private RPL') can therefore only operate a drone of Class 1A or 1B, ie below 7 kg, E factor of less than 15 kJ, and must fly it below 400 ft and only in R-VLOS (see chapter 16).

The simple pictorial below illustrates VLOS and E-VLOS operations.

R-VLOS is specific to private operations for which a RPL is not necessary. A detailed pictorial for R-VLOS can be found on page 270.

---

[11] CATS 101.01.5.

Chapter 14: Some key points 259

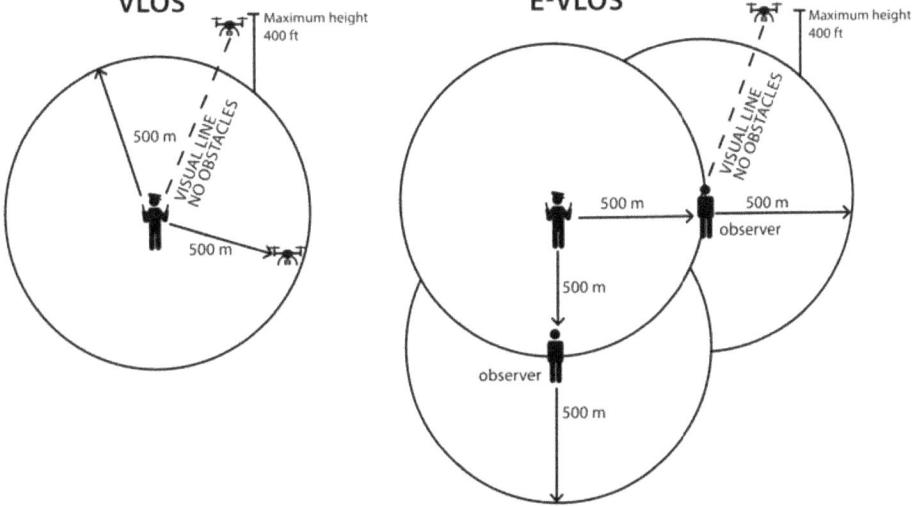

Chapter 15

. . . .

Drone pilots

15.1 THE REMOTE PILOT LICENCE

Air law is an important element of the general requirements for the issue of the RPL and is likely to acquire even more weight because of the complexity of ICAO's new SARPs, and SACAA's alignment.

In any event, a RPL is compulsory only for commercial, corporate or non-profit flying, and you are entitled to be called a Remote Pilot, and exercise the 'privileges'[1] of such a licence, only if you hold a RPL.

To make it quite clear: **there is no 'private RPL'**.

Of course, if you hold a RPL you can fly a drone privately (in your licence category and rating—see below), but you will not do so because you hold a RPL but because the purpose of the operation is private, as explained before.

What are the RPL categories of licence and ratings?

There are three categories of RPLs. They do not depend upon the type of operation you conduct as a licensed pilot of RPAS (commercial, corporate, non-profit) but upon the actual, manufactured type of RPAS, and they look familiar, as they more or less duplicate the main physical types of aircraft:[2]

- RPL (A) (Aeroplane)
- RPL (H) (Helicopter)
- RPL (MR) (Multi-rotor)

In addition, a Remote Pilot Licence is endorsed with any or all of these three ratings:[3]

- VLOS: visual line-of-sight operations
- E-VLOS: extended visual line-of-sight operations
- B-VLOS: beyond visual line-of-sight operations

This means that you are allowed to operate only a RPA in the category and rating you hold. You may hold as many categories and ratings as there are available, if you pass the examinations.

---

[1] Refer to page 48 for a definition of 'privileges'.
[2] CATS 101.03.1 (2).
[3] CARS 101.03.1 (3). See page 88 for an explanation of rating.

What are the conditions for applying for a RPL?[4]

To be allowed to apply for a RPL you must fulfil a number of stringent conditions, namely you must:
- be at least 18 years old,
- hold a Class 3 medical certificate,[5]
- hold a restricted Certificate of Proficiency in Radiotelephony (Aeronautical) (see page 53),
- have proof of your ability to speak English at proficiency level 4 or higher (see page 53),
- have completed both theoretical and practical training (see sections 15.2 and 15.3 below),
- have passed the theoretical knowledge examination within 90 days preceding the skill test,
- have passed the skill test within 60 days of completing the flight training,
- send the application to SACAA on the appropriate form within 30 days of completing the skill test, with the fee (listed annually on SACAA's website with all other fees), and
- the skill test must include the applicable sections for the E-VLOS and B-VLOS ratings if one or more of these ratings is sought.

15.2 THEORETICAL TRAINING AND EXAMINATION

Theoretical training must take place at an ATO certified as a RTO (Remotely Piloted Aircraft System Training Organisation). This implies that an aspiring RPL pilot must first find an ATO that is certified for drone training and testing. These few RTOs are listed on the SACAA website at Information for the Industry > Remotely Piloted Aircraft Systems > ATO (on side bar).

Theoretical training leads to a 'theoretical knowledge examination': a general examination which precedes a licence examination of your choice (RPL (A), RPL (H), RPL (MR).

The general examination consists of testing your knowledge about a range of aviation syllabus features, particularly air law. Most of what is described in Part 4 of this book is therefore relevant. You are expected to know what CARS and CATS Part 101 stipulate.[6] The exam must be passed before the first licence examination:[7] in other words, once you have passed a general examination. With a RPL (A) under your belt, if you wish to get a RPL (H), you should not have to write the general examination again.

---

[4] CARS 101 Subpart 3.

[5] CARS 67.00.2 as per 20th Amendment *Government Gazette* 42362 GN 645 of 29 March 2019.

[6] CATS 101.03.3–2 (1) (a). And Part 71 when it will be in effect. Part 71 will deal with licensing.

[7] CATS 101.03.3–1 (4).

General examination syllabus[8]

- Air Law;
- Human Factors (vision, stress management, signs and symptoms of fatigue);
- Meteorology (air density, fog and mist, wind and gusts, thunderstorms, weather reports);
- Navigation (latitude and longitude, aeronautical chart information for VFR, GPS);
- Lighting.

The theoretical knowledge examination must be passed (75%) within 90 days **before** the practical skill test.[9]

Licence examination syllabus

The syllabus contains items applicable to all three categories of remote pilot licences[10] (listed below under 1) and items applicable only to each category of licence (listed under 2).[11]

1

- Construction and parts of RPAS (in one of the categories you apply for);
- Forces acting on an aircraft (as applicable to the category of licence);
- Axes and motion about the axes;
- Control of motion about the axes (as applicable to the category of licence);
- Propulsion systems (as applicable to the category of licence);
- Weight and balance (as applicable to the category of licence);
- Servo motors and servo actuators;
- Radio control link (C2 link);
- Data link (this includes the all-important FPV or First Person View);
- Wireless links general (and the crucial 'line-of-sight');
- Flight controller (autopilot system);
- Batteries;
- Functions and required actions of the RPA observer.

2

- Applicable to **RPL (Aeroplane)**: stall (boundary layer, angle of attack, aeroplane characteristics);
- Applicable to **RPL (Helicopter)**: flight controls, main and tail rotors, swashplate, rotor head, rotor blade stall, fly bar, ground effect, helicopter setup;
- Applicable to **RPL (Multi-rotor)**: different configurations and frames.

---

[8] CATS 101.03.3–2.
[9] CARS 101.03.3.
[10] CATS 101.03.3–3.
[11] CATS 101.03.3–4, 5, 6.

Chapter 15: Drone pilots 263

Examination rules

The remote pilot general examination must be passed before the first licence examination may be written.[12]

You need 75% to pass. If you fail with 65%+, you can apply for a re-mark within 30 days of notification of your result (you pay a fee that will be refunded if the re-mark is a pass). You can also rewrite after seven calendar days twice. If you fail twice, two calendar months must pass before you try a third time, or a fourth, and so on. But if you score less than 50% on the first attempt, two calendar months must pass before you try a second time.

15.3 PRACTICAL FLIGHT TRAINING

Flight training has general features and specific ones depending upon your category of RPL.[13] Unlike PPL training, the exercises need not be done in a given sequence. The training can be done in a combination of simulator and actual flying. Your RTO will advise.

Flight training syllabus and flying exercises

Items applicable to all remote pilot licences

(1) Aircraft pre-flight inspection and setup.
(2) Post-launch in-flight evaluation procedures (checking of systems directly after launch—if applicable to the category of licence).
(3) Automated flying and flight controller flight modes.
(4) First person view (FPV) flying (if applicable).
(5) Parachute-assisted landing (if applicable to the category of licence).
(6) Evasive action (manoeuvres) to avoid collisions.
(7) Post-flight inspection.

Items applicable to the Remote Pilot Licence (Aeroplane) RPL (A)

(1) Climbing and descending.
(2) Turns while maintaining altitude.
(3) Climbing and descending turns.
(4) Speed changes while maintaining altitude.
(5) Horizontal figure eight.
(6) Stalls.
(7) Recovery from a spin.

---

[12] CARS 101.03.3.
[13] CATS 101.04.4.

(8) Take-offs.

(9) Catapult launch (if applicable).

(10) Hand launch (if applicable).

(11) Approaches and landings.

(12) Hand launching (if applicable).

(13) Engine failure

  (a) At altitude

  (b) After take-off

  (c) On the approach.

(14) VTOL—Vertical take-off and landing (if applicable).

Items applicable to the Remote Pilot Licence (Helicopter) RPL (H)

(1) Tail-in hover.

(2) Tail-in hover performing squares and circles.

(3) Take-offs.

(4) Tail-in hover performing a horizontal figure eight.

(5) Tail-in hover performing a vertical rectangle.

(6) Side-on hover (both sides).

(7) Transition from hover to forward flight.

(8) Transition from forward flight to hover.

(9) Turns from level flight.

(10) Climbing and descending from level flight.

(11) Approach and landing.

(12) Nose-in hover.

(13) Autorotation.

Items applicable to the Remote Pilot Licence (Multi-rotor) RPL (MR)

(1) Tail-in hover.

(2) Tail-in hover yawing slowly to right and left.

(3) Tail-in hover, move to right then to the left.

(4) Tail-in hover, move forwards then backwards.

(5) Tail-in hover, ascend and descend.

(6) Take-offs.

(7) Tail-in hover performing a horizontal rectangle.

(8) Tail-in hover performing a vertical rectangle.

(9) Nose-in hover.

> (10) From hover fly a square box rotating (yawing) the multi-rotor in the direction of flight.
> (11) From hover fly a circle rotating (yawing) the multi-rotor nose-in to the centre of the circle.
> (12) Transition from hover to forward flight.
> (13) Climbing and descending from level flight.
> (14) Turns from level flight.
> (15) Speed control in level flight.
> (16) Approach and landings.
> (17) Actions after failure of a motor.

Skill test

As already mentioned, the skill test is taken within 60 days of completing your training, conducted with a RPA in the same category for which you want a RPL, with an accredited examiner. The skill test must include testing for E-VLOS and B-VLOS ratings if any is sought. The test form, if passed, must be sent to SACAA within 30 days.[14]

15.4 MAINTAINING A REMOTE PILOT LICENCE

Your RPL is **valid for two years**, that is until the last day of the 24th month from the date of issue.[15]

However, 90 days before your RPL expires, you have to do a **revalidation** check with an accredited examiner, in the same category aircraft as your RPL. Revalidation is valid for 24 months.

If you do the revalidation more than 90 days before expiry or within 36 months of expiry, your RPL will be reissued for 24 months starting from the date of the check.

Your revalidation check form must be sent to SACAA within 30 days of the check, with the relevant fee.

You must keep a **pilot logbook**, like any pilot, which is a record of all your flight time, instrument time, simulation time and instruction time. If you have an electronic logbook, you must print it out at least every 90 days. The logbook must always be ready for inspection.[16]

---

[14] CARS 101.03.5.
[15] CARS 101.03.6.
[16] CARS 101.03.7.

Chapter 16

. . . .

Piloting drones

We have already dealt with the classification of RPAS. What about their operations? What rules apply and to whom? For clarity, rules are presented in two sections:

Rules specific to private RPAS operations;[1]

Rules specific to operations with a ROC (operator's certificate).

16.1 R-VLOS PRIVATE OPERATIONS

16.1.1 Rules and restrictions for R-VLOS private operations[2]

The rules are presented here as a logical sequence of checks or reminders.

Pre-flight checks

- Your RPA must be 'fit to fly'.[3]
- Pre-flighting includes:
  - checking your health,[4] and applying I'M SAFE,[5]
  - checking the weather and reading NOTAM,
  - checking the physical location of the intended flight to decide on altitude and distance permissible under R-VLOS,
  - any document you may need (drone manual, this checklist, authorisation by the owner of a property to fly over it in case the police intervene and possibly an indemnity waiver signed by the owner, even a copy of SACAA's private operation rules in case someone questions your right to operate a drone—you never know),[6]
  - ensuring 'unobstructed' visual (no physical obstacle; no cloud, no fog, no rain, no haze).

---

[1] CARS 101 Subpart 5.

[2] CARS 101.01.2. and Subpart 5, RPAS Operations (notwithstanding three regulations listed in 101.01.2 (2) that are not applicable to private operation).

[3] CARS 101.05.9 (1) (a).

[4] CARS 101.05.7.

[5] See page 104 to understand the procedure.

[6] CATS 101.05.17 provides a neat checklist of reminders.

Flight operations: general rules

- 'No person shall operate an RPAS in a negligent or reckless manner so as to endanger the safety of any person, property or other aircraft in the air or on the ground.'[7]
- 'The operator shall, in the best interest of safety, ensure that certain RPAS operations are supplemented with additional personnel for non-flying duties, such that the remote pilot can maintain control and situational awareness in respect to positioning and collision avoidance.'[8] This should not really concern a private operation, unless a group of people are flying RPAS at the same location, in which case enrolling someone to observe traffic may be a good idea. The general principle of safety applies anyway: a pilot must ensure safe operations. Example: if a group of operators fly at the same spot, each remote operator must be at least 50 m away from any other operator (see rule below). They should select a very large field.
- **RPAS are flown privately**
    - only in R-VLOS,[9]
    - only in Class 1A or 1B (mass < 7 kg, Impact energy < 15kj)
- Fly a RPA only in daylight (see page 239 for an aviation definition of day and night) and in clear weather conditions (no cloud, no haze, no fog, no rain). You may not operate a RPA at night.[10]
- Your RPA must be controlled by only one RPS (remote pilot station) at all times.[11]
- In R-VLOS there is no need for an air-band radio tuned to the frequencies in use in the airspace or area of the RPA.[12] R-VLOS operation does not require an altimeter fitted to the machine.
- Dangerous goods may not be conveyed.[13]

---

[7] CARS 101.95.9 (2).

[8] CARS 101.05.9 (3). The sub-regulation mentions an operator but in terms of the general rule stated in CARS 101.01.2 private operations fall under the sub-regulation.

[9] CARS 101.01.2 (3).

[10] SACAA website, RPAS Private Operations, 4 and Doc K-12612 state that private operations are 'only in daylight and clear weather'. CARS 101.05.12 (1) (a) mentions R-VLOS as a typical night operation, but it does not seem to mean that one can fly a RPA privately at night without a RPL. It seems to imply that a RPL holder may fly 'privately' at night and in R-VLOS. Clarity is needed from the Regulator.

[11] CARS 101.05.9 (1) (d).

[12] CARS 101.05.16 (1).

[13] CARS 101.05.5 (1).

Flight operations: airspace

- Do not fly in controlled,[14] restricted, or prohibited airspace.
- Do not fly within 10 km of or closer to an aerodrome (airport, helipad or airfield).

Flight operations: height, distance, vicinity

- Never fly more than **500 m from the remote pilot**, and **400 ft 'above the surface'**, or higher than a building or obstacle that is **within 300 m of the drone**. 400 ft is the maximum height above ground level or surface for a RPA to fly.[15]
- Do not fly a RPA:
  - 50 m or closer to any person or group of persons (like sports fields, road races, stadiums, schools, social events, open air assembly),
  - directly overhead any person or group of people,[16]
  - within 50 m of or on the length of a public road,[17]
  - over or within 50 m of any structure or building without permission from the property owner,[18]
  - over a prison, court of law, nuclear plant, police station or crime scene.[19]
- Do not use a public road as a point of landing or take-off.[20]

Flight operations: collision avoidance in flight, accidents

- Do not fly a RPA near manned aircraft.[21]
- Right of way: a RPA must always give way to manned aircraft (whether over, under or in front) unless the RPA passes well clear of the manned aircraft and the remote pilot takes into account wake turbulence so as not to cause a collision or an accident.[22] It is unlikely a manned aircraft will fly at 400 ft, unless on a climb-out or on final approach, and if that is the case, it would mean you are flying your RPA illegally—within 10 km of an airfield.

---

[14] CARS 101.05.3 (except by permission, in VMC in an ATZ and CTR below 400 ft, and only with ROC, hence not private).

[15] CARS 101.05.10 (3) (a). It is assumed that the regulator by 'above the surface' means 'above ground level' (AGL). The 500 m/300 m rule as per definition of restricted line-of-sight (CARS 1.01.1).

[16] CARS 101.05.13.

[17] CARS 101.05.15.

[18] CARS 101.05.14 (1). In the pictorial (on page 270) it is marked 'lateral exclusion'.

[19] CARS 101.05.10 (3) (d).

[20] CARS 101.05.2. Even if the local authority approves it, you also need to hold a ROC.

[21] As per the SACAA website, RPAS Private Operations.

[22] CARS 101.05.20.

- Right of way: if a RPA encounters another RPA in flight, standard right of way rules apply.[23]
- Accidents and incidents resulting in any injury or death of a person (it can be any one), damage to property, or destruction of the RPA beyond repair, must be reported as per CARS Part 12 (see page 229 for details).[24]

Flight operations: 'fun' things you cannot do

- Do not have your RPA to tow another aircraft.[25]
- Do not perform aerial or aerobatics displays.[26]
- No formation or swarm flying.[27]
- No object or substance to be 'released, dispensed, dropped, deployed, delivered'.[28]

16.1.2 Exemptions for R-VLOS private operations[29]

RPAS in private operations are exempted from complying with the following regulations:
- Time need not be recorded in UTC (translation: you use local, standard SA time).
- You do not need to keep a Flight Folio.
- You do not need a power reserve (electric charge or fuel of at least 10% of charge necessary to complete a flight. However, you must have enough charge or fuel to complete the flight as intended).
- You do not need a first aid kit.
- You do not need a hand-held fire extinguisher.

---

[23] CARS 101.05.20 (2) (3) (4) (5). The regulation implies that it is a case of RPAS encountering each other, and thus following habitual rules of right of way (see page 161).
[24] CARS 101.05.6.
[25] This and other restrictions are itemised by CARS 101.05.10 (2) and (3).
[26] CARS 101.05.10 (2) (b).
[27] CARS 101.05.10 (2) (c).
[28] CARS 101.05.4.
[29] AIC 009/2015 citing CARS 101.05.21, 22, 23 and 25.

270　Air Law

16.1.3　Visual representation of R-VLOS operational limits

The illustration below provides a representation of limits set on operating a RPA privately, always in R-VLOS.

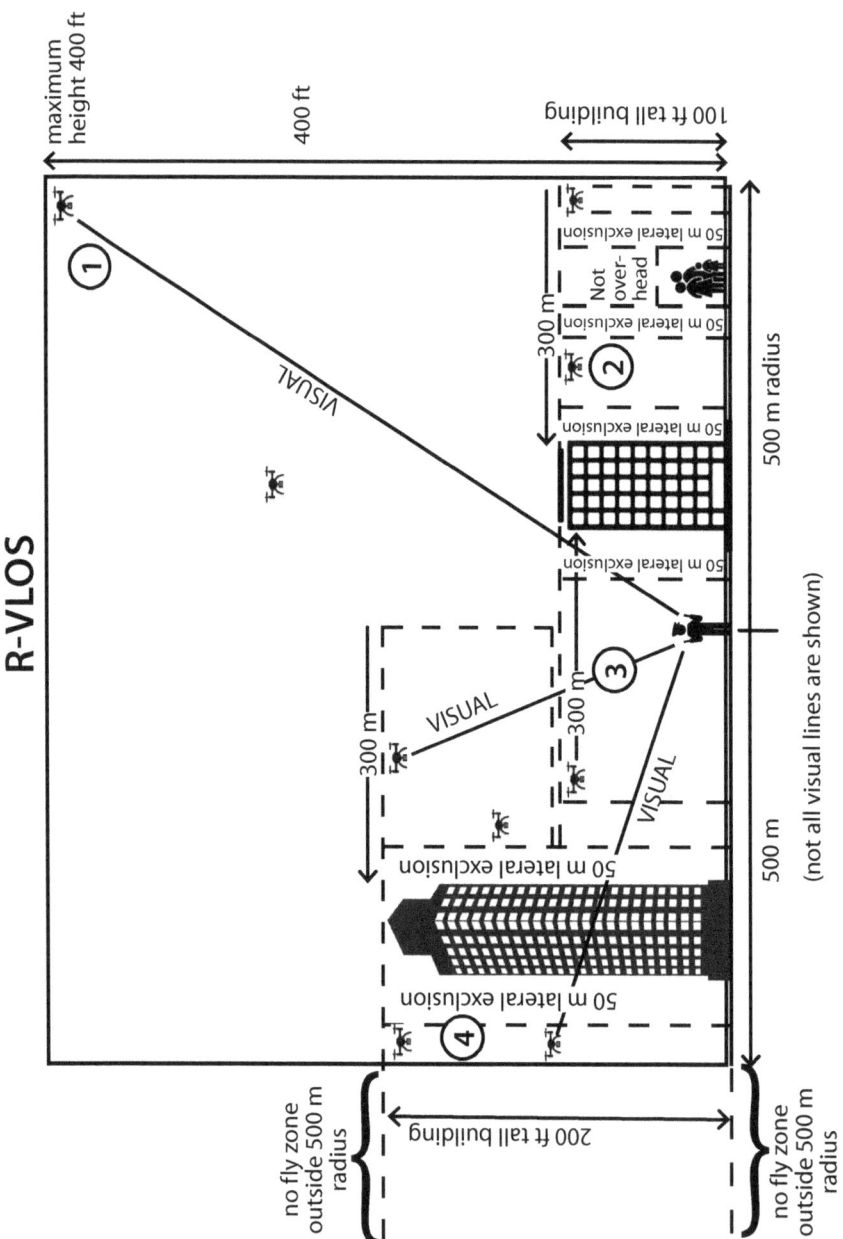

The circled numbers in the picture refer to four situations. Make allowance for the fact that the illustration is two-dimensional:

Situation 1: the RPA flies up to the maximum, vertical limit above ground of 400 ft and to the ground, the horizontal limit of 500 m. If you are at sea level, on a deserted beach, your RPA will fly to a maximum of 400 ft. If you are at a mountain lodge perched at 4 000 ft, your RPA will fly up to 4 400 ft above sea level (this sounds obvious, but better said than not).

Situation 2: the RPA must, laterally, be 50 m or more from a person, a building, an official facility, an assembly, a road, etc, and it cannot fly along/take off/land on a road (not shown in the picture). Nor can it be directly overhead people (as shown).

Situation 3: the RPA flies within 300 m of a 100 ft tall building, and stays below this height (strictly speaking, below 100 ft would be from 99 ft). The building could be any sort of obstacle that would break your visual line-of-sight of the RPA (tower, hill, radio-mast).

Situation 4: next to a 200 ft building your RPA must fly below that height (199 ft and less), as long as the building is within 300 m of the RPA. If the building in situation 3 and this one were close by, your RPA maximum height would be that of building 4 within 300 m of the RPA. You will notice that on the left of the picture the radius of 500 m from the RPS or pilot has been exceeded, hence this zone is out of flying limits.

In all situations unobstructed visual contact with the RPA must be maintained.

Note that the 50 m exclusion above a private property without permission, near or along a public road, or over a designated location is not illustrated.

16.2 KEY POINTS FOR PILOTS ABOUT ROC OPERATIONS

RPAS Operator's Certificate ROC operations is short hand for commercial, corporate and non-profit operations since all three need a ROC or Operator's Certificate (refer to page 256). In addition, a commercial operator must first obtain an Air Services Licence. Anyway, regulations and standards make frequent reference to a ROC as the deciding criterion to define a flight operation that is not private.

Flying a RPA in a non-private operation immediately means two things for you as a pilot:
- you must hold a RPL in the correct category and with the relevant rating; if you have a RPL (H), you cannot operate a RPA (A). If you only hold a VLOS rating, you cannot operate in E-VLOS.
- you are not confined to flying R-VLOS like private 'pilots' are. And that is liberating: as appropriately rated, you may fly VLOS, E-VLOS and B-VLOS. And, of course, as a RPL holder, you are allowed to operate R-VLOS.

16.2.1 Operator vis-à-vis Pilot

In the new field of RPAS the boundary between pilot and operator becomes blurred at times. At face value, the situation of a RPL pilot is simple: you are not allowed to exercise the privileges, as they are called, of your RPL by flying a RPA operated by a ROC holder if the certification has not been duly obtained by the ROC holder from SACAA. You may still fly that RPA as a private operation, if the owner lets you.

ROC operations are a fast-growing industry, with open horizons for research and development, and profit. SACAA has published on its website all regulatory documents needed, as well as clear and informative guidelines needed by operators who wish to run a legally licensed RPAS business, alongside RTO and RMT (maintenance) registration issues.

SACAA imposes exacting rules[30] for the registration and marking of RPAS (the nationality mark for RPAS is ZT), their maintenance, compliance with safety regulations, and liability[31]—on top of specific flight rules that are of direct concern to pilots.

For instance:

- an 'observer', under flight rules for E-VLOS, has to be at least 17 years of age, and there must be at least one such observer;
- training of personnel;
- rules for the safe-keeping and quality of records (kept for five years and protected from damage, theft and tampering) are stringent;
- background checks of personnel, including checks of criminal records every 24 months are mandatory;
- safe storing of the RPAS;
- safety management systems (identification of hazards, remedial actions);
- third party insurance must be complied with.

These are the legal responsibility of the ROC operator, not the RPL pilot. But it is the duty of a RPL pilot to question any infringement of the regulations by a ROC operator as, ultimately, a pilot, manning an aircraft or remotely controlling it, must ensure safety—this is a fundamental rule of aviation (see page 103).

The purpose of this book is not to advise the industry on legal procedures to register a RPAS-based commercial venture, but to provide pilots with what they need to be aware of in legal terms.

Below are some points of interest for pilots who hold a RPL and are called to conduct ROC operations and outside R-VLOS as described in the private operations section above.

---

[30] CARS and CATS 101, Subpart 4. See also CATS 47.01.3-2 (6) (d).
[31] CATS 101.02.4.

16.2.2 Pilot logbook and flight folio

Pilot logbook

A RPL pilot must maintain a logbook: 'The holder of an RPL must maintain in a pilot logbook a record **of all** his or her **flight time**, instrument time, simulation time and instruction time',[32] thus including private flights. But 'private' can be misleading as it refers both to private operations that do not require a RPL, hence no logging, and private operations by a RPL holder. If electronic, the data must be printed at least every 90 days and bound sequentially. Logbooks have to be kept for at least 60 months from the date a RPL lapses and must be available for inspection by an officer, inspector, or other authorised person.

Flight folio

The operator has to maintain a flight folio for each RPA. It is not the pilot's remit to maintain it, although, as in general aviation, the pilot may enter some details, if not all details after each flight. The specifics are below.

Flight folio[33]

'(a) aircraft registration

(b) date

(c) names (of) flight crew members

(d) duty assignment of flight crew members

(e) place of departure

(f) place of arrival

(g) time of departure (off-block time)

(h) time of arrival (on-block time)

(i) hours of flight

(j) nature of flight

(k) incidents, observations (if any)

(l) signature of remote pilot

(m) the current maintenance statement giving the aircraft maintenance status of what maintenance, scheduled or out of phase, is due

(n) all outstanding deferred which affect the operation of the aircraft

(o) fuel and oil used (if applicable)

(p) fuel and oil uplift (if applicable)

(q) battery charge status (beginning and end of the flight, if applicable).'

---

[32] CARS 101.03.7.
[33] CATS 101.05.22.

16.3 VLOS, E-VLOS AND B-VLOS OPERATIONS

Further regulations governing operations by a RPL pilot under ROC certification are described in CARS 101 Subpart 5 and CATS 101.04.5, 101.05.3, 8, 11, 12 and 17. See annexure 18.

They are to be read carefully by professional remote pilots, who should keep an eye on developing regulations and standards, and the release of a new Technical Guidance Material by SACAA.

16.4 BY WAY OF CONCLUSION

As RPAS grow into a substantial part of civil aviation for commerce and industry, and play a more complex role in intelligence gathering, security and civilian surveillance,[34] RPAS regulations and standards are likely to outgrow in volume and complexity the modest limits they currently occupy in CARS and CATS, if not in primary legislation itself. At the same time RPAS create contentious ethical issues which the attractiveness of technological advances will not be able to offset in the minds of the general public.

Whereas the birth of aviation was saluted with fervour as a great fraternal leap for humanity, linking people across continents and creating a world community of aviators, the advent of drones, first seen by the general public as amusing 'toys-for-boys', now raises serious concerns for privacy. Civilian drones are regarded with a sense of distrust because of their unfettered use by governments and corporations, to gather information and to exert surveillance and control.[35]

Although unjustified in many cases, this disquiet and occasional hostility are new. It is a public perception that aviation has not known before, even during the last World War when cities were carpet-bombed. Aviation and its beautiful aircraft have always been received with great hurrahs by the public and have put stars in the eyes of children, who dream of becoming pilots and being 'up there' one day. Drones—whatever acronym is made up to avoid calling them 'drones' in order to lend them a sheen of technological glamour—are perceived quite differently. One hopes that the beneficial use of civilian RPAS in mapping, surveying, environmental protection, search and rescue, delivery of medical supplies, and agriculture,[36] to give just a few examples, will help to balance the other dire and real concerns.

But, as always in aviation, it rests on pilots, and pilots alone, to help drones evoke the same respect and emotional admiration that aviation has elicited from the general public since its proud beginnings.

Until then, fly safely! And abide by air law.

---

[34] In respect of their military use: Gareth Evans 'UAV Innovation: What are the new concepts taking hold?' *Army Technology* (19 December 2017).

[35] Columbia Law School *The Civilian Impact of Drones* (2012).

[36] NEPAD *Drones on the Horizon: Transforming Africa's Agriculture* (2018 (?).

BIBLIOGRAPHY

Bibliography

1 LEGISLATIVE, REGULATORY AND COMPLIANCE DOCUMENTS (AVIATION)

ICAO

Most dates of issue are not indicated as updates are regular. Refer to the ICAO website for the latest versions. 'Annex' means an annex to the Convention on International Civil Aviation

Amendment 175 to the *International Standards and Recommended Practices, Personnel Licensing* (Annex 1 to the Convention on International Civil Aviation), March 2018
Annex 1 *Personnel Licensing*
Annex 2 *Rules of the Air*
Annex 3 *Meteorological Service for International Air Navigation*
Annex 6 Part I *Operation of Aircraft*
Annex 10 *Aeronautical Telecommunications*
Annex 12 *Search and Rescue*
Annex 14 *Aerodrome Design and operations*
Annex 15 *Aeronautical Information Services*
Circular 328 AN/190 *Unmanned Aircrafts Systems (UAS)*, 2011
Convention on International Civil Aviation
Doc 4444 *Procedures for Air Navigation Management Services. Air Traffic Management*
Doc 8126 *Aeronautical Information Services Manual*
Doc 8168 *Procedures for Air Navigation Services (PANS-OPS)*
Doc 8400 *ICAO Abbreviations and Codes*
Doc 8984 *Manual of Civil Aviation Medicine*
Doc 9365 *Manual of All-Weather Operations*
Doc 10019 *Manual on Remotely Piloted Aircraft Systems*
Guidelines for the Creation and Provision of Pre-flight Information Bulletins *(PIB)*, AIS-AIMSG/1-SN No. 18, Appendix
Remotely piloted aircraft system (RPAS) Concept of Operations (CONOPS) for International IFR Operations (not dated)

South Africa

The *Government Gazette* is available at www.gpwonline.co.za
Aeronautical Information Publication, Aeronautical Information Circulars, Supplements and Amendments mentioned in this book are available on the SACAA website (www.caa. co.za)

Aviation Act of 1962

Aviation Act of 1923

Civil Aviation Act of 2009, *Government Gazette* 32266 GN 461 of 27 May 2009 as updated by proclamation in *Government Gazette* 36183 GN 561 of 27 March 2012

Civil Aviation Amendment Bill of 8 October 2018, *Government Gazette* 41962 GN 640 of 8 October 2018 (bill has lapsed)

Civil Aviation Regulations *Government Gazette* 35398 GN 564 of 1 June 2012, and subsequent gazetted amendments, up to and including Twentieth Amendment of the Civil Aviation Act *Government Gazette* 42362 GN 645 of 29 March 2019

National Environmental Management: Protected Areas of 2003, *Government Gazette* 26025 GN 464 of 18 February 2004

Regulation Gazette 42581 of 17 July 2019

South African Civil Aviation Act of 1998

South African Civil Aviation Technical Standards (SA CATS); effective on the date of commencement of the Civil Aviation Regulations, 2011, with subsequent amendments as issued

White Paper on National Civil Aviation Policy *Government Gazette* 40847 GN 623 of 19 May 2017

EASA and related

European Parliament and Council, Regulation (EU) 2018/1139 *Official Journal of the European Union* 22 August 2018

Regulation EU No 1178/2011 as amended by Regulation EU No 290/2012

FAA and related

Advisory circular, Standards for airport sign systems, No 150/5340–18F, 08/16/10

Airfield Standards, Southern Region Airports Division (2018)

Airplane Flying Handbook (2016)

Basic Survival Skills for Aviation Oklahoma City, OK, Civil Aerospace Medical Institute, Airman Education Programs, no date, available at http://www.faa.gov/pilots/training/airman_education

Childs, Jerry M, Spears, William D & Prophet, Wallace W *Private Pilot Skill retention 8, 16, and 24 months after certification*, DOT/FAA/CT-83/34 (1983)

Code of Federal Regulations Title 14, Aeronautics and Space, July 2019 (these are the FAA Regulations)

Drug use trends in aviation: Assessing the risk of pilot impairment, (United States) National Transportation Safety Board, NTSB/SS-14/01 (2014)

How to Avoid a Mid Air Collision document P-8740–51

Notice N JO7110.691 Procedures A380–800 and An225 Aircraft

Schumacher, Peter M & Lease, Jered *Evaluating the effectiveness of scenario based training in the collegiate flight training environment* Final Report to the FAA/Industry Training Standards (UNED, 2007)

Other

Australia, Civil Aviation Safety Regulations, 2018
Botswana, Civil Aviation Act, 2011
Namibia, Civil Aviation Act, 2016
Namibia, Civil Aviation Regulations, 2001, 2006
Namibia, Civil Aviation Technical Standards, 2008
Swaziland, CAA-AC- PEL018A, Advisory Circular, 2011
Zimbabwe, Civil Aviation Authority of Zimbabwe, Statutory Instrument 271 (2018)
Zimbabwe, Syllabus for the Private Pilot Licence (2002)

2 AVIATION

(collective) 'Use of standard phraseology by flight crew and air traffic controllers clarifies aircraft emergencies' (March–April 2000) 26(3) *Flight Safety Foundation, Airport Operations*
Columbia Law School *The Civilian Impact of Drones* (report) (2012)
Evans, Gareth 'UAV Innovation: What are the new concepts taking hold?' *Army Technology* (19 December 2017), available at https://www.army-technology.com/features/uav-innovation-new-concepts-taking-hold/
Flight, First Aero Weekly in the World, from the archives of www.flightglobal.com
ICLG *The International Comparative Legal Guide to: Aviation Law2019* 7 ed (2019)
Jeppesen *ICAO recommended airport signs, runway and taxiway markings* 27/02/2004
Kemlo, Dylan *VFR Fixed Wing RT* (Talking Radio, 2009)
Kent, Phillip *Drone Law* (Kent & Co, 2017)
Lempp, Dietlind *The Pilot's Radio Handbook* 18 ed (Woodstock: self-published, 2015), (at time of writing 20 ed 2019), available at http://radiobooks.co.za
Marais, Phillip *Understanding CATS & CARS* 6 ed (2016), available at http://www.understandingaviation.com
NEPAD *Drones on the Horizon: Transforming Africa's Agriculture* (?, 2018)
Nell, Gerhardt *Aeronautical Radio License Course* (self-published, 2003)
Paredes, Ivan http://www.cockpitchatter.com/shedding-light-on-night-flying/
Pratt, Jeremy M *Air Law* 1 ed (Airplan Flight Equipment, 2016) and *PPL 4* 3 ed revised (Airplan Flight Equipment, 2011)
Rhodes-Houghton, Rob 'Teaching ADM/SRM', SACAA website, November 2011
Saul-Pooley, Dorothy et al *Air Law and Meteorology* 14 ed (Elstree Aerodrome: Pooleys-Air Pilot Publishing, 2017)

Seals, Lilith A *Air Law for Private Pilots* 18 ed (self-published, 2018)
SKYbrary online resource www.skybrary.aero
Worthington, G D P *The Private Pilot's Handbook* 11 ed (W J Flesch & Partners, 1991)

3 LITERATURE

Bandura, Albert *Social Foundations of Thought and Action* (Prentice Hall, 1986)
Claxton, William J *The Mastery of the Air* 1 ed 1914 (Blackie & Son Ltd, 1930)
Craig, Paul A *The Killing Zone. How and Why Pilots Die* 2 ed (McGrawHill, 2013)
Fitzgerald, F Scott *The Great Gatsby* (1925)
Grahame-White, Claude *The Story of Aviation* (Small, Maynard and Company, 1911)
Keyhoe, Donald E *Flying with Lindbergh* (Putnam's Sons, 1928)
Markham, Beryl *West with the Night* reprint of 1 ed, 1943 (North Point Press, 1983)
Mittelolzer, Walter, Gouzy, René & Heim, Arnold *R-A-S-T. En hydravion de Zurich au Cap de Bonne Espérance* (La Baconnière, 1927)
Nagatsuka, Ryuji *I Was a Kamikaze* translated from the French original (Amberley, 2014)
Saint Exupéry, Antoine de *Night Flight* 1 ed, translated by Stuart Gilbert (The Century Co., 1932)

ANNEXURES

Annexure 1

....

Extract of the Chicago Convention of 1944

Source: ICAO, fac-simile of the original text, showing the lofty purpose of ICAO which is the source of Air Law (page 1) and the page signed by the Union of South Africa (page 60).

CONVENTION ON INTERNATIONAL CIVIL AVIATION

PREAMBLE

WHEREAS the future development of international civil aviation can greatly help to create and preserve friendship and understanding among the nations and peoples of the world, yet its abuse can become a threat to the general security; and

WHEREAS it is desirable to avoid friction and to promote that cooperation between nations and peoples upon which the peace of the world depends;

THEREFORE, the undersigned governments having agreed on certain principles and arrangements in order that international civil aviation may be developed in a safe and orderly manner and that international air transport services may be established on the basis of equality of opportunity and operated soundly and economically;

Have accordingly concluded this Convention to that end.

FOR THE UNION OF SOUTH AFRICA:

FOR THE GOVERNMENT OF THE UNITED KINGDOM OF GREAT BRITAIN AND NORTHERN IRELAND:

FOR THE UNITED STATES OF AMERICA:

Annexure 2

IAIP organogram

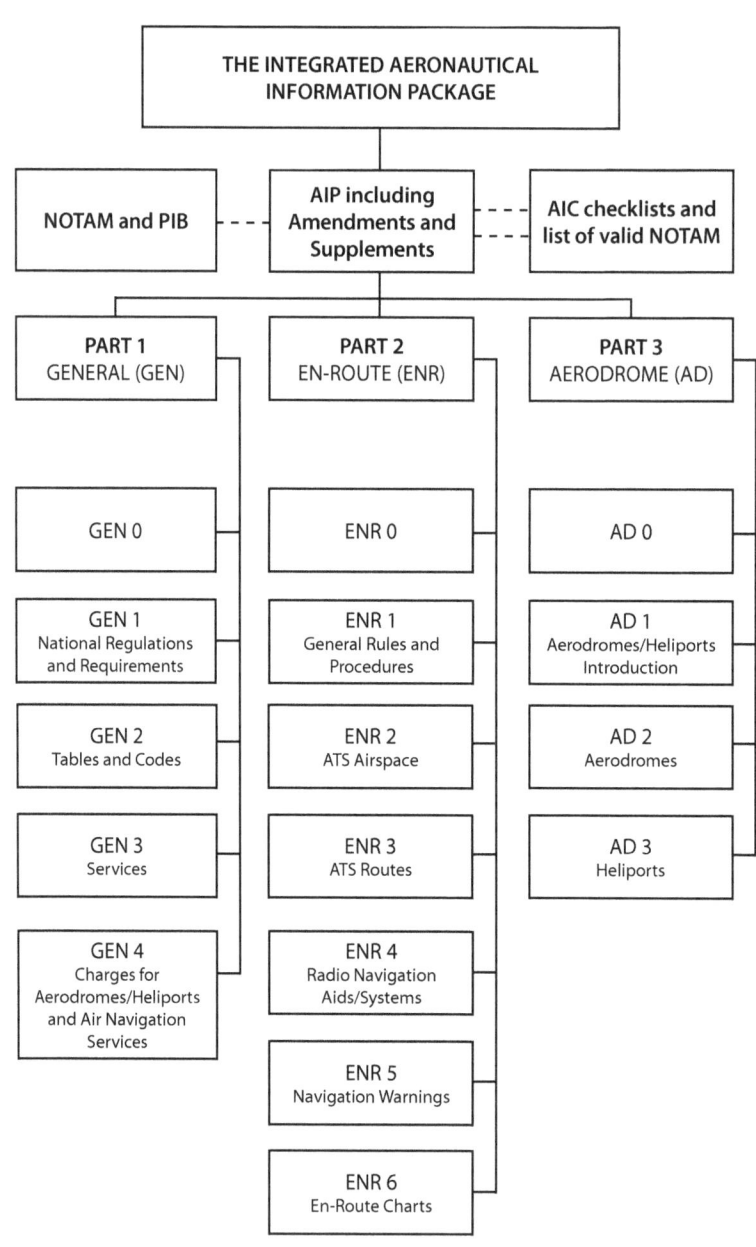

Annexure 3

Nomenclature of CARS and CATS

This is short list of Parts that are particularly relevant

Part 1 Definitions and abbreviations

Part 11 Procedures for making regulations and technical standards, granting exemptions and notifying differences

Part 12 Aviation accidents and incidents

Part 24 Airworthiness: Non-type certificated aircraft

Part 61 Pilot licensing

Part 62 National pilot licensing

Part 63 Flight engineer licensing

Part 64 Cabin crew licensing

Part 65 Air traffic service personnel licensing

Part 66 Aircraft maintenance engineer licensing

Part 67 Medical certification

Part 68 Glider pilot licensing

Part 71 Remote Pilot Licensing (*to be introduced*)

Part 69 Free balloon pilot licensing

Part 94 Operation of non-type certificated aircraft

Part 91 General aviation and operating flight rules

Part 96 Commercial operation of non-type certificated aircraft

Part 101 Remotely Piloted Aircraft Systems

Part 121 Air transport operations: Carriage on aeroplanes of more than 19 passengers or cargo more than 8 618kg

Part 127 Commercial air transport and general aviation operations: Helicopters

Part 135 Air transport operations: less than 20 passengers or cargo 8 618kg or less

Part 138 Air ambulance operations

Part 139 Aerodromes and heliports

Part 141 Aviation training organisations

Part 145 Aviation maintenance organisations

Part 149 Aviation recreation organisations

Part 172 Airspace and air traffic services

Part 174 Meteorological information services

Part 175 Aeronautical information services

Part 187 Fees and charges administration

Annexure 4

Example of NOTAM

Source: ICAO, Abbreviations and Codes, Doc 8400, 7–5

Abbreviations needed to decode are mentioned in that document.

NOTAM:

Q) LFFF/QNDAU/IV/BO/AE/ . . .
A) LFPO B) 9203312359
C) 9204010600
E) DME NOT AVBL

Meaning of NOTAM:

Item Q):

— LFFF: ICAO location indicator identifying Paris FIR in which the facility reported on is located;
— QNDAU: The letter "Q" identifies the five-letter code group as the NOTAM Code group. Second and third letters "ND identifying "distance measuring equipment" and fourth and fifth letters "AU" denoting that the facility is "not available";
— IV: Letters identifying that the information affects both IFR and VFR traffic;
— BO: Letters identifying that NOTAM is selected for pre-flight information bulletins entry and that it is operationally significant information for IFR flights;
— AE: Letters identifying that facility is serving a dual purpose as terminal and en-route aid.

Item A):

— LFPO: ICAO location indicator identifying Paris/Orly, the location of the facility being reported on.

Item B):

— 9203312359: Date/time group of the beginning of the period of validity in which the facility is not available.

Item C):

— 9204010600: Date/time group of the end of the period of validity in which the facility is not available.

Item E):

— DME NOT AVBL: Plain-language entry using ICAO abbreviations. This is the so-called free text, which makes use of abbreviations.

Annexure 5

Logbook rules and annual summary

What to fill in where. For information only.

Source: CATS 61, Appendix A

Column 1
Enter date (dd/mm/yyyy) on which the flight commences.
Column 2
Enter type of aircraft or Type or Classification of the CAA approved FSTD.
Column 3
Enter Registration Marks of aircraft or SA CAA authorisation number in the case of a FSTD.
Column 4
Enter name of pilot-in-command or SELF as appropriate and in the case of instruction, the name of the student.
Column 5
Enter details of flight.
Column 6
Instrument Time: Enter the navigational aid used.
Column 7
Instrument Time: Enter the place where the navigational aid was utilised.
Column 8
Instrument Time: Enter the actual Instrument Time Flown in hours and decimals of an hour (One hour 30 minutes is to be entered as 1.5).

Column 9

Instrument Time: Enter the FSTD Instrument Time flown in decimals of an hour (10 minutes is to be entered as 0.6).

Column 10

Instructor: Enter the time flown as an Instructor for Single Engine Aircraft (SE Civil). Ensure that the same flight time is entered as pilot-in-command time Column 15 or 18 as appropriate (PIC).

Column 11

Instructor: Enter the time flown as a civilian Instructor for Multi Engine Aircraft (ME Civil). Ensure that the same flight time is entered as pilot-in-command time Column 22 or 25 as appropriate (PIC).

Column 12

Instructor: Enter the time flown as an Instructor in a Flight Simulator Training Device (FSTD).

Column 13

Flight Simulator Training Device (FSTD): Enter the actual time flown in the FSTD.

Column 14

Flight Time: Enter the Dual time flown by day for single engine aircraft.

Column 15

Flight Time: Enter the pilot-in-command (PIC) time flown by day for single engine aircraft.

Column 16

Flight Time: Enter the pilot-in-command under supervision (PICUS) time flown by day for single engine aircraft. The pilot-in-command (PIC) should verify this time by signature in the Remarks column. Column 34.

Column 17
Flight Time: Enter the co-pilot time flown by day for single engine aircraft.

Column 18
Flight Time: Enter the Dual time flown by night for single engine aircraft.

Column 19
Flight Time: Enter the pilot-in-command (PIC) time flown by night for single engine aircraft.

Column 20
Flight Time: Enter the pilot-in-command under supervision (PICUS) time flown by night for single engine aircraft. The pilot-in-command (PIC) should verify this time by signature in the Remarks column, Column 34.

Column 21
Flight Time: Enter the co-pilot time flown by night for single engine aircraft.

Column 22
Flight Time: Enter the Dual time flown by day for multi engine aircraft.

Column 23
Flight Time: Enter the pilot-in-command (PIC) time flown by day for multi engine aircraft.

Column 24
Flight Time: Enter the pilot-in-command under supervision (PICUS) time flown by day for multi engine aircraft. The pilot-in-command (PIC) should verify this time by signature in the Remarks column. Column 34.

Column 25
Flight Time: Enter the co-pilot time flown by day for multi engine aircraft.

Format of annual logbook summary

Column 26
Flight Time: Enter the Dual time flown by night for multi engine aircraft.

Column 27
Flight Time: Enter the pilot-in-command (PIC) time flown by night for multi engine aircraft.

Column 28
Flight Time: Enter the pilot-in-command under supervision (PICUS) time flown by night for multi engine aircraft. The pilot-in-command (PIC) should verify this time by signature in the Remarks column. Column 34.

Column 29
Flight Time: Enter the co-pilot time flown by night for multi engine aircraft.

Column 30
Take-offs/Landings: Enter the number of landings by day.

Column 31
Take-offs/Landings: Enter the number of landings by night.

Column 32
A pilot flying as 'pilot-in-command under supervision' or 'student pilot-in-command' shall enter flying times as 'pilot-in-command' but all such entries shall be certified by the commander or flight instructor in the 'Remarks' column of the logbook. *Examples of other remarks that may be included arc* • *Cross country* • *Take-offs/Landings*

For information only

Source CATS 61.03. 2

(1)	(2)	(3)	(4)	(5)	(6)	(7)	(8)	(9)	(10)	(11)
A/C Class or Type	Instrument		Instructor			FSTD	Single Engine Day			
	Actual Time	FSTD Time	SE	ME	FSTD		Dual	PIC	PICUS	Co-Pilot
PA 160							4.3	4.3		
C 172	3.0						15.2	12.9		
FNPT 1		3.8					18.0	4.3		
	3.0	3.8					37.5	21.5		
(1)	(2)	(3)	(4)	(5)	(6)	(7)	(8)	(9)	(10)	(11)

(12)	(13)	(14)	(15)	(16)	(17)	(18)	(19)	(20)	(21)	(22)	(23)
Single Engine Night				Multi Engine Day				Multi Engine Day			
Dual	PIC	PICUS	Co-Pilot	Dual	PIC	PICUS	Co-pilot	Dual	PIC	PICUS	Co-pilot
(12)	(13)	(14)	(15)	(16)	(17)	(18)	(19)	(20)	(21)	(22)	(23)
Total Flight Time			59.0		Hours						

Annexure 6

Syllabus of theoretical knowledge (A) (H)

Source: CATS Part 61 with promulgated Amendments 1/2016, 2/2016, 3/2016, and 1/2018.

Any change with an effective date (date at which compliance with a regulation or standard is mandatory) that may be promulgated later than July 2019 is not reflected in this document. In doubt check on the SACAA website for updates regarding the practical syllabus by looking at: Legal and Aviation Compliance > Notices: Promulgated Technical Standards

COMBINED SYLLABUS OF THEORETICAL KNOWLEDGE FOR THE PRIVATE PILOT LICENCE (AEROPLANE) AND (HELICOPTER)

Ref.	ITEM DESCRIPTION	PPL-A	PPL-H
	AIR LAW AND OPERATIONAL PROCEDURES	X	X
	ICAO	X	X
1.	The Convention on International Civil Aviation	X	X
2.	The International Civil Aviation Organization	X	X
3.	Articles of the Convention	X	X
3.1	Sovereignty	X	X
3.2	Territory	X	X
3.5	Flight over territory of Contracting States	X	X
3.10	Landing at customs airports	X	X
3.11	Applicability of air regulations	X	X
3.12	Rules of the air	X	X
3.13	Entry and clearance regulations of Contracting States	X	X
3.14	Search of aircraft	X	X
3.22	Facilitation of formalities	X	X
3.23	Customs and immigration procedures	X	X
3.25	Customs duty	X	X
3.29	Documents to be carried in aircraft	X	X
3.30	Use of aircraft radio equipment	X	X
3.31	Certificate of airworthiness	X	X

Ref.	ITEM DESCRIPTION	PPL-A	PPL-H
3.32	Licences of personnel	X	X
3.33	Recognition of certificates and licences	X	X
3.34	Journey log books	X	X
3.35	Cargo restrictions	X	X
3.36	Restrictions on use of photographic equipment	X	X
3.37	Adoption of international standards and procedures	X	X
3.39	Endorsement of certificates and licences	X	X
3.40	Validity of endorsed certificates and licences	X	X
4.0	*Annex 14 Aerodrome data*	X	X
	– definitions	X	X
	– conditions of the movement area and related facilities	X	X
4.1	*Visual aids for navigation*	X	X
	– indicators and signalling devices	X	X
	– markings	X	X
	– lights	X	X
	– signs	X	X
	– markers	X	X
	– signal area	X	X
4.2	*Visual aids for denoting obstacles*	X	X
	– marking of objects	X	X
	– lighting of objects	X	X
4.3	Visual aids for denoting restricted use of areas	X	X
4.4	*Emergency and other services*	X	X
	– fire and rescue service	X	X
	– apron management service	X	X
4.5	*Aerodrome ground lights and surface marking colours*	X	X
	– colours for aeronautical ground lights	X	X
	– colours for surface markings	X	X
5.0	SOUTH AFRICAN REGULATIONS	X	X
	Civil Aviation Regulations (CAR) and Technical Standards (CATS)	X	X

Ref.	ITEM DESCRIPTION	PPL-A	PPL-H
5.1	PART 1: DEFINITIONS AND ABBREVIATIONS	X	X
	Definitions	X	X
	Abbreviations	X	X
5.2	PART 12: AVIATION ACCIDENTS AND INCIDENTS		
	12.02.1 – Notification of accidents	X	X
	12.02.2 – Notification of incidents	X	X
	12.02.3 – Notification of accidents and incidents outside the Republic	X	X
	12.02.4 – Particulars of notification	X	X
	12.04.1 – Guarding of aircraft involved in accident	X	X
	12.04.4 – Interference with objects and marks at scene of accident	X	X
5.3	PART 61: FLIGHT CREW LICENSING	X	X
5.3.1	Subpart 61.01 – General requirements	X	X
	– Pilot licences	X	X
	– Ratings for pilots	X	X
	– Maintenance of competency	X	X
	– Medical fitness	X	X
	– Language	X	X
	– Logging of flight time (1 – 11, 17)	X	X
	– Crediting of flight time & Theoretical knowledge examinations (1 – 5, 7, 12, 13, 14, 24, 25, 26)	X	X
	– Suspension and withdrawal of privileges and appeal	X	X
	– Payment of currency fee	X	X
	– Endorsements and record keeping	X	X
5.3.2	Subpart 61.03 (A) 61.04 (H) – Private pilot licence	X	X
	61.04.1 – Requirements	X	X
	61.04.2 – Application for private pilot licence	X	X
	61.04.3 – Experience Examinations	X	X
	61.04.4 – Skill test	X	X
	61.04.5 – Issuing of private pilot licence: Privileges	X	X
	61.04.6 – Validity of private pilot licence	X	X

Ref.	ITEM DESCRIPTION	PPL-A	PPL-H
	61.04.7 – Privileges and conditions Maintenance of competency	X	X
	61.04.8 – Ratings for special purposes	X	X
	61.04.9 – Maintenance of competency: Recency	X	X
5.3.3	Subpart 61.9 – Class and Type Ratings	X	X
	– Requirements for issue of class and type ratings (1 – 7, 9)	X	X
	– Training	X	X
	– Skill Test	X	X
	61.9.8 – Validity, revalidation and renewal: Type and class ratings	X	X
5.3.4	Subpart 61.10 – Night Rating	X	X
	– Requirements for night rating	X	X
	– Experience	X	X
	– Skill test standard	X	X
5.4	PART 67: MEDICAL CERTIFICATION	X	X
	67.00.2 Classes of medical certificates	X	X
	67.00.6 Period of validity of medical certificates	X	X
	Duties of holder of medical certificate	X	X
	Foreign medical assessments	X	X
5.5	PART 91 – GENERAL OPERATING AND FLIGHT RULES	X	X
5.5.1	SUBPART 1: GENERAL PROVISIONS	X	X
	– Applicability	X	X
	– Authority of pilot-in-command and crew members	X	X
	– Authorisation of personnel to taxi aeroplanes	X	N/A
	– Search and rescue information	X	X
	– Information on emergency and survival equipment	X	X
	– Portable electronic devices	X	X
	– Endangering safety	X	X
	– Preservation of documents	X	X
	– Passenger intoxication and unruly behaviour	X	X
	– Psychoactive substances	X	X
5.5.2	SUBPART 2: FLIGHT CREW	X	X

Ref.	ITEM DESCRIPTION	PPL-A	PPL-H
	91.02.1 Crew composition and qualifications	X	X
	91.02.2 Crew member emergency duties	X	X
	91.02.3 Crew member responsibilities	X	X
	91.02.4 Recency	X	X
	91.02.5 Crew members at duty stations	X	X
	91.02.6 Laws, regulations and procedures	X	X
	91.02.7 Duties of pilot-in-command regarding flight preparation	X	X
	91.02.8 Duties of pilot-in-command regarding flight operations	X	X
5.5.3	SUBPART 3: DOCUMENTATION AND RECORDS	X	X
	91.03.1 Documents to be carried on board	X	X
	91.03.2 Aircraft flight manual	X	X
	91.03.3 Aircraft checklists	X	X
	91.03.4 Air traffic service flight plan and associated procedures	X	X
	91.03.5 Flight folio	X	X
	91.03.6 Fuel and oil record	X	X
	91.03.7 Certificate of release to service	X	X
5.5.4	SUBPART 4: INSTRUMENTS AND EQUIPMENT	X	X
	91.04.1 Use and installation of instruments and equipment by pilot	X	X
	91.04.2 Circuit protection devices	X	X
	91.04.3 Aircraft operating lights	X	X
	91.04.4 Flight, navigation and associated equipment for aircraft operated under VFR	X	X
	91.04.11 Seats, seat safety belts, harnesses and child restraint devices	X	X
	91.04.12 Stowage of articles, baggage and cargo	X	X
	91.04.13 Standard first aid kit and universal precaution kits	X	X
	91.04.14 Supplemental oxygen in the case of non-pressurised aircraft	X	X
	91.04.18 Hand-held fire extinguishers	X	X

Ref.	ITEM DESCRIPTION	PPL-A	PPL-H
5.5.5	SUBPART 6: RULES OF THE AIR – FLIGHT RULES	X	X
	91.06.1 Landing on roads	X	X
	91.06.2 Dropping objects spraying or dusting	X	X
	91.06.3 Picking up objects	X	X
	91.06.4 Towing	X	X
	91.06.6 Proximity and formation flights	X	X
	91.06.7 Right of way	X	X
	91.06.8 Following line features	X	X
	91.06.9 Aircraft speed	X	X
	91.06.10 Lights to be displayed by aircraft	X	X
	91.06.11 Taxi rules	X	X
	91.06.12 Operation on and in the vicinity of aerodrome	X	X
	91.06.13 Signals	X	X
	91.06.15 Reporting position	X	X
	91.06.16 Mandatory radio in controlled airspace	X	X
	91.06.17 Mandatory radio in advisory airspace	X	X
	91.06.18 Compliance with rules of air and air traffic control clearance and instructions	X	X
	91.06.19 Prohibited areas	X	X
	91.06.20 Restricted areas	X	X
	91.06.21 Visibility and distance from cloud	X	X
	91.06.22 Special VFR weather *minima*	X	X
	91.06.23 VFR flight determination and weather deterioration	X	X
	91.06.28 Foreign military aircraft	X	X
	91.06.29 Identification and interception of aircraft	X	X
	91.06.30 Air traffic service procedures	X	X
	91.06.31 Priority	X	X
	91.06.32 Minimum heights	X	X
	91.06.33 Semi-circular rule	X	X
5.5.6	SUBPART 7: FLIGHT OPERATIONS	X	X
	91.07.1 Routes and areas of operation	X	X

Ref.	ITEM DESCRIPTION	PPL-A	PPL-H
	91.07.2 Minimum flight altitudes	X	X
	91.07.3 Use of aerodromes	X	X
	91.07.4 Helicopter landings and take-offs	N/A	X
	91.07.9 Meteorological conditions	X	X
	91.07.10 VFR operating *minima*	X	X
	91.07.11 Mass and balance	X	X
	91.07.12 Fuel supply	X	X
	91.07.13 Re-fuelling and de-fuelling with passengers on board	X	X
	91.07.14 Smoking in aircraft	X	X
	91.07.17 Submission of air traffic service flight plan	X	X
	91.07.18 Seats, safety belts and harnesses	X	X
	91.07.19 Passenger seating	X	X
	91.07.20 Passenger movements and briefing	X	X
	91.07.23 Use of supplemental oxygen	X	X
	91.07.27 In-flight testing on passenger and cargo carrying flight	X	X
	91.07.28 Turning helicopter rotors	N/A	X
	91.07.29 Starting and running of engines	X	X
	91.07.30 Acrobatic flights	X	X
	91.07.31 Simulated instrument flight in aircraft	X	X
5.6	PART 139: AERODROMES AND HELIPORTS	X	X
	139.01.1 Applicability	X	X
	139.01.2 Use of military aerodromes and heliports	X	X
	139.01.5 Flights by night	X	X
	139.01.10 Safety measures against fire	X	X
5.7	OPERATIONAL PROCEDURES	X	X
5.7.1	ICAO Annex 12 – Search and rescue	X	X
	– definitions	X	X
	– alerting phases	X	X
	– procedures for pilot-in-command (para 5.8 and 5.9)	X	X
	– search and rescue signals (para 5.9 and Appendix A)	X	X

Ref.	ITEM DESCRIPTION	PPL-A	PPL-H
5.7.2	ICAO Annex 13 – Aircraft accident investigation	X	X
	– definitions	X	X
	– national procedures	X	X
	– Aeronautical information Package	X	X
	– AIP- GEN	X	X
	– AIP-ENR	X	X
	– AIP-ENR	X	X
	– Interpretation of NOTAMS	X	X
	– Aeronautical codes	X	X
6.0	AIRCRAFT GENERAL KNOWLEDGE	X	X
6.1	Airframe	X	X
6.1.1	Airframe structure (aeroplane)	X	N/A
	– components	X	N/A
	– fuselage, wings, tailplane, fin	X	N/A
	– primary flying controls	X	N/A
	– trim and flap/slat systems	X	N/A
	– landing gear	X	N/A
	– nose wheel, including steering	X	N/A
	– tyres, construction, markings, limitations and condition	X	N/A
	– braking systems and precautions in use	X	N/A
	– retraction systems	X	N/A
6.1.2	Airframe structure (helicopter)	N/A	X
	– Fuselage (types of construction, structural components, materials)	N/A	X
	– Rotors	N/A	X
	blades, construction	N/A	X
	rotor heads (fully articulated, semi-rigid, rigid, swashplate)	N/A	X
	– Helicopter drive systems	N/A	X
	gearboxes (main rotor and tail rotor)	N/A	X
	clutch systems (sprag/freewheel clutch, electric and mechanical clutches)	N/A	X
	– Controls	N/A	X

Ref.	ITEM DESCRIPTION	PPL-A	PPL-H
	collective	N/A	X
	cyclic	N/A	X
	yaw pedals	N/A	X
	– Landing gear (skids, wheels and tyres, braking systems and shock absorbers)	N/A	X
6.1.3	Airframe loads (A & H)	X	X
	– static strength	X	X
	– limiting loads	X	X
	– safety factor	X	X
	– control locks and use	X	X
	– ground/flight precautions	X	X
6.2	Powerplant	X	X
6.2.1	Engines – general	X	X
	– design types and principles of the four stroke internal combustion engine	X	X
	– basic construction and component	X	X
	– causes of pre-ignition and detonation	X	X
	– power output as a function of RPM	X	X
6.2.2	Engine cooling	X	X
	– air cooling	X	X
	– cowling design and cylinder baffles	X	X
	– design and use of cowl flaps	X	X
	– cylinder head temperature gauge	X	X
6.2.3	Engine lubrication	X	X
	– function and methods of lubrication	X	X
	– lubrication systems	X	X
	– methods of oil circulation	X	X
	– oil pump and filter requirements	X	X
	– qualities and grades of oil	X	X
	– oil temperature and pressure control	X	X
	– oil cooling methods	X	X
	– recognition of oil system malfunctions	X	X
6.2.4	Ignition systems	X	X

Ref.	ITEM DESCRIPTION	PPL-A	PPL-H
	– principles of magneto ignition	X	X
	– construction and function	X	X
	– purpose and principle of impulse coupling	X	X
	– serviceability checks, recognition of malfunctions	X	X
	– operational procedures to avoid spark plug fouling	X	X
6.2.5	Carburation	X	X
	– principles of float type carburettor	X	X
	– construction, components and function	X	X
	– methods to maintain correct mixture ratio	X	X
	– operation of metering jets and accelerator pump	X	X
	– effect of pressure/density altitude	X	X
	– performance as a function of pressure and temperature	X	X
	– manual mixture control	X	X
	– maintenance of correct mixture ratio	X	X
	– limitation on use at high power	X	X
	– avoidance of detonation	X	X
	– idle cut-off valve	X	X
	– air induction system	X	X
	– alternate air induction systems (turbocharger & supercharger)	X	X
	– carburettor icing, use of hot air	X	X
	– injection systems, principles and operation	X	X
6.2.6	Aero engine fuel	X	X
	– classification of fuels	X	X
	– types, grades and identification by colour	X	X
	– quality requirements	X	X
	– additives	X	X
	– inspection for contamination (water content & ice formation)	X	X
	– fuel density	X	X
	– alternate fuels, differences in specifications, limitations	X	X
	– use of fuel strainers and drains	X	X

Ref.	ITEM DESCRIPTION	PPL-A	PPL-H
	– re-fuelling precautions	X	X
6.2.7	Engine handling	X	X
	– starting procedures and precautions	X	X
	– recognition of malfunctions	X	X
	– warming up, power and system checks	X	X
	– oil temperature and pressure limitations	X	X
	– cylinder head temperature limitations	X	X
	– ignition and other system checks	X	X
	– power settings and limitations	X	X
	– avoidance of rapid power changes	X	X
	– use of mixture control	X	X
	– action in the event of detonation or pre-ignition	X	X
6.2.8	Engine Operational Criteria	X	X
	– maximum and minimum RPM	X	X
	– (induced) engine vibration and critical RPM	X	X
	– remedial action by abnormal engine start, run-up and in-flight	X	X
	– type related items	X	X
6.3	Propellers	X	N/A
	– propeller nomenclature	X	N/A
	– conversion of engine power to thrust	X	N/A
	– design and construction of fixed pitch propeller	X	N/A
	– forces acting on propeller blade	X	N/A
	– variation of RPM with change of airspeed	X	N/A
	– thrust efficiency with change of speed	X	N/A
	– design and construction of variable pitch propeller	X	N/A
	– constant speed unit operation	X	N/A
	– effect of blade pitch changes	X	N/A
	– windmilling effect	X	N/A
6.4	Systems	X	X
6.4.1	Electrical system	X	X
	– construction and operation of alternators/generators	X	X

Ref.	ITEM DESCRIPTION	PPL-A	PPL-H
	– direct current supply	X	X
	– batteries, construction, capacity and charging	X	X
	– voltmeters and ammeters	X	X
	– circuit breakers and fuses	X	X
	– electrically operated services and instruments	X	X
	– recognition of malfunctions	X	X
	– procedure in the event of malfunctions	X	X
6.4.2	Vacuum system	X	X
	– components	X	X
	– pumps	X	X
	– regulator and gauge	X	X
	– filter system	X	X
	– recognition of malfunction	X	X
	– procedures in the event of malfunctions	X	X
6.4.3	Hydraulic system	X	X
	– components of a simple system	X	X
	– reservoir	X	X
	– pressure pump	X	X
	– accumulator	X	X
	– actuator	X	X
	– pressure relief and bypass valves	X	X
	– filters	X	X
	– types of fluid	X	X
	– operation, indication, warning systems	X	X
	– auxiliary systems	X	X
6.4.4	Fuel systems	X	X
	– fuel tanks, structural components, types and supply lines	X	X
	– venting system	X	X
	– mechanical and electrical pumps	X	X
	– gravity feed	X	X
	– tank selection	X	X
	– system management	X	X

Ref.	ITEM DESCRIPTION	PPL-A	PPL-H
6.5	Instruments	X	X
6.5.1	Pitot/static system	X	X
	– pitot tube, function	X	X
	– pitot tube, principles and construction	X	X
	– static source	X	X
	– alternate static source	X	X
	– position error	X	X
	– system drains	X	X
	– heating element	X	X
	– errors caused by blockage or leakage	X	X
6.5.2	Airspeed indicator	X	X
	– principles of operation and construction	X	X
	– relationship between pitot and static pressure	X	X
	– definitions of indicated, calibrated and true airspeed	X	X
	– instrument errors	X	X
	– airspeed indications, colour coding	X	X
	– pilot's serviceability checks	X	X
6.5.3	Altimeter	X	X
	– principles of operation and construction	X	X
	– function of the subscale	X	X
	– effects of atmospheric density	X	X
	– pressure altitude	X	X
	– true altitude	X	X
	– international standard atmosphere	X	X
	– flight level	X	X
	– presentation (three needle)	X	X
	– instrument errors	X	X
	– pilot's service ability checks	X	X
6.5.4	Vertical speed indicator	X	X
	– principles of operation and construction	X	X
	– function	X	X
	– inherent lag	X	X

Ref.	ITEM DESCRIPTION	PPL-A	PPL-H
	– instantaneous VSI	X	X
	– presentation	X	X
	– pilot's serviceability checks	X	X
6.5.5	Gyroscopes	X	X
	– principles	X	X
	– rigidity	X	X
	– precession	X	X
6.5.6	Turn indicator	X	X
	– rate gyro	X	X
	– purpose and function	X	X
	– effect of speed	X	X
	– presentation	X	X
	– turn co-ordinator	X	X
	– limited rate of turn indications	X	X
	– power source	X	X
	– balance indicator	X	X
	– principle	X	X
	– presentation	X	X
	– pilot's serviceability checks	X	X
6.5.7	Attitude indicator	X	X
	– earth gyro	X	X
	– purpose and function	X	X
	– presentations	X	X
	– interpretation	X	X
	– operating limitations	X	X
	– power source	X	X
	– pilot's serviceability checks	X	X
6.5.8	Heading indicator	X	X
	– directional gyro	X	X
	– purpose and function	X	X
	– presentation	X	X
	– use with magnetic compass	X	X
	– setting mechanism	X	X

Ref.	ITEM DESCRIPTION	PPL-A	PPL-H
	– apparent drift	X	X
	– transport wander	X	X
	– operating limitations	X	X
	– power source	X	X
	– pilot's serviceability checks	X	X
6.5.9	Magnetic compass	X	X
	– construction and function	X	X
	– earth's magnetic field	X	X
	– variation and deviation	X	X
	– turning, acceleration errors	X	X
	– precautions when carrying magnetic items	X	X
	– pilot's serviceability checks	X	X
6.5.10	Engine instruments	X	X
	– principles, presentation and operational use of:	X	X
	– oil temperature gauge	X	X
	– oil pressure gauge	X	X
	– cylinder head temperature gauge	X	X
	– exhaust gas meter	X	X
	– manifold pressure gauge	X	X
	– fuel pressure gauge	X	X
	– fuel flow gauge	X	X
	– fuel quantity gauge(s)	X	X
	– tachometer	X	X
6.5.11	Other instruments	X	X
	– principles, presentation and operational use of:	X	X
	– vacuum gauge	X	X
	– voltmeter and ammeter	X	X
	– warning indicators	X	X
	– others relevant to aircraft type	X	X
6.6	Airworthiness and Emergency Procedures	X	X
6.6.1	Airworthiness	X	X
	– certificate to be in force	X	X
	– compliance with requirements	X	X

Ref.	ITEM DESCRIPTION	PPL-A	PPL-H
	– periodic maintenance inspections	X	X
	– compliance with flight manual (or equivalent), instructions	X	X
6.6.2	Limitations, placards	X	X
	– flight manual supplements	X	X
	– provision and maintenance of documents	X	X
	– aeroplane, engine and propeller log books	X	N/A
	– helicopter, engine and rotorblade logbooks	N/A	X
	– recording of defects	X	X
	– permitted maintenance by pilots	X	X
6.6.3	Emergency Procedures	X	X
	– emergency equipment and its use	X	X
	– fire extinguisher	X	X
	– engine/cabin fires	X	X
	– flammable goods/pressurised containers	X	X
7.0	FLIGHT PERFORMANCE AND PLANNING	X	X
7.1	Mass and balance	X	X
7.1.1	Terminology:	X	X
	– Arm, moment, reference datum, flight station, centre of gravity	X	X
	– Forward and aft limitations of centre of gravity, normal and utility operation	X	X
	– Lateral limitations	N/A	X
	– Maximum ramp and taxi mass	X	N/A
	– Maximum take-off mass	X	X
	– Maximum zero fuel mass	X	X
	– Empty operating mass	X	X
	– Maximum floor load	X	X
	– Limitations on maximum mass	X	X
	– Forward and aft limitations of centre of gravity, normal and utility operation	X	X
	– Mass and centre of gravity calculations	X	X
	– Aircraft mass and balance sheet	X	X
7.1.2	Loadsheet	X	X

Ref.	ITEM DESCRIPTION	PPL-A	PPL-H
	– Calculation of CG	X	X
	– Movement of CG in flight/on ground	X	X
	– Maximum load at station	X	X
7.2	Abbreviations, definitions and symbols	X	X
	– IAS, RAS, TAS	X	X
	– Vx, Vy, Vfe, Vfo, Vle, Vlo, Va, Vne, Vno, Vs, Vso (as applicable)	X	X
	– OAT, IOAT	X	X
	– ISA temperature/deviation from ISA	X	X
	– pressure altitude, density altitude	X	X
	– QNH, QFE, QNE	X	X
7.3	Runways	X	X
	– runway length	X	X
	– take-off run available (TORA)	X	N/A
	– take-off run required (TORR)	X	N/A
	– take-off distance available (TODA)	X	N/A
	– take-off distance required (TODR)	X	N/A
	– landing distance available (LDA)	X	N/A
	– landing distance required (LDR)	X	N/A
	– displaced threshold, stopway, clearway	X	X
	– slope	X	N/A
	– surface	X	N/A
7.4	Aeroplane – use of performance graphs to determine:	X	N/A
	– take-off run (TORR) no flaps, effects of mass, wind, density altitude, ground surface and gradient	X	N/A
	– take-off run (TORR) with flaps, effects of mass, wind, density altitude, ground surface and gradient	X	N/A
	– take-off distance required (TODR), no flaps, effects of mass, wind, density altitude, ground surface and gradient	X	N/A
	– take-off distance required (TODR), with flaps, effects of mass, wind, density altitude, ground surface and gradient	X	N/A
	– climb performance	X	N/A

Ref.	ITEM DESCRIPTION	PPL-A	PPL-H
	– time, distance and fuel to climb	X	N/A
	– engine performance	X	N/A
	– speed – power performance cruise	X	N/A
	– speed – power economy cruise	X	N/A
	– range – performance cruise	X	N/A
	– range – economy cruise	X	N/A
	– endurance	X	N/A
	– time, distance and fuel to descend	X	N/A
	– glide range	X	N/A
	– landing performance, effect of flaps, mass, wind, density altitude, approach speed, ground surface and gradient	X	N/A
	– landing ground roll, effect of flaps, effects of mass, wind, density altitude, approach speed, ground surface and gradient	X	N/A
	– airspeed system calibration	X	N/A
	– stall speeds	X	N/A
7.5	Helicopter – use of performance graphs to determine:	N/A	X
	– Airspeed system calibration	N/A	X
	– Density altitude chart	N/A	X
	– Wind Component Graph	N/A	X
	– IGE Hover Ceiling vs Gross Weight	N/A	X
	– OGE Hover Ceiling vs Gross Weight	N/A	X
	– Airspeed Limitations (VNE/VNO)	N/A	X
	– Engine Limit of Manifold Pressure	N/A	X
	– Maximum Continuous Power	N/A	X
	– Autorotational Performance	N/A	X
	– Height/Velocity diagram	N/A	X
	– Longitudinal Weight and Balance	N/A	X
	– Lateral Weight and Balance	N/A	X
7.6	Fuel Weight and performance	X	X
	– specific weight	X	X
	– specific gravity	X	X

Ref.	ITEM DESCRIPTION	PPL-A	PPL-H
	– fuel consumption	X	X
	– fuel performance	X	X
	– calculation of fuel requirements	X	X
7.7	Aircraft Performance	X	X
	– icing, rain	X	X
	– condition of the airframe	X	X
	– wake turbulence	X	X
	– aqua-planing	X	N/A
	– windshear, take-off, approach and landing	X	X
8.0	HUMAN PERFORMANCE AND LIMITATIONS	X	X
8.1	Basic physiology	X	X
8.1.1	The atmosphere	X	X
	– composition of the atmosphere	X	X
	– the gas laws	X	X
	– oxygen requirement of tissues	X	X
8.1.2	The heart	X	X
	– basic physiology	X	X
	– blood pressure, pulse rate	X	X
	– composition of blood and circulation	X	X
	– ailments, recognition and treatment	X	X
8.1.3	The lungs	X	X
	– physiology	X	X
	– respiration	X	X
	– ailments and treatment	X	X
	– effects of partial pressure	X	X
	– effect of increasing altitude	X	X
	– gas transfer	X	X
	– hypoxia, symptoms, prevention	X	X
	– cabin pressurization	X	X
	– effects of rapid decompression	X	X
	– time of useful consciousness	X	X
	– the use of oxygen masks and rapid descent	X	X
	– hyperventilation, symptoms, avoidance	X	X

Ref.	ITEM DESCRIPTION	PPL-A	PPL-H
	– effects of accelerations	X	X
8.1.4	Vision	X	X
	– physiology of vision	X	X
	– limitations of the visual system	X	X
	– vision defects	X	X
	– optical illusions	X	X
	– night vision	X	X
	– spatial disorientation	X	X
	– avoidance of disorientation	X	X
	– ailments and treatment	X	X
8.1.5	Hearing	X	X
	– basic physiology	X	X
	– vestibular system	X	X
	– inner ear sensations	X	X
	– effects of altitude/pressure change	X	X
	– noise and hearing loss	X	X
	– protection of hearing	X	X
	– spatial disorientation	X	X
	– conflicts between ears and eyes	X	X
	– prevention of disorientation	X	X
	– motion sickness, causes, symptoms, prevention	X	X
8.1.6	Flying and health	X	X
	– medical requirements	X	X
	– effect of common ailments and cures	X	X
	– colds and flu	X	X
	– stomach upsets	X	X
	– hypotension, hypertension, coronary disease	X	X
	– obesity	X	X
	– nutrition hygiene	X	X
	– drugs, medicines, and side effects	X	X
	– alcohol	X	X
	– tobacco	X	X
	– self medication	X	X

Ref.	ITEM DESCRIPTION	PPL-A	PPL-H
	– personal fitness	X	X
	– passenger care	X	X
	– scuba diving – precautions before flying	X	X
	– decompression sickness	X	X
	– acceleration/deceleration and vibration	X	X
	– effects of pressure change	X	X
	– incapacitation	X	X
	– faints	X	X
	– toxic hazards	X	X
	dangerous goods	X	X
	carbon monoxide from heaters/exhausts	X	X
8.2	Basic psychology	X	X
8.2.1	Human information processing	X	X
	– attention, selective attention, divided attention	X	X
	– concepts of sensation	X	X
	– cognitive perception	X	X
	– expectancy and anticipation	X	X
	– habits	X	X
8.2.2	The central decision channel	X	X
	– mental workload, limitations	X	X
	– information sources	X	X
	– stimuli and attention	X	X
	– verbal communication	X	X
	– memory	X	X
	– sensory	X	X
	– working	X	X
	– long term	X	X
	– motor skills	X	X
	– limitations	X	X
	– causes of misinterpretation	X	X
8.2.3	Stress	X	X
	– causes and effects	X	X
	– concepts of arousal	X	X

Ref.	ITEM DESCRIPTION	PPL-A	PPL-H
	– effects on performance	X	X
	– identifying and reducing stress	X	X
	– fatigue	X	X
	– sleep	X	X
	– circadian rhythms	X	X
8.2.4	Judgement and decision-making	X	X
	– concepts of pilots' judgement	X	X
	– psychological attitudes	X	X
	– behavioural aspects	X	X
	– risk assessment	X	X
	– development of situational awareness	X	X
9.0	METEOROLOGY	X	X
9.1	The atmosphere	X	X
	– composition and structure	X	X
	– vertical divisions	X	X
	– ICAO standard atmosphere	X	X
9.2	Pressure, density and temperature	X	X
	– barometric pressure, isobars	X	X
	– changes of pressure and density with altitude	X	X
	– insolation and terrestrial energy radiation	X	X
	– diurnal variation of temperature	X	X
	– adiabatic process	X	X
	– temperature lapse rate	X	X
	– stability and instability	X	X
	– effects of advection and convection	X	X
9.3	Humidity and precipitation	X	X
	– water vapour in the atmosphere	X	X
	– dew point, relative humidity	X	X
	– condensation and vaporization	X	X
	– precipitation	X	X
9.4	Pressure and wind	X	X
	– high and low pressure areas	X	X
	– troughs, ridges, cols	X	X

Ref.	ITEM DESCRIPTION	PPL-A	PPL-H
	– pressure gradient, coriolis force	X	X
	– geostrophic and surface winds	X	X
	– vertical and horizontal motion, convergence, divergence	X	X
	– effect of wind gradient and windshear on take-off and landing	X	X
	– relationship between isobars and wind, Buys Ballot's law	X	X
	– turbulence and gustiness	X	X
	– local winds	X	X
	– föhn wind	X	X
	– land and sea breezes	X	X
	– anabatic and katabatic winds	X	X
9.5	Cloud formation	X	X
	– cooling by advection, radiation and adiabatic expansion	X	X
	– cloud types (high, medium, low and vertical development)	X	X
	– formation of cloud types	X	X
	– flying conditions associated with each cloud type	X	X
9.6	Fog, mist and haze	X	X
	– visibility	X	X
	– radiation fog	X	X
	– advection fog	X	X
	– frontal fog	X	X
	– freezing fog	X	X
	– steam fog	X	X
	– valley fog	X	X
	– formation and dispersal	X	X
	– assessment of probability of reduced visibility	X	X
	– hazards in flight due to low visibility, horizontal, vertical and slant angle	X	X
9.7	Air masses	X	X

Ref.	ITEM DESCRIPTION	PPL-A	PPL-H
	– characteristics and factors affecting the properties of air masses	X	X
	– classification of air masses, region of origin	X	X
	– modification of air masses during their movement	X	X
	– development of low and high pressure systems	X	X
	– weather associated with pressure systems	X	X
9.8	Frontology	X	X
	– cold fronts	X	X
	formation	X	X
	associated clouds and weather	X	X
	flying conditions	X	X
	changes with the passage of the front	X	X
	– warm fronts	X	X
	formation	X	X
	associated clouds and weather	X	X
	weather in the warm sector	X	X
	flying conditions	X	X
	changes with the passage of the front	X	X
	– occlusions	X	X
	formation	X	X
	associated clouds and weather	X	X
	– stationary fronts	X	X
9.9	Ice accretion	X	X
	– conditions conducive to ice formation	X	X
	– effects of hoar frost, rime ice, clear ice	X	X
	– effects of icing on aircraft performance	X	X
	– precautions and avoidance of icing conditions	X	X
	– powerplant icing	X	X
	– precautions, prevention and clearance of induction and carburettor icing	X	X
9.10	Thunderstorms	X	X
	– conditions required	X	X
	– formation, trigger action	X	X

Ref.	ITEM DESCRIPTION	PPL-A	PPL-H
	– air mass, frontal, orographic	X	X
	– development process	X	X
	– hazards for aircraft	X	X
	– effects of lightning and severe turbulence	X	X
	– avoidance of flight in the vicinity of thunderstorms	X	X
9.11	Flight over mountainous areas	X	X
	– hazards	X	X
	– influence of terrain on atmospheric processes	X	X
	– mountain waves, windshear, turbulence, vertical movement, rotor effects	X	X
	– valley winds	X	X
9.12	Climatology	X	X
	– general seasonal circulation in the troposphere over Southern Africa	X	X
	– local seasonal weather and winds	X	X
	– development of a coastal low (orographic depression)	X	X
	– South Westerly Buster	X	X
	– Cape Doctor	X	X
	– Black South Easter	X	X
	– Berg winds	X	X
9.13	Altimetry	X	X
	– operational aspects of pressure settings	X	X
	– pressure altitude, density altitude	X	X
	– height, altitude, flight level	X	X
	– QNH, QFE, standard setting	X	X
9.14	Weather analysis and forecasting	X	X
	– synoptic weather charts, symbols, signs	X	X
	– significant (prognostic) weather charts	X	X
	– upper wind and temperature charts	X	X
9.15	Weather information for flight planning	X	X
	– interpretation of coded information METAR, TAF, SPECI, SIGMET	X	X
	– Meteorological broadcasts for aviation	X	X

Ref.	ITEM DESCRIPTION	PPL-A	PPL-H
	– ATIS	X	X
10.0	NAVIGATION	X	X
10.1	Form of the earth	X	X
	– true north, axis, poles, direction and rate of rotation	X	X
	– cardinal and quadrantal points	X	X
	– meridians of longitude	X	X
	– prime (Greenwich) meridian	X	X
	– parallels of latitude	X	X
	– equator	X	X
	– great circles, small circles, rhumb lines	X	X
	– convergency between meridians	X	X
	– hemispheres, north/south, east/west	X	X
	– distances	X	X
	– units in use	X	X
	– derivation of nautical mile and kilometre	X	X
10.2	Time	X	X
	– Arc to time, relationship between universal co-ordinated (UTC) time, local mean time (LMT) and Standard time factor (STF)	X	X
	– definitions of sunrise and sunset times	X	X
	– official day and official night	X	X
10.3	Mapping – general	X	X
	– aeronautical maps and charts (topographical)	X	X
	– Lambert's conic conformal, (ICAO 1: 500 000 chart)	X	X
	orthomorphism	X	X
	– construction	X	X
	– convergence of meridians	X	X
	– presentation of meridians, parallels, great circles and rhumb lines	X	X
	– measurement of tracks	X	X
	– indication of magnetic variation	X	X
	– scale, standard parallels	X	X

Ref.	ITEM DESCRIPTION	PPL-A	PPL-H
	– measurement of distance in relation to map projection	X	X
	– conversion of units	X	X
	– map analysis	X	X
	depiction of height	X	X
	topography	X	X
	relief	X	X
	cultural features	X	X
	permanent features (e.g. line features, spot features, unique or	X	X
	special features)	X	X
	features subject to change (e.g. water)	X	X
	aeronautical symbols	X	X
	aeronautical information	X	X
10.4	Direction	X	X
	– true north	X	X
	– earth's magnetic field, variation – annual change	X	X
	– magnetic north	X	X
	– isogonals, agonic lines	X	X
10.5	Aircraft magnetism	X	X
	– magnetic influences within the aircraft	X	X
	– compass deviation	X	X
	– turning errors	X	X
	– acceleration/deceleration errors	X	X
	– avoiding magnetic interference with the compass	X	X
10.6	The navigation computer	X	X
10.6.1	Wind scale side	X	X
	– use of the computer to solve triangle of velocities	X	X
	– calculation of heading and groundspeed	X	X
	– drift, wind correction angle	X	X
	– finding wind velocity (W/V)	X	X
	– application of TAS and wind velocity to track	X	X

Ref.	ITEM DESCRIPTION	PPL-A	PPL-H
	– headwind and crosswind components relative to runway	X	X
10.6.2	Circular slide rule	X	X
	– IAS, CAS/RAS and TAS	X	X
	– groundspeed, distance and elapsed time	X	X
	– conversion of units (kg/lbs, USG/litres, nm/km, metres/feet)	X	X
	– fuel consumption and fuel required	X	X
	– pressure altitude true altitudes	X	X
	– density altitude	X	X
	– true altitude	X	X
	– time en route and ETA	X	X
	– one in sixty rule	X	X
10.7	Practical Navigation	X	X
	Use of South African Navigation Plotting Chart (1:500 000)	X	X
	– measurement of tracks and distances	X	X
	– dead reckoning, position, fix	X	X
	– procedure when uncertain of position	X	X
	– plotting positions	X	X
	– latitude and longitude	X	X
	– use of VOR/DME/ADF for position fixing	X	X
	– bearing and distance	X	X
	– use of navigation protractor	X	X
	– calculating headings (T), (M), (C)	X	X
	– EET and ETA	X	X
	– rate of descent and rate of climb	X	X
	– ETA for top of descent	X	X
	– fuel considerations	X	X
	– compass headings, use of deviation card	X	X
10.8	Radio navigation	X	X
10.8.1	Ground D/F	X	X
	– application	X	X

Ref.	ITEM DESCRIPTION	PPL-A	PPL-H
	– principles	X	X
	– presentation and interpretation	X	X
	– coverage	X	X
	– errors and accuracy	X	X
	– factors affecting range and accuracy	X	X
10.8.2	ADF, including associated beacons (NDBs) and use of the RMI	X	X
	– application	X	X
	– principles	X	X
	– presentation and interpretation	X	X
	– coverage	X	X
	– errors and accuracy	X	X
	– factors affecting range and accuracy	X	X
10.8.3	VOR/DME	X	X
	– application	X	X
	– principles	X	X
	– presentation and interpretation	X	X
	– coverage	X	X
	– errors and accuracy	X	X
	– factors affecting range and accuracy	X	X
10.8.4	GPS	X	X
	– application	X	X
	– principles	X	X
	– presentation and interpretation	X	X
	– coverage	X	X
	– errors and accuracy	X	X
	– factors affecting reliability and accuracy	X	X
10.8.5	Ground radar	X	X
	– application	X	X
	– principles	X	X
	– presentation and interpretation	X	X
	– coverage	X	X
	– errors and accuracy	X	X

Ref.	ITEM DESCRIPTION	PPL-A	PPL-H
	– factors affecting reliability and accuracy	X	X
10.8.6	Secondary surveillance radar	X	X
	– principles (transponders)	X	X
	– application	X	X
	– presentation and interpretation	X	X
	– modes and codes	X	X
11.0	PRINCIPLES OF FLIGHT	X	X
11.1	The atmosphere	X	X
	– composition and structure	X	X
	International standard atmosphere (ISA)	X	X
	atmospheric pressure	X	X
11.2	Lift	X	X
	– Newton's Laws of motion	X	X
	– Equation of continuity	X	X
	– IAS, CAS, TAS	X	X
	– Bernoulli's principle – venturi effect	X	X
	– airflow around a flat plate	X	X
	– airflow around a curved plate (aerofoil)	X	X
	– Description of aerofoil cross section	X	X
	Relative Airflow	X	X
	Chord line	X	X
	Mean camber line	X	X
	Camber	X	X
	Symmetrical aerofoils	X	X
	Surface area	X	X
	Shape	X	X
	Angle of Attack	X	X
	Centre of Pressure	X	X
	Lift Force	X	X
	Pressure distribution about an aerofoil	X	X
	– The lift formula – definitions	X	X
	Velocity	X	X
	Coefficient of Lift (CL)	X	X

Ref.	ITEM DESCRIPTION	PPL-A	PPL-H
	Density	X	X
	Surface area	X	X
	– Lift curve	X	X
11.3	Drag	X	X
	– Parasite (profile) drag	X	X
	form	X	X
	skin friction	X	X
	interference drag	X	X
	– Induced drag	X	X
	wingtip and trailing edge vortices	X	X
	downwash angle	X	X
	– Total Drag Curve	X	X
	– The Drag Formula	X	X
	– lift/drag ratio	X	X
	– aerofoil shapes and wing planforms	X	X
	– aspect ratio	X	X
11.4	Thrust	X	N/A
	– The propeller blade as an aerofoil	X	N/A
	– The thrust force	X	N/A
	– Thrust curve	X	N/A
	– Thrust Horse Power (THP)	X	N/A
11.5	Flying controls	X	X
	– the three planes	X	X
	– pitching about the lateral axis	X	X
	– rolling about the longitudinal axis	X	X
	– yawing about the normal axis	X	X
	– primary effects of the elevator (stabilators), ailerons and rudder	X	N/A
	– effect of speed, slipstream and location of centre of gravity	X	N/A
	– effects of cyclic, collective and rudder pedal inputs	N/A	X
	– further effects of the elevator (stabilators), ailerons and rudder	X	N/A

Annexure 6: Syllabus of theoretical knowledge (A) (H)

Ref.	ITEM DESCRIPTION	PPL-A	PPL-H
	– spiral dive recovery	X	N/A
	– Control in pitch, roll and yaw	X	X
	cross coupling, roll and yaw	X	X
	mass and aerodynamic balance of control surfaces	X	N/A
	effect of rotor configuration on control power	N/A	X
	adverse aileron yaw	X	N/A
11.6	Trimming controls	X	X
	– basic trim tab, balance tab and anti-balance tab	X	N/A
	– purpose and function	X	X
	– method of operation	X	X
11.7	Flaps and slats	X	N/A
	– simple, split, slotted and Fowler flaps	X	N/A
	– purpose and function	X	N/A
	– operational use	X	N/A
	– slats, leading edge	X	N/A
	– purpose and function	X	N/A
11.8	Flight mechanics	X	X
	– Forces acting on an aircraft	X	X
11.8.1	Straight and level flight	X	X
	– lift and mass	X	X
	– thrust and drag	X	X
	– methods of achieving balance (use of trim)	X	X
	– balance and couples (Lift/Weight and Thrust/Drag)	X	X
	– relationship between power required and power available	X	X
	– Understanding of power curves	X	X
	range and endurance	X	X
	effects of configuration, weight, temperature and altitude	X	X
11.8.2	Climbing	X	X
	– forces	X	X
	– maximum rate and maximum angle of climb	X	X

Ref.	ITEM DESCRIPTION	PPL-A	PPL-H
	– effects of configuration, weight, temperature and altitude, wind	X	X
	– use of power curves	X	X
11.8.3	Descending	X	X
	– descending without power	X	N/A
	– forces	X	X
	– effects of configuration, weight, temperature and altitude, wind	X	X
	– effect of power	X	X
11.8.4	Turning	X	X
	– forces	X	X
	– load factor	X	X
	– turn rate and turn radius	X	X
	– effects of weight, speed, angle of bank, wind, configuration	X	X
	– effect of torque	N/A	X
	– use of power curves	X	X
	– Advanced turning	X	X
	reduction of performance during climbing and descending turns	X	X
	steep turns	X	X
11.9	The stall	X	X
	– boundary layer	X	X
	– laminar and turbulent flow	X	X
	– stalling angle of attack	X	X
	– disruption of smooth airflow	X	X
	– reduction of lift, increase of drag	X	X
	– movement of centre of pressure	X	X
	– blade stall	N/A	X
	– symptoms of development	X	N/A
	– aircraft characteristics at the stall	X	N/A
	– factors affecting stall speed and aeroplane behaviour at the stall	X	N/A

Ref.	ITEM DESCRIPTION	PPL-A	PPL-H
	– stalling from level, climbing, descending and turning flight	X	N/A
	– inherent and artificial stall warnings	X	N/A
	– recovery from the stall	X	N/A
	– effect of weight and flaps	X	N/A
	– basic stalling speed	X	N/A
11.10	Avoidance of spins	X	N/A
	– wing tip stall	X	N/A
	– the development of roll and autorotation	X	N/A
	– recognition at the incipient stage	X	N/A
	– recovery technique	X	N/A
	– full spin recovery technique	X	N/A
11.11	Stability	X	X
	– definitions of static and dynamic stability	X	X
	– longitudinal, lateral and directional stability	X	X
	– effect of location of centre of gravity and speed	X	X
11.12	Load factor and manoeuvres	X	X
	– structural considerations	X	X
	– manoeuvring and gust envelope	X	X
	– limiting load factors, (aeroplane – with and without flaps)	X	X
	– changes in load factor in turns and pull-ups	X	X
	– vibrations, control feedback	N/A	X
	– manoeuvring speed limitations	X	X
	– in-flight precautions	X	X
	– H/V diagram, take-off and landing	N/A	X
11.13	Stress loads on the ground	X	X
	– side loads on the landing gear	X	X
	– landing	X	X
	– taxiing, precautions during turns	X	X
12.0	Helicopter Aerodynamics	N/A	X
12.1	Helicopter terms	N/A	X
	– Plane of rotation	N/A	X

Ref.	ITEM DESCRIPTION	PPL-A	PPL-H
	– Axes of rotation	N/A	X
	– Rotor shaft axis	N/A	X
	– Tip path plane	N/A	X
	– Rotor disc	N/A	X
	– Disc loading	N/A	X
	– Blade loading	N/A	X
12.2	The forces diagram and associated terminology	N/A	X
	– Pitch angle	N/A	X
	– Induced airflow	N/A	X
	– Relative airflow to the blade	N/A	X
	– Angle of attack	N/A	X
	– Drag-blade	N/A	X
	– Total reaction-blade	N/A	X
	– Rotor thrust	N/A	X
	– Rotor drag	N/A	X
	– Torque	N/A	X
	– Mass	N/A	X
	– Uniformity of rotor thrust along blade span	N/A	X
	– Blade twist	N/A	X
	– Blade taper	N/A	X
	– Coning angle	N/A	X
	– Centrifugal force	N/A	X
	– Limits of rotor RPM	N/A	X
	– Centrifugal turning moments	N/A	X
12.3	Helicopter Controls	N/A	X
12.3.1	Collective lever	N/A	X
	– collective pitch changes	N/A	X
	– relationship with rotor thrust and rotor drag	N/A	X
12.3.2	Cyclic stick	N/A	X
	– cyclic pitch changes	N/A	X
	– rotor disc attitude	N/A	X
	– rotor thrust tilt	N/A	X
12.3.3	Yaw pedals	N/A	X

Ref.	ITEM DESCRIPTION	PPL-A	PPL-H
	– fuselage torque	N/A	X
	– tailrotor drift	N/A	X
	– tailrotor roll	N/A	X
12.4	Rotor blade freedom of movement	N/A	X
12.4.1	Feathering	N/A	X
	– the feathering hinge	N/A	X
	– pitch angle	N/A	X
12.4.2	Flapping	N/A	X
	– the flapping hinge	N/A	X
	– alleviation of bending stresses	N/A	X
	– flapping to equality	N/A	X
12.4.3	Dragging	N/A	X
	– the drag hinge	N/A	X
	– drag dampers	N/A	X
	– leading/lagging	N/A	X
	– periodic drag changes	N/A	X
	– blade C of G (conservation of angular momentum)	N/A	X
12.4.4	Vertical flight	N/A	X
	– take-off	N/A	X
	– vertical climb	N/A	X
	– vertical descent	N/A	X
12.5	Hovering	N/A	X
12.5.1	Outside – Inside ground effect	N/A	X
	– factors affecting ground cushion	N/A	X
	– re-circulation	N/A	X
12.5.2	Forces in balance	N/A	X
	– in the hover	N/A	X
	– in forward flight	N/A	X
	– influence of centre of gravity	N/A	X
	– influence of rotor shaft tilt	N/A	X
12.5.3	Translational lift	N/A	X
	– effect of horizontal airflow on induced flow	N/A	X

Ref.	ITEM DESCRIPTION	PPL-A	PPL-H
	– variation of total flow through the disc with forward flight	N/A	X
12.6	The relationship between pitch angle and angle of attack	N/A	X
12.6.1	Power requirements	N/A	X
	– rotor profile power	N/A	X
	– power absorption – tail rotor and ancillary equipment	N/A	X
	– rotor profile power variation with forward speed	N/A	X
	– induced drag	N/A	X
	– parasite drag	N/A	X
	– rotor profile drag	N/A	X
	– total power required	N/A	X
	– power available	N/A	X
12.7	Transition from and to the hover	N/A	X
	– symmetry and asymmetry of rotor thrust	N/A	X
	– main rotor flapback	N/A	X
	– tail rotor flapback and methods of removal	N/A	X
12.8	Factors affecting maximum forward speed	N/A	X
	– design limits of cyclic stick	N/A	X
	– airflow reversal	N/A	X
	– retreating blade stall	N/A	X
	– symptoms and recovery actions	N/A	X
	– flow separation	N/A	X
12.9	Factors affecting cyclic stick limits	N/A	X
	– All up mass (AUM)	N/A	X
	– Density altitude	N/A	X
	– Centre of gravity position	N/A	X
	– The flare – power flight	N/A	X
12.10	Helicopter specific hazards	N/A	X
12.10.1	Vortex Ring State (Settling with Power)	N/A	X
	– tip vortices	N/A	X
	– comparison between induced flow and rate of descent flow	N/A	X

Annexure 6: Syllabus of theoretical knowledge (A) (H)   327

Ref.	ITEM DESCRIPTION	PPL-A	PPL-H
	– development	N/A	X
	– change in relative airflow along blade span – root stall and turbulence	N/A	X
12.10.2	Blade sailing	N/A	X
	– rotor RPM and blade rigidity	N/A	X
	– effect of adverse wind	N/A	X
	– minimising the danger	N/A	X
12.10.3	Autorotation – vertical	N/A	X
	– rate of descent airflow	N/A	X
	– effective airflow	N/A	X
	– relative airflow	N/A	X
	– inflow and inflow angle	N/A	X
	– autorotative force	N/A	X
12.10.4	Blade regions	N/A	X
	– stalled region	N/A	X
	– driven region	N/A	X
	– driving region	N/A	X
	– rotor drag	N/A	X
	– effect of mass and altitude	N/A	X
	– control of rotor RPM	N/A	X
12.10.5	Autorotation – forward flight	N/A	X
	– factors affecting inflow angle	N/A	X
	– effect of forward speed on rate of descent	N/A	X
	– effect of forward speed on the three regions	N/A	X
	– turning	N/A	X
	– the flare	N/A	X
	– rotor RPM increase from movement of autorotative section	N/A	X
	– increase in rotor thrust	N/A	X
	– reduction in rate of descent	N/A	X
	– autorotation for range and endurance	N/A	X
	– height/velocity avoidance graph	N/A	X
12.10.6	Rollover	N/A	X

Ref.	ITEM DESCRIPTION	PPL-A	PPL-H
	– dynamic roll-over and avoidance of	N/A	X
	– static rollover	N/A	X
	– effect of centre of gravity	N/A	X
12.10.7	Operating with limited power	N/A	X
12.10.8	Overpitch	N/A	X
12.10.9	Ground resonance	N/A	X
12.10.10	Mast bumping	N/A	X

Annexure 7

. . . .

Practical syllabus for flight instruction PPL (A)

Source: CATS Part 61 with promulgated Amendments 1/2016, 2/2016, 3/2016, and 1/2018.

Any change with an effective date (date at which compliance with a regulation or standard is mandatory) that may be promulgated later than July 2019 is not reflected in this document. In doubt check on the SACAA websites for updates regarding the practical syllabus by looking at : Legal and Aviation Compliance > Notices: Promulgated Technical Standards

Note that according to SACAA 'this document is based on Appendix 1 to JAR-FCL 1.125 (Amendment 4 2–C–2 01.09.05)'.

Note that "E" stands for emergency procedures.

Exercise	ITEM DESCRIPTION
Exercise 1	Familiarisation with the aircraft
	– characteristics of the aircraft
	– cockpit layout
	– systems
	– check lists, drills, controls
Exercise 1E	Emergency drills
	– action in the event of fire on the ground and in the air
	– engine cabin and electrical system fire
	– systems failure
	– escape drills, location and use of emergency equipment and exits
Exercise 2	Preparation for and action after flight
	– flight authorisation and aircraft acceptance
	– serviceability documents
	– equipment required, maps, etc.
	– external checks
	– internal checks
	– harness, seat or rudder panel adjustments
	– starting and warm up checks

Exercise	ITEM DESCRIPTION
	– power checks
	– running down system checks and switching off the engine
	– parking, security and picketing (e.g. tie down)
	– completion of authorisation sheet and serviceability documents
Exercise 3	Air experience
	– Flight exercise
	– introduce student to fixed-wing flight
Exercise 4	Effects of controls
	– primary effects when laterally level and when banked
	– secondary effects of aileron and rudder
	– effects of:
	– airspeed
	– slipstream
	– power
	– trimming controls
	– flaps
	– other controls, as applicable
	– operation of:
	– mixture control
	– carburettor heat
	– cabin heating/ventilation
	– airmanship
Exercise 5	Taxiing
	– pre-taxi checks
	– starting, control of speed and stopping
	– engine handling
	– control of direction and turning
	– turning in confined spaces
	– parking area procedure and precautions
	– effects of wind and use of flying controls
	– effects of ground surface
	– freedom of rudder movement
	– marshalling signals

Annexure 7: Practical syllabus for flight instruction PPL (A)

Exercise	ITEM DESCRIPTION
	– instrument checks
	– air traffic control procedures
	– airmanship
Exercise 5E	Emergencies
	– Brake and steering failure
Exercise 6	Straight and level
	– at normal cruising power, attaining and maintaining straight and level flight
	– flight at critically high airspeeds
	– demonstration of inherent stability
	– control in pitch, including use of trim
	– lateral level, direction and balance, trim
	– at selected airspeeds (use of power)
	– during speed and configuration changes
	– use of instruments for precision
	– airmanship
Exercise 7	Climbing
	– entry, maintaining the normal and max rate climb, levelling off
	– levelling off at selected altitudes
	– en route climb (cruise climb)
	– climbing with flap down
	– recovery to normal climb
	– maximum angle of climb
	– use of instruments for precision
	– airmanship
Exercise 8	Descending
	– entry, maintaining and levelling off
	– levelling off at selected altitudes
	– glide, powered and cruise descent (including effect of power and airspeed)
	– side slipping (consideration of aircraft limitations)
	– use of instruments for precision flight
	– airmanship

Exercise	ITEM DESCRIPTION
Exercise 9	Turning
	– entry and maintaining medium level turns
	– resuming straight flight
	– faults in the turn – (in correct pitch, bank, balance)
	– climbing turns
	– descending turns
	– slipping turns (or suitable types)
	– turns onto selected headings, use of gyro heading indicator and compass
	– use of instruments for precision
	– airmanship
Exercise 10A	Slow flight
NOTE:	The objective is to improve the student's ability to recognise inadvertent flight at critically low speeds and provide practice in maintaining the aeroplane in balance while returning to normal airspeed. It means that you may fly at a critically low speed **without having noticed** it, which happens, and is very dangerous.
	– safety checks
	– introduction to slow flight
	– controlled flight down to critically slow airspeed
	– application of full power with correct altitude and balance to achieve normal climb speed
	– airmanship
Exercise 10B	Stalling
	– airmanship
	– safety checks
	– symptoms
	– recognition
	– clean stall and recovery without power and with power
	– recovery when a wing drops
	– approach to stall in the approach and in the landing configurations, with and without power,
	recovery at the incipient stage

Annexure 7: Practical syllabus for flight instruction PPL (A)

Exercise	ITEM DESCRIPTION
Exercise 11	Spin avoidance
	– airmanship
	– safety checks
	– stalling and recovery at the incipient spin stage (stall with excessive wing drop, about 45)
	– instructor induced distractions during the stall
NOTE 1:	At least two hours of stall awareness and spin avoidance flight training shall be completed during the course.
NOTE 2:	Consideration of manoeuvre limitations and the need to refer to the aeroplane manual and mass and balance calculations.
Exercise 12	Take-off and climb to downwind position
	– pre-take-off checks
	– into wind take-off
	– safeguarding the nosewheel
	– crosswind take-off
	– drills during and after take-off
	– short take-off and soft field procedure/techniques including performance calculations
	– noise abatement procedures
	– airmanship
Exercise 13	Circuit, approach and landing
	– circuit procedures, downwind, base leg
	– powered approach and landing
	– safeguarding the nosewheel
	– effect of wind on approach and touchdown speeds, use of flaps
	– crosswind approach and landing
	– glide approach and landing
	– short landing and soft field procedures/techniques
	– flapless approach and landing
	– wheel landing (tail wheel aeroplanes)
	– missed approach/go around
	– noise abatement procedures
	airmanship

Exercise	ITEM DESCRIPTION
Exercise 12/13E	Emergencies
	– abandoned take-off
	– engine failure after take-off
	– mislanding/go-around
	– missed approach
NOTE:	In the interests of safety it will be necessary for pilots trained on nosewheel aeroplanes to undergo dual conversion training before flying tail wheel aeroplanes, and vice versa.
Exercise 14	First solo
	– instructor's briefing, observation of flight and de-briefing
NOTE:	During flights immediately following the solo circuit consolidation the following should be revised.
	– procedures for leaving and rejoining the circuit
	– the local area, restrictions, map reading
	– use of radio aids for homing
	– turns using magnetic compass, compass errors
	– airmanship
Exercise 15	Advanced turning
	– steep turns (45), level and descending
	– stalling in the turn and recovery
	– recoveries from unusual altitudes, including spiral dives
	– airmanship
Exercise 16	Forced landing without power
	– forced landing procedure
	– choice of landing area, provision for change of plan
	– gliding distance
	– descent plan
	– key positions
	– engine cooling
	– engine failure checks
	– use of radio
	– base leg
	– final approach

Annexure 7: Practical syllabus for flight instruction PPL (A)

Exercise	ITEM DESCRIPTION
	– landing
	– actions after landing
	– airmanship
Exercise 17A	Low level flying
	– Safety considerations
	– Selection of the appropriate speed and configuration
	– Awareness of the danger factors and their recognition
	– Transition to low level flight
	– Control of speed and height
	– Following ground contours
Exercise 17B	Precautionary landing
	– full procedure away from aerodrome to break-off height
	– occasions necessitating
	– in-flight conditions
	– landing area selection
	– normal aerodrome
	– disused aerodrome
	– ordinary field
	– circuit and approach
	– actions after landing
	– airmanship
Exercise 18A	Navigation
	Flight planning
	– weather forecast and actuals
	– map selection and preparation
	– choice of route
	– controlled airspace
	– danger, prohibited and restricted areas
	– safety altitudes
	– calculations
	– magnetic heading(s) and time(s) en route
	– fuel consumption
	– mass and balance

Exercise	ITEM DESCRIPTION
	– mass and performance
	– flight information
	– NOTAMS etc.
	– radio frequencies
	– selection of alternate aerodromes
	– aeroplane documentation
	– notification of the flight
	– pre-flight administrative procedures
	– flight plan form
	Departure
	– organisation of cockpit workload
	– departure procedures
	– altimeter settings
	– ATC liaison in controlled/regulated airspace
	– setting heading procedure
	– noting of ETAs
	– maintenance of altitude and heading
	– revisions of ETA and heading
	– log keeping
	– use of radio
	– use of navaids
	– minimum weather conditions for continuation of flight
	– in-flight decisions
	– transiting controlled/regulated airspace
	– diversion procedures
	– uncertainty of position procedure
	– lost procedure
	Arrival, aerodrome joining procedure
	– ATC liaison in controlled/regulated airspace
	– altimeter setting
	– entering the traffic pattern
	– circuit procedures
	– parking

Exercise	ITEM DESCRIPTION
	– security of aeroplane
	– refuelling
	– closing of flight plan, if appropriate
	– post-flight administrative procedures
Exercise 18B	Navigation problems at lower levels and in reduced visibility
	– actions prior to descending
	– hazards (e.g. obstacles, and terrain)
	– difficulties of map reading
	– effects of wind and turbulence
	– vertical situational awareness (avoidance of controlled flight into terrain)
	– avoidance of noise sensitive areas
	– joining the circuit
	– bad weather circuit and landing
Exercise 18C	Radio navigation
	Use of VHF Omni Range (VOR)
	– availability, AIP, frequencies
	– selection and identification
	– omni bearing selector (OBS)
	– to/from indications, orientation
	– course deviation indicator (CDI)
	– determination of radial
	– intercepting and maintaining a radial
	– VOR passage
	– obtaining a fix from two VORs
	Use of automatic direction finding equipment (ADF) – non-directional beacons (NDBs)
	– availability, AIP, frequencies
	– selection and identification
	– orientation relative to the beacon
	– homing
	Use of VHF direction finding (VHF/DF)
	– availability, AIP, frequencies

Exercise	ITEM DESCRIPTION
	– R/T procedures and ATC liaison
	– obtaining a QDM and homing
	Use of en route/terminal radar
	– availability, AIP
	– procedures and ATC liaison
	– pilot's responsibilities
	– secondary surveillance radar
	– transponders
	– code selection
	– interrogation and reply
	Use of distance measuring equipment (DME)
	– station selection and identification
	– modes of operation
	– distance, groundspeed, time to run
Exercise 19	Basic instrument flight
	– physiological sensations
	– instrument appreciation
	– altitude instrument flight
	– instrument limitations
	– airmanship
	– basic manoeuvres
	– straight and level at various airspeeds and configurations
	– climbing and descending
	– standard rate turns, climbing and descending, onto selected headings
	– recoveries from climbing and descending turns

Annexure 8

. . . .

Progress Report Sheet

Source: Morningstar Flying Club and Academy

Date					Previous Totals		Hours this Session		Total Hours	
					Dual		Dual		Dual	
Aircraft Registration					Solo		Solo		Solo	
					Total Hrs		Total Hrs		Total Hrs	
Exercise					Briefing		Briefing		Total Brief	
					De-brief		De-brief		De-brief	
General Flying / Handling	1	2	3	4	Landings		Take-offs		Weather	
Technical Knowledge/ Preparation	1	2	3	4	Instructor					
SOP's/ CL / Normal Procedures	1	2	3	4	Student					
Command ability/ Potential	1	2	3	4	Next Exercise:		Next Dual Check:			
Airmanship	1	2	3	4						

	Name	Licence Number	Signature
Student			
Instructor			

Annexure 9

Duties of PIC regarding flight preparation

Source: CATS 91.02.7

(1) The PIC of an aircraft shall not commence a flight unless he or she is satisfied that—
(a) the aircraft is airworthy;
(b) the instruments and navigation, communication and other equipment required for the particular type of operation to be undertaken, are installed and are serviceable and functioning correctly, except as provided for in the MEL, if any;
(c) the aircraft has been released to service in accordance with Part 43;
(d) the mass of the aircraft at any time does not exceed the MCM calculated from the performance information provided in the AFM referred to in regulation 91.03.2, in terms of which the operating limitations referred to in Subpart 9 are complied with;
(e) the load carried by the aircraft is properly secured, fit to be conveyed in accordance with Part 92 and is so distributed that the centre of gravity is within the limits prescribed in the AFM referred to in regulation 91.03.2;
(f) an ATS flight plan, referred to in regulation 91.03.4, has been properly completed and filed with the appropriate ATSU, if such flight plan is required in terms of regulation 91.03.4;
(g) all the documents and forms required to be carried on board are carried as specified in regulation 91.03.1;
(h) a check has been completed indicating that the operating limitations referred to in Subpart 8 will not be exceeded;
(i) the search and rescue information, referred to in regulation 91.01.4, is available on board;
(j) the requirements in respect of fuel, oil, oxygen, weather, minimum safe altitudes, aerodrome operating minima and availability of alternate aerodromes for the route being flown and any likely alternatives, whether flown under instrument or VFR, are complied with;
(k) the aerodrome operating minima are not less than the operating minima of the aerodrome being operated to or from, established by the appropriate authority of the State in which the aerodrome is located, unless such appropriate authority approves lower aerodrome operating minima;
(l) current and suitable IFR or VFR, as applicable, charts and related publications required to—
    (i) depart the place of origin;

(ii) operate on the route to the destination, or other route that a flight could reasonably be expected to be diverted to; and

(iii) arrive at the destination or any alternate,

are carried on board;

(m) the external surfaces are checked prior to take-off for any deposit which might adversely affect the performance or controllability of the aircraft, unless otherwise permitted in the AFM referred to in regulation 91.03.2, and if such deposit is found, to have it removed;

(n) according to the information available to him or her—

(i) in respect of an aeroplane, the condition of the runway intended to be used will not prevent a safe take-off at departure or a safe landing at the destination aerodrome or alternate aerodrome, as applicable; and

(ii) the weather at the departure and arrival aerodromes and *en route*, including any possible alternate aerodromes or routes, will not preclude safe completion of the flight;

(o) the RVR or visibility in the take-off direction of the aircraft is equal to, or better than, the applicable minimum;

(p) the flight crew members are properly qualified for the specific operation to be undertaken, except that for commercial air operations, the air operator shall ensure that the flight crew are properly qualified;

(q) an adequate and suitable aerodrome is available for take-off, *en route* and destination, should it become inadvisable to continue to or land at the destination aerodrome; and

(r) if flight in RVSM airspace is contemplated—

(i) the aircraft has been approved for RVSM operations;

(ii) the crew has been trained and is otherwise qualified for the flight;

(iii) the minimum required equipment pertaining to height-keeping and alerting systems is installed and serviceable; and

(iv) no airframe or operating restrictions prevent operation in the particular RVSM airspace.

(2) The PIC of an aircraft shall –

(a) not commence a flight unless he or she has ascertained through the relevant NOTAM), AIC, IAIP or IAIP Supplement that the aerodromes, navigation aids and communication facilities are adequate for the manner in which the flight is to be conducted;

(b) prior to take-off from an aerodrome at which an ATSU is in operation, determine through the aeronautical information services available from the unit or any other reliable source, that the unserviceability of any aerodrome, navigation aids or communication facilities required for such flight, will not prejudice the safe conduct of the flight; and

(c) advise an ATSU, as soon as it is practical to do so, of any inadequate facilities encountered in the course of operations.

(3) Where a load and trim sheet is required in terms of these regulations, the load and trim sheet shall be acceptable to and countersigned by the PIC before a flight commences: Provided that if the load and trim sheet is submitted to the PIC by electronic data transfer, commencement of the flight shall be deemed to be the acceptance thereof by such PIC.

Annexure 10

Aeronautical Chart Index and Classification of Airspace

Index to the World Aeronautical Chart (WAC)—ICAO 1:1 000 000

Source: AIP GEN 3.2–5, of 15 January 2019

Title of series	Scale	Name and/or number			Date Y/M/D	Source Date
World Aeronautical Chart ICAO (WAC)	1: 1 000 000	Bloemfontein	(3 397)	7th Ed	OCT 17	2006
		Bulawayo	(3 275)	4th Ed	DEC 16	2006
		Calvinia	(3 396)	6th Ed	DEC 16	2006
		Cape iown	(3 422)	5th Ed	DEC 16	2006
		Durban	(3 398)	8th Ed	OCT 17	2006
		Inhambane	(3 276)	4th Ed	DEC 12	2000
		Johannesburg	(3 300)	7th Ed	OCT 17	2006
		Kalahari	(3 274)	3rd Ed	NOV 16	1998
		Keetmanshoop	(3 302)	4th Ed	MAY 14	2002
		Livingstone	(3 177)	5th Ed	MAY 14	2009
		Maputo	(3 299)	5th Ed	DEC 16	2006
		Ondangwa	(3 179)	3rd Ed	MAY 14	2009
		Port Elizabeth	(3 421)	4th Ed	OCT 17	1998
		Tsumeb	(3 178)	4th Ed	MAY 14	2009
		Vryburg	(3 301)	6th Ed	OCT 17	2006
		Windhoek	(3 273)	4th Ed	MAY 14	2009
SA Topographical Aeronautical Edition	1: 500 000	Alexander Bay	(2 714)	5th Ed	DEC 15	2009
		Alldays	(2 126)	3rd Ed	MAR 18	2001
		Beaufort West	(3 122)	4th Ed	DEC 15	2005
		Bloemfontein	(2 924)	3rd Ed	DEC 15	2004
		Calvinia	(3 117)	2nd Ed	APR 18	2000
		Cape Town	(3 317)	4th Ed	MAR 18	2014
		Gobabis	(2 118)	1st Ed	Namib FEB 00	1985
		Grootfontein	(1 918)	1 st Ed	Namib MAY 96	1985
		Johannesburg	(2 526)	4th Ed	MAR 18	2015
		Katima Mulilo	(1 722)	1st Ed	RSA OCT 95	1982
		Keetmanshoop	(2 518)	3r d Ed	DEC 15	2009

Title of series	Scale	Name and/or number			Date Y/M/D	Source Date
		Kimberley	(2 722)	2nd Ed	JUN 16	2002
		Kroonstad	(2 726)	3rd Ed	AUG 16	2000
		Leonardville	(2 318)	1st Ed	Namib FEB 00	1983
		Luderitz	(2 514)	1st Ed	Namib JAN 03	1978
		Nelspruit	(2 530)	4th Ed	MAR 18	2010
		Ondangwa	(1 714)	1st Ed	JUN 96	1981
		Opuwo	(1 711)	1st Ed	FEB 00	1985
		Otjiwarongo	(1 914)	2nd Ed	FEB 00	1986
		Oudtshoorn	(3 320)	4th Ed	DEC 15	2007
		Musina	(2 130)	3rd Ed	MAR 18	1999
		Phalaborwa	(2 330)	4th Ed	MAR 18	2008
		Polokwane	(2 326)	3rd Ed	JUN 16	2001
		Port Elizabeth	(3 324)	2nd Ed	OCT 15	1998
		Prieska	(2 920)	4th Ed	JUN 16	2005
		Queenstown	(3 126)	2nd Ed	AUG 16	1992
		Rehoboth	(2 314)	1st Ed	OCT 98	1977
		Rundu	(1 718)	1st Ed	OCT 96	1981
		Springbok	(2 916)	5th Ed	JUN 16	2003
		Ulundi	(2 730)	3rd Ed	AUG 16	2000
		Upington	(2 718)	4th Ed	DEC 15	2009
		Vryburg	(2 522)	3rd Ed	DEC 15	2007
		Windhoek	(2 113)	1st Ed	OCT 99	1984

Annexure 10: Aeronautical Chart Index and Classification of Airspace 345

Table 1: Southern African chart index: 1:1 000 000
Source: NGI

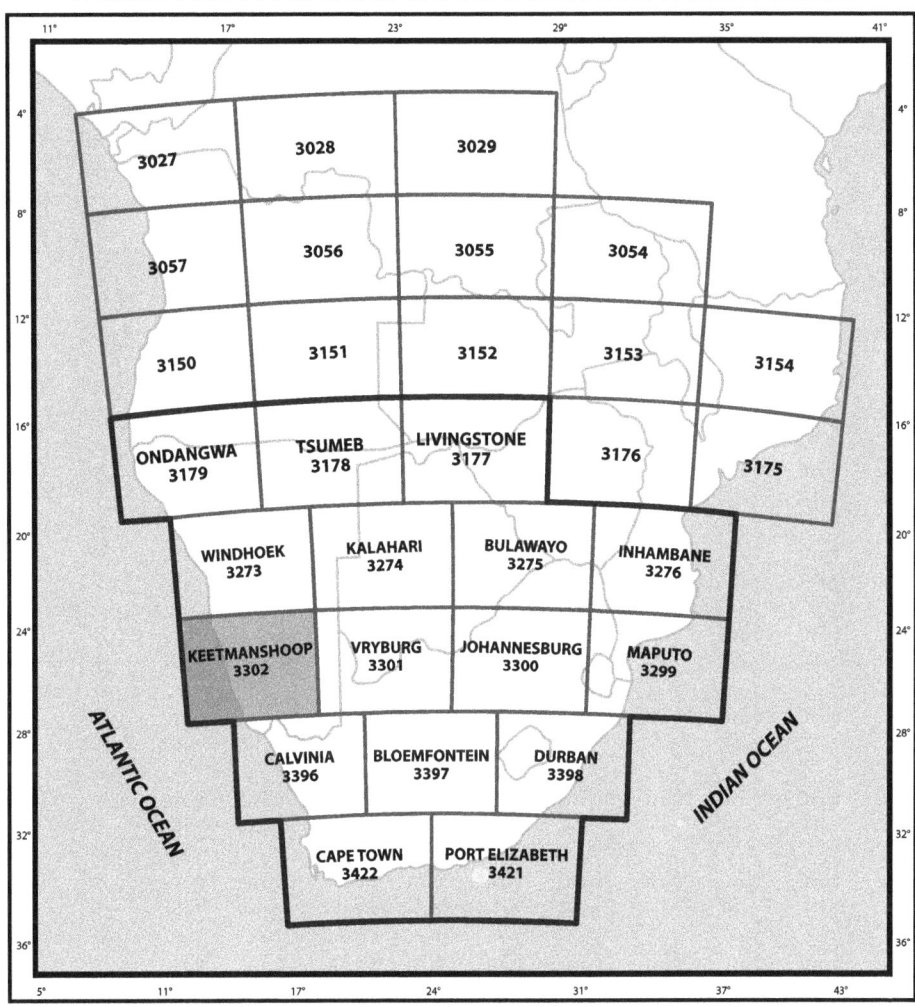

346 Air Law

Google Earth image as per WAC 1:1 000 000 (Ondangwa, Tsumeb, Livingstone not illustrated)

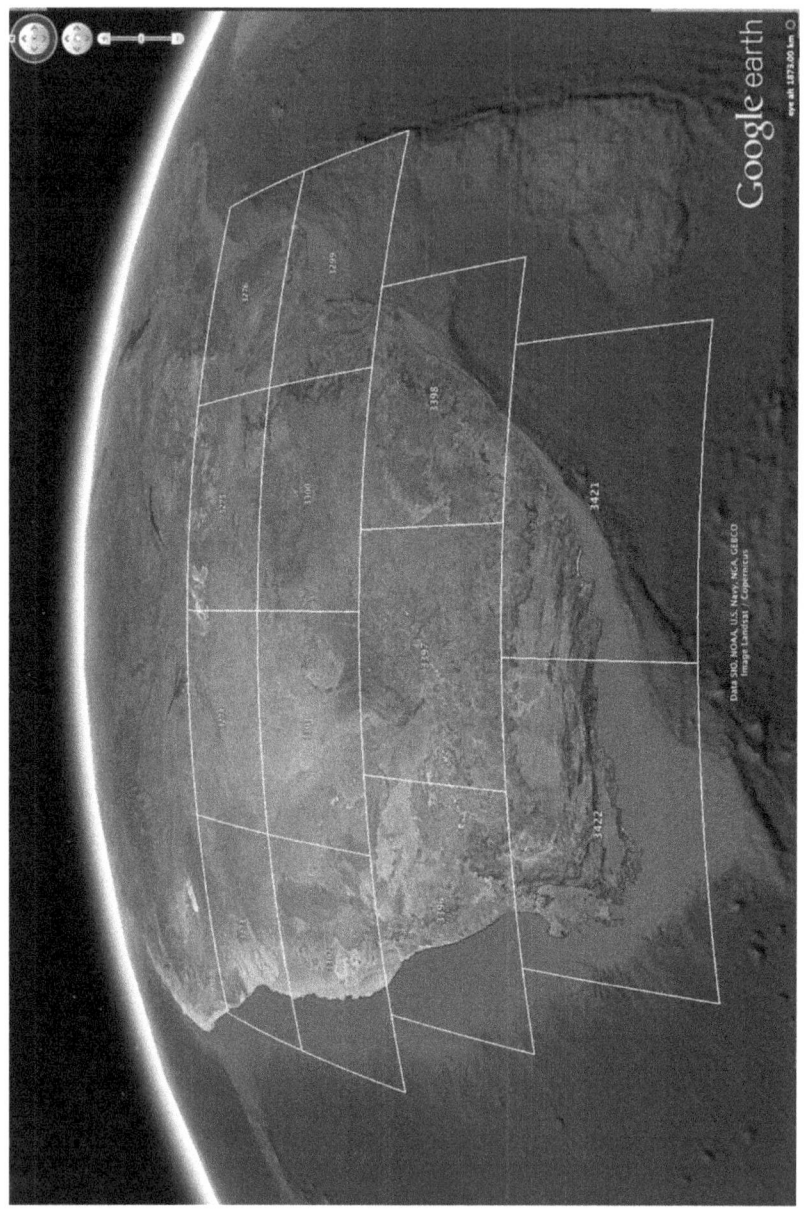

Annexure 10: Aeronautical Chart Index and Classification of Airspace 347

Table 2: Southern African chart index: 1: 500 000
Source: NGI

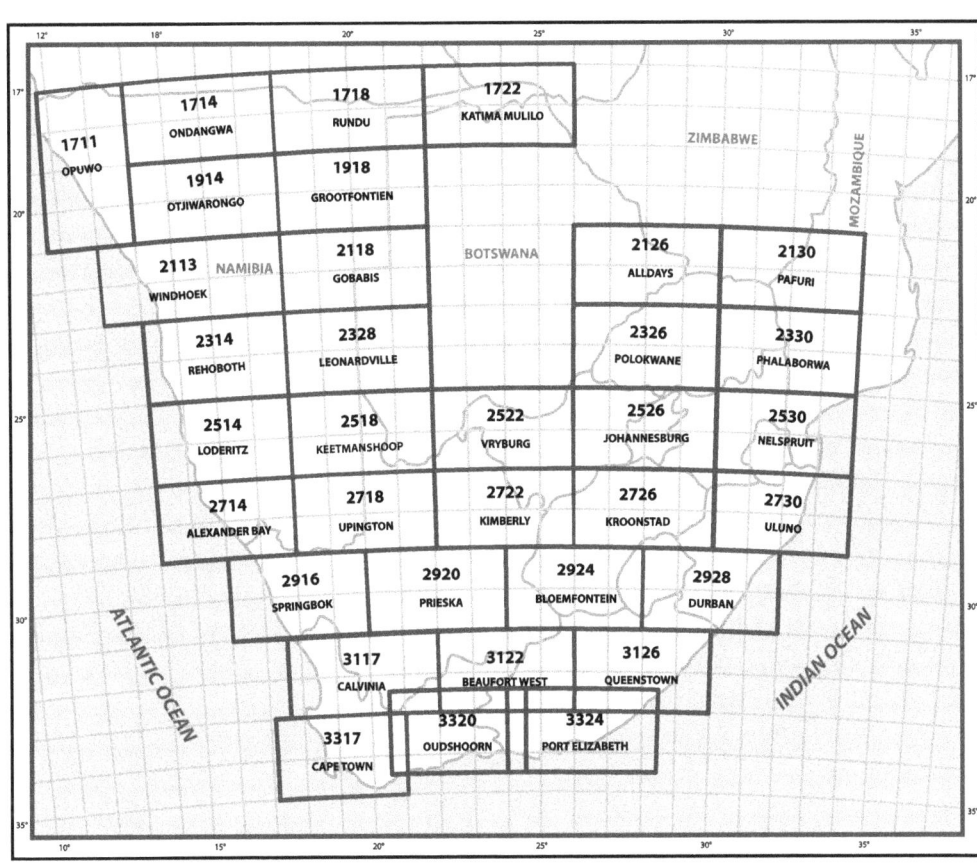

Annexure 11

Flight Plan regulation

Source: CARS 91.03.4

Air traffic service flight plan and associated procedures

(1) The owner or operator of an aircraft shall ensure that an ATS flight plan is completed if required in terms of sub-regulation (4).

(2) The items to be contained in the ATS flight plan shall be as prescribed Document SA-CATS 91.

(3) The ATS flight plan shall be filed with the appropriate ATSU unless other arrangements have been made for submission of repetitive flight plans and such unit shall be responsible for transmitting such ATS flight plan to all ATSUs concerned with the flight.

(4) The ATS flight plan shall be filed in respect of—
(a) all flights to be conducted in controlled or advisory airspace: Provided that this requirement shall not apply in respect of—
  (i) a local flight;
  (ii) a flight crossing an airway or advisory routes at right angles; or
  (iii) a VFR flight entering or departing from an aerodrome traffic zone or control zone, from or to an unmanned aerodrome and where no other controlled or advisory airspace will be entered during the flight;
(b) an international flight;
(c) all flights undertaken in terms of a Class I or Class II licence issued in terms of the Air Services Licensing Act, No. 115 of 1990 or the International Air Services Act, No. 60 of 1993;
(d) any flight within or into designated areas, or along designated routes, when so required by the appropriate ATS authority to facilitate the provision of flight information, alerting and search and rescue services; and
(e) any flight within or into designated areas, or along designated routes, when so required by the appropriate ATS authority to facilitate coordination with appropriate military units or with ATSUs in adjacent States in order to avoid the possible need for interception for the purpose of identification.

Note that AIC Series D 005/2019 of 25 APR 2019 provides a less detailed wording for (c) which does change the meaning. However for (d) the AIC refers tersely to 'a flight for which alerting action is required'; and for (e) it refers to 'all flights operating between aerodromes where an ATSU is operating'. In addition the AIC states that a flight plan 'may be filed for any flight'.

(5) An ATSU may instruct a flight for which an ATS flight plan is required in terms of sub-regulation (4) and for which an ATS flight plan has not been filed, to clear or to remain clear of controlled airspace, and not to cross the border of the Republic or to enter its airspace until such time as the required ATS flight plan has been filed.

(6) Unless otherwise authorized by the responsible ATSU, an ATS flight plan for a flight to be conducted in controlled or advisory airspace, shall be filed—
(a) for domestic flights, at least 30 minutes before departure;
(b) for international flights, at least 60 minutes before departure; or
(c) if filed during flight while outside controlled or advisory airspace for a flight to be conducted in such airspace, it shall be filed with the responsible ATSU at least 10 minutes before the aircraft is estimated to reach the intended point of entry into the controlled or advisory airspace or the point of crossing the airway or advisory route.

Note that, in relation to (a) and (b) following AIC 005/2019 already mentioned 'it is encouraged that flight plans are filed as far as in advance as possible, up to 120 hours'.

(7) The PIC of an aircraft operating an IFR or controlled VFR flight shall ensure that all changes which become applicable to an ATS flight plan before departure or in flight are reported, as soon as practicable, to the responsible ATSU. For other VFR flights, changes regarding fuel endurance or total number of persons carried on board shall, as a minimum, be reported.

(8) If an ATS flight plan has been filed with an ATSU prior to departure, and is not activated with an ATSU within one hour of original estimated time of departure or amended estimated time of departure, the ATS flight plan shall be regarded as cancelled and a new ATS flight plan shall be filed.

(9) Where an ATSU is not in operation at the aerodrome of intended landing, a report of arrival as prescribed in Document SA-CATS 91 shall be submitted to an ATSU, by the quickest means of communication available, immediately after landing, in respect of a flight for which an ATS flight plan was submitted and not as yet closed or for which search and rescue notification was requested and designated with a particular ATSU.

(10) When communication facilities at the arrival aerodrome are inadequate and alternate arrangements for the handling of arrival reports on the ground are not available, the PIC shall, prior to landing the aircraft or immediately thereafter, if practicable, transmit to the appropriate ATSU, a message comparable to an arrival report, in respect of a flight for which an ATS flight plan was submitted and not as yet closed or for which a search and rescue notification was requested with a nominated ATSU.

(11) Subject to the provisions of sub-regulation (12), the PIC shall ensure that the aircraft adheres to the current ATS flight plan filed for a controlled flight, unless a

request for a change has been made and accepted by the ATSU responsible for the controlled airspace in which the aircraft is operating, or unless an emergency situation arises which necessitates immediate action, in which event the responsible ATSU shall, as soon as circumstances permit, be notified of the action taken and that such action was taken under emergency authority.

(12) In the event of a controlled flight inadvertently deviating from its current ATS flight plan, the following action shall be taken—
(a) if the aircraft is off track, action shall be taken forthwith to adjust the heading of the aircraft to regain track as soon as practicable;
(b) if the average true airspeed at cruising level between reporting points varies, or is expected to vary, from that given in an ATS flight plan by approximately five per cent of the true airspeed, the responsible ATSU shall be so informed;
(c) if the estimated time at the next applicable reporting point, flight information regional boundary, or aerodrome of intended landing, whichever comes first, is found to be in error in excess of three minutes from that notified to the responsible ATSU, a revised estimated time shall be notified to such ATSU as soon as possible; or
(d) if the aircraft deviates from its altitude, action shall be taken forthwith to correct the altitude of the aircraft.

(13) When an automatic dependent surveillance (ADS) agreement is in place, the ATSU shall be informed automatically via data link whenever changes occur beyond the threshold values stipulated by the ADS event contract.

(14) If prior to departure it is anticipated that, subject to a reclearance in flight, a decision may be taken to proceed to a revised destination aerodrome, the appropriate ATSUs shall be so notified by the insertion in the flight plan of information concerning the revised route, where known, and the revised destination. The revised destination shall be subject to the fuel and oil provisions of regulation 91.07.12.

Annexure 12

. . . .

Fuel policy

Source: CARS 91.07.12 (1) to (9)

Note: Noteworthy details are in bold.

(1) A **pilot-in-command of an aircraft shall not commence a flight unless he or she is satisfied that the aircraft is carrying sufficient amount of usable fuel and sufficient oil** to complete the planned flight safely and to allow for deviations from the planned operation.

(2) The **pilot-in-command shall ensure** that the amount of useable (=usable) fuel to be carried shall, as a minimum, be based on

(a) the following data—
  (i) current aircraft-specific data derived from a fuel consumption monitoring system, if available; or
  (ii) if current aircraft-specific data is not available, data provided by the aeroplane manufacturer; and

(b) the operator conditions for the planned flight including—
  (i) anticipated aeroplane mass;
  (ii) notices to Airmen;
  (iii) current meteorological reports or a combination of current reports and forecasts;
  (iv) air traffic services procedures, restrictions and anticipated delays; and
  (v) the effects of deferred maintenance items and/or configuration deviations.

(3) The pre-flight calculation of usable fuel required shall include—

(a) *Taxi fuel*, which shall be the amount of **fuel expected to be consumed before take-off**; taking into account local conditions at the departure aerodrome and auxiliary power unit (APU) fuel consumption;

(b) *Trip fuel*, Which shall be the amount of fuel required to enable the aeroplane to fly from take-off or the point of in-flight re-planning until landing at the destination aerodrome taking into account the operating conditions of paragraph *(b)* of sub-regulation 91.07.12 (2);

(c) *Contingency fuel*, which shall be the amount of **fuel required to compensate for unforeseen factors**. It shall be **5 per cent** of the planned trip fuel or of the fuel required from the point of in-flight re-planning based on the consumption rate used to plan the trip fuel but in any case shall, in the case of aeroplanes,

shall **not be lower than the amount required to fly for 5 minutes at holding speed at 1 500 ft above the destination aerodrome** in standard conditions;

Unforeseen factors are those factors that could have an influence on the fuel consumption to the destination aerodrome, such as deviations of an individual aeroplane from the expected fuel consumption data, deviations from forecast meteorological conditions, extended delays.

(d) **Destination alternate fuel**, which shall be—
  (i) **where a destination alternate aerodrome is required**, the amount of fuel required to enable the aeroplane to—
    (aa) perform a missed approach at the destination aerodrome;
    (bb) climb to the expected cruising altitude;
    (cc) fly the expected routing;
    (dd) descend to the point where expected approach is initiated; and
    (ee) conduct the approach and landing at the destination alternate aerodrome; or
  (ii) where **two destination alternate aerodromes are required**, the amount of fuel, as calculated in sub-regulation 91.07.12 (3), required to enable the aeroplane to proceed to the destination alternate aerodrome which requires the greater amount of alternate fuel; or
  (iii) where a flight is operated **without a destination alternate** aerodrome, the amount of fuel required to enable the aeroplane to fly for 15 minutes at holding speed at 1 500 ft above the destination aerodrome elevation in standard conditions; or
  (iv) Where the aerodrome of intended landing is an **isolated aerodrome**—
    (aa) for a reciprocating engine aeroplane, the amount of fuel required to fly for **45 minutes plus 15 per cent of the flight time** planned to be spent at cruising level, including final reserve fuel, or two hours, whichever is less; or
    (bb) for a turbine engine aeroplane, the amount of fuel required to fly for two hours at normal cruise consumption above the destination aerodrome, including final reserve fuel;

(e) *Final reserve fuel*, which shall be the amount of fuel calculated **using the estimated mass on arrival at the destination alternate aerodrome or the destination aerodrome**, when no destination alternate aerodrome is required—
  (i) for a **reciprocating engine** aeroplane, the amount of fuel required to fly for **45 minutes**, under speed and altitude conditions specified by the Director;

(ii) for **a turbine** engine aeroplane, the amount of fuel required to fly for **30 minutes** at holding speed at 1 500 ft above aerodrome elevation in standard conditions;

(f) *Additional fuel,* which shall be the **supplementary amount of fuel required if the minimum fuel calculated** in accordance with sub-regulations 91.07.12 *(a), (b), (c), (d)* or *(e)* **is not sufficient** to—

    (i) allow the aeroplane to descend as necessary and proceed to an alternate aerodrome in the event of engine failure or loss of pressurisation, whichever requires the greater amount of fuel based on the assumption that such a failure occurs at the most critical point along the route;

        (aa) fly for 15 minutes at holding speed at 1 500 ft above aerodrome elevation in standard conditions; and

        (bb) make an approach and landing;

    (ii) allow an aeroplane engaged in EDTO to comply with the EDTO critical fuel scenario as established by the Director.

    (iii) meet additional requirements not covered above;

(g) *Discretionary fuel,* which shall be the extra amount of fuel to be carried at the discretion of the pilot-in-command.

(4) **Operators shall determine one final reserve fuel value for each aeroplane** type and variant owned or operated rounded up to an easily recalled figure.

(5) An aeroplane shall not take off or continue from the point of in-flight re-planning unless the usable fuel on board meets the requirements prescribed in paragraphs *(b), (d), (e)* or *(f)* of sub-regulation 91.07.12 (3), if applicable.

(6) The pilot-in-command shall **continually ensure that the amount of usable fuel remaining on board is not less than the fuel required to proceed to an aerodrome where a safe landing** can be made with the planned final reserve fuel remaining upon landing.

(6a) The use of fuel after flight commencement for purposes other than originally intended during pre-flight planning shall require a re-analysis and, if applicable, adjustment of the planned operation.

Note.—Guidance on procedures for in-flight fuel management including re-analysis, adjustment and/or re-planning considerations when a flight begins to consume contingency fuel before take-off is contained in the In-Flight Fuel Management TGM on the CAA website.

(7) The pilot-in-command shall request delay information from ATC when unanticipated circumstances may result in landing at the destination aerodrome with less than the final reserve fuel plus any fuel required to proceed to an alternate aerodrome or the fuel required to operate to an isolated aerodrome.

(8) The pilot-in-command shall **advise ATC of a minimum fuel state by declaring MINIMUM FUEL** when, having committed to land at a specific aerodrome, the pilot calculates that any change to the existing clearance to that aerodrome may result in landing with less than planned final reserve fuel.

354 *Air Law*

The declaration of MINIMUM FUEL informs ATC that all planned aerodrome options have been reduced to a specific aerodrome of intended landing and any change to the existing clearance may result in landing with less than the planned final reserve fuel. This is not an emergency situation but an indication that an emergency situation is possible should any additional delay occur.

(9) The pilot-in-command shall declare a **situation of fuel emergency by broadcasting MAYDAY MAYDAY MAYDAY** *FUEL,* when the calculated usable fuel predicted to be available upon landing at the nearest aerodrome where a safe landing can be made is less than the planned final reserve fuel.

Annexure 13

. . . .

Flight Authorisation Sheet

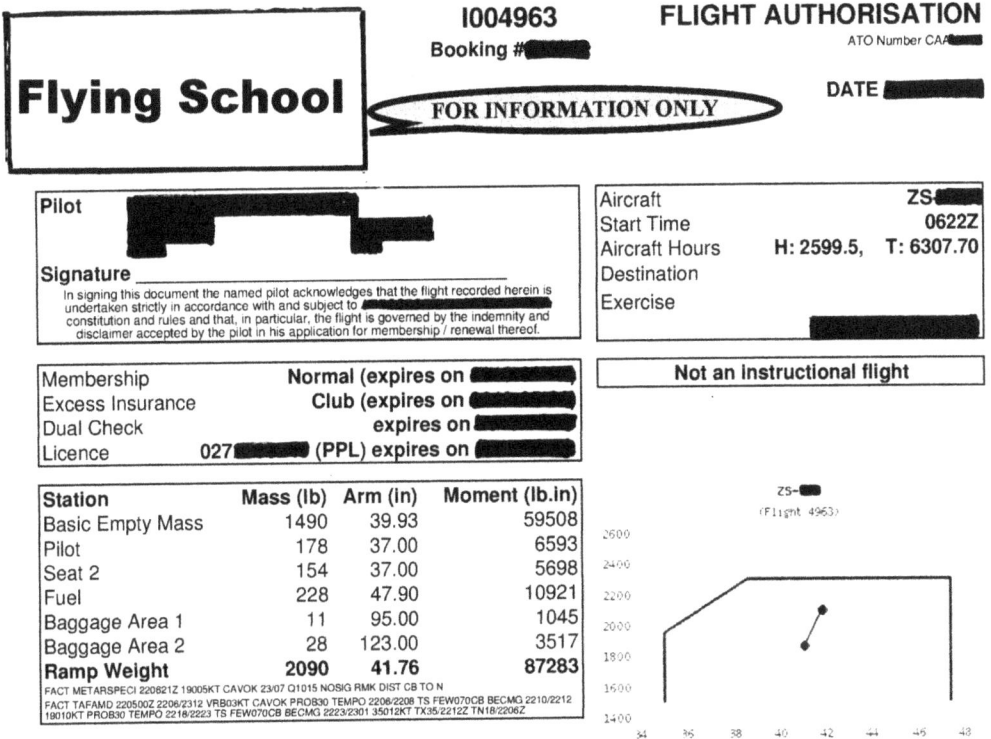

Annexure 14

Duties of PIC regarding flight operations

Source: CATS 91.02.8

(1) The PIC of an aircraft shall, whether manipulating the controls or not, be responsible for—
(a) the operation, safety and security of the aircraft, crew members, passengers and cargo in accordance with these Regulations while he or she is in command;
(b) operational control of the aircraft unless otherwise provided for in terms of Part 93, 121, 127 or 135 under an approved operational control system;
(c) the conduct of crew members and passengers carried; and
(d) the maintenance of discipline by all persons on board.

(2) The PIC of the aircraft shall have the authority—
(a) to give such commands he or she deems necessary in the interest of the safety of the aircraft, persons or property; and
(b) to disembark any person or cargo which in his or her opinion, represents a potential hazard to the safety of the aircraft, persons or property.

(3) The PIC of the aircraft shall ensure that all passengers are informed as to—
(a) when and how oxygen equipment is to be used, if the carriage of oxygen is required;
(b) the location and use of life jackets or equivalent individual flotation devices, where the carriage thereof is required;
(c) the location and method of opening emergency exits;
(d) when seat belts are to be fastened;
(e) when smoking is prohibited;
(f) when portable electronic devices may be used;
(g) the existence and location of the passenger safety features card, if carried on board; and
(h) before take-off, the location and general manner of use of the relevant emergency equipment carried for collective use and, when an emergency arises, instruct the passengers to take such emergency action as may be appropriate.

(4) The PIC of an aircraft shall—
(a) ensure that the pre-flight inspection has been carried out, and that the checklists, and where applicable, the flight deck procedures and other instructions regarding the operation of the aircraft, the limitations contained

Annexure 14: Duties of PIC regarding flight operations 357

in the AFM referred to in regulation 91.03.2 or equivalent certification document, are fully complied with at the appropriate times during a flight;
(b) decide whether or not to accept an aircraft with unserviceabilities allowed by the CDL or MEL, where applicable;
(c) determine that aircraft performance will permit the take-off and departure to be carried out safely;
(d) ensure that, before take-off and landing and whenever, by reason of turbulence, any emergency occurring during a flight or whenever deemed necessary in the interest of aviation safety the precaution is considered necessary, the PIC shall ensure that—
   (i) all persons on board the aircraft are secured in their seats by means of the seat belts or shoulder harnesses provided; and
   (ii) equipment and baggage are properly secured and all exit and escape paths are unobstructed.
(e) when replanning, whilst in flight, to proceed along a route or to a destination other than the route or destination originally planned, shall amend the OFP, if such a plan was required in terms of regulation 91.02.7(1)(f), and notify the nearest ATSU of such change;
(f) not continue towards the aerodrome of intended landing unless the latest available information indicates that at the expected time of arrival, a landing can be effected at that aerodrome or at least one destination alternate aerodrome, in compliance with the operating minima established in accordance with regulation 91.07.5;
(g) report any accident or incident involving the aircraft in accordance with Part 12, unless the PIC is incapacitated or an operator has established another means of reporting accidents or incidents, in which case the operator shall initiate the report;
(h) report any dangerous goods accident or incident involving the aircraft in accordance with Part 92;
(i) if the aircraft is endangered in flight by a near collision with any other aircraft or object, faulty air traffic procedure or lack of compliance with applicable procedures by an ATSU or a flight crew member or a failure of ATS facilities, submit an ATS incident report as prescribed by regulation 12.02.2;
(j) record any technical defect and the exceeding of any technical limitation which occurred while he or she was responsible for the flight, in the flight folio;
(k) if a potentially hazardous condition such as bird accumulation, an irregularity in a ground or navigation facility, meteorological phenomena, a volcanic ash cloud or a greater than normal radiation level is observed during flight, notify an ATSU as soon as possible;
(l) if the aircraft is equipped with an ELT, prior to engine shut-down at the end of each flight as part of the post-flight checks, tune the VHF receiver to 121,5

MHz to listen for ELT activation. If the ELT has been activated inadvertently as the result of a hard landing or for other reasons, this shall be reported—

(i) immediately through the nearest ATSU to the rescue coordination centre; and

(ii) in the appropriate flight log as maintenance may be required before it is returned to service; and

(m) report any occurrence of height keeping errors encountered in a RVSM environment, as prescribed in paragraph (7) of section 8 of technical standard 91.07.31 of Document SA-CATS 91.

(5) The PIC of the aircraft shall ensure that—

(a) breathing oxygen is available to crew members and passengers if flights in a non-pressurised aircraft are contemplated above 10 000 feet and up to 12 000 feet in excess of 120 minutes intended flight time, or above 12 000 feet; and

(b) breathing oxygen is carried in sufficient quantities for all flights at such altitudes where a lack of oxygen might result in impairment of faculties of crew members or harmfully affect passengers.

(6) The PIC of the aircraft shall not—

(a) require a crew member to perform any duties during a critical phase of the flight, except those duties required for the safe operation of the aircraft;

(b) permit any activity during a critical phase of the flight which could distract any crew member from the performance of his or her duties or which could interfere in any way with the proper conduct of those duties; and

(c) commence a flight in the event a crew member is incapacitated by any cause such as injury, fatigue, sickness or the effects of any psychoactive substance or continue a flight beyond the nearest suitable aerodrome in the event of a flight crew member becoming unable to perform any essential duties as a result of fatigue, sickness or lack of oxygen.

(7) The PIC of an aircraft which is being subjected to unlawful interference—

(a) shall notify the appropriate ATSU of this fact, any significant circumstances associated therewith and any deviation from the current flight plan necessitated by the circumstances, in order to enable the ATSU to give priority to the aircraft and to minimize conflict with other aircraft;

(b) shall attempt to land as soon as practicable at the nearest suitable aerodrome or at a dedicated aerodrome assigned by the appropriate authority unless considerations aboard the aircraft dictate otherwise; and

(c) immediately following the incident unless unable, in which case the owner or operator of the aircraft shall report the act of unlawful interference with the operation of the aircraft or the authority of the PIC—

(i) if the act of unlawful interference occurs within the Republic, to the Director; or

(ii) if the act of unlawful interference occurs within or over the territory of a foreign State, to the appropriate authority of the State and the Director.

(8) The PIC of an aircraft, that is equipped with a flight deck door, shall ensure that at all times from the moment the passenger entry doors are closed in preparation for departure until they are opened on arrival, that the flight deck door is closed and locked from within the flight deck.

Annexure 15

Annexure 15

Interception signals and phraseology

Source: CATS 91.06.29 and ICAO Annex 2

1 CATS 91.06.29

1. Principles to be observed during the interception

(1) The principles to be followed by an aircraft when intercepting another aircraft are—
(a) the interception of civil aircraft will be undertaken only as a last resort;
(b) if undertaken, an interception will be limited to determining the identity of the aircraft, unless it is necessary to return the aircraft to its planned track, direct it beyond the boundaries of national airspace, guide it away from a prohibited, restricted or danger area or instruct it to effect a landing at a designated aerodrome;
(c) practice interception of civil aircraft will not be undertaken;
(d) navigational guidance and related information will be given to an intercepted aircraft by radiotelephony whenever radio contact can be established; and
(e) in the case where an intercepted civil aircraft is required to land in the territory overflown, the aerodrome designated for the landing is to be suitable for the safe landing of the aircraft type concerned.

(2) Secondary surveillance radar or ADS-B, where available, shall be used to identify civil aircraft in areas where they may be subject to interception.

2. Action by intercepted aircraft

(1) An aircraft which is intercepted by another aircraft shall immediately—
(a) follow the instructions given by the intercepting aircraft, interpreting and responding to visual signals in accordance with the specifications in section 4;
(b) notify, if possible, the appropriate air traffic services unit;
(c) attempt to establish radio communication with the intercepting aircraft or with the appropriate intercept control unit, by making a general call on the emergency frequency 121,5 MHz, giving the identity of the intercepted aircraft and the nature of the flight; and if no contact has been established and if practicable, repeating this call on the emergency frequency 243 MHz;
(d) if equipped with SSR transponder, select Mode A, Code 7700, unless otherwise instructed by the appropriate air traffic services unit; and
(e) if equipped with ADS-B or ADS-C, select the appropriate emergency functionality, if available, unless otherwise instructed by the appropriate air traffic services unit.

Annexure 15: Interception signals and phraseology 361

(2) If any instructions received by radio from any sources conflict with those given by the intercepting aircraft by visual signals, the intercepted aircraft shall request immediate clarification while continuing to comply with the visual instructions given by the intercepting aircraft.

(3) If any instructions received by radio from any sources conflict with those given by the intercepting aircraft by radio, the intercepted aircraft shall request immediate clarification while continuing to comply with the radio instructions given by the intercepting aircraft.

3. Radio communication during interception

If radio contact is established during interception but communication in a common language is not possible, attempts shall be made to convey instructions, acknowledgement of instructions and essential information by using the phrases and pronunciations in the following table and transmitting each phrase twice.

2 ICAO Annex 2

(Refer to this annex for additional action not listed here and mentioned below)

2.1 Interception non-radio signals, by day and by night: how to understand physical signals, and how you should respond

2. SIGNALS FOR USE IN THE EVENT OF INTERCEPTION

2.1 Signals initiated by intercepting aircraft and responses by intercepted aircraft

Series	INTERCEPTING Aircraft Signals	Meaning	INTERCEPTED Aircraft Responds	Meaning
1	DAY or NIGHT – Rocking aircraft and flashing navigational lights at irregular intervals (and landing lights in the cease of a heclicopter) from a position slightly above and ahead of, and normally to the left of, the intercepted aircraft (or to the right if the intercepted aircraft is a helicopter) and, after acknowledgement, a slow level turn, normally to the left (or to the right in the case of a helicopter) on the desired heading. *Note Meteorological conditions or terrain may require the intercepting aircraft to reverse the positions and direction of turn given above in Series 1. Note 2– If the intercepted aircraft is not able to keep pace with the intercepting aircraft, the latter is expected to fly a series of racetrack patterns and to rock the aircraft each time it passes the intercepted aircraft.*	You have been intercepted. Follow me.	DAY or NIGHT – Rocking aircraft, flashing navigational lights at irregular intervals and following. *Note.– Additional action required to be taken by intercepted aircraft is prescribed in Chapter 3.3.8.*	Understood, will comply.
2	DAY or NIGHT – An abrupt breakaway manoeuvre from the intercepted aircraft consisting of a climbing turn of 90 degrees or more without crossing the line of flight of the intercepted aircraft.	You may procced.	DAY or NIGHT – Rocking the aircraft.	Understood, will comply.

Annexure 15: Interception signals and phraseology 363

Series	INTERCEPTING Aircraft Signals	Meaning	INTERCEPTED Aircraft Responds	Meaning
3	DAY or NIGHT – Lowering landing gear (if fitted), showing steady landing lights and over-flying runway in use or, if the intercepted aircraft is a helicopter, overflying the helicopter landing area. In the case of helicopters, the intercepting helicopter makes a landing approach, coming to hover near to the landing area.	Land at this aerodrome.	DAY or NIGHT – Lowering landing gear, (if fitted), showing steady landing lights and following the intercepting aircraft and, if, after overflying the runway in use or helicopter landing area, landing is considered safe, proceeding to land.	Understood, will comply.

2.2 Signals initiated by intercepted aircraft and responses by intercepting aircraft

Series	INTERCEPTED Aircraft Signals	Meaning	INTERCEPTING Aircraft Responds	Meaning
4	DAY or NIGHT – Raising landing gear (if fitted) and flashing landing lights while passing over runway in use or helicopter landing area at a height exceeding 300 m (1 000 ft) but not exeeding 600 m (2 000 ft) (in the ease of a helicopter, at a height exceeding 50 m (170 ft) but not exceeding 100 m (330 ft)) above the aerodrome level, and continuing to circle runway in use or helicopter landing area. If unable to flash landing lights, flash any other lights available.	Aerodrome you have designated is inadequate.	DAY or NIGHT – If it is desired that the intercepted aircraft follow the intercepting aircraft to an alternate aerodrome, the intercepting aircraft raises its landing gear (if fitted) and uses the Series 1 signals prescribed for intercepting aircraft. If it is decided to release the intercepted aircraft, the intercepting aircraft uses the Series 2 signals prescribed for intercepting aircraft.	Understood, follow me. Understood, you may procced.
5	DAY or NIGHT – Regular switching on and off of all available lights but in such a manner as to be distinct from flashing lights.	Cannot comply.	DAY or NIGHT – Use Series 2 signals prescribed for intercepting aircraft.	Understood.

364 *Air Law*

Series	INTERCEPTED Aircraft Signals	Meaning	INTERCEPTING Aircraft Responds	Meaning
6	DAY or NIGHT – Irregular flashing of all available lights.	In distress.	DAY or NIGHT – Use Series 2 signals prescribed for intercepting aircraft.	Understood.

2.2 Interception phraseology: how to understand verbal/radio signals, and how you should pronounce words in response

Phrases for use by INTERCEPTING aircraft			Phrases for use by INTERCEPTED aircraft		
Phrase	*Pronunciation[1]*	*Meaning*	*Phrase*	*Pronunciation[1]*	*Meaning*
CALL SIGN	KOL SA-IN	What is your call sign?	CALL SIGN (call sign)[2]	KOL SA-IN (call sign)	My call sign is (call sign)
FOLLOW	FOL-LO	Follow me	WILCO	VILL-KO	Understood Will comply
DESCEND	DEE-SEND	Descend for landing	CAN NOT	KANN NOTT	Unable to comply
YOU LAND	YOU LAAND	Land at this aerodrome	REPEAT	REE-PEET	Repeat your instruction
PROCEED	PRO-SEED	You may proceed	AM LOST	AM LOSST	Position unknown
			MAYDAY	MAYDAY	I am in distress
			HIJACK[3]	HI-JACK	I have been hijacked
			LAND (place name)	LAAND (place name)	I request to land at
			DESCEND	DEE-SEND	I require descent

---

[1] In the second column, syllables to be emphasised are underlined.

[2] The call sign required to be given is that used in radiotelephony communications with air traffic services units and corresponding to the aircraft identification in the flight plan.

[3] Circumstances may not always permit, nor make desirable, the use of the phrase "HIJACK".

Annexure 16

Search and Rescue (SAR) scenarios and procedures

Sources: ICAO Annex 12 and AIP GEN 3.6–12 to 15 (refer to them for a full description)

Note that SAR is the ICAO acronym as per Annex 12-AIP GEN uses both SR and SAR. SR is not to be confused with SRR, for a Search and rescue region, ie a region of a defined dimension where coordinated SAR is provided.

SRR: The South African Aeronautical area of responsibility as SRR covers Namibia, the Republic, Swaziland, maritime zones and part of the Antarctic down to the South Pole (for coordinates, see AIP GEN 3.6–3).

All three phases are declared by an ATSU or a Rescue Coordination Centre (RCC).

INCERFA, uncertainty phase : five scenarios

There are five possible scenarios (hence the use of 'or' in the regulations in-between each scenario) that will prompt an ATSU or RCC to declare an INCERFA:

1. An aircraft equipped with a radio and maintaining radio contact up to INCERFA has not made radio contact in the 30 minutes following
   ➢ ETA at the next reporting point;
   ➢ or at a pre-arranged or scheduled reporting time.

Important: if your aircraft has VHF only and you cannot maintain continuous radio contact with an ATSU, before you depart you must provide reporting points at which INCERFA will be declared if you fail to report on time, ie are 'overdue'; alternatively you must indicate if you want such action to be taken only if you fail to report at destination (you do so in your flight plan).

2. An aircraft is known or is believed to be in an irregular operation, if
   ➢ it is not following the correct track or maintaining the correct flight level(s); or
   ➢ is not in normal communication; or
   ➢ is unable to use appropriate navigational aids; or
   ➢ is experiencing navigational difficulties; or
   ➢ is experiencing hazardous weather conditions; or
   ➢ is experiencing impaired operating efficiency but not to the extent that the flight plan cannot be completed; or

3. An aircraft that is operating on an overdue at destination only flight plan is not in contact with the destination aerodrome within 1 hour after ETA; or

4, An aircraft operating on a flight plan where alerting action is requested after a specific time, fails to arrive or is not in contact with the ATSU by the time specified in the flight plan—and preliminary checks fail to reveal the whereabouts of the aircraft; or
5, An aircraft which is proceeding to an unmanned aerodrome but which is operating on an 'overdue action' flight plan, fails to report arrival by the time specified in the flight plan—preliminary checks fail to reveal the whereabouts of the aircraft.

ALERFA, alert phase: three scenarios

Depending upon the nature of the problem, the ATSU or RCC will upgrade the emergency from INCERFA to ALERFA in one (or more) of three scenarios:

1. Communication loss: If an INCERFA is declared due to failure to report or loss of communication, and more attempts by the ATSU to establish communication with the aircraft or enquiries to other relevant sources fail to reveal any news of the aircraft (the ATSU will try several times until it is decided that there is indeed loss of communication); or
2. Aircraft not operating as it should: If the ATSU or RCC receives information that the operating efficiency of the aircraft has been impaired but that a forced landing is not likely (do not stop reading here, but look at DESTREFA); or
3. Aircraft in jeopardy: either because it is lost or known to be operating in other than normal circumstances, and if the ATSU or RCC has good cause to believe that, for those reasons, the safe conduct of the flight is in jeopardy.
    'Other than normal circumstances' can very well include all or some of the circumstances that trigger INCERFA.

DETRESFA, distress phase: six scenarios

The ATSU or RCC will now move to the utmost phase, under six possible scenarios that build directly upon the previous situations.

1. Failure to report or loss of communication: if extensive attempts to establish communication with the aircraft and widespread unsuccessful enquiries point to the probability that the aircraft is in distress; or
2. Fuel emergency: if the fuel on board, as declared in the flight plan, is considered to be exhausted or to be insufficient to enable the aircraft to reach safety; or
3. Aircraft not operating as it should: if ATSU receives that the operating efficiency of the aircraft has been impaired to the extent that a forced landing is likely (compare with ALERFA 2) ; or
4. Forced landing, ditching, crash: if an ATSU or RCC receive information that indicates that an aircraft is about to make, or has made, a forced landing, has ditched or crashed; or
5. Missed landing time: if an aircraft that has been given approach or landing instructions at an aerodrome, fails to land within five minutes of the estimated

landing time and the ATSU is unable to re-establish communication before the five minute period lapses; or
6. Failure to report timely after take-off: if an aircraft has been instructed or is expected to report after take-off fails to do so and the ATSU is unable to re-establish communication before five minutes have lapsed.

Ground/air visual signal codes for use by survivors

The pilot of an aircraft which has crashed or force landed shall use his own discretion on whether to remain at the aircraft or to attempt to reach help. Factors which should influence his decision are—

a. if the aircraft was operating on an "overdue action" flight plan and the aircraft has crashed or force landed in a desert area, a swamp area of a very sparsely populated area, as in Botswana it is advisable to remain at the aircraft and take such of the following action as may be appropriate or possible—
   (i) take steps to conserve the strength of survivors, e.g. avoid unnecessary exertion in the sun;
   (ii) conserve available water and food supplies;
   (iii) if a usable radio transmitter is available, make transmissions using the distress procedure, giving the aircraft s position and any other pertinent data, at H + 15 and H + 45. These transmissions should be kept as short as possible to conserve battery power. (H + 15 and H + 45 are 15 and 45 minutes past the hour, e.g. 0715 and 0745, 1215, 1245 etc.) (H means 'hour').
   (iv) if automatic SR beacons are available one should be switched on for 5 minutes from H + 15 and H + 45. If, however, aircraft are seen or heard a beacon should e left on continuously.
   (v) if flares are carried they should be conserved for use when search aircraft, ships or ground search parties are known to be in the vicinity. The danger of falling flares starting veld and brush fires must be borne in mind before using the flares;
   (vi) if possible place aircraft in a conspicuous position. Engine cowls, doors or other removable parts of the aircraft should be removed, polished-up and placed where they will reflect the rays of the sun. Fine sand can be used to remove paint rom metal surfaces;
   (vii) lay out the appropriate ground/air emergency signal strips in a conspicuous place; and
   (viii) light smoke fires.
b. if the aircraft has crashed or force landed in a settled area where help is near at hand it is better to leave the aircraft to look for help. In such cases SAP stations, telephone exchanges, SA Railways station masters, etc. will render such assistance as they can. The pilot should inform the unit he has called upon for help that he is operating on an "overdue action" flight plan and ask them to advise the nearest ATSU of his whereabouts.

Annexure 17

Night Rating Training (A) (H)

Source: SA-CARS and CATS 61.10 together with Appendix 11.0

The good news: a NR is valid as long as your licence is, and there are no annual fees or revalidation. Your privileges are simple: they are those of your licence with this addition that you can exercise them now by night too. Same applies to limitations—go back to Part 2, chapter 4.2 in this book.

1 TRAINING PART

You must complete a training course with an aviation training organisation. But the theoretical knowledge course and the practical training course can be completed at different aviation training organisations.

There is a theoretical part and a practical part. The theoretical part leads to a single examination (at an ATO, online) and the practical part to a skills test. General conditions for rewrites and successful training apply (see Part 2 of this book).

1.1 Theory part and single examination

The syllabus and the examination consist of:
*air law with specific reference to
- the definition of night flying
- the privileges and limitations associated with the night rating
- the pilot-in-command's responsibilities
- the equipment to be carried on board for night flying
- aircraft lighting including navigation lights
- VFR differences from day flying
- aerodrome requirements for night flying

* Meteorology, that is
- the formation of fog
- various types of fog
- katabatic winds
- mixing, veering and backing of winds at night
- formation of ice and frost
- nocturnal thunderstorms

* Human performance, especially
- factors affecting night vision; the preservation of night vision
- visual illusions

- hypoxia
- vertigo
- autokinesis

* Lighting systems, that is
  - external aircraft lighting
  - internal cockpit lighting
  - taxiway lighting
  - runway lighting
  - approach lighting systems
  - obstruction lighting
  - aerodrome identification beacons
  - where to find information on lighting systems
  - pilot-operated lighting.

1.2 Practical Instruction

You will never fly solo in a NR training. Always dual.

Below, the headings of the practical side of your training, which does not differ from what you have learnt toward your PPL (A) and (H) with one major exception: **Flight manoeuvres and procedures with reference to instruments.**

To quote the regulation: 'Since night flying may require the pilot to operate in remote areas without a discernable horizon, the instrument flight **training requirements in South Africa exceed those of other authorities**. It is therefore important to focus the instrument training towards the pilot being able **to conduct large parts of a night flight with reference to the instruments**'.

Your instructor will ensure you are proficient at the following before letting you test.

#1 Pre-flight operations, broken into the following:
- Flight planning: minimum safe altitudes; chart preparation; weather forecasts; airport lighting and available facilities; selection of suitable alternates; flight log preparation; fuel requirements.
- Aircraft preparation: Pre-flight inspection with special attention paid to lights; torch/flashlight; oxygen if applicable.
- Pilot issues: importance of avoiding very bright lights prior to commencing the flight; the considerations attached to the IMSAFE acronym (Illness, Medication, Stress, Alcohol, Fatigue, Emotion); take-off procedures; manoeuvring on the ground at night has its own set of considerations over and above those in day time activities, and make more difficult the following actions: assessing taxi speed/hover taxi speed; position on the airport/landing area; judging distances.
- Engine run up and pre-flight vital actions carried out with the appropriate care as they are made more difficult in reduced lighting.
- Take-off roll/lift-off and directional guidance during and after take-off

and importance to transfer your attention to the attitude indicator the second you are airborne.
- "The instructor will emphasise and assist the student to develop procedures and habits to minimise the dangers associated with night ground operations".

#2 In-flight manoeuvres and procedures: the instructor will teach you how to become proficient with manoeuvres with sole reference to instruments. You will do most of your instrument training in the day time under a hood or equivalent designed to prevent you from seeing anything else but the six basic instruments. You will learn how to scan them methodically and continuously, and not get "fixated" on one in particular.

Recovery training from unusual attitudes (stall, wing drop) will be done eyes closed, under the hood; your instructor will place the aircraft in a given unusual (read: dangerous) attitude, at the command "recover!" you will open your eyes, recognize the attitude from looking at the instruments, and recover, promptly. This is in imitation of a real situation in a pitch dark night when the sensations perceived by our body and mind are unreliable: TRUST YOUR INSTRUMENTS.

Once you are done with under the hood training, you will fly dual at night with your instructor, with reference to instruments while having outside visual reference since night flying is under VFR.

You will also learn how to fly circuits and do a cross country at night.

*The manoeuvres you must show proficiency at, with sole reference to your instruments are:
- Climbing and descending at specified speeds
- Straight and level flight
- Turning including timed turns : 'rate 1 turn" is quite a chunk of this part of training.
- Recovery from stalls
- Recovery from unusual attitudes
- Flight on limited panel: the instructor will simulate instrument failure by blocking out this or that instrument, or more.

* Cross-country/navigation training, consisting of:
- Visual cues such as city lights, coast lines, beacons, and how not to trust one reference light but always cross-check with another one, and not mistake a star for an airplane light, etc., all sorts of visual light illusions
- Radio navigation aids (this is quite a chunk of your training)
- GPS/GNSS
- Approach and landing procedures
- Locate and identify the airfields/landing areas at night
- Joining the traffic pattern
- Flying in the circuit

- Assess and maintain of the correct approach path (runways can look dramatically different at night in terms of height and depth)
- Identify and use of the various lighting systems associated with night flying
- Assess the cues required to implement the round out and flare for the landing; hover, in the case of a helicopter;
- Conduct go-around/missed landing—judging promptly a go around at night is far more critical as it is easier to misjudge heights (visual illusion)
- Conduct after landing actions.

*Non-normal emergency operations the aim of which is to learn how to deal with abnormal situations at night, stay calm, and aviate:
- Engine failure
- Alternator/Electrical failure—which leads to other failures: instruments, radio, flaps, undercarriage.
- Vacuum pump failure—the most insidious as instruments linked to it "die" gradually, leading to failure of the attitude gyro and the heading/direction indicator
- Instrument failure
- Radio failure
- Navigation system failure
- Aircraft landing light failure
- System malfunctions applicable to the aircraft such as undercarriage failure
- Lost procedures
- Airport lighting failures
- Rapid weather changes

2 REQUIREMENTS

In order to apply for the Night Rating you must (beside having a valid licence and a valid medical, you never know: you may have forgotten to pay the annual fees or skipped the medical anniversary date that falls exactly on the skills test evening . . . it happens).

* hold a valid pilot licence

* submit proof of having passed the theoretical examination, and completed no less than 5 hours of theoretical instruction on the material described above, at an ATO

* submit proof of having completed the practical training at an ATO and, still at an ATO
- have flown not less than 10 hours of instrument instruction, out of those 10 hours no more than 5 hours may be accumulated in an approved FSTD (flight simulator);

A maximum of 5 hours instrument time can be credited towards the 10-hour requirement for a helicopter pilot if the applicant is the holder of an instrument or night rating on aeroplanes and *vice versa*, that is: the reverse applies

➢ and (A) have done not less 5 take-offs and five landings by night as pilot manipulating the controls of the aircraft while under dual instruction; or (H) not less than 5 circuits with 5 take-offs and five landings by night as pilot manipulating the controls of the aircraft under dual instruction; and

➢ a **dual** cross-country flight by night consisting of at least (A) a total distance of not less than 150 NM with two full-stop landings at two different aerodromes **away from base** are made; or (H) a total distance of not less than 75 NM in the course of which landings at two different aerodromes away from base are made.

* have passed the prescribed skills test (regulation 61.10.4), that is: within the 30 days immediately preceding the date of application, the skills test must be conducted in an aircraft of the applicable category, and must include a minimum of 3 take-offs, 3 circuits and 3 landings by night; the instrument component of the skills test can be done by day.

It happens also that the navigation part is done on a different night, due to weather conditions (fog coming up at night, as it often does).

The application is standard procedure (skills test report, all document listed above, proof of payment) 8.

Remember that the test counts as a revalidation for your PPL licence, but make sure to abide by the rules of a revalidation, and pay the correct fee. In doubt double-check with your ATO.

Annexure 18

Drone Operations

Source: CARS 101 Subpart 5 RPAS OPERATIONS
Valid at July 2019

WEATHER CONDITIONS

101.05.1 No person shall operate an RPAS in weather conditions that do not allow unobstructed visual contact to be maintained with the RPA by other airspace users and by the operator unless in B-VLOS or night operations approved by the Director in their operations manual.

Landing on roads

101.05.2 No person shall use a public road as a place of landing or take-off of an RPA, except—
(a) by the holder of an ROC and as approved by the Director in the operator's operations manual; and
(b) when approved by the relevant local authority.

Controlled airspace

101.05.3 (1) No RPAS may be operated in controlled airspace, except by the holder of an ROC and as approved by the Director in the operators' operations manual.
 (2) The Director may approve an RPA operation in controlled airspace as contemplated in subregulation (1) only in—
(a) VMC in an ATZ and CTR below 400ft; and
(b) subject to compliance with the conditions prescribed in Document SA-CATS 101.

Releasing object or substance

101.05.4 No object or substance shall be released, dispensed, dropped, delivered or deployed from an RPA except by the holder of an ROC and as approved by the Director in the operators' operations manual.

Dangerous goods

101.05.5 (1) Subject to subregulation (2), no RPA shall carry dangerous goods as cargo, except by the holder of an ROC and as approved by the Director in the operations manual.

(2) The provisions of Part 92 apply, with the necessary changes, to the conveyance of dangerous goods by an RPA.

Accidents and incidents

101.05.6 (1) All accidents and incidents involving an RPA shall be reported as prescribed in Part 12, where there is—
(a) any injury or death to a person;
(b) damage to property; or
(c) destruction of the RPA beyond economical repair.

(2) All incidents involving an RPA where loss of control occurred shall be reported to the holder of the ROC.

Consumption of alcohol and drugs

101.05.7 No remote pilot, observer or RMT shall—
(a) consume alcohol less than 8 hours prior to reporting for duty;
(b) commence a duty period while the concentration of alcohol in any specimen of blood taken from any part of his or her body is more than 0,02 grams per 100 millilitres;
(c) consume alcohol or any psychoactive substance during the duty period or whilst on standby for duty; or
(d) commence duty period while under the influence of alcohol or any psychoactive substance having a narcotic effect.

C2 operational requirements

101.05.8 An RPAS shall comply with C2 operational requirements as prescribed in Document SA-CATS 101.

CATS 101.05.8
C2 OPERATIONAL REQUIREMENTS

(1) A prospective operator of an RPAS shall develop the C2 performance requirements safety case for approval of the Director.
(2) The following C2 functions shall be considered for the safety case—
(a) Downlink
   (i) Link health telemetry [for BVLOS operations]
   (ii) System health
(b) Telemetry
   (i) RPA flight dynamics
   (ii) Situation awareness [for BVLOS operations]
   (iii) Data records
(c) Uplink
   (i) Flight Control
   (ii) RPA System control
   (iii) Automatic Identification System update [for BVLOS operations]
   (iv) RPAS hand over
   (v) Link health telemetry [for BVLOS operations].

(3) The RPAS operator shall present the target values of the C2 Performance requirements that were obtained from the safety case of the C2 functions to the Director.
(a) Continuity
(b) Integrity
(c) Availability
(d) Latency of the C2 data link.

Precautions and safety considerations

101.05.9 (1) No person shall operate an RPAS unless—
(a) the RPA is in a fit-to-fly condition;
(b) the pilot is the holder of a licence issued in terms of this Part;
(c) the remotely piloted aircraft station is compatible and interoperable with the aircraft it is connected to in all phases of flight; and
(d) the RPA is being controlled by only one RPS at any given moment in time.

(2) No person shall operate an RPAS in a negligent or reckless manner so as to endanger the safety of any person, property or other aircraft in the air or on the ground.

(3) The operator shall, in the best interest of safety, ensure that certain RPAS operations are supplemented with additional personnel for non-flying duties, such that the remote pilot can maintain control and situational awareness in respect to positioning and collision avoidance.

General restrictions

101.05.10 (1) No person shall operate an RPA unless they have in their possession—
(a) a valid RPA Pilot Licence;
(b) a copy of the ROC and associated OpSpec;
(c) the certificate of registration for each RPA in operation;
(d) a copy of the RLA; and
(e) user manual for the RPA and the remote pilot station.

(2) No RPA shall—
(a) tow another aircraft,
(b) perform aerial or aerobatic displays;
(c) be flown in formation or swarm;

(3) Except by the holder of an ROC, and as approved by the Director, no RPA shall be operated—
(a) above 400ft above the surface
(b) within a radius of 10km from an aerodrome:
(c) within restricted or prohibited airspace; or
(d) adjacent to or above a nuclear power plant, prison, police station, crime scene, court of law, national key point or strategic installation.

Beyond visual line-of-sight

101.05.11 (1) An RPA shall not be operated beyond visual-line-of-sight unless by the holder of an ROC and as approved by the Director in the operations manual.

(2) The Director may approve B-VLOS operation subject to the operator meeting the requirements prescribed in Document SA-CATS 101.

(3) Approved B-VLOS operations may only be conducted in VMC, below 400ft above surface level, unless otherwise approved by the Director.

Night operations

101.05.12 (1) An RPA may not be operated at night except—
(a) in R-VLOS operation; or
(b) by the holder of an ROC, and as approved by the Director in terms of subregulation (2).

(2) The holder of an ROC intending to operate an RPA at night, shall, as a minimum have each RPA approved under their ROC for night operations subject to compliance with the requirements prescribed in Documents SA-CATS 101.

(3) An RPA may not be operated at night in controlled airspace except as approved by the Director as prescribed in regulation 101.05.3.

Operations in the vicinity of people

101.05.13 No person shall operate an RPA directly overhead any person or group of people or within a lateral distance of 50 m from any person, unless—
(a) the operator is the holder of an ROC and the operation has been approved by the Director in their operations manual; or
(b) such person is the operator of the RPA or such person is under the direction of the operator of the RPA; or
(c) such person or group of people forms part of the operations of the RPA, and is under control of the operator of the RPA, and adequate provisions have been made for their safety.

Operations in the vicinity of property, structures and buildings

101.05.14 (1) No RPA shall be operated within a lateral distance of 50m from any structure or building, unless—
(a) the operator is a holder of an ROC and the operation has been approved by the Director in their operations manual; or
(b) permission is obtained from the owner of such structure or building.

(2) An operator conducting an operation as contemplated in subregulation (1) shall take such measures as are necessary to ensure the safety of all persons on the ground accessing such building or in the vicinity of such structure.

Operations in the vicinity of public roads

101.05.15 No person shall operate an RPA over a public road, along the length of a public road or at a distance of less than 50 m from a public road unless—

(a) such person is the holder of an ROC and the operation has been approved by the Director in the operator's operations manual; or
(b) in the case of operations over a public road, such road has been closed for public use; and
(c) reasonable care has been taken to ensure the safety of road users and pedestrians in the event of loss of control of the RPA.

Radio communication requirements

101.05.16 (1) Except for R-VLOS operations, no RPAS shall be operated unless the pilot has a functioning air-band radio in his possession, tuned to the frequency or frequencies applicable to the ATSU providing services or controlling such area or airspace or to aircraft in such area or airspace.

(2) The air-band radio shall have the required output and be configured in such a way that the range, strength of transmission and quality of communication extends beyond the furthest likely position of the RPA from the pilot.

(3) For VLOS E-VLOS and B-VLOS operations, the pilot shall, using the registration of the RPA as a call-sign, make the required radio calls, indicating the altitude, location and intended operation of the RPA in that area and at such intervals as are required in order to ensure adequate separation from other aircraft is maintained.

(4) For approved RPA operations in controlled airspace, the pilot shall maintain radio contact, using the registration of the RPA as a call-sign, with the relevant ATSU, and acknowledge and execute such instructions as the ATSU may give at any time during the operation of the RPA.

Pre-flight preparation

101.05.17 A pilot shall complete the pre-flight preparations prior to each flight, as prescribed in Document SA-CATS 101.

Duties of the pilot

101.05.18 (1) The pilot is accountable for safe operation of the RPAS.

(2) The pilot of an RPA shall, on each flight, operate such aircraft in accordance with the manual.

(3) The pilot of an RPA is responsible for separation and avoidance of the RPA from other aircraft and any other obstacles and hazards.

(4) The pilot of an RPA shall pilot such RPA in a manner so as to minimize hazards to persons and property on the ground, and other aircraft in the air.

(5) The pilot shall ensure that at least one observer is used for E-VLOS operations.

Flight operations

101.05.19 (1) The RPAS shall be operated in such a way that safe separation from other aircraft is maintained and that adequate obstacle clearance is ensured, during all phases of the flight.

(2) The pilot of an RPA shall ensure that the take-off and landing area is safe and of the appropriate dimensions, free from obstacles and has adequate surface conditions, with regard to the type of operation, the size of the aircraft, the aircraft's performance and external factors.

Right of way

101.05.20 (1) Notwithstanding the provisions of subregulations (2) to (5), an RPA shall give way to manned aircraft.

(2) The RPA shall avoid passing over, under or in front of manned aircraft, unless it passes well clear and takes into account the effect of aircraft wake turbulence.

(3) When two aircraft are approaching head-on or approximately in a way that there is danger of collision, each aircraft shall alter its heading to the right.

(4) When two aircraft are converging at approximately the same level, the aircraft which has the other aircraft on its right, shall give way.

(5) An aircraft which is being overtaken has the right of way, and the one overtaking shall alter its heading to keep well clear.

Use of time

101.05.21 (1) For the purposes of reporting and recording time, Co-ordinated Universal Time (UTC) shall be used and shall be expressed in hours and minutes and, when required, seconds of the 24-hour day beginning at midnight.

(2) A pilot shall have a time piece synchronised with UTC prior to operating a RPAS in controlled airspace and at such other times during the flight as may be necessary.

(3) Wherever time is utilised in the application of data link communications, it shall be accurate to within 1 second of UTC.

Flight folio

101.05.22 (1) The owner or operator of an RPA shall ensure that the RPA has a flight folio or any other similar document which meets the requirements of and contains the information as prescribed in Document SA-CATS 101, and the flight folio shall be accessible at the remote pilot station all times during flight.

(2) The flight folio shall be kept up-to-date and maintained in a legible manner by the remote pilot.

(3) All entries shall be made immediately upon completion of the occurrence to which they refer.

(4) In the case of maintenance being undertaken on the RPA, the entry shall be certified by the person responsible for the maintenance.

(5) Without detracting from the generality of subregulation (1), the remote pilot shall—
(a) maintain fuel or charging records to enable the Director to ascertain that, for each flight under his or her control, the requirements of regulation 101.05.23 are complied with;
(b) enter the fuel, charging and oil records referred to in subregulation (5)(*a*) in the flight folio; and
(c) maintain oil records to enable the Director to ascertain that trends for oil consumption are such that an RPA has sufficient oil to complete each flight.

Power reserves

101.05.23 (1) During VLOS operations, the remote pilot shall ensure that the aircraft has enough fuel or electrical charge to complete the flight, plus a reserve of at least 10%.

(2) During B-VLOS operations, the remote pilot shall ensure that the aircraft has enough fuel or electrical charge to complete the intended flight plus a reserve of at least 10%.

First aid kits

101.05.24 (1) No owner or operator of an RPA shall operate the aircraft unless a first aid kit consisting of the medical supplies as prescribed in Document SA-CATS 91 is available within the remote pilot station and within 300m of the take-off and landing points. A single kit may be used to comply with both these requirements.

(2) The owner or operator shall carry out periodical inspections of the first aid kit to ensure that, as far as practicable, the contents thereof are in a condition necessary for their intended use.

(3) The contents of the first aid kit shall be replenished at regular intervals, in accordance with instructions contained on their labels, or as circumstances require.

(4) The first aid kit shall be readily accessible to all crew members involved in the operation.

Hand-held fire extinguishers

101.05.25 No owner or operator of an RPA shall operate the RPA unless—
(a) a hand-held fire extinguisher is available at the remote pilot station and within 300m of the take-off and landing points;

(b) a hand-held fire extinguisher suitable for use with electronic equipment and any power generating equipment in use is available in the remote pilot station; and

(c) a hand-held fire extinguisher suitable for use on the RPA is available within 300m of the take-off and landing points.

QUESTIONS AND ANSWERS

Questions

Note: Unless specified, questions are related to PPL(A)
Part 1 Chapters 1, 2, 3

1 ICAO means
a   International Civil Aeronautical Organisation
b   International Civil Aviation Organization
c   International Civil Air Organisation
d   International Convention for Aviation Organisation

2 Between ICAO and SACAA regulations
a   there are no differences
b   there are differences
c   there is no alignment
d   their alignment is compulsory

3 The head of SACAA is a civil servant called
a   the Chief Executive Officer
b   the Commissioner of Civil Aviation
c   the Director of Civil Aviation
d   the Minister of Transport

4 The law currently framing civil aviation is called
a   the Civil Aviation Act of 2009
b   the Civil Aviation Bill of 2009
c   the Civil Aviation Regulations of 2009
d   the Air Law Act of 2009

5 CARS is the acronym for
a   Civil Aviation Regulations
b   Civil Aviation Rules
c   Civilian Aviation Rules
d   none of the above

6 CATS is the acronym for
a   Civil Aviation Terminology and Standards
b   Civil Aviation Temporary Services
c   Civil Aviation Technical Standards
d   Civil Aviation Technical Services

7 The South African CAA or SACAA is a state agency that
a   reports to ICAO
b   reports to the Transport Minister
c   reports to Parliament
d   is fully independent

8 AIP means
a   Aviation International Publication
b   Aeronautical Information Package

c Aviation Information Publication
d Aeronautical Information Publication

9 AIP means information of
a a lasting character
b a fixed-time value
c great importance to air navigation
d a temporary character

10 Amendments to AIP are
a for additional information
b information on permanent changes
c corrections of errors in AIP so amended
d temporary changes

11 What does AIRAC mean?
a Air Regulation and Aviation Control
b Aeronautical Information for Air Control
c Aviation Information Regulation and Control
d Aeronautical Information Regulation and Control

12 A temporary change of long duration to AIP is called a
a Supplement
b Superior amendment
c Significant change
d NOTAM

13 Is it true or false that a NOTAM is (mark two correct answers)
a distributed by the Aeronautical Fixed Service (AFS)
b short notice but for permanent change
c temporary nature and short duration
d an acronym for Notice to Aviation Management

14 The 6 categories of NOTAM are
a A, B, C, D, E, F
b CAT I, II, II
c important, medium importance, low importance, military, heliports, "trigger"
d Class 1, 2, 3,4 5, 6

15 AIP GEN contains (among other things) (mark two correct answers)
a abbreviations and codes
b airport charts
c differences between ICAO and SACAA regulations
d syllabuses for general aviation licences

16 Where will you find information on prohibited areas?
a in AIP GEN
b in AIP AG vol 2
c in AIP ENR

d   in CATS

17   Where will you find general and detailed information regulating specific airports?
a   in AIP GEN
b   in AIP AD
c   in CARS
d   in AIP ENR

18   Your personal physician or general practitioner
a   may issue your medical certificate of fitness (SPL, PPL)
b   may do so only if he/she is a designated aviation medical examiner
c   may override a decision of a DAME
d   may certify you "fit to fly"

19   The applicable class of medical certificate for CPL (A) is
a   class 2
b   class 1
c   class 4
d   a medical declaration suffices

20   Class 2 is relevant to (indicate correct answers (s))
a   PPL (H)
b   CPL (A)
c   SPL (A)
d   paraglider pilot

21   Class 1 is relevant to (indicate correct answer (s))
a   an Instrument rating
b   Class II test pilot rating
c   CPL A and H
d   ATPL

22   Regarding the validity of a medical certificate, which statement is true ?
a   class 1 is, below 60 years of age, subject to a 45 years of age standard change from 12 months to 6 months?
b   class 2 is valid for 5 calendar years if you are 30 years of age?
c   class 2 is valid only 12 months at a time from a pilot's 50th birthday date
d   you have 15 days and no more before the date of expiration of your certificate to apply for an extension by contacting a DAME

23   If a condition appears that is likely to impact the validity of your medical certificate, whom must you inform?
a   your physician
b   your medical practitioner
c   the DAME of your choice
d   SACAA

24   Which of the following conditions renders you unfit to fly (indicate correct answer (s) if applicable) on a particular day
a   you did scuba diving 48 hours before commencing operational duty
b   you switch on autopilot and take a sip of light cold wine

c you gave blood one day before commencing operational duty
d you are fatigued

25 Which of the following conditions makes you unfit to act as PIC and demand that you report them without undue delay to the designated body (indicate correct answer(s) if applicable) who will advise on your fly-ability

a surgical operation
b pregnancy
c absence due to illness for more than 21 days
d drug-induced sedation

26 What do you understand by "without undue delay"? That

a you must report within 24 hours
b you report to whom ever the law says you have to report to, and as soon as you are capable to do so
c a delay is not due to you
d any delay that cannot be justified is unacceptable

27 What do you understand by "impairment"? That (indicate the correct answer(s))

a you cannot be paired with another student due to feeling ill?
b it is a health condition due to impaired hearing
c a sudden incapacitation
d a subtle incapacitation

28 What do you understand by "co-morbidity"?

a you suffer from a terminal illness
b you are suicidal
c you suffer from a disease or disorder correlated to a main health disease or condition, that is not a cause for being declared unfit to fly because it is just a correlated situation and not the main one
d you suffer from a disease or disorder in addition to a main health disease or condition, that may be a cause for being declared unfit to fly

29 How do you understand the expression "fitness" in the context of your medical certification?

a you are fit as "in good shape"
b you are certified fit for the licence you hold
c your certificated fitness is valid for the time the certificate is valid, regardless of any health factor that may arise before it is supposed to lapse
d unrelated to psychology

30 Under what Part of CARS and CATS does medical certification fall?

a 61
b 62
c 67
d 91

Questions

Part 2 Chapter 4

1. Where do you train legally for a PPL? At
   a. a flying school
   b. an Aviation Training Organisation
   c. an Approved Training Organisation
   d. an Approved Flight Training Organisation

2. You are 16 years of age, and hold a SPL, do your privileges allow you (indicate correct answer)
   a. to fly solo after completing successfully exercise 14
   b. to fly solo with a passenger
   c. to fly solo with your instructor
   d. to fly solo on a sight seeing flight

3. You are 15 years of age, and hold a SPL, which statement(s) about limitation are false
   a. I cannot fly solo
   b. I cannot fly without a written authorization from my instructor
   c. I cannot fly VMC by day
   d. after an emergency landing other than at an aerodrome I can take off again in the same serviceable aeroplane in order to return to base

4. An endorsement, to be legal, must contain at least four specifications, which are (indicate the correct answer(s))
   a. the date of the test
   b. the name of the ATO
   c. the aircraft registration and type
   d. the name and licence number of the examiner

5. SPL theoretical training leads to a number of PPL examination papers, among which (indicate the correct answer (s))
   a. Aircraft General
   b. Air Law and Procedures
   c. General Cross-Country
   d. Meteorology

6. The pass mark is ... % and a re-mark can be applied for if you get between ... % and ... % (choose the correct combination)
   a. 75% 60% 75%
   b. 70% 60% 74%
   c. 75% 65% 75%
   d. 75% 70% 74%

7. If you fail twice a PPL exam, with a score above 50%, how much time must you wait before sitting it for a third time?
   a. within 14 days after date of failure
   b. 7 calendar days after date of failure

c 1 calendar month from the last day of the month if which you failed
d 2 calendar months

8 **If you fail for the first time an examination mentioned below you may rewrite (indicate the correct statement(s))**
a for PPL theoretical examinations, within 14 days after date of failure
b for the Restricted Radiotelephony Operator's Certificate, within 14 days after date of failure
c for the Restricted Radiotelephony Operator's Certificate, within 30 days after date of failure
d for a Night Rating, 7 calendar days after date of failure

9 **You want a better mark although you have passed the given theoretical PPL examination. What can you do?**
a you rewrite this examination
b you ask for a re-mark
c you have the examination cancelled
d you wait for all credits to lapse

10 **How much time in terms of period are you given to pass all your theoretical examinations after obtaining the first credit (= pass)?**
a one year
b ten months
c eighteen months
d thirty six months

11 **You are foreign-born from a country where English is not the first language, in which of the following case(s) are you exempt from sitting the examination for an Oral Proficiency Certificate**
a you hold a Matric, O or M level, with a pass in English first language with a minimum symbol of D or its equivalent, you meet automatically the Language Proficiency Requirement as mandated by ICAO
b you hold a SAQA recognized 2 year tertiary qualification with English either as a subject or English as the language of tuition
c you hold a foreign CAA language certification in English
d you hold a Permanent Residence Visa in South Africa

12 **What is the minimum level of Oral Proficiency in the English language you must hold not to have to undergo remedial training?**
a 4
b 5
c 3
d 6

13 **In terms of Oral Proficiency, what combination (s) below is (are) correct ?**
a "Operational" level 4, valid for 3 years at a time
b "Extended" level 5, valid for 6 years at a time
c "Operational" level 4 with retesting every 4 years
d "Expert" level 6 with retesting every 6 years

14 **PPL practical flight instruction leading up to the Skills Test contains**
a 20 exercises
b 19 exercises

c   no dual check after the first solo
d   no dual check after exercise 14 duly completed

15 Define a solo flight as a

a   flight time during which the student pilot is the sole occupant of the aircraft and in which there is no other person present in the aircraft, be it an instructor, a safety pilot, another student pilot or any other pilot
b   flight time during which the student pilot is the sole occupant of the aircraft and in which there is no other person present in the aircraft, apart from an instructor who is not allowed to manipulate the controls
c   flight time during which the student pilot is the PIC
d   flight time during which the student pilot is in the left seat

16 At what cut-off number of hours in the course of your PPL flight training prior to solo will you be declared a "potential safety risk" ? (multiple correct answers)

a   at no solo after 30 hours of dual (A)
b   at no solo after 45 hours of dual (H)
c   at no solo after 45 hours of dual (A)
d   at no solo after 40 hours of dual (H)

17 To be allowed to be released on your first solo you must have fulfilled at series of conditions among which (mark the correct answers(s))

a   I have undergone a minimum of 10 hours of dual flying
b   I hold a SPL
c   I have passed all my theoretical exams
d   I am proficient at executing a go-around manoeuvre with full flaps

18 You are allowed to attempt your first solo (indicate the false statement(s), not the true one(s)) if

a   you are a day shy of 16 years of age on the day of the solo
b   your medical lapses at the end of the month in which your first solo is due to take place
c   you are proficient at handling your aircraft in case of a simulated engine failure
d   you have done exercise 15 ahead of exercise 14 due to your natural skills

19 A first solo flight entails (indicate the false statement(s))

a   being tested by your instructor in the right seat
b   doing three take-off and landings
c   handling an engine failure that is, at this stage, not simulated
d   doing only one take-off and one landing

20 Your cross-country navigation in the course of your training is defined as follows (indicate the false statement)

a   one triangular cross-country flight of at least 200 NM, on which at least one point must be not less than 50 NM from base and must include full-stop landings at two different aerodromes away from base
b   one triangular cross-country flight of at least 150 NM, on which at least one point must be not less than 50 NM from base and must include full-stop landings at two different aerodromes away from base
c   one triangular cross-country flight of at least 250 NM, on which at least one point must be not less than 50 NM from base and must include full-stop landings at two different aerodromes away from base

d   one triangular cross-country flight of at least 150 NM, on which at least two points must be not less than 50 NM from base and must include full-stop landings at two different aerodromes away from base

21   How much time do you have once you have passed all your theoretical examinations, to complete your PPL training and test?

a   36 months counting from the final successful examination
b   18 months counting from the final successful examination
c   2 years counting from the final successful examination
d   18+36 months counting from the final successful examination

22   You will undergo a pre-test Ground Evaluation. What best defines it?

a   an oral examination which probes in detail your knowledge of CARS, CATS, AIP and other aspects of aviation
b   a computer-based multi-choice paper
c   a written examination of some length without access to documentation
d   a detailed questionnaire set according to a uniform standard with access to documentation

23   Regarding your PPL Skills Test, which one of the conditions below for being able to test is false?

a   my last dual instruction is not older than 30 days
b   I have completed 45 hours flight time in an aeroplane (type certificated or not) with a MCM in excess of 420 kg
c   of which 45 hours, I have completed 15 hours including 5 hours cross-country
d   of which 45 hours, 15 hours were dual instruction

24   During your Skills Test your examiner will grade all required items on a scale from (indicate the correct answer)

a   1 to 5 – 5 being Excellent
b   1 to 5 – 1 being Excellent
c   4 to 1 – 4 being bottom
d   1 to 4 – 4 being Excellent

25   Your Skills Test can take place over more than one flight. Which statement is correct in this regard:

a   the navigation part is done on a different day within one month of the initial flight after the first flight
b   due to unforeseen circumstances the flight test cannot be completed and has to be completed within 30 days after the first flight
c   the navigation part can be done on a different day but within 14 days after the first flight
d   the navigation part can be done on a different day but within 30 days after the first flight

26   The navigation part of the Skills Test is defined as a flight

a   not less than 200 nautical miles total distance and must include take-offs and landings at two aerodromes away from base. At least one of the aerodromes from which the aircraft takes off for this flight shall be an aerodrome at which an Air Traffic Services Unit (ATSU) is in operation

b   not less than 150 nautical miles total distance and must include take-offs and landings at two aerodromes away from base. At least one of the aerodromes from which the aircraft takes off for this flight shall be an aerodrome at which an Air Traffic Services Unit (ATSU) is in operation
c   not less than 150 NM, on which at least one point must be not less than 50 NM from base and must include full-stop landings at two different aerodromes away from base. At least one of the aerodromes from which the aircraft takes off for this flight shall be an aerodrome at which an Air Traffic Services Unit (ATSU) is in operation
d   not less than 200 NM, on which at least one point must be not less than 50 NM from base and must include full-stop landings at two different aerodromes away from base. At least one of the aerodromes from which the aircraft takes off for this flight shall be an aerodrome at which an Air Traffic Services Unit (ATSU) is in operation

27 Should you fail the Skills Test, which of these actions is/are illegal
a   you carry on training at a different ATO
b   you undergo remedial ground and flight training at your ATO
c   you continue flying solo with your SPL
d   you take passengers for a flight since you are recent anyway

28 What do you understand by the expression "co-pilot"?
a   your instructor is on the left seat, to show you some interesting manoeuvres, and you on the right
b   you hold a PPL, you can act as co-pilot of an aeroplane for which you have a valid class or type rating, and in which a co-pilot is not a requirement
c   you fly solo from base to a destination aerodrome where another student comes on board and fly solo back to departure point. Both of you are co-pilots.

29 Flight time for the operation of aeroplanes, is the total time from the moment an aeroplane first moves for the purposes of taking off until the moment it finally comes to rest at the end of the flight". Is then flight time similar to (mark correct answer (s)):
a   block to block time
b   chock to chock time
c   flying time

30 Indicate the document(s) you need to produce (among others) together with your Application for Initial Issue of your PPL
a   a valid medical certificate
b   a summary of your flying logbook
c   the Skills Test Report
d   proof of fee payment

Questions

Part 2 Chapter 5

1 The date of application for the initial issue of your PPL is

a   the date of your Skills Test
b   the date on which the CAA receives your application on the prescribed form
c   the date on which you send the application to the CAA
d   the date of issue

2 You can use the privileges of your PPL

a   from the day you passed your Skills Test
b   from the date of issue
c   from the day of delivery to you
d   once you have received it and signed it in permanent black ink

3 A PPL is valid

a   for life
b   10 years
c   5 years
d   none of the above

4 Competency is maintained by (indicate the correct answer(s)

a   undergoing a first revalidation test 12 months from the date of initial issue
b   undergoing further revalidations every 24 months from the date of re-issue
c   paying the currency fee each year
d   staying recent

5 Having undergone a successful revalidation you must

a   send to CAA the prescribed form and documents within 14 days following the test
b   send to CAA the prescribed form and documents within 30 days following the test
c   send to CAA the prescribed form and documents within 7 days following the test
d   send to CAA the prescribed form and documents without undue delay

6 You anticipated or skipped a revalidation, and have tested successfully, which of these three statement(s) is (are) correct?

a   if you tested within 90 days immediately before expiry of competency, the new date will be calculated from the beginning of the month following the date of expiry
b   if you tested more than 90 days before expiry of competency, the new date will be calculated from the beginning of the month following the date of revalidation
c   if you tested more than three (3) months before expiry of competency, the new date will be calculated from the beginning of the month following the date of expiry

7 The currency fee is paid

a annually
b at each except the first revalidation
c at the same time as a medical certification
d only when competency is tested

8 Part of CARS dealing with Fees and Charges is

a 91
b 97
c 187
d 129

9 One of the statements below is not a PPL privilege. Identify it.

a you may charge a passenger for fuel cost only (not a remuneration)
b you may act as PIC under SVFR after being authorized by ATS
c you may fly internationally
d you may act as co-pilot if you hold the appropriate valid class rating or type rating

10 You are not permitted to fly if your aggregate flying time exceeds (indicate correct answers)

a 400 hours, during the preceding 90 days
b 1000 hours, during the preceding 12 months
c for pilots not subject to an approved flight time and duty period scheme, 10 hours within a 24 hour period
d 700 hours, during the preceding 6 months

11 As a PPL pilot which one of the following rule(s) that applied to your SPL status still apply to you in terms of inability to fly (identify them)

a having done scuba diving 24 hours before
b having donated blood 72 hours before
c having consumed alcohol 8 hours before
d having a blood concentration in excess of 0,02g/100ml

12 In terms of recency, which of the following is/are false?

a I can fly PIC with passengers by day if I have done competent take-offs and landings by day or by night up to 3 months before
b I can fly PIC with passengers by night if I have done five take-offs and landings by night in the preceding 90 days
c I can fly PIC with passengers by day if I have done three take-offs and landings by night in the preceding 90 days
d I can fly PIC with passengers by night if I have done three take-offs and landings by night in the preceding 90 days

13 You have used FSTD. How many minimum take-offs and landings done on a simulator counts towards your recency?

a FSTD take-offs and landings in a simulator approved for that purpose do not count as actual take-offs and landings for the purpose of carry passengers
b 5
c 3

Air Law

14 What is your understanding of the word "currency" in an aviation context? Identify the incorrect answer(s).
a currency refers to currency fee
b currency refers to the legal maintenance of recency
c currency refers to the maintenance of competency of a licence or a rating by adhering to revalidation rules
d currency related to competency works within time frames set by CARS

15 You had dental surgery under drug-induced sedation, the requirement is that
a you can only return to flying after 24 hours
b you can only return to flying after 72 hours
c you can return to flying after 72 hours after under DAME so advises
d you have to wait 24 hours and you need not contact a DAME

16 What rating are you allowed to add to your SPL without a rating pre-requisite in Integrated Training?
a a Night Rating
b an Instrument Rating
c none of the above
d both

17 Which list below is a list of ratings?
a Night, Agricultural, Class, Type
b Category, Special Type, Instrument, Commercial
c Type, Class, Category, Special Purposes
d Warbird, Transport, Type, Variant

18 What does the acronym SEA (L) refer to exactly?
a a single-engine single pilot seaplane
b a single-engine piston aeroplane (L) for single pilot operation
c a single-engine aeroplane in the light (L) wake turbulence category
d a single-engine aeroplane that is not a seaplane for single pilot operation

19 Aeroplanes that require operation with more than one pilot necessitate
a a Class Rating
b a Type Rating
c a Special Purposes Rating
d a CPL

20 What is the prerequisite to undergo a Class Rating training multi-engine?
a 100 hours of solo
b 100 hours as PIC
c 100 hours as pilot-in-command and a CPL
d 100 hours as PIC and a CPL

21 You hold a PPL (A). You may apply for a CPL

a   if you have revalidated twice successfully
b   if you have 200 hours of flight time only
c   if the Director decides so
d   if you hold a NR in addition to other requirements

22 Which phrase below best defines a conversion in the context of ratings?

a   conversion is a rating for pilots who have not yet demonstrated proficiency
b   conversion is mandatory if you want to endorse your licence with a variant of the same model of aircraft in the same class
c   conversion is another word for mentoring

23 One or more the following is/are not a Rating for Special Purposes, which is it/are they?

a   Agricultural
b   Seaplane
c   Post-maintenance test flight
d   Flight instructor

24 A Notification of Conversion applies to (more than one correct answer)

a   familiarisation
b   differences training
c   type rating
d   aeroplanes only

25 Which one or several of the following does not qualify for applying for an Aerobatics Rating?

a   PPL (A)
b   SPL (A)
c   SPL (H)
d   PPL (H)

26 After completing a conversion what is the deadline for submitting your application?

a   within 15 days from the date of completion
b   within 30 days from the date of completion
c   without undue delay
d   as it is endorsed in my logbook by the instructor it is n/a

27 What is a Category A3 aircraft in terms of Regulations for Air Services?

a   an aircraft with a heavy (level 3) wake turbulence
b   an aeroplane with an approach speed of 141 KTS or more, but less than 166 KTS IAS
c   any aircraft excluding a helicopter with a maximum certified mass exceeding 2 700 kg and but not exceeding 5 700 kg

28 The four performance classes for aeroplanes are

a   I, II, III, IV (with single-engine at top of numerical order)
b   A, B, C, D (with single-engine at top of alpha order)
c   H, M, L, Super Heavy
d   none of the above

29 In terms of certification which one of the following aircraft is not certified under Part 21?

a   a rotorcraft of the normal category
b   a very light aeroplane
c   a powered paraglider
d   a manned free balloon

30 For how long must you keep your logbook?

a   for the whole validity period of your licence plus 60 months
b   for at least to 60 months after your licence has become invalid
c   no need to keep it after the licence has lapsed
d   upon termination of validity it must be sent to SACAA in terms of the preservation of pilot licences regulations with regard to legal safekeeping

Questions

Part 3 Chapter 6

1 Indicate which explanation of the acronym I'MSAFE is erroneous
a   I for me, M for medication, S for stress, A for alcohol, F for fatigue, E for eating
b   as above but I for Ill
c   as above in a, but I for and F for food
d   as above in a, but S for sleeplessness

2 What is the permissible alcohol blood concentration?
a   as per breathalyser testing
b   0,2 gr per 100 ml
c   0,02 mg per 100 ml
d   0,02 gr per 100 ml

3 In terms of terminology VMC signifies
a   variable meteorological conditions
b   visual meteorological conditions
c   that you cannot fly at night
d   the same as VFR

4 FIRs under the South African State's responsibility are
a   FAJA, FACA, FAJO
b   FACA, FAJA, FACO
c   FAJA, FAPA, FAJO

5 Which of the following airspace is prefixed with the nationality letters?
a   control zones
b   danger areas
c   control areas
d   ATZ

6 Which statement is the correct definition for advisory airspace ?
a   an airspace of defined dimensions, within which air traffic advice is available
b   an airspace within which air traffic advice is available
c   an airspace of advertised dimensions, within which air traffic service is available
d   an airspace of defined dimensions, within which air traffic advisory service is available

7 Which statement accurately describes controlled airspace ?
a   an airspace of defined dimensions within which an air traffic control service is provided to IFR flights in accordance with the airspace classification
b   an airspace of controlled dimensions within which an air traffic control service is provided to VFR flights in accordance with the airspace classification
c   an airspace of defined dimensions within which an air traffic control service is provided to IFR flights and to VFR flights in accordance with the airspace classification

395

d   an airspace of controlled dimensions within which an air traffic control service is provided to IFR flights and to VFR flights in accordance with the airspace classification

8 In which combination of airspace classes is VFR not permitted?
a   B C D G
b   A B C D
c   D F G E
d   B C D E

9 Which combination of airspace classes has only controlled ones?
a   C D F G
b   A B E F
c   C D E A
d   C E F G

10 Is this a correct definition of FAPs, FARs and also FADs?
Airspace areas that are declared in terms of lateral and vertical limits, the type of restriction or hazard involved, the times at which it applies and other pertinent information.
a   Yes
b   No

11 Which statements is/are not correct? (indicate multiple answers if applicable)
a   an ATZ is established at an aerodrome for the protection of controlled traffic, and extends from ground level to a specified upper limit, with variable lateral limits and can be of Class C, Class D or Class G in South Africa
b   an ATZ is established at an aerodrome for the protection of controlled traffic, and extends from ground level to a specified upper limit, with variable lateral limits and is of Class C in South Africa
c   a CTR has lateral limits of at least 5NM from the centre of the aerodrome in direction from which approach is made, and extends from the ground to a specified upper limit, where controlled traffic (IFR and VFR) is separated by radar, and is Class C in South Africa
d   a CTR has lateral limits of at least 25NM from the centre of the aerodrome in direction from which approach is made, and extends from the ground to a specified upper limit, where controlled traffic (IFR and VFR) is separated by radar, and is Class C in South Africa

12 What is visibility?
a   the ability, as determined by atmospheric conditions and expressed in units of distance, to see and identify prominent unlighted objects by day and prominent lighted objects by night, forward from the cockpit
b   the ability, as determined by atmospheric conditions and expressed in units of distance, to see and identify prominent unlighted objects by day and prominent lighted objects by night
c   the ability, as determined by atmospheric conditions and expressed in units of distance, to see and identify prominent unlighted objects by day

13 Complete the regulation "Every VFR flight shall be so conducted that the aircraft is flown with visual reference to the surface by day and to identifiable objects by night and at no time above more than . . .
a   half the sky covered below 20 000 ft
b   three eights of cloud within a radius of ten NM of such aircraft

c   four eights of cloud within a radius of 5NM of such aircraft
d   three eighths of cloud within a radius of five NM of such aircraft

14 Outside a CTR and ATZ who is responsible to determine if weather conditions allow for VFR?

a   the operator
b   the PIC
c   the ATC
d   the ATSU

15 You are in controlled airspace (not a CTR) under VFR, the weather deteriorates, what action do you take as PIC?

a   you request clearance to continue in VMC, land at the nearest aerodrome or leave the airspace concerned
b   you continue flying and land at the nearest aerodrome without undue delay and notify the appropriate ATC
c   none of the above
d   you operate under IFR being instrument rated

16 Aeroplanes SVFR flights are (indicate the erroneous statement or statements)

a   once cleared, allowed by day and night
b   by day only without a clearance
c   by day and by night after a clearance is obtained
d   with a cloud ceiling of at least 600 m and visibility of at least 1 500 ft

17 Operating in airspace C (not a CTR or ATZ) which combination is true?

a   at or above 10 000 ft above AGL, forward flight visibility 8 km
b   at or above 10 000 ft above MSL, forward flight visibility 8 km
c   below 10 000 ft MSL and above 3 000 ft above MSL, forward flight visibility 8 km

18 Your aeroplane is in a CTR and on approach under VFR. In which of the conditions cited below are your permitted to operate?

a   forward flight visibility 5 km, ground visibility 1 500 m, ceiling 1 500 ft, distance from clouds 600m horizontal, 500 ft vertical
b   forward flight visibility 5 km, ground visibility 5 000 m, ceiling 1 500 ft, distance from clouds 600 m horizontal, 500 ft vertical
c   forward flight visibility 5 km, ground visibility 1 500 m, ceiling 1 000 ft, distance from clouds 600 m horizontal, 500 ft vertical
d   forward flight visibility 5 km, ground visibility 5 000 m, ceiling 1 500 ft, distance from clouds 500 m horizontal, 600 ft vertical

19 When are you allowed to land on a road?

a   if you hold a PPL
b   while practicing a precautionary
c   for the purpose of saving human lives
d   if no adequate airfield is available

20 Must you file a flight plan in all circumstances noted below? (indicate the false option, or options, that is: not in the case of . . .)

a   a local flight
b   an international flight

398 Air Law

    c   VFR entering or departing from an ATZ or CTR
    d   a flight crossing an airway or advisory route at right angles

21 Filing a domestic flight plan. Which statement is not correct ?
    a   filing is possible 10 minutes before ETD
    b   filing is possible 120 hours before ETD
    c   filing is possible up to 30 minutes before ETD
    d   filing in flight is possible up to 10 minutes prior to entry

22 To avoid its cancellation a flight plan can be activated (multiple correct answers)
    a   up to two hours after departure
    b   before start up
    c   within one hour of departure
    d   in flight within sixty minutes of departure

23 As per CARS 'when no destination alternate aerodrome is required' the final reserve fuel for a reciprocating engine aeroplane should be enough to fly for
    a   30 minutes
    b   15 minutes
    c   45 minutes
    d   30 minutes at holding speed at 1 500 ft

24 Complete this definition of trip fuel by supplying the 4 key missing words or combination of words in the blank spaces.
Trip fuel includes fuel for … and … from aerodrome elevation to initial cruising level/altitude, taking into account the expected departure routing; fuel from … to …, including any step climb/descent; fuel from top of descent to the point where the approach is initiated, taking into account the expected arrival procedure; and fuel for approach and landing at the destination aerodrome.

25 Navigation lights are (indicate false answers)
    a   green on right, red on left, white at the back
    b   white at the back, green on left, red on right
    c   green on right, red at the back, white on left
    d   green with a 140 angle, red with a 140 angle, white with a 110 angle of coverage

26 The rotating beacon should be switched on
    a   with engines running while operating on the movement area
    b   only at night
    c   to indicate the extremity of your aircraft at night on the movement area

27 Your aircraft is not pressurised and you are cruising, alone, at 10 500 ft, in which scenario (s) must you have supplemental oxygen equipment stored and able to dispense oxygen supply.
    a   your planned leg at that altitude is estimated at 75 minutes
    b   you plan to stay at that altitude for 125 minutes
    c   you are about to descend
    d   you are climbing to 12 500 ft

28 If you enter G in your flight plan (item 10) to indicate your communication and navigation equipment, does it mean that you have
    a   a certified GPS
    b   "general" equipment, that is to say a VHF radio and a transponder mode A

c   a non-certified GPS
d   none of above is correct

29 An aircraft must be equipped with compulsory instruments for a VFR flight. In the list below, which one is not compulsory?

a   a magnetic compass
b   an airspeed indicator
c   a sensitive pressure altimeter with a subscale setting
d   a stabilised direction indicator

30 An aircraft must be fitted with extra compulsory instruments and equipment in VFR at night or in IMC on a flight operated by a single pilot. In the list below complete the requirements by filling the blank spaces

a   a headset with boom microphone and has a . . . button
b   means of displaying charts readable in . . . light
c   in IMC, a serviceable automatic flight control system with a least . . . hold and . . . mode

31 An aircraft hand-held fire extinguisher is of the type

a   APW
b   Dry chemical CO2
c   Halon 1211
d   Multi-purpose Dry chemical

32 A First Aid Kit contains a minimum of 15 items. Two of the statements below are erroneous. Indicate them.

a   there must be one FAK per ten passengers
b   disposable gloves are included in the 15 items
c   a biohazard disposal waste bag is included in the 15 items
d   a disposable resuscitation aid is included in the 15 items

33 A Universal Precaution Kit is compulsory

a   on all general aviation flights up to 20 passengers
b   only on corporate flights with one cabin attendant
c   only on-air transport flights with one cabin attendant
d   on general aviation flights with a maximum certificated passenger seating of 20 or more and one cabin attendant

34 On a domestic flight which one of these documents need not be carried on board?

a   the certificate of registration
b   the general declaration
c   the mass and balance report
d   the flight folio

35 Which combination of document and validity is incorrect?

a   the certificate of release to service, 100 hours or 1 year
b   the mass and balance report, 2 years
c   the certificate of registration until invalidated or cancelled

Questions

Part 3 Chapters 7 and 8

1. **The manoeuvring area is that part of an aerodrome used for (indicate the incorrect answer(s))**
   a take-off and landing
   b taxiing
   c loading or unloading passengers or cargo
   d refuelling

2. **The movement area includes (indicate les correct answer(s))**
   a the area designated for taking off and landing
   b the apron
   c the runway strips
   d the hangar area

3. **You are taxiing, you see a directional white flashing light. What do you do?**
   a you stop and wait for radio instructions
   b you continue taxiing up to the holding point and await radio instructions
   c you taxi back to your apron where you departed
   d you taxi back to the beginning of the taxiway

4. **You have a series of red flashes directed at you as you are about to line up. How do you acknowledge the message?**
   a you call on the correct frequency and enquire
   b you move ailerons or rudder to acknowledge and continue lining-up
   c you look at potential risks from incoming traffic and when suitable line-up
   d you clear the area

5. **You are taxiing, a small truck towing a light aircraft is coming at you from the left, you**
   a cede priority because it is coming from the left
   b cede priority because the truck is towing an aircraft
   c do not cede priority because it is not coming from the right
   d proceed because there is no danger of collision

6. **While taxiing you observe another aircraft approaching head-on, you**
   a turn to the right and expect the other to do the same
   b turn to the left and expect the other to turn to the right
   c stop and cede priority
   d turn to the left and expect the other to do the same

7. **At a controlled aerodrome, in order to taxi on the manoeuvring area, you**
   a must only obey rules of right of way
   b obtain clearance from ATC to taxi and comply with instructions

c   inform ATC and other aircrafts of your intention and start taxiing
d   none are correct

8 Under what conditions can someone else taxi the aircraft whose PIC you are? (if you chose d, mark only d)

a   that person has a SPL
b   that person has a PPL
c   that person has been declared "competent" by an instructor
d   all answers are correct

9 What does this picture tell you about runway 27?

a   it has a temporarily displaced threshold with a pre-threshold area unfit for movement
b   it has a permanently displaced threshold with pre-threshold area available for taxi and take off but not for landing
c   it has a permanently displaced threshold with pre-threshold area unfit for taxi and take off but available for landing as the arrows indicate
d   the aerodrome manager is having the runway markings repainted

10 What do the yellow chevrons mean (shown in white here)?

a   runway 27 has a parking area over the yellow chevrons
b   the yellow chevrons indicate pre-threshold unfit for normal movement of aircraft
c   the yellow chevrons should be white because runway markings are white

d   the chevrons indicate an area to expedite lining-up

11 While on taxiway bravo you notice an information sign with a yellow background and black numeral 15 with an arrow to the right. It means that
a   taxiway 15 is coming up on your right
b   runway 15 is to your right
c   it is a location sign for taxiway 15
d   you are to leave taxiway bravo and follow taxiway 15

12 What is the accurate definition of en route, or en-route?
a   phase of a flight from departing from the circuit to the commencement of the approach and landing phase
b   phase of a flight from the end of the take-off and initial climb phase to the commencement of the approach and landing phase
c   phase of a flight from the take-off and initial climb phase to the commencement of the approach and landing phase
d   phase of a flight from the take-off and initial climb phase to the commencement of the landing phase

13 On or in the vicinity of an aerodrome in uncontrolled airspace (indicate the correct answer (s))
a   all turns are to the left except on taking off
b   all turns are to the left
c   all turns are to the right
d   all turns are to the right if in force

14 Flying across an aerodrome, if allowed, is done at
a   minimum safe altitude
b   2 000 m AGL minimum
c   1 000 ft AGL minimum
d   2 000 ft AGL minimum

15 You are flying in an ATZ with a tower in operation. You need
a   to maintain a continuous radio watch on the aerodrome frequency
b   not obtain clearances
c   not watch for visual signals since tower is in operation and you have radio contact
d   to recycle your transponder

16 A Flight Information Service should as a rule
a   provide information on weather and reported traffic
b   assign you a squawk code and instruct you en route
c   ensure separation to avoid collision hazards
d   deliver clearances

17 Two aircrafts in the same category are converging at approximately the same level. SZ-POP has aircraft ZU-PIP on its right. Normally,
a   POP gives way to PIP by altering course to the left
b   PIP gives way to POP
c   POP moves left and PIP right to avoid collision

18 You are in a C172 and are about to be overtaken by a Cherokee. Normally,
a   you have right of way and the Cherokee changes course
b   the Cherokee has right of way

c   as the Cherokee is descending, she has right of way
d   as you are climbing, you have right of way

19 In a converging situation involving two aircraft in different categories, which statement is correct?
a   a power-driven heavier-than-air aircraft has right of way on same carrying an underslung load
b   a glider gives way to a helicopter
c   a helicopter gives way to a glider
d   none

20 You are at a FL. In which sequence of cruising then descending is this combination correct?
a   transition altitude transition level
b   transition level transition layer
c   transition layer transition level

21 A number of aerodromes are listed in the AIP regarding the radius within which a specified transition altitude is declared. This radius is:
a   25 km
b   25 NM
c   5 NM
d   1 500 ft

22 Outside areas of declared aerodromes that have a specified radius applicable to a transition altitude, the uniform transition altitude under VFR is
a   2 000 ft
b   1 500 ft
c   2 500 ft
d   a and b correct

23 When at Flight Level the altimeter subscale is set to
a   1012.3 hPa
b   1013.5 hPa
c   1013.2 hPa
d   local QNH

24 Aircraft A is IFR on track 359M. Aircraft B is VFR on track 179M. Their minimum flight separation is
a   1 000 m
b   2 000 ft
c   500 ft
d   1 000 ft

25 Aircraft A is on track 175T, variation 7° W. IFR FL available are
a   105, 125, 165
b   180, 210, 230
c   80, 120, 280
d   30, 50, 85

26 VFR FL easterly MT include
a   25, 35, 115
b   25, 55, 140

c   45, 105, 185
d   15, 135, 195

27 Tracks applied in the semi-circular rule are
a   M
b   T
c   M for IFR only
d   T for VFR only

28 You are flying along a railway track, which statement reflects the fact you are applying the law? (two correct answers, indicate them)
a   I am at 1 000 ft AGL, the track is below the tip of my right wing
b   I am at 1 500 ft AGL, the track is about 2 NM on my right
c   I am at 500 ft AGL, the track is about 1 NM on my right
d   I am at 500 ft AGL, the track is about 1 NM on my left

29 You are over a "rock in the bundu" festival with large crowds, you want to circle over them. You are allowed to
a   operate at 1 000 ft over the highest obstacle within a radius of 2 000 ft from your aircraft
b   operate at 3 000 ft above surface
c   operate only by prior permission of the organizers
d   drop leaflets

30 The National Parks and World Heritage Sites legislation states that the generic clearance above the highest point in order to fly over such sites is
a   2 500 m
b   2 500 ft
c   500 m
d   500 ft

31 What are the correct answer(s) regarding maximum speed?
a   below FL 100 uncontrolled airspace : 250 KIAS
b   in a CTR or ATZ : 160 KIAS reciprocating engine
c   in Cape Town SRA : 180 KIAS
d   in Johannesburg SRA : 200 KIAS

32 TIBA means
a   Traffic Information By Aircraft
b   Traffic Information Between Aircraft
c   Traffic Identification By Aircraft
d   Traffic Information Broadcast by Aircraft

33 Which frequency is the default frequency for a TIBA report?
a   124.8 kHz
b   124.8 MHz
c   124.4 MHz
d   124.4 kHz

34 Operating in controlled airspace a PIC must (mark the wrong answer(s))
a   establish a two-way radio contact before entering
b   maintain a continuous radio watch

c recycle the transponder code to 7500 upon entry
d vacate the airspace in case of radio failure even though a FP (flight plan) is active and procedures in such occurrence are complied with due to high risk of collision

35 An acrobatic flight is permitted provided that (indicate the wrong answer)

a the manoeuvre is concluded and the aeroplane is on an even keel at a height of not less than 3 000 ft above ground or water
b it is not over any populous area or public gathering
c the manoeuvre is concluded and the aeroplane is on an even keel at a height of not less than 2 000 ft above ground or water
d within 5NM of an aerodrome licensed in terms of Part 139, unless at a height not less than 4 000 ft AGL

Questions

. . . .

Part 3 Chapters 9, 10, 11, 12

1   Which statement(s) is (are) correct with regard to flying on a flight plan (FP)?
a   you have gone inadvertently off track, you get back onto your track as soon as practicable
b   your altitude deviates, you regain the filed altitude right away, and you advise ATSU
c   your IAS between two reporting points is expected to vary by 5% or less, you inform ATSU
d   your TAS between two reporting points is expected to vary by 5% or more, you inform ATSU

2   En route you decide to change your FP – which is/are correct?
a   you cannot, you must cancel your FP
b   you can file a new plan by radio, while in controlled airspace, by contacting ATSU
c   you inform ATSU of the changes
d   a change of destination cancels automatically item RMK/SAR

3   Which definition(s) is (are) correct?
a   urgency must be declared when the calculated usable fuel predicted to be available upon landing at the nearest suitable aerodrome, where a safe landing can be made, is less than the planned final reserve fuel
b   urgency must be declared when an aircraft experiences difficulties which compel the pilot to land without requiring immediate assistance
c   an urgency signal consists of a signal sent by radiotelephony consisting of the spoken words 'PAN-PAN, PAN-PAN, PAN-PAN'
d   in declaring an emergency the PIC may use frequency 121.5 kHz

4   In an emergency the relevant ATSU
a   will give priority to an aircraft in distress
b   will declare DESTREFA at the PIC's request
c   will treat urgency and emergency calls with equal urgency
d   will ask you to recycle your squawk code to 7600

5   If you are intercepted by day which one of the following is the correct sequence and meaning of : visual or radio interceptor's instruction → meaning → intercepted aircraft's response
a   rocking wings while in front and to the left of your aircraft→follow me to alanding terrain→rocking wings
b   abrupt break-away upwards of 90 or more without crossing your line of flight→follow me away immediately from prohibited airspace→rocking wings
c   rocking wings while in front and to the right of your aircraft, and flashing of navigational lights as applicable→follow me to a landing terrain→rocking wings and steady landing light on
d   PRO-SEED→you may proceed→VILL-KO (in the case an interceptor has signalled to an intercepted a landing field)

Questions: Part 3 Chapters 9, 10, 11, 12

6 Which transponder code is correct?

a   7500 emergency
b   7600 radio communication failure
c   7700 unlawful interference
d   7500 interception

7 About SAR alerting system, which statement is correct?

a   INCERFA means: interception phase
b   DESTREFA means: distress phase
c   DISTREFA means: distress phase
d   ALERFA means: first alert

8 First phase in alerting has three main causes (indicate the correct answer(s))

a   an aircraft overdue at "a destination only" FP has not made contact with destination ATSU within 30 minutes of ETA having elapsed
b   an aircraft overdue at "a destination only" FP has not made contact with destination ATSU within 60 minutes of ETA having elapsed
c   an aircraft which is operating on a FP stipulating alerting action after a specified time fails to arrive or is not in contact with the ATSU by the time specified in the FP and preliminary checks fail to reveal the whereabouts of the aircraft
d   an aircraft which is proceeding to an unmanned aerodrome but which is operating on an "overdue action" flight plan, fails to report arrival by the time specified in the flight plan and preliminary checks fail to reveal the whereabouts of the aircraft.

9 You crashed, you are alive and not incapacitated. Which visual signals using the strips do you lay on the ground to require assistance and to require medical assistance (enter the correct alpha designators in sequence)

a   V
b   X
c   N
d   Y

10 What do you understand by "transmitting blind"?

a   you are flying at night and are lost, and relying only on radio and nav aids to operate safely
b   you are unable to establish a two-way communication with your ATSU and rely on the "blind transmission" of your transponder
c   you do not have a two-way contact with your ATSU and are therefore using a general frequency, communicating "blindly" with all other aircraft
d   you are unable to establish a two-way communication with your ATSU but continue to transmit on the established frequency

11 You have radio failure in controlled airspace, you are approaching to land without two-way communication and no response from ATSU by day. Of the following actions(among others) you must take, which one is unlawful?

a   you recycle your transponder code to 2000 when in sight of airfield
b   you make a relevant blind broadcast to traffic with position and intention
c   you make the same broadcast to tower, twice
d   you preferably join on the downwind leg

408 Air Law

12 There are several types of instrument approach. Which regulation does not apply?

a a non-precision approach procedure is an instrument approach procedure which utilizes lateral guidance but does not utilize vertical guidance
b an approach procedure with vertical guidance is an instrument approach procedure which utilizes lateral and vertical guidance but does not meet the requirements established for precision approach and landing operations
c an approach procedure with a change in reference from flight-level to a height of 3 000 feet above the ground is an instrument approach which utilizes transition-level
d a precision approach procedure is an instrument approach procedure using precision lateral and vertical guidance with minima as determined by the category of operation

13 SAR is itemized on your FP. It is cancelled at stated destination
a when you land at a controlled aerodrome
b when you land safely at an uncontrolled aerodrome
c when you are over your destination aerodrome and are so deemed to have arrived safely
d none of the above

14 From the air, while over the airfield, you observe in the signal area a red panel with a yellow diagonal cross. It signals that:
a the two crossing runways are functional but there is possible danger in their adjacent areas marked in red
b landing is prohibited and is likely to be prolonged
c fire hazard
d SAR operation underway

15 From the air, while over the airfield, you observe in the signalling area this panel, what does it mean?

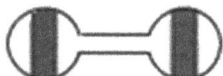

a both runways have just been re-tarred, macadam wet, exercise extreme caution when applying brakes
b you may take off or land on the runway (s) only
c runways are closed
d you may use the taxiway in between the two runways as a runway owing to the fact the runways are closed for re-tarring

16 From the air, while over the airfield, you observe in the signalling area this panel, what do you make of it?

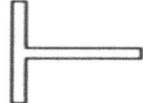

a I can land on the vertical bar and exit by the taxiway depicted horizontally
b I must beware of gliders in operation over the side of the vertical cross arm (crossbar)
c I must land on the shaft with a touch down at the point where cross arm (crossbar) and shaft meet

d   I must land on the shaft and toward the crossbar (cross arm)

17 While flying you receive a directional flashing green beam signal emitted by tower. What do you do?

a   I proceed onto finals and to landing
b   I return for landing
c   I call tower and ask for confirmation that the reported traffic ahead of me has vacated runway as the directional signal indicates
d   I begin orbiting

18 If a non-military aerodrome is equipped with an aeronautical light beacon, the light signal it emits is:

a   steady red
b   steady green
c   white flashes
d   white and red flashes

19 You are on final approach, the aerodrome is fitted with a PAPI, you have checked the AIP and NOTAM for this particular aerodrome and no unserviceability is reported. You now observe that the four lights of the system, on the left of the runway, are all lit white. What is your understanding of this?

a   all clear, I am on the correct glide slope
b   I am too high
c   the lights are broken
d   I am too low

20 You are on approach, landing or you have landed. Right of way rules apply. Which of these is (are) correct?

a   a landing aircraft has right of way over all other aircraft
b   as your aeroplane is lower than a helicopter, both on approach and both having declared intention to land, you have right of way
c   as your aeroplane is lower than a glider and both of you are on finals, you have right of way
d   a helicopter is compelled to land, you give way

21 On arrival there is a marshal. She has both arms raised straight over her head. What does it signal?

a   straighten your aircraft
b   move to this bay
c   the width of your aircraft is too large for this bay
d   cut off engine

22 What does this marshalling signal mean?

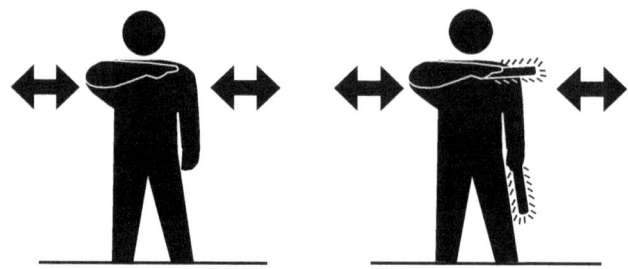

 a turn left
 b turn right
 c turn off right engine
 d turn off left engine

23 Regarding the flight folio filled in after each flight, which of the following is not correct in terms of the regulatory information that must be provided by the PIC.
 a off-block time
 b name of flight crew
 c reference of aircraft radio station licence
 d fuel and oil uplift

24 Which of the below choices are correct rules in terms of the legal period allowed for logging flight time?
 a 7 days in the case of flights not for hire and reward (Part 91 operations)
 b 21 days in the case of international commercial air transport operations
 c 48 hours after return to base in the case where a pilot is engaged in flight operations
 d away from the base where the pilot logbook is normally kept d 7 days in the case of flight training

25 In flight you experienced a near collision. Within which period must you submit an incident report?
 a within 7 days
 b within 14 days
 c within 21 days
 d within 24 hours

26 Is this statement absolutely correct? Incident means an occurrence, other than an accident, associated with the operation of an aircraft, which affects or could affect the safety of aircraft operations.
 a yes
 b no

27 If your aircraft sustains structural failure during an occurrence that adversely affects the structural integrity, performance or flight characteristics of your aircraft, but no one is fatally injured, does the said occurrence qualify as an

a   incident
b   accident
c   hazard

28 Whom does the PIC (if not incapacitated) notify of an accident? (indicate correct answers)

a   the Executive Manager: Aircraft Accident and Incident Investigation
b   an ATSU
c   the nearest police station
d   the Director of SACAA

29 An accident occurs near your base airfield. Is the chairperson of the flying club allowed to have access to the scene because it involves one of the members? (indicate the valid answer (s))

a   yes
b   no
c   yes if authorized by the Executive Manager: Aircraft Accident and Incident Investigation following due consultation
d   yes if the chairperson is an accredited representative

30 Can a guard as instructed by the owner of an aircraft that has crashed be positioned at the scene of an accident in order to safeguard valuables without being prevented to do so by the investigator-in-charge?

a   yes
b   no

Questions

Part 3 Chapter 13

Since the aim is not to prepare you for the Night Rating, and given the rather short NR theoretical examination paper which combines Air Law, Operations, and more, this questionnaire looks at essentials directly relevant to Air Law. Human limitations (disorientation, illusions), flying the circuit and navigation at night, as well as the instrument part of the Night Rating syllabus do not belong here. This is a basic tool to test your knowledge. Nonetheless it can be of help to students or private pilots preparing for this advanced rating. Finally, some night flying questions do pop up at the PPL Air Law examination.

1 The definition of night is

a the period from 15 minutes after sunset to 15 minutes before sunrise, sunset and sunrise being as given in the publication "Times of Sunrise, Sunset and Local Apparent Noon of the South African Astronomical Observatory" or a similar publication issued by a recognised astronomical observatory

b the period from 15 minutes before sunset to 15 minutes after sunrise, sunset and sunrise being as given in the publication "Times of Sunrise, Sunset and Local Apparent Noon of the South African Astronomical Observatory" or a similar publication issued by a recognised astronomical observatory

c the period from 15 minutes after sunset to 15 minutes after sunrise, sunset and sunrise being as given in the publication "Times of Sunrise, Sunset and Local Apparent Noon of the South African Astronomical Observatory" or a similar publication issued by a recognised astronomical observatory

2 Night duty means

a a period of not less than 4 hours between 22h00 and 7h00 of the next day
b a period of not less than 4 hours between 20h00 and 06h00 of the next day
c a period of not less than 4 hours between sunset and sunrise of the next day
d a period of not less than 4 hours between 22h00 and 05h00 of the next day

3 How recent must you be to carry a passenger at night ?

a you must have personally within the 90 days immediately preceding the flight, carried out at least three take-offs and three landings by night in the same class

b you must have personally within the 3 months immediately preceding the flight, carried out at least three take-offs and three landings by night only in the same class

c you must have personally within the 90 days immediately preceding the flight, carried out at least three take-offs and three landings by night or by day in the same class

d you must have personally within the 3 months immediately preceding the flight, carried out at least three take-offs and three landings by night or by day in the same class

4 To fly at night you must carry supplementary equipment. Which is (are)

a a supplementary fire extinguisher of the prescribed type
b a means to display charts that allows you to read them in ambient light
c a serviceable electric torch for each crew member
d a torch with red light facility affixed to your forehead

Questions: Part 3 Chapter 13   413

5 **What is the point of navigational lights at night ? They are meant**
a to help you avoid spatial disorientation in case of a night induced visual illusion
b to indicate the relative path of your aircraft in the air or on the ground
c to substitute for the beacon light
d to supplement strobes

6 **You can operate at night (indicate erroneous statement(s))**
a without a beacon if the navigation lights are serviceable
b without a beacon if the aircraft is fitted with serviceable strobes
c without a beacon if the landing light has two separately energised filaments

7 **Which one of these three statements is completely accurate?**
a a VFR flight shall be so conducted that the aircraft is flown with visual reference to the surface by day and to identifiable objects by night and at no time above more than three eighths of cloud within a radius of five nautical miles of such aircraft
b a VFR flight by night shall be so conducted that the aircraft is flown with visual reference to identifiable ground and at no time above more than three eighths of cloud within a radius of five nautical miles of such aircraft
c a VFR flight shall be so conducted that the aircraft is flown with visual reference to the surface by day and to identifiable objects by night and at no time above more than three eighths of cloud within a 10NM radius of such aircraft

8 **Flying at night is dangerous because of terrain. Which formulation(s) of the relevant regulation is (are) correct?**
a except when necessary for take off and landing an aircraft at night under VFR will fly at a height of at least 1 000 ft above the highest terrain or obstacle where the height of such terrain or obstacle does not exceed 5 000 ft above sea level within 5 NM of the aircraft in flight
b except when necessary for take off and landing an aircraft at night under VFR will fly at a height of at least 2 000 ft above the highest terrain or obstacle where the height of such terrain or obstacle does not exceed 5 000 ft above sea level within 5 NM of the aircraft in flight
c except when necessary for take off and landing an aircraft at night under VFR will fly at a height of at least 2 000 ft above the highest terrain or obstacle where the height of such terrain or obstacle exceeds 5 000 ft above sea level within 5 NM of the aircraft in flight

9 **Is it correct to say that minimum lighting facilities at an aerodrome for night operations are at least : runway edge, threshold and runway end lights?**
a Yes
b No
c Neither

10 **Here are the colours for runway lighting. Which combination is correct ?**
a edge= white,   green=threshold,   red=end
b blue=edge,   green=threshold,   red=end
c blue=end,   green=threshold,   yellow=edge

11 **If there are centre line lights on a runway what colour are they ?**
a white turning bright orange at end
b yellow turning red at end
c white turning red at end

414 Air Law

12 If taxiways are lit what combination of colours can you expect ?
a edge, blue centre line, yellow
b centre line, green edge, white
c centre line, green edge, blue

13 Which aircraft lights will you switch on before start? (indicate correct answser(s)
a the navigation lights
b the strobes
c the landing light
d the rotating beacon

14 In case an aerodrome is equipped with a pilot-operated lighting facility, you will do the following clicks on your PTT on the designated frequency
a five clicks on, seven clicks off
b five clicks on, three clicks off
c as per AIP

15 Should you trespass into a restricted zone, apart from possible interception, what sort of visual ground signal may you expect?
a a red flare discharged from a signal pistol, followed by another after 10 sec
b a directional beam, steady red
c a series of projectile bursts, red and green lights or stars, at 10 second intervals

16 You are intercepted at night. You have complied with the SAAF Gripen's instructions to follow her to a landing field you deem suitable. The interceptor is circling, has lowered landing gear, and has switched on a steady landing light. What is your response?
a you circle and overfly, you lower the gear if applicable, you switch on your landing light steady if carried and proceed to land
b you flash your landing light while flying over the airfield at a height exceeding 1 000 ft but not exceeding 2 000 ft, and proceed to land
c you flash your landing light or any other light while flying over the airfield at a height exceeding 1 000 ft but not exceeding 2 000 ft, await the interceptor's next instruction

17 You are on final approach at night, the aerodrome is equipped with a serviceable PAPI. You observe the four lights of the wing bar are red. What do you determine and what action do you take?
a you are way too high and you descend trying to catch the slope
b you are too low and power up immediately to avoid terrain
c you begin flaring

18 Do SVFR apply at night ?
a yes
b no

19 How to you maintain NR validity?

a   by currency payment of an annual fee
b   by passing a two-yearly competency test after the age of 40
c   by renewing it every five years after the age of 60
d   none of the above

20 Does the fact a NR is an advanced rating exempt you from limitations placed on the permissible aggregate of flight time?

a   yes
b   no

Answers

Students are encouraged to understand the reason for each answer by going back to the relevant chapter or by looking at the index.

. . . .

Chapters 1–13

Q Part 1 Chapters 1, 2, 3: answers

1b; 2b; 3c *Note: If the Act is amended after May 2019, the title will revert to 'Commissioner', in which case correct answer will be: b (as noted on page 13, note 24, this proposed change has now lapsed in Parliament);* 4a; 5a; 6c; 7b; 8d; 9a; 10b; 11d; 12a; 13ac; 14a; 15ac; 16c; 17b; 18b; 19b; 20ac; 21acd; 22c; 23c; 24bcd; 25abcd; 26d; 27cd; 28d; 29b; 30c

Q Part 2 Chapter 4: answers

1b; 2a; 3d; 4abcd; 5abd; 6d; 7b; 8d; 9d; 10c; 11abc; 12a; 13ab; 14b; 15a; 16ad; 17abd; 18ad; 19abc; 20b; 21a; 22d; 23b; 24d; 25c; 26a; 27acd; 28b; 29ab; 30abcd

Q Part 2 Chapter 5: answers

1b; 2d; 3b; 4ab; 5b; 6ab; 7a; 8c; 9a; 10abcd; 11abcd; 12cd; 13c; 14ac; 15c; 16a; 17ac; 18b; 19b; 20b; 21d; 22b; 23acd; 24ab; 25bcd; 26b; 27d; 28d; 29c; 30b

Q Part 3 Chapter 6: answers

1b; 2d; 3b; 4a; 5b; 6d; 7c; 8b; 9c; 10a; 11ac; 12b; 13d; 14b; 15a; 16abcd; 17b; 18b; 19c; 20acd; 21bcd; 22bcd; 23c; 24 take-off climb top of climb top of descent; 25bcd; 26a; 27bd; 28d; 29d; 30 a: transmit b: ambient c: altitude heading; 31c; 32ac; 33d; 34b; 35b

Q Part 3 Chapters 7 and 8: answers

1ab; 2abc; 3c; 4d; 5b; 6a; 7b; 8d; 9b; 10b; 11b; 12b; 13bd; 14d; 15a; 16a; 17a; 18a; 19c; 20b; 21b; 22a; 23c; 24c; 25c; 26d; 27a; 28bd; 29b; 30b; 31abc; 32d; 33b; 34cd; 35a

Q Part 3 Chapter 9, 10, 11, 12: answers

1ad; 2b; 3abc; 4a; 5d; 6b; 7b; 8bc; 9ab; 10d; 11a; 12c; 13a; 14b; 15b; 16d; 17b; 18c; 19b; 20bd; 21b; 22b; 23c; 24acd; 25d; 26a; 27b; 28abc; 29bcd; 30a

Q Part 3 Chapter 13: answers

1a; 2b; 3a; 4bc; 5b; 6ac; 7a; 8ac; 9a; 10a; 11c; 12c; 13ad; 14c; 15c; 16a; 17b; 18b; 19d; 20b

Index

A
accidents
  access to scene 235
  definition 230–231
  drones 268–269
  guarding of wreckage 235–236
  interference with wreckage 236
  notification of 233
  notification particulars 234
  reporting of 229
acrobatic flights 182
aerodromes
  alternate, adequate and suitable in VFR 122–123
  controlled 153
  information on aeronautical chart 124
  lights, signals and markings 214
  meaning of 'adequate' 123
  meaning of 'suitable' 123
  minimum lighting facilities 245
  night flying 244
  operating minima (AOM) 120–121
  preflight selection of 121
  private-use 125
  rules in traffic zone 213–214
  signalling area 156
  signalling panel 156
Aeronautical Information Circulars (AIC) 19
  definition 24
Aeronautical Information Publication (AIP) 19, 20–21, 25–27
  Aerodromes (AD) 27
  amendments 21
  En route (ENR) 26
  General (GEN) 26
  supplements 21
Aeronautical Information Regulation and Control (AIRAC), supplements 21
air ambulance 207
aircraft
  categories of 96–97
  definition of 'operator' 130
  definition of 'owner' 131
  documents and records 144
  inspection of 130
  pre-flight checks 132
  type certification 97
  verification of airworthiness 131
airfields
  conditions at 124
  private-use 125
  unlicensed 126
air law, distinguished from aviation law 10
airmanship, definition 59
air service, definition 255
airspace
  advisory 108, 183
  classifications 109–111
  controlled 108–109, 183, 192, 206
  designation of 107–108
  drones 268
  evaluation of 106
  information 183
  uncontrolled 109, 183
airworthiness, definition 131
alcohol consumption 85, 104–105
altimeters
  settings 165, 166–169
  transition altitudes 166, 167–169
  transition levels 166
anaesthetics 86
application dossier 75–77
  attachments 76
approach
  application of transition levels 209–210
  cancellation of search and rescue 210
  closure of flight plan 210
  controlled airfield 211
  instrument 208–209
  resetting of altimeter 209
  right of way 211–212
  uncontrolled airfield 210–211
apron, definition 150
arrival report
  format 225
  if flight plan has been filed 224–225
  rules 225

ASHTAM 25
authorisation sheet 147
aviation law, distinguished from air law 10
aviation medical report 30
aviation medicine *see* certificate of fitness
aviation time, Zulu time 157

B
baggage 142
benzodiazepine 86
BIRDTAM 25
blood donation 85
Bravo time 157
brown book *see* licence

C
Cape Town Convention *see* Convention on International Interests in Mobile Equipments, 2001
Cape Town Flight Information Region (FACA) 22
cargo 142
certificate of airworthiness 131–132
certificate of fitness 28
　age limitations 33–35
　application procedure 35–36
　classes of 31–33
　curtailment of privileges 34
　definition 29
　general requirement 31
　guidelines 30
　tests 35–36
　validity of 33–35, 81
certification of aircraft
　in terms of approach speed 98
　in terms of performance 98
　in terms of wake turbulence 97
charts 107
　line features 178
　symbols 178
checklists 146
　definition 24–25
Chicago Convention *see* Convention on International Civil Aviation, 1944
child restraint devices 141
chocks 148

circuit breakers 141
civil aviation authority 10
Civil Aviation Regulations (CARS) 12, 13–19
Civil Aviation Technical Standards (CATS) 12, 14
clearance quantum 176
cognitive learning method 4–5
collision avoidance
　acrobatic flights 182
　converging aircraft 164
　drones 268
　formation flights 181–182
　objects 181
　overtaking aircraft 162–163
　right of way 161–164, 211–212
　rules for communication 182–189
　rules of the air 159–161
　semi-circular rule 169–173
　setting altimeters 164
　speed limits 180–181
　terrain 173–180
communication equipment
　capability 137–138
　master minimum equipment list (MMEL) 137
　minimum equipment list (MEL) 136–137
　specification in flight plans 138
communication rules 182–189
　advisory airspace 183, 188
　aircraft with VHF only 189
　controlled airspace 183, 185–187
　emergency 194
　uncontrolled airspace above 1 500 ft 185
　uncontrolled airspace at or below 1 500 ft 183–184
competency maintenance 77
　application for extension 80, 82
　check report 81
　drones 265
　failure of revalidation test 83
　loss of currency 82
　new expiry date 80
　remedial actions after failure 83

submission of form 80
  time limits for second and later revalidations 82
  time limits to revalidate 81–82
  when check to be performed 81
compulsory instruments 139–141
confidential aviation hazard report system (CAHRS) 232
confirmation bias 19
Convention on International Civil Aviation, 1944 8–9
Convention on International Interests in Mobile Equipments, 2001 8
converging aircraft 164
conversion, when compulsory 92
conversion training
  class and type 92–93
  differences training distinguished from familiarisation 93
  endorsement for class or type rating 95
  endorsement for other ratings 96
  endorsement for warbird rating 96
  notification of differences or familiarisation 95
  what constitutes 92
Coordinated Universal Time 157
co-pilot, definition 68, 70
crash, actions after 204–205
currency
  competency-related 83
  distinguished from recency 86
currency fees 79, 81

D

debriefs 60
designated aviation medical examiner (DAME) 29
differences training, distinguished from familiarisation 93
direction indicator 157
Director of Civil Aviation 13–14
disabled pilots 28
distress
  communication rules 194
  priority over all other communications 199
  signals 199

VFR aircraft 198
documents and records
  authorisation sheet 146
  instrument markings 147
  mass and balance sheet 146
  placards 147
  required on board 144–146
  waiver of liability or indemnity form 146–147
drones, *see* Remotely Piloted Aircraft Systems (RPAS)
drug use 9

E

electronic devices on board 147
emergency
  communication rules 194
  declaration of 125, 197–199
  ground/air signalling codes 205
emergency and survival equipment 17–18
EMPIC software 30
English language certification *see* language proficiency certificate
en route
  definition 158
  end of 208
  safe altitude 175
ensure, definition 103
European Aviation Safety Agency (EASA) 10
examination papers 51–53
examination pass mark 51
examinations
  failure in 55–57
  pre-solo 61
  re-marking after failure 57
  rewriting after failure 55–57
  time-lines 55, 57–58
exercises 48

F

familiarisation, distinguished from differences training 93
fatigue 85, 105
fire extinguishers 141
first aid kit (FAK) 142–143

fitness, definition 29
flight authorisation sheet 113
flight folio 225–227
   drones 273
flight levels, and magnetic track 172–173
flight plans
   amendment of 129
   change en route 192–193
   changes to 193
   communication and navigation
      capability 138–139
   definition 126
   deviation from 130, 192–193
   electronic filing 128
   filing of 122, 126–127
   methods of filing 128
   right bestowed by 130
   self briefing service 128
   validity of 129
   in VFR 127
   when closed 130
   when to be activated 129
   when to be filed 128–129
   Zulu time 157
flight simulator 71
flight time
   beginning of 148
   definition 67, 149
   end of 220
   helicopters 149
   limitations 85
   permissible aggregate 85, 104
   recording of 46, 67–68, 227–228
forced landing, actions after 204–205
formation flights 181–182
fuel pump 157
fuel supply
   distress phase (DETRESFA) 203
   final reserve fuel 133, 194
   quantity 133
   refuelling 134
   usable fuel 133–134
fuses *see* circuit breakers

G

game reserves *see* protected areas

ground evaluation, questionnaire 72–73

H

handiflight pilots 28
hazards
   confidential aviation hazard report
      system (CAHRS) 232
   confidential reporting of 232
   definition 231
   identification of 232
helicopter pilots, condition of recency 80
helicopters
   flight time 149
   night flying 243
'high' density altitude 126
historic aircraft 98

I

I'M SAFE test 44, 104–106, 266
incidents
   definition 230
   notification of 232–233
   notification particulars 234
   reporting of 229
indemnity form 147
Instrument Flight Rules
   changing from Instrument to Visual
      Flight Rules 190–192
   classes of airspace requiring 109
   compulsory instruments and equipment
      in 139
   compulsory instruments single pilot or
      at night in 140
   flight levels in 171
   fuel 133
   instrument approach procedures
      208–209
   RCF procedures in 206
instrument markings 147
Integrated Aeronautical Information
   Package (IAIP) 19–20
interception 199–202
   signals 247
International Civil Aviation Organization
   (ICAO) 8

regulations and standards distinguished from SACAA 13

J
Johannesburg Flight Information Region (FAJA) 22, 108
Johannesburg Oceanic Flight Information Region (FAJO) 22, 108

L
landing light 157
language proficiency certificate 50, 53–54
liability *see* waiver of liability form
licence
   duplicate 76
   expiry date of maintenance of competency 77
   notification of changes to personal details 77
   signature on receipt 76
   validity of 78–79
light beacons 215
lights
   encountering aircraft 247
   operating 135, 148
light signals 150–151
   from tower 218–219, 247
limitations 49, 88
   general 84, 85
   human performance 84, 85
   recency 84, 86, 86–87
line features 178–179
logbook 227–228
   drones 265, 273
   dual flight time 70
   endorsements 46–47, 60, 96
   flight time 46, 66–67, 227–228
   inspection of 68
   PIC flight time 69
   retention of 67

M
magnetic track table 171
manoeuvres-based training 4
mass and balance sheet 146
master minimum equipment list (MMEL) 137

medical certificate *see* certificate of fitness
medical declaration 33
medical flights call signs 207
medical self-declaration 33
medication 104
meteorological aerodrome report (METAR) 113
meteorological conditions
   determination of minima in VFR 111–112, 114–115
   night flying 238
minimum en-route altitude (MEA) 176
minimum equipment list (MEL) 137
minimum flight altitudes 174
   en-route safe altitude 175
minimum heights 178
   national parks 180
   over people 179–180
   world heritage sites 180
minimum off-route altitude (MORA) 175, 176–177
   clearance diagram 177
   grid 177
   route 177
minimum safe altitude (MSA) 176
minimum sector altitude (MSA), definition 176
movement area 135

N
nationality letters 2
national parks 180
navigation equipment 136–137
   capability 138–139
   compulsory instruments 139–141
   specification in flight plans 138
navigation lights, angle of coverage 246D
night flying
   aerodrome lighting 244
   compulsory instruments 140
   definition of day 239
   definition of night 239
   definition of night duty 239
   facilities 125
   general requirements 241–243
   height and terrain 244

helicopters 243
human performance 238
instruments 238
lights to be displayed by aircraft 242
meteorology 238
minimum heights 178
passengers 243
simulators 238
single-pilot extra requirements 241–242
special purpose rating 95
visual flight rules 240
weather and wind 243
night rating 13
notice to airmen (NOTAM) 19, 22–24
  checklist 24–25
  definition 22
numbers, transmission of 172

O

occurrences *see* accidents; incidents
operating rules of the air 160–161
oral proficiency interview (OPI) 54
overtaking aircraft
  definition 162
  left hand circuit 163
  right-hand circuit 162
oxygen supply, supplemental oxygen 135–136

P

Paris Convention, 1919 8
passenger briefing 157
permissible aggregate *see* flight time
pilot-in-command (PIC), definition 68
pilot-in-command under supervision (PICUS), definition 68
pilotless aircraft *see* drones
placards 147
potential safety risk 63
practical flight instruction
  airmanship 59
  debriefs 60
  endorsements 46–47, 60
  flying exercises 58–59
  student prefixes 59–60
Practical Syllabus of Flight Instruction 59

precision approach path indicator (PAPI) 214–215
pre-flight checks
  external surfaces 132
  fuel supply 132–133
Pre-flight Information Bulletins (PIB) 22
private-use airports 125
privileges 48, 84, 88
prohibited or restricted areas 193
protected areas 180
psychoactive substances 16, 85
pyrotechnical signals (flares) 218

R

radio communication failure (RCF)
  action before landing at aerodrome 214
  controlled airspace 206
ratings
  aerobatics 182
  category 89
  class 89–90
  conversion training 92
  definition 88
  examination 91–92
  night 237–239
  revalidation 92
  special purposes 89, 93–95
  training prerequisites 91
  type 89, 90–91
recency
  condition 80
  distinguished from currency 86
reduced vertical separation minimum (RVSM) 171–172
refuelling, flammable gas and liquids 134
remotely piloted aircraft, definition 252
Remotely Piloted Aircraft Systems (RPAS)
  see also ROC operations
  drones 5, 251
    R-VLOS private operations
      applications for remote pilot licence 261
      commercial drone operation 255
      corporate drone operation 255–256
      examination rules 263
      flight folio 273

flight training syllabus and flying
    exercises 263–265
general examination syllabus 262
licence examination syllabus 262
line-of-sight 257, 260
logbook 265, 273
maintenance of remote pilot
    licence 265
non-profit drone operation 256
privacy concerns 274
private drone operation 254–255
remote operator certificate (ROC)
    254
remote pilot licence (RPL) 254,
    260
revalidation check 265
R-VLOS private operations
    266–271
size 257
skill test 265
systems classification 258
theoretical knowledge examination
    for remote pilot licence 261
theoretical training for remote pilot
    licence 261
VLOS, E-VLOS and B-VLOS
    operations 274
Required Visual Reference (RVR) 113
restricted or prohibited areas 193
revalidation 47
revalidation check *see* competency
    maintenance
right of way, collision avoidance 161–164,
    211–212
risk management analysis 104–106
roads, taking-off or landing on 125
ROC operations 271–272
    flight folio 273
    logbook 273
    operator vis-à-vis pilot 272
rule of redundancy 36
runway
    illuminated signs 245
    information signs 156, 216, 246B
    lights 246A
    mandatory signs 156, 216, 246B
    markings 154, 215–216
runway visual range (RVR) 113, 121
R-VLOS private operations
    accidents 268–269
    aerial or aerobatics displays prohibited
        269
    airspace 268
    collision avoidance 268
    exemptions from regulations 269
    flight operations' rules 267
    formation or swarm flying prohibited
        269
    height, distance, vicinity 268
    operational limits 270–271
    pre-flight checks 266
    release of object or substance prohibited
        269
    towing prohibited 269

S

safe altitudes *see* minimum flight altitudes
safety belts and harnesses 141
scenario-based training 4
scuba diving 85
search and rescue (SAR)
    alert phase (ALERFA) 203
    cancellation of 210, 224
    controlled airfield as destination 211
    distress phase (DETRESFA) 203
    inadequate facilities for closing and
        cancelling procedures 211
    rules of 202
    uncertainty phase (INCERFA) 203
    uncontrolled airfield as destination
        210–211
secondary surveillance radar (SSR) 182
semi-circular rule
    flight levels 169–171
    magnetic track 170–173
signals
    aeronautical light beacons 215
    ground/air signalling codes 205
    interception 247
    light signals from tower 218–219, 247
    marshalling 222–224
    precision approach path indicator
        (PAPI) 214–215

pyrotechnical signals (flares) sent from
    tower 218
  runway markings 215–216
  unauthorised entry 247
  visual ground signals and markings
    216–217
skills test 47, 55
  failure of 75
  grading system 74
  navigation element 73, 74
  pre-test ground evaluation 72–73
  report 73, 74
  standards 73–74
  when may be taken 70–72
solo flight
  definition 61
  dual check after solo 65
  dual competency check flight before
    first solo 64–65
  dual progress check 62–63
  failing to meet standards 63–64
  first 60
  legal requirements 61–62
  potential safety risk 63
  rules 66
  unsatisfactory progress after solo 65–66
solo navigation flight 66
South African Civil Aviation Authority
    (SACAA) 11–12
  objects of 12
  regulations and standards distinguished
    from ICAO 13
South African Weather Service (SAWS)
    113
special rules areas (SRA)
  communication rules 183
  speed limits 181
speed limits 180–181
  special rules areas (SRA) 181
squawk code 129, 138, 157, 182, 206
Standards and Recommended Practices
    (SARPs) 9–10
sterile flight deck 207
stowage 142
stress 104

student-pilot-in-command (SPIC),
    definition 68
student pilot licence (SPL) 43–44
  application for 44–45
  date of application 45
  maintenance of 46
student prefixes 59–60
syllabi
  flight instruction 50
  radio telephony 50, 53
  theoretical knowledge 50

T

taxiing
  controlled aerodromes 153
  definition 149
  light signals 150–151
  manoeuvring area 149, 153
  movement area 149, 153
  right of way 151, 152–153
  rules 152–153, 220–221
taxiways 149–150
  illuminated signs 245
  information signs 156, 246B
  lights 246A
  mandatory signs 156, 246B
terminal aerodrome forecast (TAF) 113
theoretical syllabus 50
thresholds
  definition 154
  displaced 155–156, 216
traffic information broadcast by aircraft
    (TIBA) 183–184
training, syllabi 50
transition altitude 165–169
transition level 166, 168, 209–210
transponder 157, 182, 199, 206
turbojet or turbofan mentor programme 93
type acceptance certificate 97

U

uncertainty phase (INCERFA), reasons for
    declaration 203
unfitness
  reporting medical issues 36–37
  requirement to observe prohibitions
    38–39

uniformity in standards 9–10
universal precaution kit 142, 143
urgency
  declaration of 194–197
  definition 197
  priority over other aircraft 197
  signals 195

V
validity of licence
  definition 79
  maintenance of 79
  rules 80
vaping 134
visibility, definition 111
Visual Flight Rules 3
  absolute rule 114
  changing to instrument flight rules 190–192
  classes of airspace in 109
  flight levels in 17
  night flying 240
visual ground signals and markings 246C
Visual Meteorological Conditions (VMC)
  altimeter setting under 168–169
  drone operations under 376
  helicopter a night under 140
  minima for classes of airspace under 110
  student pilot by day only under 49
  transition altitude and level under 168–169
see weather
vortex effect 97

W
waiver of liability form 147
wake turbulence
  categories 97
  right of way 211
weather
  aerodrome operating minima IFR 120–121
  aeroplane (or aircraft excluding helicopters) VFR minima 117–118
  AIRMET 114
  at departure, en route, and at destination 112–113
  deterioration in controlled airspace 115–116
  determination of meteorological minima in VFR 111–112
  helicopter VFR minima 119–120
  night flying 238
  SIGMET 114
  special VFR (SVFR) minima 116
wind sock 157
world heritage sites 180
wreckage
  guarding of 235–236
  interference with 236

Z
Zulu time 157

www.ingramcontent.com/pod-product-compliance
Lightning Source LLC
Chambersburg PA
CBHW061123010526
44114CB00029B/2990